Interest in theories of religion has never been greater. While anthropologists, archaeologists, classicists, evolutionary biologists, philosophers, psychiatrists and scholars of religion have presented new theories in academic publications, 'New Atheists' such as Richard Dawkins and Daniel Dennett have brought the debate to wider audiences. For everyone eager to understand the current state of the field, *Contemporary Theories of Religion* surveys the neglected landscape in its totality.

Michael Stausberg brings together leading scholars in the field to review and discuss seventeen contemporary theories of religion. Each chapter provides students with background information on the theoretician, a presentation of the theory's basic principles, an analysis of basic assumptions and a review of previous critiques. In a concluding section entitled 'Back and forth', Stausberg compares the different theories and points to further avenues of discussion for the future.

Michael Stausberg is Professor of Religion at the University of Bergen (Norway). Recent publications include *Zarathustra and Zoroastrianism* (2008) and *Theorizing rituals* (co-editor, 2 vols, 2006–7). He is the European editor of the journal *Religion*.

Contemporary Theories of Religion

A critical companion

Edited by

Michael Stausberg

Routledge
Taylor & Francis Group

LONDON AND NEW YORK

First published 2009
by Routledge
2 Park Square, Milton Park, Abingdon, Oxon OX14 4RN

Simultaneously published in the USA and Canada
by Routledge
270 Madison Ave., New York, NY 10016

Routledge is an imprint of the Taylor & Francis Group, an informa business

Typeset in Sabon by
Bookcraft Ltd, Stroud, Gloucestershire
Printed and bound in Great Britain by
TJ International Ltd, Padstow, Cornwall

British Library Cataloguing in Publication Data
A catalogue record for this book is available from the
British Library

Library of Congress Cataloging in Publication Data
A catalog record for this book has been requested

ISBN10: 0-415-46346-7 (hbk)
ISBN10: 0-415-46347-5 (pbk)
ISBN10: 0-203-87592-3 (ebk)

ISBN13: 978-0-415-46346-1 (hbk)
ISBN13: 978-0-415-46347-8 (pbk)
ISBN13: 978-0-203-87592-6 (ebk)

Contents

Figures

Contributors

Gregory D. Alles is Professor of Religious Studies at McDaniel College, Westminster, MD, USA. His publications include *The Iliad, the Ramayana, and the work of religion* (1994) and the edited volume *Religious studies: a global view* (2008).

Gustavo Benavides teaches at the Department of Theology and Religious Studies at Villanova University, Pennsylvania, USA. His research and publications deal with the theory and historiography of religion. He is co-editor of *Numen: International Review for the History of Religions* and of the series *Religion and society* and *Religion and reason.*

Peter Beyer is Professor of Religious Studies in the Department of Classics and Religious Studies at the University of Ottawa, Canada. His research specializations include religion and globalization, social theory of religion, religion and transnational migration and religion in Canada. His books include *Religions in global society* (2006). He is the co-editor of *Religion, globalization and culture* (2007) and *The world's religions: continuities and transformations* (2009).

Joseph Bulbulia is a Senior Lecturer in the Faculty of Humanities and Social Sciences at Victoria University in Wellington, New Zealand. His research considers the place of religious culture and cognition in the evolution of large-scale cooperative society. He is a co-editor of *The evolution of religion: studies, theories and critiques* (2008).

Matthew Day teaches at the Department of Religion at Florida State University, Florida, USA. He is editor of the journal *Method & Theory in the Study of Religion.*

Steven Engler teaches at the Department of Humanities, Mount Royal College, Calgary, and is adjunct at the Department of Religion, Concordia University, Montreal, Canada. He is the North American editor of the journal *Religion*, co-editor of the *Numen* book series *Studies in the history of religions* and editor of the *Key thinkers in the study of religion* book series. He is the co-editor of *Historicizing 'tradition' in the study of religion* (2005).

Marcus Frean is a Senior Lecturer in the Faculty of Engineering and Computer Science at Victoria University of Wellington, New Zealand. He has longstanding interests in the evolution of cooperation.

Mark Quentin Gardiner is a Philosophy Instructor in the Department of Humanities, Mount Royal College, Calgary, Canada. He works primarily in the area of philosophical semantics and in contemporary metaethics. He is the author of *Semantic challenges to realism: Dummett and Putnam* (2000).

Armin W. Geertz is Professor in the History of Religions at the Department of the Study of Religion, the University of Aarhus, Denmark. His main interests are cognitive theory in the study of religion, the religions of indigenous peoples, recent developments in contemporary religiosity and method and theory in the comparative study of religions. His books include *The invention of prophecy: continuity and meaning in Hopi Indian religion* (1992). He is a co-editor of *Perspectives on method and theory in the study of religion* (2000), *New approaches to the study of religion* (2 vols, 2004) and of the series *Religion, cognition and culture*.

Aaron W. Hughes is Associate Professor of History and the Gordon and Gretchen Gross Professor of Jewish Studies at the University at Buffalo, SUNY, USA. He works in the areas of Jewish thought and critical discourses in religion. His books include *Jewish philosophy A–Z* (2005), *Situating Islam: the past and future of an academic discipline* (2007), *The art of dialogue in Jewish philosophy* (2008) and *Defining Judaism* (forthcoming).

Jeppe Sinding Jensen is Associate Professor, Department for the Study of Religion, Aarhus University. His research interests include semantics and cognition in religious narrativity, myth and cosmology and method, theory and the philosophy of science in the study of religion. He is the author of *The study of religion in a new key: theoretical and philosophical soundings in the comparative and general study of religion* (2003) and the co-editor of *Rationality and the study of religion* (2003). He is the co-editor of the series *Religion, cognition and culture*.

Benson Saler is Professor Emeritus of Anthropology at Brandeis University, Massachusetts, USA. He is the author of *Los Wayú (Guajiro)* (1988),

Conceptualizing religion: immanent anthropologists, transcendent natives, and unbounded categories (1993, 2000), *Understanding religion* (forthcoming) and co-author of *UFO crash at Roswell: the genesis of a modern myth* (1997).

Robert A. Segal is Sixth Century Professor in Religious Studies, University of Aberdeen, Scotland. His books include *The Poimandres as myth* (1986), *Explaining and interpreting religion* (1992), *Theorizing about myth* (1999) and *Myth: a very short introduction* (2004). He is the editor of *The myth and ritual theory* (1998), *The Blackwell companion to the study of religion* (2006) and *Myth: critical concepts* (4 vols, 2007).

Hubert Seiwert is Professor of the Study of Religion at the University of Leipzig, Germany. His books include *Popular religious movements and heterodox sects in Chinese history* (2003).

Michael Stausberg is Professor of the Study of Religion at the University of Bergen. Besides theory in the study of religion, his main research interests are Zoroastrianism, the history of the study of religion and the interface between religion and modern tourism. His books include *Zarathustra and Zoroastrianism* (2008). He is a co-editor of *Theorizing rituals* (2 vols, 2006–7). He is the European editor of the journal *Religion* and co-editor of the series *Religion and reason*.

Donald Wiebe is Professor of the Philosophy of Religion in the Faculty of Divinity, Trinity College, in the University of Toronto, Canada. His research interests include philosophy of the social sciences with particular reference to method and theory in the study of religion and the history of the academic and scientific study of religion. He is author of *Religion and truth: towards an alternative paradigm for the study of religions* (1982), *The irony of theology and the nature of religious thought* (1991) and *The politics of religious studies* (1998). He is the editor of the series *Toronto studies in religion*.

1

There is life in the old dog yet

An introduction to contemporary theories of religion

Michael Stausberg

The early modern humanist recovery of ancient worlds and overseas expansion, later radicalized in colonialism, created an explosion in the amount of information available to European audiences. Transforming that information into knowledge was an effective way of dealing with it, since knowledge potentially establishes control and thereby grants power over what is known. The relationship between information (facts, data) and knowledge is a complex one. Information is generated and selected by means of prior knowledge and expectations. New information, however, may lead to a change in previously accepted knowledge and generate new expectations.

The incipient study of religion(s) tried to account for the massive influx of information on religious phenomena around the world by such means as interpretation, classification, typologies, and historical genealogies. Generality is a feature of scientific knowledge (see Chalmers 1990: 26–9), and, since its beginnings, the academic study of religion(s) sought to make statements about religion(s) in general, addressing such questions as:

- Can and ought religions be ranked, and if so, according to which scale of values?
- Do religions change? If so, do they change according to any regular principles we might discover, such as evolution or degeneration?
- Do religions change in terms of their own internal dynamics, or do they change in terms of their relations to other cultural systems or religions – say, by imitation or direct opposition? (Strenski 2003: 177 [based on Tylor, Frazer, and Müller])

Any attempt to address such questions obviously requires empirical data. However, the questions themselves are theoretical. Although the study of religion(s) appears to be characterized by an aversion to theory,[1] it cannot avoid an intricate interplay of data and theory. The 'raw' data become 'theory-laden as soon as they are placed on the table' (Engler 2004: 299).

The table manners are the methods engaged in research, and the cutlery used at this table is the conceptual apparatus of the trade. Theory in religious studies, in this basal sense, refers to 'the myriad conceptual tools used to "see" religion' (Deal and Beal 2004: xi). Observing, describing, interpreting and accounting for anything in terms of its being 'a religion' posits the category of religion; this category is invariably informed ('laden') by a theory of what can be communicated as 'religion'. The discussion about what exactly, in the academic study (or science) of religion(s), can be legitimately communicated as 'religion' raises questions of definition and theory of religion. These questions have been on the table since the beginnings of the modern academic study of religion(s). Sometimes they have been its main course, sometimes a side dish, a starter, or dessert. And on occasion they were relegated to the wine list or served as an aperitif. Where the question of definition is routinely rehearsed, theory is clearly perceived as being less savoury. This volume tries to give it a more central place on the table. On the menu are not the myriad tools, but the 'real thing': theories of religion. At this point, the reader may wonder: what is a theory?

Theories of theory

The meaning of the very word 'theory' is not theory-free. In fact, there are several competing ideas, if not theories, on theory in the philosophy of science. In the social sciences, 'there has been a perennial debate about what theory actually is or entails' (Turner 2000: 6). This is less so in religious studies, but theorizing about religion is necessarily entrenched in that problematic.

There are different ideas and practices of theory in different sciences and disciplines. More often than not, the ideal of theory is derived from popular ideas of physics, which for many seems to incarnate the idea of science *par excellence*. Physics has served as the model for much theory of science, and physical theories as the epitome of theory. But physics does not represent all of natural science; nor do theories in physics, such as gravitational theory, exhaust the notion of theory in the natural sciences. Biology, which has recently been called 'a science of specific solutions' (North 2003: R719),[2] presents a very different picture,[3] and the theory of evolution, with its theorem of natural selection, to take one example, presents other kinds of challenges, given that the process conceptualized by the theory at the same time generates ever-changing environments, resulting in a much greater degree of complexity to be accounted for in the models developed by theorizing.[4] In the social sciences one also finds different notions of theory,[5] including critical metatheory, i.e. theorizing the implications of theory, or even anti-theory (see below). While there is theory in all sciences and branches of scholarship, in the US 'Theory' (with a capital T!) commonly refers to literary theory,[6] even though hardly any scientists or philosophers would recognize 'what is done, said, published under the name of "theory" in some American departments of literature' as either science in a scientific sense or theory in a philosophical sense (Derrida 1994: 81).

It is obvious, but nevertheless worth recalling, that theories are invariably situated in intellectual, institutional, ideological, and political contexts. They are social facts as much as their objects or subject matter (see Jensen 2003: 298), and as social facts they are public and coercive in that they 'are also responsible for the way we think' (Jensen 2003: 301). Moreover, since minds make sense by creating stories and narratives (Turner 1996), most theories and explanations/interpretations, at least in the humanities, are also narrative structures. Finally, theories operate with metaphors and rhetorical tropes that give them specific twists (see Tweed 2006: 46). Likewise, theorists are situated in specific contexts; they cannot assume an omniperspective position (Tweed 2006: 13–20).

Four main questions for theories of religion

While religions are the subject matter of theories of religion, religion is their theoretical object. In order to give a full account of their object, theories of religion[7] can be reasonably expected to address the following four interrelated main questions that I will here briefly comment on, partly in order to dispel some common misconceptions.

1. The **specificity** *of religion(s)*

Any theory of religion is expected to determine whether there is anything special about religion, something unique to religion. Other terms that are invoked in order to address this question are the *content*, *components*, *typical* or *regular features* of religion. Only if religion can be said to have or to be identified with any specific *properties*, to possess its own *regularities*, or to be communicated as a specific *code*, can one be sure to be able to recognize religion in observation, unless one makes it a point to analyze only instances of religion identified by social actors as 'religion'[8] (much as art historians would analyze only products that are explicitly referred to as 'art' by the respective audience).

The question addresses the specific and specifiable ways religion *is* and *works* as distinct from, or as compared to, other 'systems', 'domains', 'spheres', 'forms', 'constructs', 'classes', 'figures' or 'maps'.

Speaking of specific properties of religion or conditions for identifying something as 'religion' does not necessarily imply that religion is a separate and timeless entity. Even on the level of public and private ascriptions to a culturally postulated and constructed realm of 'religion', regularities of ascriptions determining what counts as religion can be observed (Beckford 2003). These are then culture- and time-bound discursive properties.

In earlier theorizing the problem of specific properties of or conditions for identifying religion was addressed under the guise of the *sui generis* character of religion.[9] This, I believe, has resulted in an unnecessary confusion. To begin with, to posit the uniqueness of religion, its *sui generis* character, does not a priori preclude reductionist, naturalist, realist, or constructionist positions (see Engler 2004: 308). Moreover, it is one thing to say that religion is peculiar and quite another to say that religion is a 'thing' or fact totally apart, as it were an insular phenomenon. While the latter interpretation would preclude religion's having any interface with other 'systems', 'domains', or social facts such as society or economy (which are likewise human and conceptual constructions), possible effects of religion on these 'spheres' can only be conceptualized if religion is taken to operate *as* religion, as an independent variable (see Segal 2005: 52).

Another key term in the debate on this issue is *essentialism*, which, since postmodernism, is commonly regarded as a bad thing. One way to avoid essentialism is to talk about *typical features* (Saler 2008). Among these features some may well be more relevant for the identification of the categories in question than others. As long as one recalls that the regularities observed and attributed by the scholars (i.e. second-order observations) are strategic and epistemological conceptualizations relative to classification and are not grounded in ontological or timeless metaphysical assumptions, one may not need to give up the quest for regular features. It may legitimately be considered that there are possibly not only typical but also characteristic features or regularities, though these are defined from a given position, and that there may be not only sufficient, but also necessary conditions – necessary for various purposes and in various contexts.

If there are good arguments that there cannot be any specific properties of religion, no specifiable conditions for identifying religion, theorizing religion can stop at this point. This could in itself be the result of theoretical work and cannot be verified in a purely empirical manner. This would then amount to a negative theory of religion.

2. The **origins** of religion(s)

Essences are often conceived of as being determined by ontological–metaphysical origins. While this line of thinking may be characteristic of religious discourses, this is not how these terms tend to be conceptualized in theories of religion. 'Origin' as understood here refers to an emerging quality, or a mechanism, which makes the specifiable conditions come to the fore. Origin in this sense is historically indeterminate – religion can emerge (originate) at any time, provided certain conditions are met. These conditions need to be specified by a theory. Origin-talk points to the factors that contribute to establish the regularities of religion observed, interpreted, explained or redescribed by scholars.

Origin therefore needs to be distinguished from 'beginnings'. The latter category refers to the determinate period(s) in (evolutionary) history, when religion first can be said to be documented. In many cases, the quest for the origin of religion is conceptualized in terms of establishing its beginnings. I find this problematic, because this presupposes a definition of the origins and the regularities. One cannot define when a fact has been established without knowing what the fact is like and how it can possibly arise in the first place.

Nor should the emerging origin of religion be confused with the historical genealogy of the category 'religion'. While the latter is irrelevant to the former,[10] the latter is not irrelevant as such, since it could potentially amount to a historical theory explaining a mode of classification. Explaining the genealogy of the classification is not the same as proving the classification to be wrong.

3. The **functions** of religion(s)

The notion of 'function' is relational in a double sense. It is observer-relative – it is the observer who assigns functionality – and it relates social facts to other social facts, in a causal and purposeful manner, claiming the utility of one fact with respect to another. It therefore refers to causal relations within a normative model (Searle 2006: 17). As with all other aspects of theories of religion, speaking of functions invokes second-order statements. The functions analyzed by the observer can be operational without being perceived or realized ('cognized') by the actors (see Rappaport 1968: 237–8). Similarly, Robert Merton introduced the distinction between manifest (deliberate, intentional) and latent functions, where the latter category refers to further unintended consequences of actions (see Merton 1957).

Speaking of functions does not require the idea that religion 'as such' has agency; rather, the ascriptions to religion by social actors observed by scholars can, when analyzed with regard to their regularities, be said to function within models.

It is important not to confuse functions with *effects*. The former notion is normative; the latter is empirical. Consider the following examples. While religion may arguably function to generate social cohesion, the activities of religions often point to disruptive effects; whereas religion may function to cement social hierarchies, religions may also stir rebellion. Based on their normative notions, protagonists of functionalism will claim that the religions showing these effects are atypical or malfunctioning.[11]

In addition, finding empirical evidence for effects should not be confused with analyzing functions. There may be ample evidence that being religious has positive effects for mental health (see Koenig 1998), but this is not the same as saying that it is the function of religion to promote mental health. The effect of religion on health, i.e. a positive correlation, may well be a by-product of some other trait in or function of, or associated with, religion.

4. The **structure** *of religion(s)*

Looking at any textbook on any religion, one finds chapters on agents, rituals, myths, institutions, etc. Are these the aspects, dimensions, elements, components, recurrent patterns or building blocks of religion? Are all of them necessary or just some? Do they mutually confirm and sustain each other or are they independent of each other? The question is whether, how, and possibly also why these elements (aspects, dimensions, components, recurrent patterns, or building blocks) hang together, are parts of joint constructs and attributions, whether they are interdependent (and if so, how) or just arbitrary assemblies. At issue is what else could be called the *coherence, integrity, system-character, dimensions,* or *design* of religion.[12] Note that theorizing possible structures of religious facts or constructs does not need to proceed from a structuralist methodology.

Not all theories of religion suggest answers to these four questions. In fact, very rarely does any one theory even address them all. Moreover, not all of these questions need to be answered positively in any given theory of religion. In other words, one would expect a theory of religion to contain propositions on the distinctiveness and functionality of religion, but theories of religion can in principle come up with arguments that do not ascribe any generic functions or structures to religion. Note also that theoretical accounts more often than not are accounts of *how* rather than *why* things are as they are (or came to be as they now appear to be).

Further questions

Many more questions with regard to religion can be posited. Think of issues and problems such as the *meaning, costs and benefits, development, evolution*[13] and *heritability* of religion. Is religion an evolutionary *adaptation* or rather a *by-product* or *spandrel*? What is the *attraction* of religion to people, and what about the *persistence* of religion? Are there several *species, kinds,* or *types* of religion, and how is one to evaluate *differences between religions* in general? Are there, or does it make sense to speak about, *fake, pseudo-* or *quasi-religions?* This relates to the problem of *naturalness* of religion. These are all important questions.[14]

I have singled out the four issues above as the key questions for any given theory of religion, since, taken together, they will make sense of religion as a whole by accounting for (1) religions' specific modes of operation (if any), (2) the conditions for their emergence (if any), (3) the ways in which they relate to other domains (if they do so at all), and (4) the mechanisms by which their regularities can be said to fit together (if they can be said to do so).[15]

Arguably, scientific theories have appeared as a result of the loss of given certainties. This loss of the plausibility of traditional truth claims is generally described as a feature of the process of modernization. Modern sciences on the one hand help to accelerate that process, while on the other hand compensating for it by generating truth claims and institutions of truth-production (such as the modern university) of a different order. It has been said that religion first had to be perceived as a 'problem' for it to be then addressed by way of theorizing (Strenski 2006: 1–3). At present, however, this claim remains a premise more than a result of an empirical study. Problems tend to appear in the course of or as a result of theorizing rather than as its starting point. Critical and creative theorizing is not constrained a priori by matters of general concern and collective consciousness.

Lay theories and academic theories

In that connection, it should be pointed out that scholars are by no means the only group of people thinking about religion. Sets of general propositions or theorems interpreting and explaining religion are entertained privately, in thought and conversation, and they permeate the public sphere, including the media and politics.[16] Everybody has some sort of theory, although the shape, level of articulation, frequency of application, degree of universality, and level of endorsement of such lay theories (also called implicit, naïve, popular, or folk theories) vary across populations and cultures (see Levy, Chiu, and Hong 2006). Lay theories are also part of various religious and anti-religious discourses. Recall the discourses on spirituality, religion and terrorism, or religion and the economy that often carry with them specific understandings, theorems, and explanations about religions.

Lay theories have complex relationships with academic (professional) theories, including parallels, overlap, borrowings, and competition. While they do not necessarily differ in their basic theorems – religion as the cement guaranteeing social cohesion and religion as generator of meaning are competitors on the lay and the professional theory market – there are several requirements for a theory to qualify as an academic (professional/expert) theory.[17] To begin with, academic theories are put forward by members of the academy, who articulate them in their capacity as trained professionals, i.e. in compliance with what is considered good practice in their respective disciplines. Criteria for the scientific status of theories are variously discussed in the philosophy of science and differ in accordance with the respective view on theory one subscribes to.[18] Take the claim that academic theories put a greater emphasis on coherence, consistency, formality, explicitness, causality (Furnham 1988: 3–4), explicit and reflected background assumptions, rationality, exposure to mutual criticism, sensitivity to data, validity and reliability of the data, and testability.[19] Moreover, academic theories aspire to a greater degree of complexity. This implies a distinction between the various levels on which phenomena are situated. A theory of religion, for instance, would ideally distinguish between biological, ecological, sociological, psychological, semantic, cognitive, and ontological levels or dimensions of the social facts it seeks to make sense of and account for. Moreover, a fuller theory might need to distinguish between ultimate and proximate causes, i.e. the larger (distal) causes and those (psychological or social) mechanisms that trigger the processes actually under observation.

Classical and contemporary theories of religion

Theories of religion have been in the baggage of the modern study of religion(s) since its beginnings. Naturalist (Preus 1987), Enlightenment (Rudolph 1985), and Romantic (Kippenberg 2001) theories of religion have all in some way or another laid the groundwork for the history of religious studies. The century from the 1860s to the 1960s saw the appearance of a series of theories of religion that have become common points of reference. A list of theorists (not all of whom have produced comprehensive or separate theories of religion) includes the likes of Karl Marx, Max Müller, Edward B. Tylor, William Robertson Smith, James G. Frazer, Émile Durkheim, Sigmund Freud, Max Weber, Bronislaw Malinowski, Carl G. Jung, Edward E. Evans-Pritchard, Mircea Eliade, Clifford Geertz, and Peter Berger. There are by now several textbook accounts of these theories (see Thrower 1999; Kunin 2003; Drehsen, Gräb, and Weyel 2005; Pals 2006; Strenski 2006).[20]

Further theories were published in the 1970s and 1980s (Bataille 1974 [posthumous]; Mol 1976; Luhmann 1977; Crosby 1981; Greeley 1982; Stark and Bainbridge 1987; Hick 1989 [2004]). Some of these theories even stirred debate. None, however, has to date achieved the status of a classic theory in religious studies, i.e. a recurrent point of reference in scholarly discussions and syllabi. Luhmann and Stark published revised theories around the turn of the century.[21] Although this tends to be generally overlooked, the present volume shows that the production of theories of religion has continued, and even intensified, from the 1990s to the present day. The current volume invites discussion of these theories. Rather than being a closed chapter in the past history of the field, theorizing about religion is and hopefully will remain an ongoing preoccupation.

Approaches, ideas, theories

In this connection, it may be useful to distinguish between theoretical approaches, theoretical ideas, and theories. Note that this distinction implies no value judgement, but refers to different degrees of generalization and explication. 'Theoretical approaches' refers to scholarly work based on or related to a corpus of shared theoretical or methodological assumptions or key problems in religious studies – take feminist, postcolonial, or cognitive approaches as examples. Such approaches tend to imply theoretical ideas about religion, but are not necessarily explicated as theories of religion by single theorists.[22] Apart from such general approaches, scholars tend to come up with theoretical ideas about religion that lay claim to make sense of or account for religion in general, or at least some of the main questions (as outlined above) related to religion. Some examples of theoretical ideas about religion proposed in recent scholarship include hunting (Lease 2004), commitment (Irons 2008), costly/hard-to-fake signalling (Sosis 2003; Bulbulia 2008), (meta-) contextualizing (Hastrup 2004), meaning-making (Jensen 2004), discourse (Lincoln 2003), social formation (McCutcheon 2001), and semiotic construction and displacement (Murphy 2003). These can be called embryonic theories or starting points for further theorizing that may or may not result in larger theoretical constructs (theories). Most theories start with seminal theoretical ideas, generally outlined in articles or chapters before receiving fuller treatment.[23] The present volume focuses on such fuller accounts, i.e. theoretical ideas that have been systematized and unfolded, and often illustrated with empirical data. However, the threshold that separates theories from theoretical ideas is gradual and difficult to demarcate and often refers less to content than to the degree of elaboration.[24]

The seventeen theories discussed in the present volume present (more or less) fully-fledged theories of religion, and the chapters discuss whether the respective theories can be said to have lived up to the expectations thus created. Apart from the claim to present general accounts, the theories selected for inclusion were all presented in the form of a monograph (book).[25] Admittedly, this is a purely formal and admittedly somewhat arbitrary criterion. However, the book-length articulation of a theory requires a larger degree of conceptualization and explication than what can be achieved in an article or in a chapter. It therefore serves as an index of whether a theoretical idea has passed a first threshold towards achieving the status of a theory.

The authors were asked to comment on the structure of the book in question, since this often is analogous, if not isomorphous, to the architecture of the theory. The authors, in turn, were selected for their documented expertise in matters of theory. In order to warrant a high degree of intellectual fairness, they were mostly assigned to the various chapters because of a critical sympathy with the main thrust of the allotted theories (but not necessarily the theorist!). The chapters are arranged chronologically with respect to publication date of the books.

This is not the place for a sociology of knowledge of theorizing religion. However, some comments are in order. To begin with, the androcentrism endemic to theorizing religions seems to remain firmly established. All theorists and all authors are men.[26] Moreover, theories of religion are in the majority produced in the US (11 out of 17 in terms of place of work, 10 out of 17 in terms of nationality). It is also worth mentioning that only five of the contemporary theorists (Lawson, Pyysiäinen, Rue, Tweed, Riesebrodt) hold positions in religious studies departments. This is true also for classical theories. Think of anthropologists such as Tylor, Frazer, Malinowski, Evans-Pritchard, and Geertz, sociologists such as Durkheim, Weber, and Berger, and psychologists such as Freud and Jung. The disciplinary and institutional backgrounds of the contemporary non-religious studies theorists include anthropology with a focus on cognitive studies and evolutionary theory (Atran, Boyer, Guthrie) or cybernetics (Rappaport), archaeology in combination with neurology (Lewis-Williams), evolutionary biology (Dawkins, Wilson), classical philology in combination with ethology (Burkert), nuclear medicine, psychiatry, and neurology (Newberg), philosophy (Dennett, McCauley), and sociology with a focus on rational choice economics (Stark and Finke) or systems theory (Luhmann).

A comparison with the classical theories indicates the increasing impact of the natural and behavioural sciences on contemporary theories of religion. Even three of the religious studies theorists draw inspiration from cognitive sciences (Lawson, Pyysiäinen) or evolutionary theory (Rue). This is also in marked contrast to the dominance of late or post-Marxist theorizing that was dominant from the 1960s to the 1980s. It is not the case that shared disciplinary and metatheoretical backgrounds predict the outcome of theorizing: biological approaches, for example, result in conflicting theories and interpretations of religion with regard to such fundamental questions as origin, function, qualities, benefits/costs, etc.[27] but also with regard to key concepts.[28] Moreover, the potential of the disciplinary approaches is far from exhausted by the theories so far produced. Economic theory, to take just one example, could probably also yield theories of religion other than the rational choice theory put forward by Stark and Finke. So could cognitive science.

The vast majority of the contributors to the present volume are either trained in the study of religion(s) or are based in departments of religion. The present volume thus attempts to bring the discussion of theories of religion more firmly 'home' to the study of religion(s), a field that should have an inherent interest in these matters.

Only one of the seventeen theories discussed in the present volume has grown out of empirical work on a religious site (Tweed), while another one has remote origins in an earlier fieldwork project (Rappaport) and a third theory has emerged from reflections on the meaning of neolithic excavation sites (Lewis-Williams). Rather than taking bottom-up approaches, the remaining theories take more top-down points of departure, in that they start from the puzzle that is religion in general. While religion is their subject, with the exception of Riesebrodt, their frames of references or theoretical framework are taken from the fields and disciplines listed above. In retrospect, *Rethinking religion* by Thomas Lawson and Robert McCauley (1990), which draws on Chomsky's generative linguistics theory, can be said to have opened the door to the sort of trans-disciplinary conversation that the present volume aims to provoke.[29] *Rethinking religion* also contains still-pertinent reflections on the relations between interpretation and explanation in the study of religion(s) and a survey of earlier theories of religion; similar surveys can be found in some other works.[30]

Transcendentalist and non-transcendentalist theories

Several scholars have distinguished between two main groups of definitions and theories of religion. The pairs have been referred to as Christian vs. secular (Jensen and Rothstein 2000), theological/insider vs. non-theological/outsider (Kunin 2003), those of believers vs. those of nonbelievers (Guthrie 1993), theological vs. naturalist (McCutcheon 2001), religious vs. naturalistic (Hick 2004 [first edition 1989]; Thrower 1999) or religious studies vs. social scientific (Segal 2005). All these binary pairs point to some characteristic differences and all are flawed in one way or another. Given its recent popularity as a positive marker of identification, let us take a brief look at the label 'naturalism'.

Naturalism is a problematic term in relation to the study of religion, for it implies ideological premises and positions[31] that one need not endorse in order to theorize religion beyond transcendentalism, i.e. beyond the idea that religion is the result of an intervention (creation; hierophany) of a transcendental reality. A non-transcendentalist (immanent) position seeks to explain transcendentalist positions rather than building an explanation of religions on a transcendental foundation. While one generally adduces philosophical reasons for this position, such as the claim that transcendentalist theories cannot be tested but can only be affirmed, that they are purely deductive and are not based on empirical analysis, or that they cannot be falsified but only verified, we are ultimately dealing with a metaphysical divide here. Transcendentalists theorize religion in terms of the superhuman (or supernatural), where the human responds to a superhuman reality, whereas non-transcendentalists theorize religion in human terms – be it on the basis of biology, symbolization, cognition, communication, rationality, culture, or other qualities and dimensions of the human.[32] For the transcendentalist position, then, the cause of religion is given by its transcendental origin, granting it a unique (*sui generis*) quality.[33] Consequently, a transcendentalist theory of religion can merely interpret religion (see the title of Hick's *An interpretation of religion* [1989/2004]), yet may be explanatory within the given framework (i.e. explain traits of religion, even if religion as such is treated as transcendentally given).[34] Non-transcendentalist theories, on the other hand, are not constrained by the assumption of a prior existence of something naturally grasped as religion. This type of theory seeks to establish conditions or causes.[35] It is the latter group of theories that are discussed in the present volume, and while *sui generis* theories may still be cherished by many American scholars (at least if we are to believe McCutcheon), no new academic theories of this sort appear to have been produced in the relevant period.

Fundamental challenges

At present, theorizing religion has turned into nothing short of an equation with two unknowns. A series of critiques that can with some justification be subsumed under the label 'postmodern' have raised serious doubts about both the validity of the concept of religion and the legitimacy of theory.

One can safely state that the discussions beginning in the 1980s have pulled the rug out from under any naïve realistic understanding of the term and the concept 'religion'. It has become increasingly clear that (1) in scholarly discourse, 'religion' serves as an analytical category, a conceptual tool, a map used by scholars to navigate their discursive territory,[36] (2) that the term has dramatically changed its semantic and pragmatic dimensions in the modern period, (3) that it is a contested term, and (4) that the term carries a large and largely also limiting and embarrassing (religious, ideological, political) baggage.[37] Critical scholarship has pointed out a number of dangers associated with using the term, including reification, epistemological ambiguities, ethnocentric bias, metaphysical and theological presuppositions, implicit

Protestant values, orientalist misrepresentations, imperialist and colonialist genealogies and agendas, methodological anachronisms, and its historical conjunction with other, equally problematic terms such as 'the secular' or binaries such as public and private (see e.g. Asad 1993; Dubuisson 1998; Fitzgerald 2000, 2007a,b).

There are two ways to relate to these insights. The weaker version takes them as an exhortation for scholars to become 'relentlessly self-conscious' (Smith 1982: xi) by critically (and theoretically) relating to their conceptual apparatus, scholarly strategies, and manoeuvres. The stronger programme is not content with these moves but holds that the only intellectually accountable way to avoid such problems with 'religion' is to actually get rid of the term and the concept altogether.[38] The campaign against 'religion' has so far not resulted in any substantial numbers of scholars abandoning the term or the concept. The theories discussed in the present volume are a case in point. But it is important to keep in mind the question whether the theories discussed in the present volume acknowledge and address this issue at all.

Not satisfied with critiques of 'religion', postmodernist critiques have attacked the concept of theory itself. It is one thing to criticize theories for their shortcomings in accounting for their subject area or theoretical object or with regard to criteria often adduced to evaluate theories and quoted above. It is quite another to unveil subjective and ideological, including religious and political, agendas underlying theories and the effects and consequences of their application. Neither of these crucial exercises warrants 'massive cynicism about theories' (Strenski 2006: 287; see also McCutcheon 2001: 114).

However, the very project of theory (or the caricature sometimes made of it) has in recent decades been challenged by, among others, philosophers such as Derrida, Foucault, and Rorty. This complex debate cannot even be summarized here. Some main points include the alleged totalizing, hierarchizing, universalizing, reifying, and essentializing character of theories, the apparent impossibility of grounding objective truth claims and universal values, the inherent 'phallogocentrism' (Derrida 1994: 86), the declared impossibility of assuming a neutral or Archimedean point of departure for theorizing or for adjudicating among competing theories and claims, the dubious character of the Grand Narratives often implied by theories, and the alleged futility of achieving 'the closure of an ensemble of totality on an organized network of theorems, laws, rules, methods' (Derrida 1994: 86). Along this path, the ironist, the critic, the writer replaces the theorist. Postmodernists emphasize incommensurability, differences, multitude, fragmentation, indeterminacy, etc. Postmodern and poststructuralist thinkers such as those mentioned above hold that their projects are different from theory.[39] Any redescription of their discourse in terms of a theory would probably have a walkover in refuting such claims (for religious studies see Segal 2006), but any such refutation will not convince the anti-theoreticians, since they articulate their claims in radically different philosophical idioms, linked to quite distinct epistemologies and ontologies. At present, I see no commensurability between postmodernist anti-theoretical and theoretical discourses.[40] The present volume is certainly not intended to make a case for the futility of theories of religion, as a cabinet of intellectual folly – though some may read it in that manner – but is produced in a spirit (call it 'modernist' if you will) that valorizes theory, critique, and discussion as means of doing science. Theorizing is here understood as a means not of achieving closure but as an act of reopening the issues. Even if the study of religion(s) is not a major producer of theories of religion, where there are academic theories of religion out there, it is our professional duty to discuss them. It remains for me to thank all the authors for their willingness to contribute to an ongoing dialogue.[41]

Notes

---

1   The empirical training of scholars in the field contributes to suspicion of theory; one primarily achieves prestige and status in the profession by mastering an empirical field.

2   See also North 2003: R719: 'It was all very well for Einstein to take the observation that the speed of light appears to be the same whatever frame of reference it is measured in, and deduce the Lorentz transformations of length and time between reference frames. But it is fairly rare in biology to be able to make accurate predictions by pure mathematical reasoning from general basic laws, or infer precisely defined general laws from observations (Mendel providing an exception here)'.

3   The relation of the physical to the biological sciences is a debated topic in the philosophy of science.

4   Day 2007 points to some of the implications of the challenges of biological theory (as interpreted by Alexander Rosenberg) for the claims that can realistically be made for a cognitive science of religion.

5   Mjøset 2001 distinguishes between five main conceptions of 'theory' in the social sciences:

   1   The 'deductive-nomological' notion of theory. The project of theory is to deduce theorems from a limited number of axioms; it is based on the correspondence theory of truth (i.e. the theorems are verified or falsified by their correspondence with facts or data); it is grounded in realism; although very few, if any, non-trivial laws were ever uncovered in the social sciences, this notion of theory has remained something like the regulatory ideal of theory in the social sciences (and religious studies).

2   The 'law-oriented' notion of theory aims at law-like regularities within specific contexts, or middle-range theories. This project appears as a weaker version of the deductive-nomological notion, adapted to the realities of social sciences, but retaining the deductive-nomological model as the ultimate regulative idea.

3   The 'idealizing' notion of theory that aims at constructing idealized models of human action and behaviour, which can then be calculated via mathematical modelling or game-theories and predicted with regard to an idealized world. This notion presupposes an underlying correspondence between the knowledge and motivation of the scientist and the actor in the model.

4   Unlike the above-mentioned models the 'constructivist' notion of theory regards the differences between science and everyday knowledge as fuzzy, a matter of degree rather than of principle. This notion favours a plurality of theories which are conceived as incomplete and bounded processes and social and historical products in their own right; the constructivist notion points to motives and contexts; it is often characterized by ideas of pragmatic or non-representational realism.

5   The notion of 'critical' theory implies the role of the scholar as participating in a power struggle committed to universal ethical principles challenging various knowledge interests underlying other varieties of scientific or non-scientific theories.

6   The identification of theory with literary theory is taken so much for granted that books with titles such as *The future of theory* (Rabaté 2002) or *How to do theory* (Iser 2006) do not even need to carry a qualifying subtitle which would indicate that they address literary theory. Note that both books can be rewarding reading for scholars of religion(s)!

7   Tulving (in Gazzaniga 1991: 89) distinguishes between theories *of* and theories *about* something. A theory *about* something (in his case, memory) would be 'concerned with selected, restricted sets of phenomena and thereby escape facing the problem of complexity', being more like a local theory, whereas a theory *of* something should tell 'what it ... is, and how its phenomena must be what they are because of what the theory says they should be, or how it is precisely sensible that they are what they are'. A theory *of* religion in that sense may not be feasible (see Pyysiäinen 2003: viii), but the ideal remains to say something about what religion is rather than what some associated phenomena are. In any case, I would not want to overemphasize that distinction.

8   This is, if I understand him correctly, the strategy advocated by Beckford 2003.

9   See Pyysiäinen 2004: 67–80 for an explanation of the *sui genesis* thesis in terms of a theory of metarepresentation.

10   Claiming otherwise would amount to committing the genetic fallacy.

11   Function is also normative with regard to the benchmark point of reference. Luhmann (2002: 49) distinguishes between the function (*Funktion*) of religion for society in general and the accomplishment, benefit, effect, or performance

(*Leistung*) of religion for other societal systems. Consider this example: that religious ceremonies facilitate coping in cases of death does not say anything about the function of religion for society.

12   The analysis of structure does not necessarily imply an evolutionary perspective. In terms of evolutionary theory the possibility of analyzing a domain as a specific design is often regarded as a criterion for its qualifying as an adaptation.

13   'Development' here refers to historical change, or the historical malleability of religion, whereas 'evolution' points to the constraints imposed by the theory of evolution on religion.

14   See Strenski 2003: 176–8 for a list of important and typical questions taken from some standard approaches in the study of religion(s).

15   Segal 2005 takes origins and functions as the main questions, but does not offer any reasons for this selection.

16   See Furnham 1988 for lay theories in psychology, psychiatry, medicine, economics, statistics, law, and education. I am not aware of a study of lay theories in religion, but see now Schlehofer, Omoto, and Adelman 2008 on lay definitions of 'religion' and 'spirituality' among 64 older adults living in three retirement communities in Los Angeles County.

17   Boyer 2002: 6–57 discusses 12 widespread lay theories of religion.

18   For the study of religion(s) Pye has argued that '[t]heories of religion may be described as scientific in so far as they are rational, empirical, explanatory, and testable' (2000: 211).

19   Given that there is no reality independent of interpretation and theory, theories can only be tested by theory and not against a 'theory-free' realm of the 'pure' unmediated reality (see Jensen 2003: 179).

20   Unfortunately, Georg Simmel and Ernst Cassirer are generally neglected in works on classical theories of religion in English.

21   See the chapters by Gregory Alles and Peter Beyer in this volume.

22   See Connolly 1999 for a survey of seven main approaches (anthropological, feminist, phenomenological, philosophical, psychological, sociological, theological).

23   Some theories – both classical and contemporary ones – rely on one main principle.

24   See also Strenski 2006: 342 for a healthy realism: 'Nowhere can the study of religion claim to own anything remotely approaching a Darwinian *theory* of evolution or a Newtonian *theory* of the physical universe.' Yet, *pace* Strenski, I think that there are constructs in the study of religion that are theories rather than merely theoretical ideas.

25   In hindsight, Hatzfeld 1993; Hervieu-Léger 1993; Greeley 1995; Hinde 1999; and Kirkpatrick 2005 could have been included. Unfortunately, the planned chapter on Piette 2003 did not make it through. All books, especially edited volumes, have their history ...

26   The editor could be blamed for selecting only male contributors; in my defence let it be said that I invited some female colleagues, but none were available.

27 See also Dennett 2006: 82–93, who outlines six main possible theoretical options within the evolutionary framework (sweet-tooth theories, symbiont theories, sexual-selection theories, money theories, group-selection theories, and pearl theories).

28 The concept of 'meme', for example, is of fundamental importance for some theories (Dawkins, Dennett), but rejected by others (Atran, Wilson).

29 See the chapter by Steven Engler and Mark Q. Gardiner in the present volume.

30 Lawson and McCauley (1990: 32–44) distinguish between intellectualist, symbolist, and structuralist theories; Guthrie (1993: 10–38) discusses three groups within 'humanistic' theories of religion: the 'wish fulfillment group', the 'social functionalist or group solidarity group', and the intellectualist group, plus some eclectic and synthesizing theories; Smith (1995: 1068–70, an anonymous entry on 'types of theories of religion') distinguishes between emotivist theories, intellectualist theories, symbolist theories, structuralist theories, ideological theories, and cognitive theories; Riesebrodt (2007: 75–107) outlines the following theories: religion as the divine gift of reason, religion as experience of revelation, religion as projection, religion as proto-science, religion as affect and control of affects, religion as a function of the brain, religion as sacralized society, religion as an interest in salvation, religion as a ware.

31 Think of the following varieties: methodological naturalism, i.e. the idea that neither the data for a scientific study nor a scientific theory can properly refer to supernatural beings; metaphysical naturalism, i.e. the idea that nature is all there is, that there simply are no supernatural beings; classificatory naturalism, i.e. the idea that there are in fact natural divisions among things in nature. All these varieties of naturalism seem equally problematic as starting points for the study of religion(s).

32 Note that it would be wrong to characterize non-transcendentalist theories as 'humanistic' and transcendentalist theories as anti-humanistic, if humanism is understood as a political project.

33 It can be said that the first and the second of the main questions outlined above are collapsed in this theoretical model.

34 To some extent, this type of theory is a 'hermeneutics of faith'.

35 To some extent, this type of theory is a 'hermeneutics of suspicion'.

36 That should not be confused with the idea, as famously worded by J.Z. Smith and sheepishly reproduced as a mantra by many epigones, that it is 'solely the creation of the scholar's study' (Smith 1982: xi) or that 'it is a term created by scholars' (Smith 1998: 281). In actual fact, however, many actors were and are involved in 'creating' that term, including missionaries, colonial administrators, politicians, and various others. No ivory tower, not even in Chicago, can be so huge as to overlook that obvious fact. But Smith is right to point out that religion is an observer-related (second-order) category and that religion cannot be observed directly; observation is always mediated by prior categorization and theory; see also Engler 2004.

37 More controversial is the claim, made by McCutcheon, that specific varieties of the term are devised and marketed in specific institutional contexts to bolster the academic enterprise known as religious studies.

38   Dubuisson 1998 (English translation 2003) suggests introducing the term/ concept 'cosmographic formation'. See the review symposium (edited by S. Engler and D. Miller) in *Religion* 36 (3) (2006).

39   It remains for their epigones to redescribe their anti-theories as theories and their anti-methods (such as deconstruction) as methods. This is part of the process of canonization and normalization in science.

40   Anti-theory here does not refer to theory-blind empiricism, 'but the kind of scepticism of theory which is theoretically interesting' (Eagleton 2003: 54).

41   Special words of thanks to Steven Engler (very special thanks indeed!), Jeppe Sinding Jensen, and Greg Alles.

References

Asad, T., 1993. *Genealogies of religion: discipline and reasons of power in Christianity and Islam*. Johns Hopkins University Press, Baltimore.

Bataille, G., 1974. *Théorie de la religion*. Edited by Thadé Klossowski. Gallimard, [Paris].

Beckford, J.A., 2003. *Social theory and religion*. Cambridge University Press, Cambridge.

Boyer, P., 2002. *Religion explained: the human instincts that fashion gods, spirits and ancestors*. Vintage, London.

Bulbulia, J., 2008. Free love: religious solidarity on the cheap. In: Bulbulia, J., Sosis, R., Harris, E., Genet, R., Genet, C. and Wyman, K. (Eds.), *The evolution of religion: studies, theories, and critiques*. Collins Foundation Press, Santa Margarita, 153–60.

Chalmers, A.F., 1990. *Science and its fabrication*. University of Minnesota Press, Minneapolis.

Connolly, P. (Ed.), 1999. *Approaches to the study of religion*. Continuum, London, New York.

Crosby, D.A., 1981. *Interpretive theories of religion*. Mouton, The Hague, Paris, New York.

Day, M., 2007. Let's be realistic: evolutionary complexity, epistemic probabilism, and the cognitive science of religion. *Harvard Theological Review* 100 (1), 47–64.

Deal, W.E. and Beal, T.K., 2004. *Theory for religious studies*. Routledge, New York, London.

Dennett, D.C., 2006. *Breaking the spell: religion as a natural phenomenon*. Viking, New York.

Derrida, J., 1994. Some statements and truisms about neologisms, newisms, postisms, parasitisms, and other small seismisms. In: Carroll, D. (Ed.), *The states of 'theory': history, art, and critical discourse* Stanford University Press, Stanford, 63–94.

Drehsen, V., Gräb, W. and Weyel, B. (Eds.), 2005. *Kompendium Religionstheorie*. Vandenhoeck & Ruprecht, Göttingen.

Dubuisson, D., 1998. *L'Occident et la religion. Mythe, science et idéologie*. Éditions Complexe, Brussels. (English translation, 2003, *The Western construction of religion: myths, knowledge, and ideology*. Johns Hopkins University Press, Baltimore.)

Eagleton, T., 2003. *After theory*. Allen Lane, London.

Engler, S., 2004. Constructionism versus what? *Religion* 34, 291–313.

Fitzgerald, T., 2000. *The ideology of religious studies*. Oxford, New York.

Fitzgerald, T. (Ed.), 2007a. *Religion and the secular: historical and colonial formations*. Equinox, London.

Fitzgerald, T., 2007b. *Discourse on civility and barbarity: a critical history of religion and related categories*. Oxford University Press, Oxford.

Furnham, A., 1988. *Lay theories: everyday understanding of problems in the social sciences*. Pergamon, Oxford.

Gazzaniga, M.S., 1991. Interview with Endel Tulving. *Journal of Cognitive Neuroscience* 3 (1), 89–94.

Greeley, A.M., 1982. *Religion: a secular theory*. The Free Press, London and Collier Macmillan, New York.

Greeley, A.M., 1995. *Religion as poetry*. Transaction Publishers, New Brunswick, London.

Guthrie, S.E., 1993. *Faces in the clouds: a new theory of religion*. Oxford University Press, New York, Oxford.

Hatzfeld, H., 1993. *Les racines de la religion. Tradition. rituel, valuers*. Seuil, Paris.

Hastrup, K., 2004. Religion in context: a discussion of ontological dumping. In: Antes, P., Geertz, A.W. and Warne, R.R. (Eds.), *New approaches to the study of religion*. Volume 2, *Textual, comparative, sociological, and cognitive approaches*. Walter de Gruyter, Berlin, New York, 253–70.

Hervieu-Léger, D., 1993. *La religion pour mémoire*. Éditions du Cerf, Paris. (English translation, 2000, *Religion as a chain of memory*. Polity Press, Cambridge.)

Hick, J., 2004. *An interpretation of religion: human responses to the transcendent*. Second edition; originally published 1989. Yale University Press, New Haven, London.

Hinde, R.A., 1999. *Why gods persist: a scientific approach to religion*. Routledge, London, New York.

Irons, W., 2008. Why people believe (what other people see as) crazy ideas. In: Bulbulia, J., Sosis, R., Harris, E., Genet, R., Genet, C. and Wyman, K. (Eds.), *The evolution of religion: studies, theories, and critiques*. Collins Foundation Press, Santa Margarita, 51–7.

Iser, W., 2006. *How to do theory*. Blackwell, Malden, Oxford, Victoria.

Jensen, J.S., 2003. *The study of religion in a new key: theoretical and philosophical soundings in the comparative and general study of religion*. Aarhus University Press, Aarhus.

Jensen, J.S., 2004. Meaning and religion: on semantics in the study of religion. In: Antes, P., Geertz, A.W. and Warne, R.R. (Eds.), *New approaches to the study of religion*. Volume 1, *Regional, critical and historical approaches*. Walter de Gruyter, Berlin, New York, 219–52.

Jensen, T. and Rothstein, M. (Eds.), 2000. *Secular theories of religion: current perspectives*. Museum Tusculanum Press, Copenhagen.

Kippenberg, H.G., 2001. *Discovering religious history in the modern age*. Princeton University Press, Princeton.

Kirkpatrick, L.A., 2005. *Attachment, evolution, and the psychology of religion*. Guilford Press, New York.

Koenig, H.G., 1998. *Handbook of religion and mental health.* Academic Press, San Diego.

Kunin, S.D., 2003. *Religion: the modern theories.* Johns Hopkins University Press, Baltimore, London.

Lawson, E.T. and McCauley, R.N., 1990. *Rethinking religion: connecting cognition and culture.* Cambridge University Press, Cambridge.

Lease, G., (2004). Hunting and the origins of religion. In: Bulbulia, J. and Morris, P. (Eds.), *What is religion for?* Victoria University of Wellington, Wellington, 211–21.

Levy, S.R., Chiu, C.-y. and Hong, Y.-y., 2006. Lay theories and intergroup relations. *Group Processes and Intergroup Relations* 9 (1), 5–24.

Lincoln, B., 2003. *Holy terrors: thinking about religion after September 11.* University of Chicago Press, Chicago, London.

Luhmann, N., 1977. *Funktion der Religion.* Suhrkamp, Frankfurt am Main.

Luhmann, N., 2002. *Die Religion der Gesellschaft.* Edited by André Kieserling. Suhrkamp, Frankfurt am Main.

McCutcheon, R.T., 2001. *Critics not caretakers: redescribing the public study of religion.* State University of New York Press, Albany.

Merton, R.K., 1957. *Social theory and social structure.* Free Press, Glencoe.

Mjøset, L., 2001. Theory: conceptions in the social sciences. *International Encyclopedia of the Social and Behavioral Sciences,* Elsevier, Oxford, 15641–7.

Mol, H., 1976. *Identity and the sacred: a sketch for a new social-scientific theory of religion.* Blackwell, Oxford.

Murphy, T., 2003. Elements of a semiotic theory of religion. *Method and Theory in the Study of Religion* 15 (1), 48–67.

North, G., 2003. Editorial: biophysics and the place of theory in biology. *Current Biology* 13 (8), R719–R720.

Pals, D.L., 2006. *Eight theories of religion.* Oxford University Press, New York.

Piette, A., 2003. *Le fait religieux. Une théorie de la religion ordinaire.* Economica, Paris.

Preus, J.S., 1987 (1996). *Explaining religion: criticism and theory from Bodin to Freud.* Scholars Press, Atlanta.

Pye, M., 2000. Westernism unmasked. In: Jensen, T. and Rothstein, M. (Eds.), *Secular theories of religion: current perspectives.* Museum Tusculanum Press, Copenhagen, 211–30.

Pyysiäinen, I., 2003. *How religion works: towards a new cognitive science of religion.* Brill, Leiden.

Pyysiäinen, I., 2004. *Magic, miracles, and religion: a scientist's perspective.* AltaMira, Walnut Creek.

Rabaté, J-M., 2002. *The future of theory.* Blackwell, Oxford.

Rappaport, R.A., 1968 (1975). *Pigs for the ancestors: ritual in the ecology of a New Guinea people.* Yale University Press, New Haven, London.

Riesebrodt, M., 2007. *Cultus und Heilsversprechen. Eine Theorie der Religion.* C.H. Beck, Munich.

Rudolph, K., 1985. *Historical fundamentals and the study of religions. Haskell lectures delivered at the University of Chicago.* With an introduction by Joseph M. Kitagawa. Macmillan/Collier Macmillan, New York, London.

Saler, B., 2008. Conceptualizing religion: Some recent reflections. *Religion* 38 (3), 219–25.

Schlehofer, M.M., Omoto, A.M. and Adelman, J.R., 2008. How do 'religion' and 'spirituality' differ? Lay definitions among older adults. *Journal for the Scientific Study of Religion* 47 (3), 411–25.

Searle, J.R., 2006. Social ontology: some basic principles. *Anthropological Theory* 6 (1), 12–29.

Segal, R.A., 2005. Theories of religion. In: Hinnells, J.R. (Ed.), *Routledge Companion to the Study of Religion.* Routledge, London, 49–60.

Segal, R.A., 2006. All generalizations are bad: postmodernism on theories. *Journal of the American Academy of Religion* 74 (1), 157–71.

Smith, J.Z., 1982. *Imagining religion: from Babylon to Jonestown.* University of Chicago Press, Chicago.

Smith, J.Z., 1995. *The HarperCollins Dictionary of Religion.* HarperSanFrancisco, San Francisco.

Smith, J.Z., 1998. Religion, religions, religious. In: Taylor, M.C. (Ed.), *Critical terms for religious studies.* University of Chicago Press, Chicago, London, 269–84.

Sosis, R., 2003. Why aren't we all Hutterites? Costly signaling theory and religious behavior. *Human Nature* 14 (2), 91–127.

Stark, R. and Bainbridge, W.S., 1987 (1996). *A theory of religion.* Rutgers University Press, New Brunswick, NJ.

Strenski, I., 2003. Why it is better to know some of the questions than all of the answers. *Method and Theory in the Study of Religion* 15 (2), 169–86.

Strenski, I., 2006. *Thinking about religion: an historical introduction to theories of religion.* Blackwell, Malden, Oxford, Victoria.

Thrower, J., 1999. *Religion: the classical theories.* Edinburgh University Press, Edinburgh.

Turner, B.S., 2000. Introduction. In: Turner, B.S. (Ed.), *The Blackwell companion to social theory.* Second edition. Blackwell, Oxford, 1–18.

Turner, M., 1996. *The literary mind.* Oxford University Press, New York, Oxford.

Tweed, T.A., 2006. *Crossing and dwelling: a theory of religion.* Harvard University Press, Cambridge, MA.

2

Religion as superhuman agency

On E. Thomas Lawson and Robert N. McCauley,
Rethinking religion (1990)

Steven Engler and Mark Quentin Gardiner

Lawson and McCauley's *Rethinking religion: connecting cognition and culture* (*RR*) 'launched the cognitive science of religion'; it 'inaugurated the field of cognitive studies of religion' (McCauley and Lawson 2002: ix; Liénard and Boyer 2006: 817). It offers a 'theory of religious ritual systems as well as a framework for a larger theory of religious systems' (171).[1] The book's 'principal theoretical object is the shared knowledge about their religious systems (both the system of ritual acts and the accompanying conceptual scheme) of persons who are participants in those systems' (5). It proposes that human minds are constrained to think about action in certain ways and that religious ritual is subject to these same constraints. *RR* attempts to show how the resulting 'symbolic-cultural systems' can be explained scientifically, i.e., 'by means of *systematically related, general principles*' that work at a different level from religious phenomena and that 'are empirically culpable beyond their initial domain of application' (2, 27; original emphasis). As a theory of religion, *RR*'s originality consists in its axiomatic connection between culture (the domain of relatively non-structured religious commitments) and cognition (the domain of structured representations of action): religion becomes subject to formal analysis when it extends from the former into the latter, above all in the case of ritual.

RR has broad implications for four main reasons. First, its theory is cognitivist (following Sperber 1975): it studies 'the (usually) unconscious representations of cultural and social forms (and their underlying principles) which participants share' (3). Influenced in part by Noam Chomsky's generative grammar, its analysis of the tacit knowledge of ritual participants focuses on general cognitive mechanisms for the representation of action, leading to 'a theory of religious ritual competence rather than … a theory of actual ritual acts' (77). In contrast to later work in the cognitive science of religion, *RR* downplays evolutionary and biological factors in their account of this tacit knowledge. Second, *RR* proposes a clear criterion for distinguishing religious ritual from other sorts of actions: 'all religious systems involve commitments to culturally postulated superhuman beings' (123). Third, following from the first two points, *RR* underlines the importance of (theory of) ritual in (theory of) religion. It defines 'a religious system as a symbolic-cultural system of ritual acts accompanied by an extensive and largely shared conceptual scheme that includes culturally postulated super-human agents' (5). *RR* emphasizes the *humanlike agency* of these beings in its characterization of religion: 'it is the putative action of culturally postu-lated superhuman agents that is central to understanding the dynamics of religious ritual systems' (6). Fourth, *RR* attempts to provide a coherent semantic framework for analyzing the meaningfulness and significance of religious ritual (137–69).

These elements of *RR* have met different fates in the subsequent liter-ature. First, an increasing number of scholars have investigated cognitive aspects of religion, with little further exploration of the book's competence approach, and with an overwhelming emphasis on evolutionary and biolog-ical factors. In relation to the second and third points, *RR*'s emphasis on 'culturally postulated superhuman agents' has come to serve as the defining characteristic of religion in subsequent cognitivist work. The concept of 'superhuman,' vague in *RR* itself, has been fleshed out in terms of 'counter-intuitiveness' (Boyer 1994, 2001; Pyysiäinen 2003), anthropomorphism (Guthrie 1993, 2001)[2] and 'hyperactive agency detection' (Barrett 2000, 2004). In more recent work, McCauley and Lawson have integrated the concepts of counter-intuitiveness and hyperactive agency detection, placing greater emphasis on evolutionary biology as a premise (2002: 22–3, 39). In relation to the fourth point, *RR*'s discussion of semantics has been almost entirely ignored. We give this aspect of *RR* special attention here, given its importance to the book's argument and its neglect in the critical literature.

Summary

RR is the most important of several fruits of the exemplary collaboration between philosopher Robert N. McCauley and scholar of religion E. Thomas Lawson (McCauley and Lawson 1984, 1996, 2002; Lawson and McCauley 1993). Lawson (Professor of Comparative Religion, Western Michigan University) has worked on religion in Africa and theory of religion. McCauley (Professor of Philosophy, Emory University) has worked on philosophy of psychology and of science more generally.

Their respective areas of expertise allowed them to contextualize their theory to an unusual extent. The first chapter of *RR* examines views of the relation between explanation and interpretation and situates its theory in the interactionist camp: the two 'are different cognitive tasks ... [that] supplement and support one another' (30). This move is crucial, given that their theory analyzes the interface between *cognitive* constraints on representations of action and *culturally* postulated religious commitments. The second chapter offers valuable overviews and critiques of intellectualist, symbolist, and structuralist theories of religion, arguing that none pays sufficient attention to the analogy between linguistic and symbolic-cultural systems. The third chapter evaluates views of the relation between ritual and language, arguing for an approach that draws on similarities between language and ritual as formal systems. The fourth chapter develops the metatheoretical frame, reviewing Chomsky on language and Sperber on symbolic systems. The fifth chapter (summarized in this section) sets out the theory of ritual. The sixth chapter (critiqued below) lays out a semantic framework for making sense of 'meaning' within this theoretical frame. The final chapter discusses implications for linking cognition and culture. Arguably (see Platvoet 1993), *RR* suffers from the fact that so much time is spent situating the theory in polemical relation to competing views, with only two chapters setting out the theory itself.

RR's theory begins with a cognitivist premise:

[H]uman beings are likely to have some reasonably ordered system for the (cognitive) representation of actions. Consequently, any theory of participants' representations of their religious ritual actions should commence with some account of such a system for the representation of action, generally. ... [A]n understanding of the underlying principles organizing such systems of representations will help clarify the relation of cognitive systems and symbolic-cultural systems, that is, they will help show how what is 'in the head' connects to what is outside of it. (6, 12)

RR analyzes competence not performance, tacit knowledge of ritual systems not actual examples or conditions of ritual practice. In this sense, the theory has 'a fundamentally *normative* dimension': it analyzes not actual ritual(s) but humans' sense of what constitutes a correct ritual, i.e., 'the principles which underlie an idealized participant's judgments and intuitions about the "well-formedness" of ritual' (65; original emphasis).

In developing this approach, *RR* draws on Chomsky's generative linguistic theory. It argues, contra Chomsky, (i) that a competence approach to theory (i.e., one that specifies constraints on a given domain of representations) has purchase beyond the domain of language and (ii) that putative mental structures are not sufficient to explain the systematic features of ritual (65–77, 138, 151–2, 179–84).

RR analyzes ritual as a sub-type of action: representations of ritual are constrained by the same cognitive systems invoked to represent all actions. Hence, its theory of ritual is rooted in a detailed analysis of how human beings represent action in general. Basic representations include the agent who initiates the action, the object or patient upon whom the action is performed, and the instrument used to perform the action. Formal descriptions involve a 'formation system' that includes a nuanced set of elements: participant, action complex, agent, object, quality, property, act, action quality, action property, and action condition (87, 92, 100). The 'object agency filter' is postulated as a cognitive mechanism that ensures that 'only what counts as agents from an ontological standpoint can fulfill the role of an agent in an action' (98).

The representation of religious ritual systems consists of this same 'action representation system' with one important addition: 'All religious rituals involve superhuman agents at some point or other in their representation' (124). 'Superhuman' is defined in relative terms: 'The theoretical significance of the notion of superhuman properties concerns agents' abilities to do things that human participants cannot' (124). Regarding cases of religious ritual where it is the patient or instrument, not the agent, that is believed to be superhuman, *RR* holds that the action of some superhuman agent is a precondition: providing the capacity to a human agent to act on a supernatural patient; or emphasizing a superhuman property of the instrument. For example, rituals of ordination are analytically prior to the agency of Catholic priests, and this is prior to any ritual involving holy water.

These additional elements yield two fundamental principles for the analysis of ritual, enabling the generation of a typology of ritual forms. The 'Principle of Superhuman Agency' holds that 'rituals where superhuman agents function as the agent in the ritual ... will always prove more central to a religious system than those where the superhuman agents serve some other role' (125). 'Special-agent rituals' are thus the cornerstone of *RR*'s theory of ritual. The 'Principle of Superhuman Immediacy' holds that 'the fewer enabling actions to which appeal must be made in order to implicate a superhuman agent, the more fundamental the ritual is to the religious system in question' (125).

RR's analysis of the representation of religious ritual leads to theoretically interesting conclusions (e.g., that special-agent rituals do not need to be repeated, that special agents cannot be substituted for, etc.) and, ambitiously, to making predictions (e.g., 'Where *novel rituals* arise in a particular religious system those rituals will conform to the structural constraints that the formation rules of the action representation system impose' [112; original emphasis]). Although *RR*, like all cognitive theories of religion, suffers from a relative lack of empirical support, McCauley and Lawson (2002) and others (e.g., Abbink 1995; Vial 1999; Barrett and Lawson 2001) have taken steps in this direction.

Biology

In insisting that evolutionary/biological constraints are not sufficient to explain all the systematic properties of ritual systems (138; see 65–77, 151–2, 179–84), *RR* diverges from the subsequent development of the cognitive science of religion (e.g., Boyer 2001; Atran 2002; Pyysiäinen 2003).[3] This difference has fundamental implications for the project of *RR*'s subtitle: 'connecting cognition and culture.'

The evolutionary/biological route taken by other cognitive theories of religion has resulted in an explanatory gap between universal cognitive constraints and contingent cultural variability: the latter remains a largely unexamined space of possibilities broadly constrained by the 'evolutionary landscape' of the former (Atran 2002). In contrast, *RR* includes a certain relation between the two in its premises: 'ritual systems have both cultural *and* cognitive dimensions'; 'analyses of these two domains will reflect and mutually inform one another' (68, 42; original emphasis).

Symbolic-cultural systems are analyzed via their cognitive representations; that is, *RR* studies 'minds rather than the systems themselves' (183). However, where Chomsky is held to have taken 'the biological route,' emphasizing 'universal, *biologically based* constraints' on cognitive representations, Lawson and McCauley 'eschew this strong nativist route,' holding that 'with religious ritual systems, the nativist route seems implausible in the extreme'; rather, 'symbolic-cultural systems ... arise in virtue of human social interaction' (180, 75, 183–4; original emphasis). That is, *RR*'s connection between cognition and culture is a theoretical premise not an analytical result. It is as if a book by Anthony Giddens or Pierre Bourdieu were subtitled 'connecting agency and structure.'

This emerges from *RR*'s primary concern with the representation of action in general, not of religious ritual, or religion, in particular:

> The principles which underlie religious ritual systems do not seem to be unique to that domain. ... [W]hat distinguishes religious rituals from both other sorts of rituals and everyday actions overwhelmingly concerns the peculiar conceptual commitments *which characterize religion generally*. There is very little reason to think that these commitments result from anything innate. (79; emphasis in original)

RR analyzes a sub-set of actions (religious ritual) characterized by beliefs in *culturally* postulated superhuman beings. Where ritual includes these commitments in representations of action, it brings them under the sway of cognitive constraints. Religious commitments are cultural not cognitive, but they are predictably shaped by tacit constraints when they appear within religious ritual systems.

Once we accept the analogy between ritual and language, issues of meaning and truth become central. Given its de-emphasis on biology, *RR* turns instead to a 'semantic account that focuses on the overarching cognitive constructs with which we bring order to the world' (152). This 'reflexive holism' (critiqued below) is fundamental to *RR*'s project of 'bootstrapping our way up theoretically from the cognitive to the cultural' (183).

Criticisms

At the most general level, some have criticized *RR*'s cognitive approach. Cognitive approaches to the study of religion are explicitly limited in their objectives and scope, yielding specific strengths and weaknesses: 'if the cognitivists offer a better analysis of ritual structure, they say very little about the social and political uses of ritual' (Vial 1999: 144). Hence, it is beside the point to argue, as, for example, Levine (1998) does, that *RR*'s cognitive approach is of little value because it tells us nothing about the meaning or function of rituals. Harvey Whitehouse (drawing on Maurice Bloch's concept of deference) argues that *RR*'s cognitive approach, in its attempt to show how rituals may 'conform in various ways to implicit intuitive expectations,' fails to explain 'aspects of ritualization that would seem rather directly to *challenge* certain of these expectations': specifically, cognitive constraints lead humans to posit 'intentional meanings lurking behind *all* actions. In the case of ritual actions, however, the search for intentional meaning is inevitably frustrated because the actions in question do not originate in the intentions of the ritual actor' (Whitehouse 2006: 662–3, original emphasis; cf. Bloch 2005, 2006; see also Humphrey and Laidlaw 1994). This raises important questions about action, though arguably beyond the narrow focus that informs *RR*'s argument.

Others point to the need to clarify the 'innateness' of ritual competence: *RR* needs to offer a 'plausible account of the constraints' on such tacit knowledge, given the rejection of the nativist route (Proudfoot 1992: 133); by shifting the ground of tacit knowledge of ritual forms from hard-wired to socio-cultural, *RR* problematizes 'innateness' (Platvoet 1993), though the choice to bracket this thorny issue may have strategic advantages. Boyer (1991) calls for more empirical clarification of the argument, especially with reference to intuitions of the 'well-formedness' of rituals.

Others have taken issue with *RR*'s approach to ritual. Caroline Humphrey and James Laidlaw make several points: Jainism offers a counter-example to *RR*'s claim that 'religions without commitments to culturally postulated superhuman agents are … extremely unlikely to have rich … ritual systems'

(7–8; Humphrey and Laidlaw 1994: 82–3, n.4); *RR* offers 'no definition or characterization of ritual action as such … because ritual is for them a derivative term'; it does not 'seriously consider the possibility of secular ritual, or whether anything other than the "religious" postulate of superhuman agents distinguishes ritual from other modes of action' (Laidlaw and Humphrey 2006: 272–3). (To be fair, *RR* nowhere denies the possibility of non-religious ritual.) More generally, *RR*'s idealized approach to ritual (e.g., 65, 77, 152) leaves it ill-prepared to deal with issues of ritual dynamics: Carlo Severi, for example, notes *RR*'s 'disregard of actual ceremonial interaction as a possible source of structure' (2006: 590). Platvoet (1993) notes that *RR*'s characterization of ritual in terms of the action representation system defines certain forms of religious action, e.g., prayer, as non-ritual.[4] (*RR* holds that 'the actions of superhuman agents … which are constitutive of a religion's ritual system are never denoted by intransitive verbs' [92–3].)

Others criticize *RR*'s basic characterization of religion. Humphrey and Laidlaw argue that its definition excludes Theravada Buddhism (1994: 82–3, n.4); though *RR* specifically discounts Theravada Buddhism along with Marxism as 'hardly prototypical' (7); and Hans Penner suggests that the Buddha serves as a superhuman agent, bringing this putative counter-example back into the fold (2002: 159). Stewart Guthrie argues that 'the term superhuman does not fit agents such as demons and ghosts … which often are better described as subhuman,'[5] and he suggests that his own evolutionary emphasis on anthropomorphism answers a question that *RR* does not: 'why should humans posit humanlike, but not exactly human, beings at all? The Lawson–McCauley approach offers no apparent answer. Rather, it substitutes the problem of humanlike agents for the problem of religion' (Guthrie 1996: 414). On a related note, Scott Atran and Ara Norenzayan include *RR* among cognitive theories that

> do not account for the emotional involvement that leads people to sacrifice to others what is dear to themselves, including labor, limb, and life. Such theories are often short on motive and are unable to distinguish Mickey Mouse from Moses, cartoon fantasy from religious belief. (2004: 714; see Atran 2002: 13–14)

Jeremy Carrette argues that Lawson and McCauley's divergence from Chomsky, their connecting cognition and culture, constitutes an 'ideological move toward computation and the essentialism of brain functions': 'cognitive science, in its computational processing form, relates to the ideology of the machine and political totalitarianism' (2005: 255–6, see 2007: 163–203). Carrette does not analyze or critique *RR*'s argument but rather 'the wider ideology it supports' (2005: 255). This shift from internalist to externalist analysis raises important issues, but it fails to note, for example, that *RR* is careful not to assert a biological basis for ritual competence.

These various critiques have four main thrusts: *RR* is committed to a necessarily limited (though empirically promising) cognitivist perspective; it requires additional clarification and empirical support, some of which is addressed in McCauley and Lawson's later work (especially 2002); its approach to ritual stands in tension with other important work in ritual theory, though some rapprochement may be possible (Laidlaw and Humphrey 2006: 283); and its ideological resonance with broader developments in the political economy of knowledge is worth examining further.

Semantics

The sixth chapter of *RR*, 'Semantics and ritual systems,' attempts to provide a coherent semantic framework to underpin the meaningfulness of religious (or 'symbolic') language. Lawson and McCauley set an important, though neglected, precedent in recognizing the need for a thorough semantic framework. We argue here that their account is flawed, but that it sets an important precedent.

RR's discussion of semantics presupposes the three central elements of the book's theory of ritual: agents, actions, and the objects of actions. Although this account of ritual is discussed at length, little of semantic significance turns on it, beyond the view that ritual, involving agent intentionality, falls under the same general category as language. Thus, ritual can be studied and theorized about just as language is: i.e., in terms of both syntax and semantics.

RR first explains and critiques the traditional semantic approach (mainly Fregean, though he is not acknowledged), which finds the core of meaning in a 'mapping' or one-to-one relation between certain semantically simple terms (e.g., names of logical 'atoms') and metaphysically basic objects (e.g., basic Lockean sense data). In the course of describing this view, *RR* describes the traditional view in various terms: (i) 'extensionalist,' as it takes the meaning of linguistic items to be given by metaphysical objects rather than by further linguistic description (i.e., as per an 'intensionalist' semantics); (ii) 'referential,' as the so-called mapping function is essentially a 'reference relation' between word (term) and object (referent); (iii) 'atomistic,' as the basic items – whether words or objects – are irreducible; and (iv) 'empiricist,' as the epistemic access to the metaphysical objects which serve as the referents of linguistic terms is presumed to be observational. Lawson and McCauley seem to treat these four terms as equivalent, or at least as standing or falling together. This is problematic, as it is quite possible to advocate a semantic framework that contains some of these elements but not others. This confusion is similar to another, discussed below, that leads them to see 'reflexive holism' as the only viable alternative to the 'traditional' view.

Lawson and McCauley rightly critique this traditional view. First, they argue that such a semantics is untenable for religious language because the purported referents of the terms are metaphysically 'unusual': i.e., not obvious, epistemological distant, disputed, etc. The danger here, though not stated explicitly, is that if, as a matter of fact, such entities failed to exist, then the terms of religious language would be literally meaningless. The problem is that meaning would fail if a semantics tied it to the existence of an entity that did not exist. On such an account, whether people believe or not in the entity wouldn't make any difference, as it is the actual entity, not representations of, beliefs about, or commitments to it, which does the semantic work. The second main problem for the traditional approach is that such an 'extensionalist' semantics is inadequate even for 'natural language.'[6] They do a nice job explaining why such a semantics is inadequate even for relatively unproblematic language. These problems are well known to philosophers from the works of Frege and Russell, through Wittgenstein, Quine, Putnam, Davidson, Rorty, etc. By drawing attention to this well-established semantic critique, *RR* effectively challenged theorists of religion to stop using an outdated and much-criticized account of the meaning of (religious) language. For the most part, this gauntlet has lain ignored in the dust.

The structure of *RR*'s two critiques reveals a crucial ambiguity. On the one hand, Lawson and McCauley argue that a traditional semantics fails for religious language because of the differences between religious and non-religious discourse. On the other hand, they argue that it fails because of a similarity between the two. The discourses are different, so they require a different semantics, and, as the underlying semantics of 'natural' language is 'atomistic,' then the underlying semantics of religious language must be 'holistic.' However, the discourses are both language, and semantic holism is required (all the way down) because atomism is incapable of adequately explicating meaning. This ambiguity resurfaces in a deeper problem that we address below.

RR presents semantic 'holism' as the alternative to 'atomism.' According to holism, the meaning of any term is given, at least in part, by its relation to other terms (whose meaning must also be given by reference to other terms, etc.): linguistic meaning forms a Quinean 'web'; meanings are 'primarily functions of their positions in the web and, secondarily, of their relationships to those statements with which they have the most direct connections' (144).[7] Thus, looking for the referents of religious terms in the 'real' world misses the point; look rather, *RR* says, to how the term is related to others within the 'conceptual scheme' of the religious discourse.

The main weakness of holistic approaches, according to *RR*, is that the web may be free floating, i.e., have no connection at all with anything outside of itself. As such, it would not be 'stable,' but rather be 'completely unconstrained' and face 'epistemic chaos' (147). *RR* thus opts for a form of referential holism, or holistic referentialism.

RR argues that, in 'natural' language, reference is probably best understood in relation to 'basic levels' rather than to 'logical atoms' (150–3).[8] Terms at the basic level, although they ultimately ground the meaning of other parts of speech, have 'no epistemic privilege' (i.e., are not 'innate' in the Cartesian sense of being epistemologically incorrigible) and are almost certainly responsive to cultural differences. ('Snow' would be unlikely to function at a basic level for native Hawaiians in the seventeenth century.) They can also vary within a community: the basic level for experts might be different from that of the laity, e.g., 'atom' might be at a basic level for a physicist, but not for a child. A web of meaning anchored to such 'basic' terms provides 'innate perceptual biases' that function as relatively stable and fruitful 'models' or 'theories' of the world.[9] Because such terms have 'no epistemic privilege' (i.e., are not innate, incorrigible, necessary, a priori, universal, etc.) and play predominately an ordering and systematizing role, we can 'often entertain multiple (and not fully consistent) models and theories for the *same* domain,' and different models are sometimes 'competitors' and sometimes 'make their peace' (153).

Once the referential groundings for a semantic framework are thus divorced from a foundational epistemological 'sense datum' approach, the door is open for non-obvious objects to play that role, including unobservable entities such as quarks, gravitational forces, or culturally postulated superhuman agents. However, this view, which implicitly extends the discussion to include religious systems, counts against their argument. They suggest here that reference can be made to unobservable entities (or, rather, that an adequate semantics can invoke grounding referents of a 'non-obvious' sort). However, if this is the case, then one of the major criticisms of the 'traditional' approach is obviated, and the necessity of a holism seems diminished. That is, *RR* criticizes the traditional approach because it makes reference to entities that are metaphysically unusual, but then it argues that semantic holism does a better job of dealing with religion because it allows for reference to such metaphysically unusual entities as superhuman beings.

The direction that *RR* takes at this point is problematic. Lawson and McCauley suggest that such a 'basic levels' approach would be inadequate for religious language, however promising it might be for 'natural' language.

Presumably this is because the differences between 'dog' and 'god' are too great. In the examples they explore, the basic levels are still fundamentally observational in nature, whereas, in the case of religious language, many, at least, are not. Possible candidates for the 'referents' needed to ground the web of meaning of religious language, according to *RR*, must be free of observational constraints.[10]

From this point, *RR* makes a problematic leap: 'The only sort of reference available to such systems, then, is self-reference' (156). There are three fundamental problems with this conclusion that meaning is self-referential in the case of religious ritual systems.[11] First, it presupposes a false dichotomy: either reference is to observational entities or it is reflexive. There are all kinds of accounts (particularly in contemporary metaethics and philosophy of science) of how reference to objective and independent but non-observable entities and properties might be understood (e.g., a scientific realist's account of the status of electrons). Hence, the attempt to ascribe some sort of meaning to rituals does not necessitate a choice between the traditional semantics that *RR* rightly rejects and the reflexive holism that it proposes.

Second, *RR* assumes that only some sort of reference relation can provide the grounding required to avoid 'epistemic chaos.' However, there are holistic semantic theories that attempt this in non-referential ways. For example, Donald Davidson's more familiar holism (resulting from reflection on radical interpretation) suggests that interpreting the language of others be constrained by a broad conformance to rationality, even where the 'standards of rationality' adopted by the interpreter are criticizable and perhaps even socially embedded (e.g., Davidson 1984). Robert Brandom (1994), alternatively, argues that meaning can be grounded on the basis of the correctness of a set of standard inferences, even where the inferences are culturally relative.[12]

Third, no informative account is given of what a 'reflexive' reference might be. *RR*'s usage is distinct from standard examples of reflexivity from philosophical logic (e.g., trivial truths like 'This sentence has five words' and semantic paradoxes like 'This sentence is false.'). It is very difficult to imagine what self-referentiality would mean for religious terms. All that seems left is to make them refer to the entire 'conceptual scheme,' but this borders on incoherence. What, on Lawson and McCauley's account, is the referent of the term 'Olorun'? The traditional account, as they read it, would have this term refer to something reducible to a set of observationally accessible properties and objects; i.e., a face-value reading would have it refer to an objectively, though supernaturally, existing entity. A free-floating holist eschews 'reference' in this sense, but could say that 'Olorun' 'refers' to the relational/functional position it occupies in the web of language in which it is embedded. Lawson and McCauley can't mean this, however, as such a position would be indistinguishable from the epistemologically chaotic holism that they explicitly reject. It is this rejection that motivates their quest for some form of grounding through reference. As *RR* stands, it seems impossible to make sense of *reflexive* holism, and this is a serious weakness.[13]

On a different note, a basic tension arises in Lawson and McCauley's account of semantics based on its presupposition of obvious and clear-cut distinctions between domains of discourse. They unproblematically distinguish at least three domains of discourse: 'natural' language (which seems, again, to mainly be about medium-sized, observationally obvious public objects); 'scientific' language (which, with its apparent reference to unobservable entities as well as mysterious and non-obvious causal forces, seems as problematic as religious discourse); and 'symbolic' or religious language. As mentioned above, their initial argument that reflexive holism is the most promising semantic framework for understanding religious phenomena is ambiguous: it rests on acknowledging a relevant distinction between religious and natural language, while, at the same time, insisting on their similarity. Later, they resurrect reference for religious language (reinforcing the analogy with natural language, an analogy that serves as a metatheoretical axiom, thus requiring a similar semantics). However, they propose an exceedingly strange form of reference, one that remains unclear if not indefensible. Their motivation in doing so appears to be to distinguish religious language from natural language, mainly in order to enable the two to play different normative roles in such things as explanation and in making sense of the world, as well as to account for the *prima facie* distinctiveness of the use, evocation, and, for the most part, insular nature of religious language.

In the end, one is left wondering whether Lawson and McCauley can truly have it both ways: either religious language is language, embedded in other language and explicable according to the *same* semantic framework as any other bit of language; or else there are clear *semantic* differences between religious and non-religious discourse. But, such a result could only be shown if there were a semantic theory, neutral to types of discourse, able to generate such distinctions. It is difficult to see how 'reflexive' holism could do the job when, by their own admission, it is the wrong semantic model for 'natural' language.

Holistic semantic approaches, particularly Davidson's, were intended to provide an account of meaning at its most basic level, i.e., one considerably deeper than attempts to articulate a distinction between domains of discourse. The sort of bifurcation of types of meaning that is presupposed by *RR*'s distinction between religious and natural language is reminiscent of the attempt to understand religious phenomena in terms of metaphor, i.e., a type of 'meaning' distinct from normal meaning, a view that has come under harsh critique in theory of religion (e.g., Penner 2002; Frankenberry 2002b). The idea that religious language refers in some special symbolic, metaphorical, or other non-literal manner is impossible to clarify adequately for the purposes of the scholarly study of religion. Davidson's holistic arguments are incompatible with such an approach. Lawson and McCauley also reject such a 'metaphorical' approach to the study of religion. Yet, in the end, the alternative that they offer, reflexive holism, seems similarly impossible to clarify in a manner that would ground the sort of theoretical approach that they champion.

Conclusion

Lawson and McCauley's semantic account of the meaning of ritual (and of religion) is flawed, and this cuts the ground out from under their theory. On the other hand, sustained attention to semantics is missing entirely from other theories of ritual and of religion. With rare exceptions, theorists of religion limp bravely on, apparently unaware that their work is hamstrung by the lack of an adequate account of just *how* it is that religious language (and, arguably, religious ritual) *means* anything. Almost all work in the field implicitly accepts the traditional Fregean semantic view, despite the fact that rejecting this view, as modeled by *RR*, is the first step toward any adequate account of religious meaning. In this sense, Lawson and McCauley's false start continues to set an exemplary precedent: better a flawed foundation than none at all. The few attempts to address this much-needed dimension of theories of religion have drawn almost exclusively on the work of philosopher Donald Davidson (e.g., Godlove 1989; Frankenberry 2002a; Jensen 2003, 2004). Although more promising than both the traditional view critiqued by *RR* and the 'reflexive holism' that it proposes as an alternative, this direction faces significant problems of its own (Gardiner and Engler 2008). In the end, *RR* stands as a foundational work among cognitive theories of religion, though a different legacy may prove more important to the further development of theories of religion: despite its problems, *RR*'s attention to semantics set a benchmark in a foundational area that begs for further work.

Acknowledgements

Work on this chapter was supported in part by a research fellowship from Brazil's Coordenação de Aperfeiçoamento de Pessoal de Nível Superior (CAPES).

Notes

1 All page number citations without author/date refer to *RR*. Valuable reviews include Boyer (1991), Glazier (1994), Maguire (1991), Platvoet (1993), and Proudfoot (1992); valuable synopses include Vial (1999: 138–43), Barrett (2000: 32–3), Pyysiäinen (2003: 85–9), Laidlaw and Humphrey (2006: 272–4), and Kreinath, Snoek, and Stausberg (2007: 263–6). Pyysiäinen (2001) attempts, in part, to generalize *RR*'s approach in service of a more general theory of religion. McCauley and Lawson (2002) further developed their views in dialogue with the work of Harvey Whitehouse (1995, 2000). See Engler and Gardiner (forthcoming) for an overview of critiques of cognitive approaches to religion. The authors thank Robert N. McCauley for comments; we of course take full responsibility for any remaining errors in interpretation.

2 See Benson Saler's chapter in this volume.

3 On Boyer/Pyysiäinen and Atran see, respectively, the chapters by Jeppe Sinding Jensen and Joseph Bulbulia in this volume.

4 In earlier work, Lawson (1976) proposed prayer as a type of ritual that offers fruitful parallels with language.

5 In later work, Lawson and McCauley, following the dominant trend in cognitive theory of religion, talk of 'counter-intuitiveness' more than 'superhuman.'

6 The meaning of 'natural language' is not clear here. Presumably *RR* means 'non-religious language.' However, it is difficult to see how that distinction is to be drawn semantically.

7 The Quinean approach eliminates the temptation to reify either meanings or claims. The meaning of a speech act is given by its relation to other speech acts. To grasp the meaning of a claim is to grasp the role it plays in the overall structure of intentional action. That's all there is to meaning: there is no mysterious *thing* called the meaning of a claim (nor is there any mysterious *thing* called the 'claim').

8 Logical atoms are indefinable and irreducible, such as G.E. Moore's famous 'good' or 'yellow.' 'Basic levels' are determined empirically by cognitive psychology. For example, 'dog' is not a logical atom, because it could be defined, for example, as a domesticated canine mammal; however, it is more 'basic' than any of these terms. The 'basic level' is that of which 'subjects unhesitatingly report the ability to generate an image' and 'most rapidly recognize'; it is 'the highest level at which subjects report standard patterns of interaction'; it is 'typically the least complex (both phonemically and orthographically)', is 'the most remembered,' and is 'most likely to be first learned' (150–1). In light of work since *RR*, the concept of basic levels offers a promising basis for exploring the semantic implications of discussions of 'counter-intuitiveness,' defined in terms of the violation of 'ontological categories' (Boyer 2001: 60–1), 'intuitive expectations' (Pyysiäinen 2003:17–22), or 'innate, modular expectations' (Atran 2002: 96).

9 Lawson and McCauley often refer to these 'models' as 'conceptual schemes,' seemingly invoking the 'scheme/content' distinction famously critiqued and rejected by Davidson. Here again, *RR*'s discussion stands in tension with current

debates in philosophical semantics. See Godlove (1989) for an exploration of the implications of Davidson's critique for theory of religion.

10   Further evidence of this necessity is given by religious beliefs' immunity from revision by experience in a variety of senses: e.g., how no future experience could possibly force revision of a religious belief, how religious systems can be 'explanatory' of everything, etc.

11   Robin Horton criticized *RR* for its portrayal of religion as the 'building up of elaborate self-referential structures, apparently as ends in themselves' (1993: 350).

12   Both Davidson's and Brandom's positions are similar to the 'basic levels' approach advocated by Lawson and McCauley for 'natural' (but not religious) language: 'basic concepts,' 'conceptions of rationality,' and 'correctness of inference' are remarkably similar in each system, in that they seem to play analogous roles in the resulting semantics, though none of them is 'epistemically privileged' in any obvious sense.

13   Many of *RR*'s 'arguments' in support of reflexive holism are of an odd type: 'notice how such an approach would solve problem x'; and 'see how such an approach seems parallel (or merely analogous?) to recent research in field y.' Though such comments are intriguing, this is hardly the type of evidence that moves the philosopher or semantic theorist.

References

Abbink, J., 1995. Ritual and environment: the *Mosit* ceremony of the Ethiopian Me'en people. *Journal of Religion in Africa* 25, 163–90.

Atran, S., 2002. *In gods we trust: the evolutionary landscape of religion.* Oxford University Press, Oxford.

Atran, S. and Norenzayan, A., 2004. Religion's evolutionary landscape: counter-intuition, commitment, compassion, communion. *Behavioral and Brain Sciences* 27, 713–70.

Barrett, J.L., 2000. Exploring the natural foundations of religion. *Trends in Cognitive Sciences* 4, 29–34.

Barrett, J.L., 2004. *Why would anyone believe in God?* AltaMira Press, Walnut Creek.

Barrett, J.L. and Lawson, E.T., 2001. Ritual intuitions: cognitive contributions to judgements of ritual efficacy. *Journal of Cognition and Culture* 1 (2), 183–201.

Bloch, M., 2005. Ritual and deference. In: Bloch, M. (Ed.), *Essays on cultural transmission.* Berg Publishers, Oxford, 123–37.

Bloch, M., 2006. Deference. In: Kreinath, J., Snoek, J., and Stausberg, M. (Eds.), *Theorizing rituals: issues, topics, approaches, concepts.* Brill, Leiden, Boston, 495–506.

Boyer, P., 1991. Review of Lawson, T.E. and McCauley, R.N., *Rethinking religion. American Anthropologist* (n.s.) 93 (4), 984–5.

Boyer, P., 1994. *The naturalness of religious ideas: a cognitive theory of religion.* University of California Press, Berkeley.

Boyer, P., 2001. *Religion explained: the evolutionary origins of religious development.* Basic Books, New York.

Brandom, R., 1994. *Making it explicit*, Harvard University Press, Cambridge, MA.

Carrette, J., 2005. Religion out of mind: the ideology of cognitive science and religion. In: Bulkeley, K. (Ed.), *Soul, psyche, brain: new directions in the study of religion and brain-mind science*. Palgrave Macmillan, Gordonsville, VA, 242–61.

Carrette, J., 2007. *Religion and critical psychology: religious experience in the knowledge economy*. Routledge, London and New York.

Davidson, D., 1984. *Inquiries into truth and interpretation*. Oxford University Press, Oxford.

Engler, S. and Gardiner M.Q., forthcoming. A critical response to cognitivist theories of religion. In: King, R. (Ed.), *Theory/religion/critique: classic and contemporary approaches*. Columbia University Press, New York.

Frankenberry, N.K. (Ed.), 2002a. *Radical interpretation in religion*. Cambridge University Press, Cambridge.

Frankenberry, N.K., 2002b. Religion as a 'mobile army of metaphors.' In: Frankenberry, N. K. (Ed.), *Radical interpretation in religion*. Cambridge University Press, Cambridge, 171–87.

Gardiner, M.Q. and Engler, S., 2008. Review essay: Frankenberry, N.K. (Ed.), *Radical interpretation in religion*. Method and Theory in the Study of Religion 20 (2), 185–90.

Glazier, S.D., 1994. Religion in Latin America: behavioral and cognitive approaches. *Reviews in Anthropology* 23, 313–21.

Godlove, T.F., Jr., 1989. *Religion, interpretation, and diversity of belief: the framework model from Kant to Durkheim to Davidson*. Cambridge University Press, Cambridge, New York.

Guthrie, S.E., 1993. *Faces in the clouds: a new theory of religion*. Oxford University Press, Oxford.

Guthrie, S.E., 1996. Religion: what is it? *Journal for the Scientific Study of Religion* 35 (4), 412–19.

Guthrie, S.E., 2001. Why gods? A cognitive theory. In: Andresen, J. (Ed.), *Religion in mind: cognitive perspectives on religious belief, ritual, and experience*. Cambridge University Press, Cambridge, 94–111.

Horton, R., 1993. *Patterns of though in Africa and the West: essays on magic, religion and science*. Cambridge University Press, Cambridge.

Humphrey, C. and Laidlaw, J., 1994. *The archetypal actions of ritual: a theory of ritual illustrated by the Jain rite of worship*. Oxford University Press, Oxford.

Jensen, J.S., 2003. *The study of religion in a new key: theoretical and philosophical soundings in the comparative and general study of religion*. Aarhus University Press, Aarhus.

Jensen, J.S., 2004. Meaning and religion: on semantics in the study of religion. In: Antes, P., Geertz, A.W., and Warne, R.R. (Eds.), *New approaches to the study of religion*. Volume 1, *Regional, critical and historical approaches*. Walter de Gruyter, Berlin, New York, 219–52.

Kreinath, J., Snoek, J., and Stausberg, M., 2007. *Theorizing rituals: annotated bibliography of ritual theory, 1966–2005*. Brill, Leiden, Boston.

Laidlaw, J. and Humphrey, L., 2006. Action. In: Kreinath, J., Snoek, J., and Stausberg, M. (Eds.), *Theorizing rituals: issues, topics, approaches, concepts*. Brill, Leiden, Boston, 265–83.

Lawson, E.T., 1976. Ritual as language. *Religion* 6, 123–39.

Lawson, E.T. and McCauley, R.N., 1990. *Rethinking religion: connecting cognition and culture*. Cambridge University Press, Cambridge (= *RR*).

Lawson, E.T. and McCauley, R.N., 1993. Crisis of conscience, riddle of identity: making space for a cognitive approach to religious phenomena. *Journal of the American Academy of Religion* 61 (2), 201–23.

Levine, M.P., 1998. A cognitive approach to ritual: new method or no method at all. *Method & Theory in the Study of Religion* 10, 30–60.

Liénard, P. and Boyer, P., 2006. Whence collective rituals? A cultural selection model of ritualized behavior. *American Anthropologist* 108 (4), 814–27.

Maguire, J.F., 1991. Review of Lawson, T.E. and McCauley, R.N., *Rethinking religion*. *Journal for the Scientific Study of Religion* 30 (3), 344–6.

McCauley, R.N. and Lawson, E.T., 1984. Functionalism reconsidered. *History of Religions* 23, 372–81.

McCauley, R.N. and Lawson, E.T., 1996. Who owns culture? *Method & Theory in the Study of Religion* 8, 171–90.

McCauley, R.N. and Lawson, E.T., 2002. *Bringing ritual to mind: psychological foundations of cultural forms*. Cambridge University Press, Cambridge.

Penner, H.H., 2002. You don't read a myth for information. In: Frankenberry, N.K. (Ed.), *Radical interpretation in religion*. Cambridge University Press, Cambridge, 153–70.

Platvoet, J.G., 1993. Review of Lawson, T.E. and McCauley, R.N., *Rethinking religion*. *Numen* 40 (2), 189–91.

Proudfoot, W., 1992. Review of Lawson, T.E. and McCauley, R.N., *Rethinking religion*. *The Journal of Religion* 72 (1), 132–3.

Pyysiäinen, I., 2002. Introduction: cognition and culture in the construction of religion. In: Pyysiäinen, I. and Anttonen, V. (Eds.), *Current approaches in the cognitive science of religion*. Continuum, London, New York, 1–13.

Pyysiäinen, I., 2003. *How religion works: towards a new cognitive science of religion*. Brill, Leiden, Boston.

Severi, C., 2006. Language. In: Kreinath, J., Snoek, J., and Stausberg, M. (Eds.), *Theorizing rituals: issues, topics, approaches, concepts*. Brill, Leiden, Boston, 583–93.

Sperber, D., 1975. *Rethinking symbolism*. Cambridge University Press, Cambridge.

Vial, T.M., 1999. Opposites attract: the body and cognition in a debate over baptism. *Numen* 46, 121–45.

Whitehouse, H., 1995. *Inside the cult: religious innovation and transmission in Papua New Guinea*. Oxford University Press, Oxford.

Whitehouse, H., 2000. *Arguments and icons: divergent modes of religiosity*. Oxford University Press, Oxford.

Whitehouse, H., 2006. Transmission. In: Kreinath, J., Snoek, J., and Stausberg, M. (Eds.), *Theorizing rituals: issues, topics, approaches, concepts*. Brill, Leiden, Boston, 657–69.

3

Anthropomorphism and animism

On Stewart E. Guthrie, Faces in the clouds (1993)

Benson Saler

Stewart E. Guthrie's theory of religion was first set forth in an essay entitled 'A cognitive theory of religion,' published in 1980 in the journal *Current Anthropology* (21 [2]: 181–203). Guthrie later elaborated and refined his views in a number of publications, and he continues to do so. Thus far, his most extensive statement in one place is found in his book, *Faces in the clouds: a new theory of religion*. Published by Oxford University Press in a hardback edition in 1993, it was reissued by the same publisher in paperback in 1995. It expands and to some extent modifies the theory set forth in the 1980 essay. That theory pivots on the claim that human beings universally tend to respond to environmental ambiguities by recourse to human-like and animal-like models. This chapter explores Guthrie's theory as it developed in the 1980 essay and in the 1993 book.

It is widely supposed that the new cognitive science of religion began in 1990, with the publication of E. Thomas Lawson and Robert N. McCauley's *Rethinking religion: connecting cognition and culture* (see, for instance, Liénard and Boyer 2006: 815).[1] Without detracting from the importance of Lawson and McCauley's foundational book, however, it should be noted that some of the central ideas and understandings in the current cognitive science of religion were set forth by Guthrie in 1980.

This chapter is organized as follows. After a brief biographical introduction to Guthrie, it situates and describes the 1980 essay. Then it addresses the 1993 book, along with some of the criticisms of that work.

Stewart Elliott Guthrie

Stewart Elliott Guthrie received a Bachelor of Arts degree in the humanities from the University of Iowa in 1963. During the following academic year he was an Exchange Fellow at the University of Tübingen. After returning from Germany, he enrolled in the PhD program in anthropology at Brown

University, but soon transferred to Yale University, where he received a PhD in anthropology in 1976.

In preparation for ethnographic fieldwork in Japan, Guthrie spent the academic year 1969–70 in the Japanese language program at the Stanford Inter-University Center in Tokyo. The principal published work stemming from his research in Japan is a book, *A Japanese new religion: Rissho Kosei-kai in a mountain hamlet*, published in 1988 as the first volume in the Michigan Monograph Series in Japanese Studies.

Some of the background: Tylor and Horton

Guthrie's theoretical approach did not spring *de novo* from ruminations about religion. Rather, it was nurtured by a number of insights published in a diversity of sources. Guthrie himself declares that his theory 'is indebted most to [Robin] Horton and intellectualism' (1993: 37). It will prove instructive to consider both as background for the emergence of Guthrie's approach.

The term 'intellectualism' in religious studies is pre-eminently associated with the theorist Edward Burnett Tylor (1832–1917). Tylor's appointment as Reader in Anthropology at Oxford in 1884 was the first appointment of an anthropologist as such in a British university. His major statement about religion is found in a two-volume work, *Primitive culture* (1871). Tylor states there that his evolutionary approach emphasizes 'the intellec- tual ... side of religion,' to the explicitly confessed near-neglect of other aspects of that phenomenon (1958 [1873, 1871] vol. II: 444–5). His task, Tylor tells us, is 'not to discuss Religion in all its bearings.' Rather, it is 'to portray in outline the great doctrine of Animism, as found in what I conceive to be its earliest stages ... and to show its transmission along the lines of religious thought' (1958 II: 445). In doing so, however, Tylor does far more than outline a theory about the evolution of religion. As J. Samuel Preus points out:

> [W]e see that Tylor is writing the history of the mind. Repeatedly, he refers to his project as describing 'the course of mental history,' the 'laws of intellectual movement,' the 'history of laws of mind,' the 'history of opinion,' 'intellectual history,' and so on. (Preus 1987: 133)

In Tylor's theoretical account, our ancient forebears were moved by curiosity. Puzzled by dreams, trances, visions, and death, they invented, largely from their sensory experiences, ideas about animating principles and ghost-souls. Then, through the workings of a psychological process that we call stimulus generalization, they extended the idea of individual souls out to the non-human world, and they further developed ideas about independently existing spirits. In this way, they propounded what Tylor regards as the two complementary aspects of 'the great doctrine of Animism,' beliefs in souls and beliefs in other spiritual beings. According to Tylor, animism, so conceived, is at the core of all religions (Saler 1997).

Guthrie follows Tylor in emphasizing the intellectual aspects of religion, in regarding animism as an important matter that needs to be analyzed and explained relative to 'the course of mental history,' and in conceptualizing religion as universally founded on certain panhuman psychological processes. Beginning with a virtual paraphrase of Tylor, Guthrie (1993: 5) remarks that '[i]n explaining religion, I shall not explore its social uses.' He goes on to justify his approach by declaring that 'Showing that religion may be useful … does not show why religion arises and is believed. If religion did not arise for its own reasons or were not believable, its potential social uses could not create it.' Guthrie differs from Tylor, however, with respect to certain crucial details. In doing so, as pointed out above, he acknowledges being intellectually stimulated by Robin Horton, another theorist who appreciates Tylor while diverging from him in significant ways.

Horton, a British-trained social anthropologist whose principal fieldwork was among the Kalabari people of the Niger delta, incorporates a sensitivity to social organization into his overarching intellectualist perspective. While Tylor's famous 'minimum definition' of religion pointed to a belief in spiritual beings as the crucial definitional factor, Horton (1960: 211) characterizes religion as 'an extension of the field of people's social relationships beyond the confines of purely human society.'

In addition to his training as a social anthropologist, Horton also has something of an academic background in chemistry and in the philosophy of science. He draws upon that background in what is probably his most famous publication, a two-part essay entitled 'African traditional thought and Western science,' which appeared in the journal *Africa* in 1967. The first part of that essay outlines what Horton sees as similarities between Western science and traditional African thought as found in certain African religions. The second part of the essay describes what Horton regards as significant differences.

Both Western science and traditional African worldviews, Horton argues, seek to explain selected workings of the world by recourse to theory. Theory in both cases, moreover, yields understandings that contribute to human abilities to affect events or to have a sense of affecting events. Salient in both Western science and traditional African religion, Horton maintains, is the postulation of unobservable entities to explain observable phenomena. Electrons and spirits are among his examples. Structurally, moreover, theories in both cases are formatted by means of nesting models. That is, the least abstract explanatory models incorporate features of the workaday world, while at higher levels of abstraction models explain more and more with less and less. Thus, for instance, entities postulated at lower levels of abstraction are seen as 'special manifestations of those postulated at the higher level' (Horton 1967: 610). This is well known and routinely accepted in modern Western science. Recognition of it as a structural principle in traditional African religions, Horton argues, allows us to understand what may otherwise be a puzzling phenomenon among peoples such as the Kalabari, Ibo, and Tallensi. He refers to the postulation of both multiple spirits and a supreme god. These, on Horton's analysis, are complementary. While the spirits are treated as independent entities at lower levels of abstraction, at higher levels they are considered to be 'manifestations or dependents of the supreme being' (Horton 1967: 61). The spirits serve to set events into relatively limited causal contexts. The supreme being, in comparison, serves to set events into the widest possible context (Horton 1967: 62). This structural understanding, Horton contends, supports Evans-Pritchard's claim that '[a] theistic religion need be neither monotheistic nor polytheistic. It may be both. It is the question of the level, or situation, of thought, rather than of exclusive types of thought' (quoted in Horton 1967: 62).

In part two of his essay, Horton considers differences between traditional African systems of thought and modern Western science. I deal here with only one of the suggested differences, a contrast between a reliance on personal idioms in African systems and a preference for impersonal idioms in Western science. That difference seems most relevant to Guthrie's theorizing, which has much to say about the nature and functions of anthropomorphism in religion and in other aspects of human life.

Horton suggests that a personal idiom, an idiom of sentient beings, is appropriate for traditional African theoretical models because of the great and constraining influence of kinship and social organization on African culture and behavior. In the West, in comparison, there is more personal mobility and greater fluctuations in the nature and significance of daily, face-to-face social encounters. These, he thinks, dispose Westerners to appreciate the stable aspects of inanimate phenomena in comparison to the changeable social order. Horton surmises that this renders it appropriate in the West to utilize inanimate phenomena in theory construction. He is careful, however, to caution that if we were to convert a distinction between personal and impersonal entities into 'the crux of the difference between tradition and science,' we would handicap ourselves in achieving an adequate understanding of either. The difference between 'non-personal and personalized theories,' he states, 'is more than anything else a difference in *the idiom* of the explanatory quest' (Horton 1967: 69–70, emphasis added). Underlying the different idioms, Horton argues, are important resemblances in explanatory goals and in the theoretical structures that serve those goals.

Horton and Guthrie

Guthrie discusses Horton in both his 1980 essay and the 1993 book. I rely on the latter here.

Guthrie considers Horton's definition of religion – 'the extension of the field of people's social relationships beyond the confines of purely human society' – as a step in the right direction (Guthrie 1993: 33). It maintains that humans conceive of a *social relationship* with part of the non-human world. *This, indeed, is the crux of Guthrie's own theory*. But Guthrie pushes this line of thought further than does Horton. While agreeing with Horton that religion is (among other things) 'a social relationship' (Guthrie 1993: 35), and that conceptualized social relations are central to a religious worldview, Guthrie adds that 'faith is not in a doctrine but in a person' (1993: 36). That is, in extending the field of social relationships beyond the confines of the purely human (and pets and domestic animals), some non-human phenomena are treated as *persons or as having certain salient characteristics of human persons*. Most typically, they are credited with will, intelligence, and the capacity to receive and send messages. Non-human phenomena are, in short, anthropomorphized. If, moreover, some objects appear to be what we would deem inanimate, they are in effect animated, since abilities to exercise will and intelligence and to send and to receive messages are normally associated with being 'alive' (even if that may mean having some form of life after death). Anthropomorphism and animism, as Guthrie conceives them, are more than 'idioms.' In his theory, they are products of a universal human strategy, much of it unconscious, for coping with ambiguity in efforts to make sense of the world.

The 'nub' of his own theory of religion, Guthrie writes, 'is that belief in gods organizes experience as significantly as possible by positing for nonhuman things and events the highest actual organization we know: that of human beings and their society' (1993: 36). Horton, Guthrie charges, does not fully appreciate this, and he tends to view religious models as 'merely opportune' (1993: 36). From Guthrie's perspective, indeed, Horton misses the point in his contrast of modern Western science and traditional African religion. In religion, Guthrie maintains, anthropomorphism 'is fundamental and characteristic' (1993: 7), whereas in science, to the extent that we encounter anthropomorphism at all, it does not have 'a central role' (1993: 7). And while scientists are supposed to doubt doctrines, to doubt a doctrine in religion is to doubt a social relation, and to doubt a social relation is to undermine it (1993: 36). Skepticism, a virtue in science, is a vice in religion (1993: 36). Contrary to Horton, Guthrie argues that 'religious conservatism and scientific progressivism derive ... not so much from characteristics of the differing communities in which they are found (the communities may be the same) as from the entailments of religious and nonreligious belief' (1993: 36).

Overall, Guthrie opines that Horton's account 'seems voluntaristic and overly rationalistic, and seems to give too much weight to conscious explanations and too little to unconscious perception and interpretation' (1993: 36). Interestingly enough, these charges, directed here at Robin Horton, are charges that the contemporary cognitive science of religion levels at various theories of religion that preceded it.

The 1980 essay

As noted earlier, Guthrie's 1993 book expands on and to some extent modifies his seminal 1980 essay, 'A cognitive theory of religion.' In what immediately follows, I briefly describe the main point of that essay. In addition, I note some of the differences between the book and the essay. Finally, I assess the significance of the essay with respect to the development of the cognitive science of religion.

In his essay, Guthrie (1980: 181) defines religion as 'systematic application of human-like models to nonhuman, in addition to human, phenomena (e.g., in the discovery of "messages" in plagues and droughts, as well as in human language).' Religion is thus, 'among other things, a form of anthropomorphism' (1980: 181). As the phrase 'among other things' indicates, Guthrie acknowledges that there is more to religion than anthropomorphism. He holds, however, that the systematic application of human-like models is fundamental to religion, and that 'if the various phenomena that have been called "religion" have anything in common,' it is that (1980: 181, n.4). Indeed, while he claims that anthropomorphism is to be found in virtually all domains of human life, he maintains that anthropomorphism is usually neither central nor systematic in non-religious domains. Rather, outside of what we recognize as religion, it is typically *ad hoc* and opportunistic.

Guthrie initially accepts a broad, dictionary definition of anthropomorphism: the 'interpretation of what is not human or personal in terms of human or personal characteristics' (*Webster's Third New International Dictionary*, cited in Guthrie 1980: 181). In developing his argument in the essay (as well as in the book), however, Guthrie focuses on certain aspects of anthropomorphism, without ruling out the possible importance of others. The factors that he emphasizes include the attribution of will, purpose, and intelligence to the non-human world and, above all, the attribution of postulated capacities to send and receive messages. As Guthrie puts it:

What exactly do I mean by 'human-like' models? A few characteristics seem most nearly to distinguish humans from nonhumans. These ... are – despite some symbolism in chimps and gorillas – language and symbolism generally and resulting capacities for formal and symbolic statements about, and using, social relations among other things. 'Religion', then, means applying models to the nonhuman world in whole or in part that credit it with a capacity for language ... and for associated symbolic action. (Guthrie 1980: 189)

The above described points are repeated in more expansive form in the 1993 book. Some of the differences between book and essay are these:

1   In both publications Guthrie considers theories of religion advanced prior to his own, and he ventures opinions about their relative strengths and weaknesses. But, as one may expect, the treatment of antecedent theories is more substantial in the book than in the essay.

2   Guthrie says more about the psychological foundations of anthropomorphism in the book than in the essay. Further, he says a good deal more in the book, substantively as well as theoretically, about the ubiquity or pervasiveness of anthropomorphism in human life. Thus, for instance, the book contains a 29-page chapter (plus a number of photographs) addressed to 'Anthropomorphism in the arts,' and a 24-page chapter concerned with 'Anthropomorphism in philosophy and science.' Indeed, the book is the most comprehensive and sophisticated treatment of anthropomorphism of which I am aware.

3   While Guthrie mentions animism in the 1980 essay, his discussion of it is more intellectually engaging, and more obviously central to his theorizing, in the 1993 book.

4   While Guthrie expresses phylogenetic interests and sensitivities in the 1980 essay – as, for instance, in a suggestive analogy that he draws between religion and magic on the one hand and human languages and non-human animal call systems on the other, and in treating the threat displays of chimpanzees to rainstorms and waterfalls as something of an analog to human religion – his observations in the 1993 book are richer in that regard and should prove of more interest to scholars concerned with the evolutionary landscape of religion.

5   In the 1980 essay, Guthrie partially expounds an innatist argument, especially to the effect that a notable feature of religion is its linguistic approach to the world at large, and that such an approach is nurtured by inborn dispositions. But he also endorses Clifford Geertz's traditional anthropological claim of an 'extreme generality of man's innate ... response capacities' (Geertz 1966: 13, quoted in Guthrie 1980: 187). Guthrie, indeed, adds that 'the meanings of phenomena for us (unlike the apparent case for insects, for example) are not built into them, but conferred on them' (1980: 187). That strikes me as too one-sided a statement, and one out of harmony with the position on innate constraints

taken by the contemporary cognitive science of religion and, indeed, out of harmony with some of Guthrie's theorizing in the essay. The 1993 book, on the other hand, broadens and strengthens the intuitivist and innatist perspectives of the essay, and it does so consistently. It argues that anthropomorphism and animism stem from adaptive predispositions. As perceptual phenomena, Guthrie argues, they are predominantly unconscious, involuntary, and primitive.

Having already touched on Guthrie's discussions of Tylor and Horton in the 1993 book, I will deal to some extent with the other points noted above in my exposition of that work. Here, however, I relate certain ideas expressed in the 1980 essay to present-day themes in the cognitive science of religion.

Guthrie's characterization of the application of human-like models to the world clearly implicates what we today term the attribution of agency. While Guthrie does not employ that vocabulary in his 1980 essay, he is obviously positing what Lawson and McCauley, Justin Barrett, Pascal Boyer, Scott Atran, and other distinguished contributors to the cognitive science of religion (many of whom draw upon him) mean when they invoke the terms 'agency' and 'agent.' Not only does Guthrie argue – in 1980! – that the systematic attribution of what we now call agency is crucial to the existence and persistence of religion, but he maintains that such attribution is both natural and unsurprising. Because of universal and pre-eminent human preoccupations with other humans, he writes, we can readily appreciate why 'Ambiguous phenomena are commonly measured against a human-like template' (1980: 188). Anthropomorphism, indeed, betokens a prudent bet. Adapting Pascal's wager, Guthrie argues that although human-like models may be applied mistakenly, 'they are a good risk; it is usually better to err many times by applying them when they do not obtain than to err once by failing to apply them when they do' (1980: 190). We humans, Guthrie suggests – and here he sets forth claims now voiced by numbers of others – are not only disposed to be sensitive to the possibilities of human-like intentional agents in the environment, *but we are given to over-detecting them*, and doing so may ultimately be in our best interests.

Most importantly, as Luther Martin (2003: 221) notes, 'Guthrie's insight that religious thought and behavior are to be understood as "closely related variants of ordinary cognitive processes" (Guthrie 1980: 181) lies at the core of all subsequent cognitive studies of religion' (see also Boyer 1994a: 91–2). Numbers of Guthrie's predecessors had recognized the existence of anthropomorphism in religion. But Guthrie stresses its ubiquity in human life because it is *a product* of panhuman cognitive processes operating in an otherwise ambiguous world. It is found outside of what we conventionally call religion, but it is systematic and central in religion. In sum, he maintains in the 1980 essay, anthropomorphism exists and persists as a central organizing factor in religion because the world is chronically uncertain to human perception, because humans and their works are of maximal importance to other humans, and because under conditions of uncertainty a prudent conceptual strategy can be summed up by the words 'better safe than sorry.' These same points are crucial to his argument in the 1993 book.

The 1993 book

The central argument

In the Introduction, Guthrie sets forth his central argument succinctly and lucidly. I can do no better than to describe his main points in his own words:

> I claim religion consists of seeing the world as humanlike and arises because doing so is a good bet even though, like other bets, it may fail. My account has three aspects. One is ethnographic. It shows that we find plausible, in varying degrees, a continuum of humanlike beings from gods, spirits, and demons, to gremlins, abominable snowmen, HAL the computer, and Chiquita Banana. We find messages from many of these beings, or glimpses or traces of them, in a wide range of phenomena such as weather, earthquakes, plagues, traffic accidents, and the flight of birds.
>
> A second and central aspect of my account is analytic. It shows why such figures and messages are plausible. They are plausible for four nested reasons: our world is ambiguous and perpetually inchoate; our first need therefore is to interpret it; interpretation gambles on the most significant possibilities, and the most significant possibilities are humanlike. The third aspect of my account offers evidence for these claims, from cognitive science among other sources. (Guthrie 1993: 4)

Guthrie affirms in the book as well as in the 1980 essay that we may best understand religion 'as systematic anthropomorphism' (1993: 3). Anthropomorphism, whether systematic or not, he argues, is commonplace as a universal human phenomenon. It is such because it is a result of efforts to resolve perceptual uncertainty, as when, for example, we mistakenly interpret the sound of a tree branch brushing our window as the malign actions of a burglar. Anthropomorphism amounts to a residual category for such typically erroneous interpretations, albeit we may judge them erroneous only if we attempt to test them against recognized alternative possibilities. We do not set out to anthropomorphize the world, Guthrie maintains, but we are highly sensitive to the likelihood of human-like agency, and this sensitivity may sometimes lead us into error.

Animism

Guthrie's discussion of animism is multifaceted and dispersed throughout the book (see the index at 1993: 276). But his principal account of it is found in Chapter 2, 'Animism, perception, and the effort at meaning.'

Guthrie notes that the term 'animism' has several contemporary uses. For the most part, however, in studies of religion it usually means belief in spirit beings, while in psychology it often refers to the attribution of life to non-living phenomena (1993: 39). The tendency, moreover, to attribute the quality of being alive to non-living things, and thus credit the environment with an organization that it may not actually enjoy, is not distinctly human. Cats may see fluttering leaves as prey, dogs may hear sirens as howls, and so on. Guthrie deems the inclination to animate that we share with other animals a strategy for increasing meaning, a strategy that is almost never conscious (1993: 39).

The relationship between animism and anthropomorphism is variable, although we often both anthropomorphize and animate at the same time. 'We animate but do not anthropomorphize,' Guthrie writes, '... if we say an automobile purrs like a kitten, and anthropomorphize but do not animate if we speak to our pet turtle. If we speak to the automobile, however, we both animate and anthropomorphize' (1993: 39–40).

Guthrie holds that the animism usually described in studies of religion and the animism that is normally described in psychological studies are related – so much so that he feels confident in offering a single account for both. This account, he writes, 'holds that distinguishing what is alive from what is not is intrinsically difficult and that animism stems in part from this difficulty. The difficulty has two sources: animals in their natural environments typically are hard to see, and criteria for life are uncertain' (1993: 41). His argument as to why animism exists is very similar to his argument about why anthropomorphism exists. In his view, animism is the product of a perceptual strategy: when in doubt as to whether something is alive, assume that it is. Like anthropomorphism, then, animism is not itself a strategy. Rather, it is a product of a strategy, a strategy of scanning the world with the most important models available to us. Guthrie's posit of this strategy is nurtured by three linked convictions: perception is interpretation (we don't merely 'see,' but, as Wittgenstein points out, we 'see as'); interpretation seeks significance; and significance normally bears a correspondence to the degree of organization that we perceive (1993: 41).

In pursuing his argument, Guthrie discusses various traits often assigned to animistic beings, and he relates these to phenomena in the natural world, including phenomena associated with non-human animals and with plants. Thus, for instance, he relates the invisibility frequently credited to gods, spirits, and ghosts to animal and plant camouflage, to mimicry, to habitat and spatial ambiguity, to false warning (as when harmless insects bear the bright colors of poisonous species), and so on. Invisibility and ambiguity, he maintains, 'are not unique to gods, ghosts, or other spirits, nor merely products of the human imagination. Rather, they, and deceit generally, pervade the relations of animals, including humans, with each other and with plants' (1993: 50).

Naturalism

As the quotation above suggests, Guthrie opts for a naturalistic under-standing of religion. That is, he attempts to explain why we have religion by positing evolved, panhuman processes – processes, he notes, that we share to some extent with other species – that presumably would be in place even if we had no religion. Of central importance to his argument is the affirmation of perception as interpretation. Sensory cues, he holds, require us to make choices – 'bets' – as to what they may mean, because such cues can be variously interpreted. Interpretation is usually rapid and for the most part unconscious, which may very well give us the illusion that no choice is actually involved. While the appearance of certainty may doubtless be useful to us – the suppression of uncertainty can enable purposeful behavior – such an extreme naïve realism is given the lie by studies of perception conducted by cognitive psychologists, animal behaviorists, art historians, and others. To adapt an expression favored by some existentialist philosophers, *there is no avoiding of choices*, in perception as elsewhere. Guthrie supports this central tenet of the book by numerous citations to the work of scholars in diverse fields. The best bets, he maintains, are those with the highest informational payoffs and lowest risks. Anthropomorphism and animism, though by Guthrie's definition mistaken, are seen by him as products of a universal human strategy, a form of Pascal's wager, for maximizing payoffs and minimizing risks. Religion is thus grounded in dispositions or stratagems that have adaptive values.

Criticisms

Faces in the clouds was widely reviewed. All of the dozen or so reviews that I have read say favorable things about the book, although many reviewers also express opinions to the effect that Guthrie's theory does not cover all that needs to be covered in explaining religion. The most extensive cata-logue of claimed deficiencies is found in a review by Gustavo Benavides (1996). Benavides faults Guthrie either for not considering various questions or for not considering them adequately. The considerations so invoked sum to a sizeable list, and even Benavides himself exclaims 'Too many ques-tions perhaps' (1996: 459). In the end, however, Benavides concludes that

'Despite all these caveats – raised, it should be stressed, by a reviewer who is sympathetic to Guthrie's position – this book is to be welcomed for its ambition, for its attempting to provide a cognitive theory of religion, and for its emphasizing the role of practical concerns in the genesis of religion' (1996: 459).

A more realistic review, in my opinion, is furnished by Pascal Boyer (1994a). Boyer mentions two matters (see below) that he thinks that Guthrie does not really explain. I disagree, inasmuch as I think that Guthrie does offer explanations (as, I hope, my exposition of his theory makes clear), though I concede that more needs to be said about each. Otherwise, however, Boyer succinctly points to the book's importance for students of religion:

> Most importantly, Guthrie stresses the continuity of religious represen-
> tations and everyday cognition, a theme that is not really common in
> religious studies. ... Such careful attention to psychological findings and
> hypotheses is rare, and is the main reason why the book will be indis-
> pensable to all students of religion. Obviously, there are problems, too;
> for instance, it is not always clear why the 'search for complexity' in
> cognitive processes should result in projection of *human* characteris-
> tics, and why only *some* characteristics of humans tend to be projected
> repeatedly. These, however, are questions for future investigation, and
> Guthrie's book shows how they should be approached in a general
> study of religious ideas. (Boyer 1994a: 91–2)

I published brief comments on Guthrie's 1980 essay in the same issue of *Current Anthropology* in which that essay appeared (Saler 1980). While I was very favorably impressed by Guthrie's discussion of anthropo-morphism as it relates to religion, I opined that his essay did not deal adequately with frequently encountered attributions to gods and spirits of *non-human* qualities. I supposed, indeed, that gods and spirits are rendered objects of worship, veneration, or propitiation not only because of their imagined abilities to send and receive messages and to do other things that humans do, but also because of beliefs about their *departures* from our humanity – their invisibility, their immortality, their remarkable powers, and so forth. Boyer (1994b) productively analyzes certain of these as examples of counter-intuitive beliefs.

In fairness to Guthrie, it must be acknowledged that he is not only aware of the departures of religious beings from our humanity, but that in both essay and book he takes some account of such departures. He does so in two ways. First, he suggests that departures from our humanity may not be all that counter-intuitive. To cite one example, there is Guthrie's theorizing about invisibility as described earlier in this essay. He relates the claimed invisibility of some gods to the difficulty of seeing or identifying animals in various habitats because of camouflage, mimicry, and other natural factors. And he claims that the gods typically differ from humans not in absolute terms but in degrees. Second, following Horton (1967: 68), Guthrie (1980: 200) allows that the requirements of theorizing may induce us to conceptualize our explanatory elements in ways that seem appropriate or best suited for the explanatory tasks that they serve.

While the ideas described above are welcome moves in the direction of accounting for the important (and often dramatic) non-human qualities or aspects of gods and other religious figures, I think that more is needed by way of explaining the multi-dimensionality of such beings. Not only that, but Guthrie explicitly limits his explanatory efforts to only certain aspects or dimensions of religion. While this self-imposed limitation is, I think, a reasonable strategy, it results in a theory that fails to address a number of matters that other students of religion deem interesting and important. Miles Richardson (1996: 179), for example, notes in his review of the book that Guthrie 'has all but ignored the performance, ritual aspect of religion,' a consideration that prompts Richardson to ask, 'Where is the reality of religion?' For this reason, as well as for what I regard as an inadequate treatment of the non-human features of the gods, I deem Guthrie's theory to be a more powerful theory of anthropomorphism than of religion. One may evaluate the power of any theory in terms of how much it explains. Guthrie, I think, persuasively explains a great deal about anthropomorphism, both as an *ad hoc* phenomenon in many instances and as a more systematic enterprise in the case of religion. But his theorizing is less inclusive when projected against the complexity that generations of scholars attribute to religion.

Guthrie's theory is, to be sure, an important effort to explain certain recurrent ideational features of religion, and all students of religion can benefit by studying it. In my opinion, nevertheless, its full promise, even as an intellectualist exercise, has yet to be realized. Happily, however, Guthrie is still working on it. Among other things, I hope that he will expand his theorizing to take better account of the criticism that I proffered in 1980. If people were to conceptualize the gods as human and nothing more, it would be unlikely that anyone would worship them. Guthrie, however, cogently directs our attention to the '*human-like*' qualities of the gods, thus indicating that they differ from us in some respects. But what may be involved in the differences requires further exploration and explanation.

Acknowledgements

I am greatly indebted to Stewart E. Guthrie for comments on an early draft of this essay.

Note

1 On Lawson and McCauley's theory see the chapter by Steven Engler and Mark Q. Gardiner in this volume.

References

Benavides, G., 1996. Review of S.E. Guthrie's *Faces in the clouds*. *Journal of the American Academy of Religion* 64 (1), 457–59.

Boyer, P., 1994a. Review of S.E. Guthrie's *Faces in the clouds*. *Method & Theory in the Study of Religion* 6 (1), 91–2.

Boyer, P., 1994b. *The naturalness of religious ideas: a cognitive theory of religion.* University of California Press, Berkeley and Los Angeles.

Geertz, C., 1966. Religion as a cultural system. In: Banton, M. (Ed.), *Anthropological approaches to the study of religion.* Tavistock, London, 1–46.

Guthrie, S.E., 1980. A cognitive theory of religion. *Current Anthropology* 21 (2), 181–203.

Guthrie, S.E., 1988. *A Japanese new religion: Rissho Kosei-kai in a mountain hamlet.* University of Michigan Center for Japanese Studies, Ann Arbor.

Guthrie, S.E., 1993. *Faces in the clouds: a new theory of religion.* Oxford University Press, Oxford, New York.

Horton, R., 1960. A definition of religion, and its uses. *Journal of the Royal Anthropological Institute* 90 (2), 201–26.

Horton, R., 1967. African traditional thought and Western science. *Africa* 37, 50–71, 155–87.

Lawson, E.T. and R.N. McCauley, 1990. *Rethinking religion: connecting cognition and culture.* Cambridge University Press, Cambridge.

Liénard, P. and P. Boyer, 2006. Whence collective rituals? A cultural selective model of ritualized behavior. *American Anthropologist* 108 (4), 814–27.

Martin, L., 2003. Religion: a new approach to the study of culture. *Culture and Religion* 4 (2), 207–31.

Preus, J.S., 1987. *Explaining religion: criticism and theory from Bodin to Freud.* Yale University Press, New Haven.

Richardson, M., 1996. Review: a latter-day Tylorean theory of religion. *Current Anthropology* 37 (1), 178–9.

Saler, B., 1980. Comments on S.E. Guthrie's 'A cognitive theory of religion.' *Current Anthropology* 21 (2), 197.

Saler, B., 1997. E.B. Tylor and the anthropology of religion. *Marburg Journal of Religion* 2 (1), 1–6, online at www.uni-marburg.de/fb11/religionswissenschaft/journal.

Tylor, Edward B., 1958 (1873, 1871). *The originas of culture and religion in primitive culture,* Volumes I and II of the 1873 edition of *Primitive culture.* Harper and Brothers, New York.

4

From need to violence

On Walter Burkert, Creation of the sacred (1996)

Gustavo Benavides

Killing, eating, sacrifice

Defending his understanding of sacrifice in an exchange with Jean-Pierre Vernant at a conference on sacrifice in antiquity, Walter Burkert said that he was in search of a 'philosophy of the continuity of the living.'[1] This concern with continuities has been central in Burkert's work; it has led him back in time, from the study of the myths and rituals of Greece to those of ancient Near Eastern cultures, to the sacrificial practices of Paleolithic hunters, to the ritual displays of apes; it has also taken him forward, to the present. According to Burkert, religion is connected with the propagation and maintenance of life, with procreation and sexuality. But just as reproduction is intimately connected with – indeed, presupposes – death, Burkert understands religion in its relation to death, specifically, in its relation to killing. This connection is studied in early articles such as 'Greek tragedy and sacrificial ritual' (1966), in which Burkert considers how the tradition of a goat sacrifice 'leads back to the depths of prehistoric human development' (1966: 121 = 2007: 31), and, in more general terms, how 'in the ambivalence of the intoxication of blood and the horror of killing, in the twofold aspect of life and death,' 'the rites of sacrifice touch the roots of human existence' (1966: 113 = 2007: 24).

These issues received full scale treatment in *Homo necans* (1972/1997), the book that spread Burkert's name beyond the narrow circle of scholars of Greek religion.[2] Published in the same year as René Girard's *La violence et le sacré*, Burkert's *Homo necans* dealt with an issue that was difficult to address in a dispassionate manner in the quarter of a century that followed the end of the Second World War. Aware, in fact, that his book does not deal with the more edifying aspects of Greek culture, Burkert concludes the Preface to *Homo necans* by quoting the Delphic 'Know thyself' – this 'knowing oneself' referring to the need to move beyond illusion in order to achieve clarity about the human condition.[3] Using, in addition to the traditional tools of classical scholarship, Karl Meuli's cross-cultural research on ceremonial offerings – 'Griechische Opferbräuche' (1946)[4] – as well as Konrad Lorenz's ethological approach to violence,[5] Burkert focused on the central role played by sacrificial killing in the rituals and myths of ancient Greece. Taking as point of departure the commonalities between the ritual aspects of prehistoric hunting and the alimentary components of sacrificial killing, Burkert points, once again, to the role of death in the maintenance of life. Unlike Girard, who focuses on the connection between ritual killing and scapegoating, Burkert never loses sight of the centrality of eating in sacrificial acts – an emphasis that contradicts Jean-Pierre Vernant's claim that whereas he, Vernant, is interested in the eating of the sacrificial victim, Burkert is interested in the killing.[6] For Burkert, ritual violence is ultimately connected to practical concerns – especially to the eating of meat, as he emphasizes in writings such as 'Glaube und Verhalten: Zeichengehalt und Wirkungsmacht von Opferritualen' (1981), *Anthropologie des religiösen Opfers* (1984) and 'The problem of ritual killing' (1987). In fact, in 'Glaube und Verhalten,' he criticizes Girard for overlooking the centrality of eating in Greek sacrifice (1981: 110); while in *Anthropologie des religiösen Opfers* he writes that the desire for meat points to 'the Paleolithic in us.'[7] As concerned with historical as with evolutionary continuities, in the 'Afterword' to the second edition of *Homo necans* he writes that meat-eating provides the thread that connects phenomena as apparently disparate as chimpanzees' hunting, the sacrifices offered to Zeus and the Christian Eucharist (1972/1997: 342). This concern with continuities across cultures as well as species, expressed in the exchange with Vernant referred to at the beginning of this essay, continues to play an important role in *Creation of the sacred*.

From contingency to necessity

While *Homo necans* grew out of Burkert's need to account for the centrality of violence in Greek myth and ritual, *Creation of the sacred*, originally delivered as the Gifford lectures in 1989, seeks to render intelligible a range of practices and beliefs prevalent well beyond the eastern Mediterranean world, the area that has been the object of Burkert's research over decades. In theoretical terms, too, *Creation of the sacred* is an expansion of *Homo necans*, for while the earlier book proposes a theory of sacrifice, the latter develops a general theory of religion. What both books have in common, besides their having grown out of the author's familiarity with the eastern Mediterranean world, is their concern with practical – in fact, elementary – matters, since Burkert regards religion as emerging out of the desire for biological survival. Whether this leads to regarding religion as contributing to 'inclusive fitness' or 'providing a heightened endurance in the face of catastrophe,' as maintained by sociobiologists, are hypotheses that Burkert discusses briefly; even briefer is his reference to ecological approaches, which would have benefited from a consideration of Roy Rappaport's distinction between 'cognized' and 'operational models.'[8]

In summary, Burkert understands 'religion' as that 'which cannot be verified empirically,' being 'manifest in actions and attitudes that do not fulfill immediate practical functions,' but which nevertheless 'manifests itself through interaction and communication' in two directions: 'toward the unseen and toward the contemporary social situation.' Religion involves a 'claim for priority and seriousness,' a characteristic that makes it 'vulnerable to laughter and derision' (1996: 5–7). In the end, religion is to be understood as a hybrid between biology and culture, developing through adaptation to the landscape provided by the evolutionary process – an approach that can be pursued with help of the concept of 'scenic complement';[9] as well as by making use of the 'dual inheritance' theory postulated by Robert Boyd and Peter Richerson (1985, 2005).

In *Creation of the sacred*, Burkert explores the processes whereby contingency becomes necessity. More precisely, he deals with the mechanisms whereby what is subject to change is made to appear as changeless. Referring to Niklas Luhmann, Burkert discusses the role played by religion in the 'reduction of complexity' (Luhmann [1977] 1982: 20). Religion validates choices, distinctions, power, hierarchies, although in some cases religion is involved in counteracting an unjust social order by the postulation of a transcendent gift system.[10] Religion provides 'orientation within a meaningful cosmos for those who feel helpless vis-à-vis infinite complexity' (1996: 26), in a way that seems to resemble Mircea Eliade's theories about the functions of sacrality, but which is not encumbered with the reification of '*le sacré*' or of 'meaning' that characterizes Eliade's approach to religion. In this regard, Burkert's view is closer to Rappaport's understanding of sanctity as 'the quality of unquestionable truthfulness imputed by the faithful to unverifiable propositions' (Rappaport 1971: 69). Ways of dealing with what is ultimately unverifiable is indeed what religion provides, for in a world in which one can use language in order to lie, one requires the validation provided by oaths, and oaths require guarantors, namely, gods. Gods are to be understood, therefore, as having come into being in order to serve as ultimate points of reference; as being created by the fear of uncertainty, of contingency, of the capacity to lie.

Religious bodies

The more solemn an oath is, the more it becomes necessary to anchor the utterance in gestures, in touch, in sacrifice, as if the finality of death could remove an utterance from the realm of contingency, moving it to that of finality. Fear plays a role here, too, as the death of the sacrificial victim or the trampling of the testicles of the sacrificed animal can be understood as prefiguring what would happen to the one who breaks the oath sanctified by death (1996: 173–4).[11] When words are accompanied by gestures and, even more so, when words are replaced by gestures, movements, or specific postures, one engages in elementary forms of communication, forms which, in principle, preclude deceit (169–72). This happens, as we have seen, when one swears an oath. Gesture, movement, posture, and location are also crucial to mark one's rank, to issue orders, to ask for favors, to beg for one's life. Approached from an evolutionary perspective, these bodily practices have played a central role in Burkert's theory of religion – as they do, with less emphasis on the evolutionary component, in Rappaport's *Ritual and religion in the making of humanity* (1999). At the level of pure submission, these postures can be seen in two scenes, separated by millennia: one, a Greek gem that represents the Trojan Dolon pleading for his life; the other, a picture of Pakistani soldiers pleading for theirs. The pictures, reproduced in Burkert's *Structure and history in Greek mythology and ritual* (1979: 47) and also referred to in *Creation of the sacred* (1996: 87),[12] show how the defeated mark their submission and plead for their life by grabbing the knees of their captors. These non-linguistic, gestural forms of communication, particularly those involving dominance and subordination, are placed by Burkert in an evolutionary context, as he compares human rituals of greeting – embraces, patting of shoulders, kissing of hands – with those found among chimpanzees and other apes (1996: 86–7).

Dealing with the other end, the one occupied by the relationship between humans and their gods, Burkert refers to liturgical practices involving bowing, bending, kneeling, throwing oneself on the floor, all of which have also been used to mark one's lowly rank in front of a ruler – as already pointed out by Detlev Fehling in his *Ethologische Überlegungen auf dem Gebiet der Altertumskunde* (1974) – or a god, as it can be observed to this day in temples and assemblies across the world. It is also to the animal world that one has to turn when considering how rank is displayed, as it is among primates that one finds relations of dominance and submission, displayed either by posture, permanent or momentary size, or by the physical location of the body. The complementary ritual displays of power and submission in which humans engage follow the same principles. In the case of power displays, the rulers must show that their power surplus allows them to advertise their presence in a manner that those in a subordinate position cannot afford. Indeed, those in subordinate positions must appear not just as inoffensive, but also as willing to endure the violence that their superiors may want to inflict on them – a violence that usually involves having labor or the product of labor extracted from one. Before dealing with the labor-related implications of these displays, we must consider how animal size, shape, anatomical

details, color, design, can be regarded as having been produced over generations for analogous purposes; the same being true of movements that advertise an animal's fitness to attack or to elude a predator; or of the sounds
produced by an animal; or of the smell it exudes – this latter component
being consistently neglected even by scholars who work with evolutionary
models. Sedimented over generations, these shapes, movements, sounds, and
smells are activated when needed, becoming the building blocks of power
displays or of apotropaic rituals. In the case of humans at least, these rituals
seem to acquire a life of their own, being enacted at regular intervals despite
the absence of imminent danger, thus becoming some of the building blocks
of religion.

On fear

Exaggerated fear of not fulfilling a vow, of not performing a ritual in the
proper manner, or of the gods in general, may have been regarded as
superstitio; but fear has been traditionally understood as having a place
in one's dealing with the gods, just as violence has a place in the way in
which the gods deal with humans, much as this may appear as alien to us
moderns. Fear is central, as it is through fear that boundaries are maintained, whether these boundaries mark the distance between humans and
gods, or the choice between permissible and non-permissible actions, or the
border between one's field and that of one's neighbor.[13] Having devoted
so much attention to sacrificial killing, Burkert never tires of emphasizing
the centrality of fear and violence in religion. He quotes Statius about fear
having created the gods – *'primus in orbe deos fecit timor'*[14] – but instead of
developing a metaphysics or a theology of fear, or of violence, à la Girard, he
tries to account for it from the point of view of survival, pointing out how
'anxiety, fear and terror are not just free-floating emotions brought on by
psychological fantasy,' but 'have a clear function in protecting life' (1996:
31). The same applies to deception, as Burkert points out in 'Ritual zwischen
Ethologie und Postmoderne,' an address he delivered in 2003. In this essay,
Burkert considers the role of lying in assuring one's survival, mentioning
the significance of the emergence of lying in children and to some extent
in chimpanzees. This is an issue that deserves further research, since religion could be understood as having emerged in order to counteract not just
contingency in the abstract, or *anomie* in general, but rather the capacity to
engage in deception. Given that the capacity to lie depends on the ability to
develop a theory of mind and to engage in meta-representations, the ability
to engage in ever more complex forms of deception increasing in direct
proportion to our meta-cognitive abilities, one may conclude that since it is
among humans that meta-representational deceit reaches its peak, it is also

humans who are likely to generate imaginary beings who, besides being able to deceive, sometimes at an unimaginable level, are able to pierce through the veil of human deception.[15]

To get

Why would one lie, however? Merely to exercise one's capacity to play with meta-representations or to activate one's theory of mind? Or is it that one must engage in deceit – or seek to see through it – for the same reason that one engages in power display – or tries to get around it – namely, in order to have access to food and sexual mates? From the time of *Structure and history in Greek mythology and ritual* (1979) to that of *Creation of the sacred* (1996), Burkert has made use of the sequence of 31 functions identified by Vladimir Propp in *Morphology of the folktale* (1928): the steps the hero goes through, from the initial gap/absence/loss to the moment the hero receives his reward. In the simplified version proposed by Burkert, the hero goes through 22 steps, and in a still shorter version, he goes through 9 (1996: 63). Ultimately, the entire sequence can be reduced to one verb: 'to get' (1979: 15). Whatever the adventures undergone, the violence and the fear inflicted or endured, the goal is to obtain something precious, overcoming scarcity. It is for the sake of 'getting,' or of defending what one has already got, or of increasing it, fearful of scarcity, that hierarchies are established. In many cases, to be sure, one wastes what those one commands have extracted from the claws of scarcity; or one outright destroys it, thereby showing that one's capacity to get is unlimited. But in order to be able to have access to what somebody else's work has produced – that is, to be able to compel someone to work – hierarchies have to be surrounded by a mix of fear and awe. To achieve the former one needs access to brute force; for the latter one needs ritual – but, as the history of words such as 'awful' and 'awesome' reminds us, it is not always ease to distinguish between brute force and its aesthetic/ritual surplus.[16]

Discussing how the ruler's power is validated by his submission to the gods, Burkert writes that 'submission and sovereignty inhabit the same hierarchic structure' (1996: 95), going on to quote Horace addressing Rome: 'Because you keep yourself subordinate to the gods, you rule the empire'[17] (1996: 97). Because of the importance of this interplay of submissions, present as much in the Rome of Augustus as in the United States of G.W. Bush, one misses here a recognition of the role played by labor in the emergence of the need for submission in the first place; and, at an even more elementary level, one misses a recognition of the role of scarcity[18] as the source of the hierarchies that mobilize and allocate labor among humans[19] – the humans who use their meta-representational capacities to create not just increasingly complex tools and to generate linguistic forms, but also tools to make tools and to generate language about language. The neglect of the role of work at the center of this process is regrettable – it is, in fact, doubly regrettable, given that Burkert had devoted insightful pages to the connection between religion and work in 'Ursprungsgeschichte der Technik im Spiegel antiker Religion' (1967),[20] based on his inaugural lecture at the Technical University of Berlin, almost three decades before he delivered the Gifford lectures. Since the purpose of this essay is to present a critical overview of Burkert's theory of religion, rather than the speculations of the chapter's author, it may be sufficient to point out here that beings condemned to work and capable of meta-representations are likely to imagine, on the one hand, scarcity-free utopias and, on the other, beings who are capable of even greater meta-representational feats, that is, gods.

Not unrelated to utopian hopes is the manner in which human beings resort to the supernatural in the quest to keep catastrophe at bay; in the desire for the maintenance and, more often, the restoration of health. This quest involves transactions with the gods, built around divination, prayers, and sacrifices, most of these practices requiring the activities of mediators: shamans, seers, specialists of various kinds. These transactions are frequently of a *do ut des* nature – 'I give so that you give in return' – in a manner that in some cases involves shaming the divine recipient of the offering (1996: 136). Mediators as much as their clients have traditionally thought in terms of purity, pollution, and guilt. Burkert writes about religious explanations being based on a 'surplus of causality' (1996: 128) – the surplus that would explain natural disasters such as hurricanes by pointing, for example, to moral transgressions of a sexual nature: the kind of explanation that would have prompted entire communities to engage in expiatory rituals, but which are now received with indignation in the West, even in the United States, a society in which supernatural realities still play a role in the legitimization of morality and politics (Benavides 2008: 95, n.39).

Perspectives

As pointed out at the beginning of this essay, Burkert's theories of sacrifice and of religion in general grew out of his work with Greek and Near Eastern cultures,[21] his approach to this material having been enriched by his use of Karl Meuli's work, as well as ethology. Because of its historical, philological, and archaeological foundations, Burkert's understanding of religion has a factual solidity that is much greater than that found in other attempts to generate a theory of religion; his theories, furthermore, are not to be regarded, as is now the fashion, as an 'invention' but as a 'finding,' as he said in his concluding remarks at a symposium in his honor,[22] and as he repeated in his contribution to the Versnel *Festschrift*, where he defends the usefulness of categories such as 'myth and ritual' (2002: 14). The historical density one finds in Burkert's work is not to be understood as a mere collection of particulars, either; indeed, in the Preface to *Homo necans* he writes that 'a lexikon will not give us an understanding of a language if the grammar is unknown or disregarded and if the practice under discussion has not been understood' (1986 [1972]: xx–xxi). This density more than compensates for the occasional gaps in his references to research in ethology and evolutionary theory, as well as for his not having taken into account developments in cognitive approaches to religion, as he recognizes in his response to Pascal Boyer (1998b: 132).

In fact, one of the most valuable aspects of Burkert's approach to religion, as of his scholarship in general, is his willingness to engage developments in several disciplines. For instance, in 'Greek tragedy and sacrificial ritual,' he had written that, compared to men, 'the other primates are rather innocent creatures' (1966: 110 = 2007: 22); but this was corrected in later works, after it became clear that our close relatives, chimpanzees, were not only hunters, but capable of extreme, as well as calculated, violence against each other (1994: 12). Similarly, in *Creation of the sacred* we find a reference to a circular design on the wings of a butterfly, which Burkert understands as a staring eye that serves to frighten potential enemies; conversely, he understands the eye on the tail of a peacock as serving to catch the attention of prospective mates (1996: 43). Approached from an evolutionary perspective, however, there is no need to think in terms of eyes: from the point of view of 'costly' or 'hard-to-fake-signaling' theory, it is the perfect circular shape that, by advertising the health of the butterfly or of the bird, scares off potential predators and competitors, while at the same time attracting mates. This explanation, proposed by Amotz and Avishag Zahavi in *The handicap principle*, published in 1997, could not have been used in *Creation of the sacred*, as this book was published in 1996; however, one finds references to the Zahavis' work in 'Ritual zwischen Ethologie und Postmoderne' (2003: 8).

A further advantage of immersing oneself in texts, iconography, and archaeology before sacrificing on the altar of theory is that one's findings are likely to be compatible with serious hypotheses advanced in a number of disciplines. This applies to developments in cognitive science, as shown in Pascal Boyer's review of *Creation of the sacred*, in which, after writing that 'Burkert's intuitions of links between evolution and religious representations can be in fact pushed further than he suggests' (Boyer 1998: 89), he concludes by saying that 'the cognitive study of religion provides empirical support for many of the connections mentioned in Burkert's important and inspiring contribution to the anthropological study of religion' (Boyer 1998: 91).[23] The compatibility between Burkert's theories and the cognitive approach applies also to research in evolutionary psychology and, in general, to some of the theories of religion examined in this volume, such as Atran's, Pyysiäinen's and Wilson's, all of whom refer to Burkert. While historians of religion continue to make use of Burkert's work, although in most cases ignoring related work by psychologists and anthropologists, social and behavioral scientists who work on the relations among religion, group cohesion, morality, and violence, tend not to take into account historical research, even when this would provide validation for their theories.

Notes

1   'Philosophie der Kontinuität des Lebendigen' (in 1981: 130).
2   Walter Burkert was born in Bavaria in 1931. After studying classical philology, history, and philosophy in Munich and Erlangen, he taught classical philology at the Technical University of Berlin (1966–9) and then at the University of Zurich (1969–96); he has also held visiting positions at Harvard, Berkeley, and UCLA. A list of his publications, including reviews, from 1959 to 2000 can be found in the first volume of his collected articles (2001: 234–56). Two journals have devoted issues to Burkert's work: 'Review Symposium: Walter Burkert,' *Method & Theory in the Study of Religion* 10 (1), 1998, 84–132 and 'Symposium: Walter Burkert' (edited by Larry Alderink), *Religion* 30 (3), 2000, 211–92; the latter includes a 'Bibliography of Walter Burkert,' 287–92, which also lists 'Articles and symposia about Walter Burkert.'
3   See also Burkert 1990, 1992, 2002.
4   On the significance of Meuli's work, see Burkert 1992.
5   Burkert has been influenced by Lorenz's emphasis on the 'similarities, analogies, and even continuities between animals and humans in the field of anger, fighting and war,' on the connection between aggression, the maintenance of hierarchies and social solidarity (1996: 9; see also 1972: 28; 1984: 13–14), as well as on the continuities between animal and human ritual behavior (1972: 31–2).
6   See Vernant 1981: 26: 'Sans que nos raisons soient exactement les mêmes, nous plaçons l'un et l'autre une des formes les plus typiques du sacrifice grec dans la perspective de l'alimentation. Sacrifier c'est fondamentalement tuer pour manger. Mais dans cette formule, vous mettez l'accent plutôt sur *tuer*; moi, sur *manger*' (italics in the original).
7   'Der Paläolithiker in uns' (in 1984: 28). In addition to continuities, however, one must also consider discontinuities – above all, whether the egalitarianism of hunter-gatherers, and the concomitant attitude towards violence and gender relations, is not the result of the rejection of the hierarchical arrangements which reappear in chiefdoms and later social formations, and which are analogous to those found in most primate species. On this issue see Knauft 1991 (which includes comments by eight anthropologists and Knauft's response) and Boehm 1999.
8   See 'On cognized models' and 'Adaptive structures and its disorders,' both in Rappaport 1979.

9   'Szenische Ergänzung': see G. Baudy 1997 as well as 2001: 34, n.10, where he
     refers to Rudolf Bilz as the originator of this concept. Dorothea Baudy makes
     fruitful use of Bilz's and Burkert's ideas in her study of Roman rites of circum-
     ambulation (1998).

10   This is an issue that deserves further attention. Rituals of reversal and analo-
     gous phenomena are studied in Burkert 1993.

11   For a discussion of these practices in the context of a theory of magic, see
     Benavides 2006, preferably to be consulted in the corrected 2008 paperback
     edition.

12   On *hiketeia* see also Burkert 1995/2007: 197; 2003: 11.

13   On boundaries and on the fear associated with them, see Burkert 1996: 30,
     165; *Kontakte und Grenzen* 1969; on the punishments for those who transgress
     boundaries, see Werkmüller 1976.

14   Burkert 1981: 102; 1996: 31; 1997: 29; see also Michaels 1997.

15   This issue is discussed in Benavides forthcoming.

16   See Benavides 2001: 105 and forthcoming.

17   '*Dis te minorem quod geris, imperas*' (Carmina 3. 6. 5).

18   On scarcity see, however, Burkert 1996: 149 and 1987b: 47, which also pays
     some attention to the connection among redistribution, surrender, and destruc-
     tion of goods.

19   This is not unrelated to Burkert's focus on the hunting-sacrifice complex, to the
     detriment of the ritual aspects of agriculture; on the latter – Anthesteria and
     Thesmophoria – see Burkert 1997: 358–70.

20   This issue is discussed in Benavides 2000. It may be added that in *Creation of the
     sacred* (1996: 13, 191, n.50) and in 'Fitness oder Opium?' (1997: 25–6), Marx's
     understanding of religion is reduced to the 'opium thesis,' as presented in *Zur Kritik
     der Hegelschen Rechtsphilosophie* (1844 [1981]: 488); in fact, the views of religion
     proposed by Marx in the previous paragraph of the *Kritik* are not incompatible
     with Burkert's.

21   During a conversation in Zurich in March of 2000, Fritz Stolz mentioned that
     he and Burkert met once a week to read cuneiform texts: of how many theorists
     of religion could one say that?

22   'Mein Eindruck war immer der, daß es nicht um ein Erfinden gehe, sondern um
     ein Finden' (1998a: 442).

23   See Burkert 1998b and 2000 for his response to Boyer and for comments on
     cognitive approaches to religion.

Bibliography

1. Walter Burkert's writings

Collected articles

2001. *Kleine Schriften I: Homerica* [Hypomnemata Supplement-Reihe 2, I], ed. by
     Ch. Riedweg. Vandenhoeck & Ruprecht, Göttingen.

2003. *Kleine Schriften II: Orientalia* [Hypomnemata Supplement-Reihe 2, II], ed. by L.M. Gemelli Marciano. Vandenhoeck & Ruprecht, Göttingen.

2006. *Kleine Schriften III: Mystica, Orphica, Pythagorica* [Hypomnemata Supplement-Reihe 2, III], ed. by F. Graf. Vandenhoeck & Ruprecht, Göttingen.

2007. *Kleine Schriften VII: Tragica et Historica* [Hypomnemata Supplement-Reihe 2, VII], ed. by W. Rösler. Vandenhoeck & Ruprecht, Göttingen.

2008. *Kleine Schriften VIII: Philosophica* [Hypomnemata Supplement-Reihe 2, VIII], ed. by Th. A. Szlezák and K.-H. Stanzel. Vandenhoeck & Ruprecht, Göttingen [not seen].

Books and articles

1966. Greek tragedy and sacrificial ritual. *Greek, Roman and Byzantine Studies 7*, 87–121 = *Kleine Schriften VII*, 1–36.

1967. Ursprungsgeschichte der Technik im Spiegel antiker Religion. *Technikgeschichte* 34, 281–99.

1972. *Homo Necans. Interpretationen altgriechischer Opferriten und Mythen.* Walter de Gruyter, Berlin; enlarged edition, with Afterword, 1997.

1977. *Griechische Religion der archaischen und klassischen Epoche* [Die Religionen der Menschheit 15]. Kohlhammer, Stuttgart, Berlin, Köln, Mainz.

1979. *Structure and history in Greek mythology and ritual.* University of California Press, Berkeley.

1981. Glaube und Verhalten: Zeichengehalt und Wirkungsmacht von Opferritualen. In: Rudhart J. and Reverdin, O. (Eds.), *Le sacrifice dans l'antiquité* [Entretiens sur l'Antiquité classique 27]. Fondation Hardt, Vandœuvres, Genève, 91–125 [Discussion, 126–33].

1984. *Anthropologie des religiösen Opfers. Die Sakralisierung der Gewalt* [Karl Friedrich von Siemens Stiftung – Themen 40]. Siemens Stiftung, Munich.

1986. *Homo necans: the anthropology of ancient Greek sacrificial ritual and myth*, translated P. Bing. University of California Press, Berkeley.

1987a. The problem of ritual killing. In: Hamerton-Kelly, R.G. (Ed.), *Violent origins: ritual killing and cultural formation.* Stanford University Press, Stanford, 149–76 [Discussion, 177–88].

1987b. Offerings in perspective: surrender, distribution, exchange. In: Linders, T. and Nordquist, G.C. (Eds.), *Gifts to the gods* [Boreas 15], Uppsala, 43–9.

1990. Der Mensch, der tötet. Walter Burkert über 'Homo Necans' (1972). In: Ritter, H. (Ed.), *Werkbesichtigung Geisteswissenschaften.* Insel Verlag, Frankfurt, 185–94.

1992. Opfer als Tötungsritual: Eine Konstante der menschlichen Kulturgeschichte? In: Graf, F. (Ed.), *Klassische Antike und neue Wege der Kulturwissenschaften. Symposium Karl Meuli (Basel 11.–13. September 1991).* Verlag der Schweizerischen Gesellschaft für Volkskunde, Basel, 170–89.

1993. Kronia-Feste und ihr altorientalischer Hintergrund. In: Döpp, S. (Ed.), *Karnevaleske Phänomene in antiken und nachantiken Kulturen und Literaturen. Stätten und Formen der Kommunikation im Altertum I* [Bochumer Altertumwissenschaftliches Colloquium 13]. Wissenschaftlicher Verlag, Trier, 11–30.

1994. *'Vergeltung' zwischen Ethologie und Ethik. Reflexe und Reflexionen in Texten und Mythologien des Altertums* [Karl Friedrich von Siemens Stiftung – Themen 55]. Siemens Stiftung, Munich.

1995. Krieg und Tod in der griechischen Polis. In: Stietencron, H. v. and Rüpke, J. (Eds.), *Töten im Krieg*. Alber, Freiburg, Munich, 179–96 = *Kleine Schriften VII*, 195–209.

1996. *Creation of the sacred: tracks of biology in early religions*. Harvard University Press, Cambridge (Mass), London.

1997. Fitness oder Opium? Die Fragestellung der Soziobiologie im Bereich alter Religionen. In: Stolz, F. (Ed.), *Homo naturaliter religiosus. Gehört Religion notwendig zum Mensch-Sein?* [Studia Religiosa Helvetica 3]. Peter Lang, Bern, 13–38.

1998a. Ein Schlußwort als Dank. In: Graf, F. (Ed.), *Ansichten griechischer Rituale. Geburtstag-Symposium für Walter Burkert*, B.G. Teubner, Stuttgart, Leipzig, 441–4.

1998b. Exploring religion in a biological landscape. *Method & Theory in the Study of Religion* 10 (1), 129–32.

2000. Response. *Religion* 30 (3), 283–5.

2002. 'Mythos und Ritual' im Wechselwind der Moderne. In: Horstmanshoff, H.F J., Singor, H.W. and Straten, F.T. van (Eds.), *Kykeon. Studies in Honour of H.S. Versnel* [Religions in the Graeco-Roman World 142]. Brill, Leiden, Boston, Cologne, 1–22.

2003. Ritual zwischen Ethologie und Postmoderne. Philologisch-historische Anmerkungen. *Forum Ritualdynamik* 2 (www.ritualdynamik.uni-hd.de).

2. Other references

Baudy, D., 1998. *Römische Umgangsriten. Eine ethologische Untersuchung der Funktion von Wiederholung für religiöses Verhalten* [Religionsgeschichtliche Versuche und Vorarbeiten 43]. Walter de Gruyter, Berlin, New York.

Baudy, G., 1997. Religion als 'szenische Ergänzung'. Paläoanthropologische Grundlagen religiöser Erfahrung. In: Stolz, F. (Ed.), *Homo naturaliter religiosus. Gehört Religion notwendig zum Mensch-Sein?* [Studia Religiosa Helvetica 3]. Peter Lang, Bern, 65–90.

Baudy, G., 2001. Blindheit und Wahnsinn. Das Kultbild im poetologischen Diskurs der Antike: Stesichoros und die homerische Helena. In: Graevenitz, G. v., Rieger, S. and Thürlemann, F. (Eds.), *Die Unvermeidlichkeit der Bilder*. Gunter Narr, Tübingen, 31–57.

Benavides, G., 2000. Towards a natural history of religion. *Religion* 30 (3), 229–44.

Benavides, G., 2001. Religious studies between science and ideology. *Religious Studies Review* 27, 105–8.

Benavides, G., 2006. Magic. In: Segal, R.A. (Ed.), *The Blackwell companion to the study of religion*. Blackwell, Oxford, 295–308.

Benavides, G., 2008. Western religion and the self-canceling of modernity. *Journal of Religion in Europe* 1, 85–115.

Benavides, G., forthcoming. Religion, at the intersection. *Historia Religionum* 1.

Boehm, C., 1999. *Hierarchy in the forest: the evolution of egalitarian behavior*. Harvard University Press, Cambridge (Mass.), London.

Boyd, R. and Richerson, P.J., 1985. *Culture and the evolutionary process.* University of Chicago Press, Chicago, London.

Boyd, R. and Richerson, P.J., 2005. *The origin and evolution of cultures.* Oxford University Press, Oxford, New York.

Boyer, P., 1998. *Creation of the sacred*: A cognitivist view. *Method & Theory in the Study of Religion* 10, 88–92.

Fehling, D., 1974. *Ethologische Überlegungen auf dem Gebiet der Altertumskunde. Phallische Demonstration – Fernsicht – Steinigung* [Zetemata 61]. C.H. Beck'sche Verlagsbuchhandlung, Munich.

Graf, F. (Ed.), 1998. *Ansichten griechischer Rituale. Geburtstag-Symposium für Walter Burkert.* B.G. Teubner, Stuttgart, Leipzig.

Knauft, B.M., 1991. Violence and sociality in human evolution. *Current Anthropology* 32, 391–428.

Kontakte und Grenzen. Probleme der Volks-, Kultur- und Sozialforschung. Festschrift für Gerhard Heilfurth zum 60. Geburtstag, Herausgegeben von seinen Mitarbeitern. Otto Schwartz, Göttingen, 1969.

Luhmann, N., 1977. *Funktion der Religion.* Suhrkamp, Frankfurt am Main.

Marx, K., 1844. *Zur Kritik der Hegelschen Rechtsphilosophie.* Karl Marx, *Frühe Schriften I,* ed. H.-J. Lieber and P. Furth. Wissenschaftliche Buchgesellschaft, Darmstadt, 1981, 488–505.

Meuli, K., 1946. Griechische Opferbräuche. In: Gogon, O.A. (Ed.), *Phyllobolia: für Peter von der Mühll.* Schwabe, Basle, 185–288 = Karl Meuli, *Gesammelte Schriften* II. Schwabe, Basle, Stuttgart, 1975, 907–1021.

Michaels, A., 1997. Religion und der neurobiologische Primat der Angst. In: Stolz, F. (Ed.), *Homo naturaliter religiosus. Gehört Religion notwendig zum Mensch-Sein?* [Studia Religiosa Helvetica 3]. Peter Lang, Bern, 91–136.

Propp, V., 1928/1968. *Morphology of the folktale,* translated L. Scott, ed. L. Wagner. University of Texas Press, Austin.

Rappaport, R.A., 1971. Ritual, sanctity, and cybernetics. *American Anthropologist* 73, 59–76.

Rappaport, R.A., 1979. *Ecology, meaning, and religion.* North Atlantic Books, Richmond.

Rappaport, R.A., 1999. *Ritual and religion in the making of humanity.* Cambridge University Press, Cambridge.

Stolz, F. (Ed.), 1997. *Homo naturaliter religiosus. Gehört Religion notwendig zum Mensch-Sein?* [Studia Religiosa Helvetica 3]. Peter Lang, Bern.

Vernant, J.-P., 1981. Théorie générale du sacrifice et mise à mort dans la *thysía* grecque. In: Rudhart J. and Reverdin, O. (Eds.), *Le sacrifice dans l'antiquité* [Entretiens sur l'Antiquité classique 27]. Fondation Hardt, Vandœuvres, Geneva, 1–21 [Discussion, 22–39].

Werkmüller, D., 1976. Recinzioni, confini e segni terminali. In: *Simboli e simbologia nell'alto medioevo* [Settimane di studio del Centro Italiano di Studi sull'Alto Medioevo 23]. Spoleto, II, 641–59 [Discussion, 661–78].

Zahavi, A. and Zahavi, A., 1997. *The handicap principle: a missing piece of Darwin's puzzle.* Oxford University Press, New York, Oxford.

5

Religion as ritual

Roy Rappaport's changing views from Pigs for the ancestors (1968) to Ritual and religion in the making of humanity (1999)

Robert A. Segal

Some theorists consider belief the heart of religion, others ritual. But over the past century and a quarter, there has been a general shift of emphasis from belief to ritual. The shift began with William Robertson Smith's *Lectures on the religion of the Semites* (1889). But for Smith the centrality of ritual held only for 'primitive' religion. Since his time, theorists of religion have come ever more to deem ritual the core of *all* religion. Belief, especially when formalized as creed, has come to be seen as abstract and artificial, as the religion of philosophers and theologians. Ritual has come to be embraced as folk religion, as religion as lived. Yet the stature that Roy Rappaport accords religious ritual is unprecedented. In, especially, his posthumously published *Ritual and religion in the making of humanity* (1999), he goes beyond the import that even theorists of religion like Victor Turner, Mary Douglas, and Clifford Geertz credit to ritual.

Roy Rappaport, whom I knew, was a successful innkeeper in New England who at the age of 40 decided to become an academic. He had fought in World War II and had received a degree from Cornell University's School of Hotel Management. On the advice of Erik Erikson and son Kai, who were guests at his inn, he decided to become an anthropologist. He enrolled at Columbia University in its school for mature students, the School of General Studies. As told by one of the editors of the posthumously published *Festschrift* for Rappaport, Columbia introduced Rappaport to an array of rival anthropological positions:

In Columbia's anthropology courses, Rappaport encountered the exciting and often competing ideas of [Marvin] Harris's cultural materialism, [Harold] Conklin's ethnoscience, [Margaret] Mead's understandings of fieldwork, [Conrad] Arensberg's political anthropology, and [Andrew]

Vayda's, [Fredrik] Barth's, and Conklin's interpretations of anthropological ecology. Exposed to Leslie White's 'general evolution,' as it was presented by [Morton] Fried, he developed his own ideas of ordered general systems, a lawful and unified order underlying the apparent multiplicity of human structures and events. Presented with Conklin's ideas on ethnoscience and ethnoecology, he developed his own comparative units of 'cognized' and 'operational' environments, which incorporated aspects of Harris's materialism. He moved Arensberg's focus on the formal characteristics of political hierarchies and their operations toward ideas about structure in adoptive systems. Drawing on all of the above plus readings in biological ecology, with Vayda he moved beyond [Julian] Stewart's cultural ecology to a human ecology that removed the conceptual separation between the subsistence culture core and secondary peripheral features. (Messer 2001: 4–5)[1]

Of all these influences, the one with which Rappaport has most commonly been associated is that of Harris, who himself subsumes Rappaport's 'ecological anthropology' under his own cultural materialism (see Harris 1980 [1979]: 94, 245–6). While rooted in Marxism, cultural materialism at once denies any dialectical contradiction and adds 'reproductive pressure and ecological variables to the conjunction of material conditions studied by Marxist-Leninists' (Harris 1980 [1979]: ix). Culture is seen as a practical means of adaptation to the environment for the purpose of securing food and other necessities: 'Culture has been regarded here ... as part of the distinctive means by which a local population maintains itself in an ecosystem and by which a regional population maintains and coordinates its groups and distributes them over the available land' (Rappaport 1968: 233).[2]

Rappaport did four months of fieldwork in the Society Islands of Polynesia and then fourteen months of fieldwork in Papua New Guinea. He did not set out to study religion, toward which he was 'ambivalent,' if not 'negative' (Messer 2001: 9). He set out to study 'the human population in the same terms that biological ecologists studied animal populations in ecosystems' (Messer 2001: 5). Spurred by the burgeoning environmental movement, he sought to learn how native peoples 'managed' their environment. He discovered that he could not understand the ecological system without understanding the ritual cycle. Ritualistic management of the pig population was the key to management of the environment.

For Rappaport, ritual means religious ritual, and religion means ritual. Rappaport's theory of religion is thus a theory of ritual. Rappaport's original approach to ritual and therefore to religion is the one in his Columbia dissertation and in turn in his first book, *Pigs for the ancestors* (1968, 1984), which was based on his fieldwork in Papua New Guinea. What changed over Rappaport's career was not his equation of ritual with religious ritual and of religion with ritual but his analysis of ritual. His original, ecological approach, while never abandoned, was transformed into the formalist approach found in his *Ecology, meaning, and religion* (1979), and then into the almost metaphysical approach found in his posthumously published *Ritual and religion in the making of humanity* (1999). The shift could scarcely have been sharper.

In 1965, Rappaport began teaching anthropology at the University of Michigan in Ann Arbor. He received his PhD from Columbia in 1966. He spent his thirty-two-year career at Michigan, becoming Leslie A. White Professor of Anthropology. In 1991, he became Director of the Program on Studies of Religion. He served as President of the American Anthropological Association (1987–9). He finished *Ritual and religion* only months before his death from lung cancer.

Pigs for the ancestors

The subtitle of *Pigs* makes clear Rappaport's ecological approach to ritual: *Ritual in the ecology of a New Guinea people.* By 'ritual' Rappaport means religious ritual: 'the term *ritual* has been taken in this study to refer to the performance of conventional acts explicitly directed toward the involvement of nonempirical or supernatural agencies in the affairs of the participants' (Rappaport 1968: 191). But the main functions that Rappaport attributes to ritual are secular. They are its 'social, demographic, nutritional, and ecological consequences' (Rappaport 1968: 191–2). By 'consequences' Rappaport means unintended consequences, or effects. To use the terms made famous by Robert Merton, Rappaport, like most other social scientists, is concerned more with latent than with manifest functions (see Rappaport 1968: 232).

Rappaport focuses not on people's beliefs but on the effect of their beliefs on their actions (see Rappaport 1984: 306).[3] The gods to whom participants direct rituals are illusory, but the rituals produced by belief in those gods have physical, not merely ideological, effects. The view that Rappaport rejects is epitomized by the line he quotes from the sociologist George Homans: 'Ritual actions do not produce a practical result on the external world – that is one of the reasons we call them "ritual"' (quoted Rappaport 1968: 2). Contrary to Homans and, more, to Marx, religious ritual improves lives materially (see Rappaport 1971b: 23).[4]

For Rappaport, the raising of pigs in abandoned gardens by the Tsembaga Maring farmers of New Guinea serves to clear the ground and make planting easier. The ritualistic killing of pigs keeps an increasing number from damaging the ground and making planting harder. The eating of pigs, which ordinarily happens only during rituals, provides protein to keep the people healthy: 'the ritual regulation of pork consumption by the Tsembaga makes an important contribution to a diet that maintains the population in adequate health at a high level of activity' (Rappaport 1968: 87). In times of stress, such as war, pigs are killed and eaten 'to provide physiological reinforcement' (Rappaport 1968: 87). Truces are celebrated with pig offerings to allies and to ancestors.[5]

In *Pigs* Rappaport sees ritual as merely the human means of maintaining the ecosystem we share with animals. Elsewhere he contends that animals, too, have rituals (see, for example, Rappaport 1974: 11). He declares that religious ritual deals not just with 'relationships occurring within a congregation [i.e., community],' as for Emile Durkheim, but also with 'relationships between a congregation and entities *external* to it' (Rappaport 1968: 1).[6] Humans alone have culture, of which religion is a part, but culture serves the same ends as claws and teeth do for animals: 'The study of man the culture-bearer cannot be separated from the study of man as a species among species' (Rappaport 1968: 242).

Rappaport appeals to cybernetics and to systems theory as well as to ecology to make his case that religion is part of a self-regulating system that works like a thermostat. Much of the book, not least the ten appendices, is devoted to measuring the various systems and subsystems he delineates. Rappaport seeks simultaneously to differentiate and to connect the array of spheres at work. He wants to show that events and processes in one sphere affect those in other spheres. His approach can properly be called holistic.[7] While the image of a society as a organism goes back to Herbert Spencer, Rappaport extends 'organicism' beyond society to the physical environment.[8]

Rappaport wrote *Pigs* to revive functionalism, which by then had been widely spurned.[9] In his foreword to *Pigs*, anthropologist Andrew P. Vayda, who was Rappaport's doctoral supervisor, lists three standard objections to functionalist explanations: (1) that functionalism cannot explain the origin of ritual or any other aspect of culture; (2) that functionalism limits itself to positive, integrative functions and ignores negative, anti-social ones; and (3) that functionalism makes claims that cannot be tested (see Vayda 1968: ix).

In response to the first objection, Vayda and in turn Rappaport note that Rappaport explicitly confines himself to explaining the function, not also the origin, of Tsembaga ritual and therefore cannot be faulted for failing to do what he never intends to do (see Vayda 1968: x): 'The systemic role of ritual in the ecology of the Tsembaga has been the focus of this study and I have offered no suggestions concerning the origin of these rituals' (Rappaport 1968: 230). In response to the second objection, Vayda notes that the search for integration amidst apparent chaos constitutes not obliviousness to disorder but a refutation of it (see Vayda 1968: x–xi).[10] In response to the third objection, Vayda and in turn Rappaport insist strongly that, whatever the untestability of some functionalist analyses, Rappaport defines 'needs' in ways that can be tested (see Vayda 1968: xi; Rappaport 1968: 230, 232).

Vayda and Rappaport both cite the philosopher Carl Hempel's then-recent (1959) essay on 'The logic of functional analysis' as the key source of the third objection (see Hempel 1965: 303–8).[11] Hempel types functionalism as a species of teleological explanation, which for him postulates needs, on the part of either society or the individual, that cannot be proved. He cites the example of neovitalism, which maintains that every living being harbors a life spirit that dictates its development. Hempel allows for invisible causes, such as a magnetic field. He objects to the neovitalist spirit because it is untestable.

Rappaport seeks to meet this objection by quantifying the variables and specifying the range within which they must operate for the system to function adequately: 'If the method of functional analysis is to meet the criticisms of Hempel (1959) and others, quantitative values must be assigned to all variables, and in the case of those variables that define the adequate functioning of the system their tolerable ranges of values must also be specified' (Rappaport 1968: 230; see also 232). But this procedure, which consumes much of the book, still does not provide a test for the claim that these variables must be present, and in the right proportion. To do so, Rappaport must find cases in which adequate functioning is absent, an absence that he can then attribute to variables falling outside the range. By *modus tollens*, a valid argument would be:

PREMISE: If variables present and if present in the right proportion, adequate functioning.
PREMISE: No adequate functioning.
CONCLUSION: Therefore variables not present or not present in the right proportion.

If, instead, Rappaport were to argue from variables outside the range to inadequate functioning, he would be committing the fallacy of denying the antecedent:

PREMISE: If variables present and if present in the right proportion, adequate functioning.
PREMISE: No variables present or present in the right proportion.
CONCLUSION: Therefore no adequate functioning.

Rappaport's attempt to meet Hempel's criticisms oddly ignores Hempel's main objection: that functionalism commits the fallacy not of denying the antecedent but of affirming the consequent (see Hempel 1965: 308–12). Claiming that religious ritual explains stability in either society or the environment is not fallacious. The claim must simply be proved. The problem is that a functionalist explanation works backwards: it starts with stability, which it attributes to religious ritual.

A valid deductive argument takes the following form:

PREMISE: If religious ritual, then stability.
PREMISE: Ritual.
CONCLUSION: Therefore stability.

But the explanation to which Hempel objects work in reverse:

PREMISE: If religious ritual, then stability.
PREMISE: Stability.
CONCLUSION: Therefore religious ritual.

This claim is invalid because the cause is deduced from the effect and not vice versa. Because the argument is deductive, the conclusion is supposed to follow necessarily from the premises. What is thus claimed is not that stability *may* be caused by ritual but that it *must* be caused by ritual. Yet how can other causes be ruled out? Since Rappaport begins with stability, he commits the fallacy by attributing stability necessarily to religious ritual. He need not account for the origin of religious ritual to avoid the fallacy. But he need start with ritual and prove that it necessarily causes stability. He cannot start with the existence of both ritual and stability and conclude that ritual necessarily causes stability. Yet this is exactly what he does, so that his meticulous measuring of variables still produces a pseudo-explanation of the ecosystem.[12]

In the second edition of *Pigs*, which has an 'epilogue' almost two-fifths the size of the original book, Rappaport tries anew to meet Hempel's objections to functionalism, but he continues to consider only the objection of untestability (see Rappaport 1984: 362–70; see also Rappaport 1979: 52–5, 66ff.). Not until *Ritual and religion* does he confront the objection of fallaciousness, but his defense there is the unexpected contention that his 'functionalism' purports to offer only a formal and not a causal relationship among variables (see Rappaport 1999: 27–8).[13]

Ecology, meaning, and religion

In the first four of the seven essays in *Ecology, meaning, and religion* (1979) – all but one of the seven reprinted, if usually revised – Rappaport remains concerned with the ecological function of religious ritual. But in the last three essays he turns from the function of religious ritual to the form. More precisely, he includes the function in the form, so that to grasp what ritual is is to grasp what it does: 'it is only when function is intrinsic to form that functional uniqueness can be claimed' (Rappaport 1974: 4). The function here becomes less ecological than communicative, though communication is still a means to an ecological end.[14] Rappaport continues to enlist cybernetics and systems theory as well as ecology.

The key essay in the collection is 'The obvious aspects of ritual,' originally published in 1974. Sensibly, Rappaport tries to identify what makes ritual ritual by differentiating it from anything else. He grants that 'no single feature of ritual is peculiar to ritual' but insists that 'the conjunction of its features' is 'unique' (Rappaport 1974: 6). These aspects, or criteria, are supposed to be anything but obvious. They include formality, performance, means to end, congregation, and community. For example, ritual must be done precisely, repeatedly, and at set times and places. But an assembly line is equally formal yet scarcely a ritual. Ritual must, in addition, be performed. But so, too, must dance. Ritual is only a means to an end. But so, too, is drama. Where, however, drama involves an audience, ritual requires a community, or 'congregation,' which does not merely witness the action but participates in it. So goes Rappaport's procedure: he identifies a characteristic of ritual but then adds another characteristic to set ritual apart from whatever else shares the first characteristic.

Ritual and religion in the making of humanity

Ritual and religion in the making of humanity constitutes a grand elaboration of the 'Obvious' essay. Adding speech acts theory to his mainstays, cybernetics and systems theory, Rappaport constructs perhaps the fullest and richest theory of ritual ever formulated.

Yet his theory is limited. Rather than accounting for the origin of ritual, he still takes its existence for granted, as he did in *Pigs*, and still confines himself to the function of ritual. In not trying to account for ritual, which would make it beholden to whatever caused it, he gives ritual more clout than it might otherwise have.

In *Ritual and religion* ritual, apparently, does almost everything, not least things that others would automatically attribute to belief. Classical theorists of religion like E.B. Tylor and J.G. Frazer viewed ritual as the *application* of belief. Turner, Geertz, and Douglas viewed ritual as the *expression* or, at best, the *instillment* of belief. Rappaport credits ritual with actually *creating* belief. Rappaport does consider myth, but for him it is secondary. Like Turner, Geertz, and Douglas, he attributes to ritual what others would attribute to myth: 'Much of what is "said" in ritual is, of course, "said" in myth or in lawbooks or in theological treatises or, for that matter, in novels, drama and poetry but, to reiterate an assertion made earlier, there are things "said" *by all liturgical rituals that cannot be said in other ways*' (Rappaport 1999: 38).[15] Like Turner, Geertz, and Douglas, Rappaport rejects the once commonplace view that ritual provides action and myth content. For him, as for the three of them, ritual itself provides content. Where others, such as Jane Harrison and Edmund Leach, confer on myth the ritual-like power of performance, Rappaport, like Turner, Geertz, and Douglas, confers on ritual the myth-like power of cognition.[16]

In fact, as the quotation shows, ritual for Rappaport not merely duplicates myth in imparting content but imparts even more content than myth does – a claim that likely exceeds any made by Turner, Geertz, or Douglas. Consequently, he considers his analysis of ritual successful when he can show not merely that ritual accomplishes its functions 'but that certain meanings and effects can best, or even *only*, be expressed or achieved in ritual' (Rappaport 1999: 30). One might call his an irreducibly ritualistic theory of ritual. His approach to function matches that to form: ritual is deciphered only when it is shown to be unique.

By 'belief' Rappaport means religious belief, just as by ritual he means religious ritual. He allows for nonreligious ritual (see Rappaport 1971b: 25; 1999: 24–6) but, in contrast to Turner, Geertz, and Douglas, ignores it. Where for Turner, Geertz, and Douglas ritual is at most the key part of religion, for Rappaport it is nearly, though not quite, the whole. He allows for religion beyond ritual but asserts that 'ritual as defined here is the ground from which religion grows' (Rappaport 1999: 26). From ritual comes the rest of religion: 'religion's major conceptual and experiential constituents, the sacred, the numinous, the occult and the divine, and their integration into the Holy, are creations of ritual' (Rappaport 1999: 3).

Rappaport's definition of ritual is imposing:

> It is clear that ritual, as a form of action or structure, may have and in a trivial sense inevitably has social and material consequences (that may or may not be 'functional'). To define ritual as a form or structure, however, *ipso facto* goes beyond the recognition of such effects [i.e., functions] for, as sets of enduring structural relations among specified but variable features or elements, ritual not only can claim to be socially or materially consequential, but to possess *logical entailments* as well. *I will argue that the performance of more or less invariant sequences of formal acts and utterances not entirely encoded by the performers logically entails the establishment of convention, the sealing of social contract, the construction of the integrated conventional orders we shall call* Logoi ... *the investment of whatever it encodes with morality, the construction of time and eternity; the representation of a paradigm of creation, the generation of the concept of the sacred and the sanctification of conventional*

order, the generation of theories of the occult, the evocation of numinous experience, the awareness of the divine, the grasp of the holy, and the construction of orders of meaning transcending the semantic. (Rappaport 1999: 27)

As in the 'Obvious' essay, so here, Rappaport seeks to circumvent the fallacy of affirming the consequent by maintaining that he is concerned only with the form and not also the function of ritual – this despite his celebration of ritual for all that it does (see Rappaport 1999: 27–8). But in fact here, too, he builds the function into the form. The functions of ritual are the same as those enumerated in 'Obvious aspects.'

To offer an example of what Rappaport means in *Ritual and religion*, the biblical patriarch Isaac, wanting Esau, his firstborn son, to succeed in life, does not merely state his wish but utilizes the ritual of a blessing to ensure it (Genesis 27). Even when the blind Isaac discovers that he has been duped into bestowing his deathbed blessing on Jacob instead, the blessing cannot be undone. The ritual is itself efficacious, no matter what the intent of either party. To take a more positive example, most couples planning to spend their lives together still partake of the ritual of marriage. The ceremony, whether civil or religious, binds the parties even if, let us say, one of them only pretends to be in love with the other.

Against Rappaport, one might note that even if Isaac's blessing, once offered, cannot be rescinded, it still does not transform Jacob into Isaac's firstborn or favorite. A wedding ceremony presupposes that the bride and groom are committed to each other and expresses, not establishes, that commitment. The ritual is hollow if the commitment is missing. And marriage, unlike Isaac's blessing, can be annulled, albeit by another ritual.

Rappaport distinguishes ritual from belief on many grounds. A ritual is public, whereas belief can be private. Ritual is certain, whereas belief can waver. But these distinctions are debatable. Are there not private rituals, including private weddings? Freud (1963 [1907]) famously compared private obsessive-compulsive acts with public, religious rituals – an essay actually cited in the bibliographies of both *Pigs* and *Ritual and religion*. Even if belief can be held privately, most beliefs are shared with others, and it is from others that most of us secure confirmation for our beliefs. The more persons who profess to have seen UFOs, the more confident others are in their own sightings. Is ritual always certain? Is there never doubt that it is the right ritual, that it is the right time and place, and that it is effective? Conversely, what of, to use the apt term, 'unshakable belief'? Rappaport asserts that ritual can implant or shore up belief, as undeniably it can. But for its part, belief can impel ritual. Belief in God spurs baptism.

Rappaport does allow for doubt in ritual: 'acceptance' in ritual of belief 'does not in and of itself ... dissolve doubt' (Rappaport 1999: 283). But ritual for Rappaport circumvents the need for ordinary justifications for belief and thereby neutralizes doubt. Rappaport now even identifies 'belief' with belief requiring justification: 'the acceptance indicated by participation in a liturgical order [i.e., a ritual] being independent of belief, ... makes it possible for the performer to transcend his own doubt, experience and reason by accepting in defiance of them' (Rappaport 1999: 283). Rappaport then notes that 'some prominent theologians have suggested that faith necessarily includes an element of doubt' (Rappaport 1999: 283). The issue, however, is not whether faith allows for doubt but whether the acceptance of faith in the face of doubt comes from ritual and not, say, from will. Does the greatest case of faith overcoming doubt – the resolve of Abraham to 'suspend the ethical,' in Kierkegaard's phrase, and kill his son – stem from any ritual rather than from will?

Rappaport roots other aspects of religion in ritual. To participate in a ritual is to accept it, so that acceptance spells obligation and therefore morality: '[O]bligation is entailed by the acceptance intrinsic to participation in ritual. Breach of obligation, it could be argued, is one of the few acts, if not, indeed, the only act that is always and everywhere held to be immoral' (Rappaport 1999: 132). Yet just as ritual seemingly presupposes belief rather than dispenses with it, so ritual seemingly presupposes morality rather than creates it. When two parties ritually shake hands after agreeing to something, the faith that they have in each other does not stem from the handshake, which merely expresses, not establishes, their mutual trust.

Rappaport argues that not even homicide is always immoral – unless it violates a ritual: 'There are conditions, so common as to require no illustration, under which killing humans is laudable or even mandatory. What is immoral is, of course, killing someone whom there is an obligation, at least tacit, not to kill' (Rappaport 1999: 132). Because parricide, matricide, and infanticide are immoral only because they violate ritualistic obligations not to kill members of one's family, Rappaport is here broadening the term 'ritual' far beyond the scope of a formal performance, to which he otherwise commendably confines it.

Having rooted morality in ritualistic obligation, Rappaport is prepared to conclude that ritual is the center of social life: 'In enunciating, accepting and making conventions moral, ritual contains within itself not simply a symbolic representation of social contract, but tacit social contract itself. As such, ritual ... is *the* basic social act' (Rappaport 1999: 138). Ritual socializes in other ways, too. Notably, it links what is private to what is public. A rite of passage turns the physiological changes in an adolescent into a change in status.

Ritual ties human beings not only to one another but also to the external world – a claim that harkens back to *Pigs*. Ritual orders experience in many ways, with Rappaport emphasizing the experience of time over the experience of space. Most straightforwardly, ritual organizes time into clear-cut divisions: the ritual of Christmas divides the year into two seasons.

Above all, ritual, here only religious ritual, connects humans to the cosmos. As in *Ecology, meaning, and religion*, so here, all rituals communicate, but only religious rituals communicate eternal, metaphysical, 'sacred' truths. Sacred truths, or 'Ultimate Sacred Postulates,' hold everywhere, are not derivative, deal with more than this world, and stir emotion. Rappaport's best example is the Hebrew Shema: 'Hear O Israel, the Lord our God the Lord is One.' Sacred truths provide certitude not only because they are unchanging but also because they lie beyond the realm of proof or disproof. Religious rituals, as the most invariant and therefore the most repetitive of rituals, are ideal for communicating eternal truths. But religious rituals are not like PowerPoint. They are not just an effective means of communicating content that is known or knowable otherwise. Somehow they establish and validate the Ultimate Sacred Postulates they instill: 'The truth of divine orders as well as divine beings is established in ritual' (Rappaport 1999: 345). Without religious rituals, there would be no Ultimate Sacred Postulates.

I do not see how Rappaport can claim this much for ritual. For example, he enlists philosopher J.L. Austin's (1962) famous notion of performative utterances, which do things, rather than constative utterances, which state things. 'The cat is on the mat' states a fact but in no way effects it. 'I pronounce you man and wife' effects marriage but does not describe it. For Austin, sentences can both state and do, but the roles are distinct. Rappaport conflates the roles. For him, a marriage ceremony does not merely transform two persons into husband and wife but somehow 'establishes' the phenomenon of marriage itself: 'We have already noted that a dubbing did more than transform a particular young man into a knight ... It further established and re-established the conventions of knighthood itself' (Rappaport 1999: 125). How, similarly, the Mass not merely invokes but 'establishes a more general conventional understanding of the relationship of humans to the divine' (Rappaport 1999: 125–6) it is hard to see. On this point, as on so many other points, Rappaport offers pronouncements, not arguments.

In a return to the theme of *Pigs*, Rappaport makes the overarching function of religion adaptation, but adaptation now to the cosmos and not just to the environment. Adaptation is now to the world that humans share with god, not just with animals (see Rappaport 1999: ch. 13). Where in *Pigs* religion keeps humans healthy, in *Ritual and religion* religion gives their lives meaning. Where in *Pigs* belief barely figures, in *Ritual and religion* it is central. But it is still the product of ritual.

At the end of the book Rappaport decries the toppling of religion by science and declares that religion must continue to play a central role in human life, with which for him it is coexistent. As his book approaches its climax, it reads less like social science and more like theology, despite Rappaport's assurance that a theologian he is not. Clearly, the declaration of the indispensability of religion and of its compatibility with science requires argument. The argument for compatibility rests on a 'postmodern' conception of science. Where modern science aspires to objectivity, postmodern science embraces subjectivity and thereby makes room for religion (see Rappaport 1999: 456–61). Against the 'modern' view of science we get no argument, only pronouncement. In his linkage of religion to adaptation and, further, to evolution, Rappaport echoes Teilhard de Chardin. The book flies off into the metaphysical stratosphere. To paraphrase *The wizard of Oz*, we're not in New Guinea any more.[17]

In his foreword to *Ritual and religion*, anthropologist Keith Hart (1999) proclaims the work of equal stature to Durkheim's *The elementary forms of the religious life* (1912). I demur. However magisterially it does so, *Ritual and religion* merely defines religion. One whole book of *Elementary forms* is devoted to defining religion, but two more books are devoted to explaining religion. Rappaport himself saw *Ritual and religion* as completing *Pigs*. But the posthumous book completes the first book only if one accepts Rappaport's retroactive categorization of *Pigs* as a mere definition of religion. Put mildly, the definitions in the books would still diverge, but at least both books would be doing the same task. For me, the task that *Pigs* does and that *Ritual and religion* does not do is to explain the phenomenon defined. For me, Rappaport's legacy rests with *Pigs*.

Notes

1   On Rappaport's life and anthropology, see, above all, Messer 2001, from which most of my biographical information comes. See also Hul 1989. For a bibliography of Rappaport's writings, see Messer and Lambek 2001: 39–45.

2   In the added epilogue to the enlarged edition of *Pigs*, Rappaport defends his ecological analysis against the charge, by Jonathan Friedman (1974: 459–60, 465–6 [on Rappaport]; 457–9, 460–6 [on Harris]), of 'vulgar materialism' (see Rappaport 1984: 304–7; see also Rappaport 1977: 43–77), which Friedman distinguishes from both classical Marxism and his own structural Marxism. For other criticisms both of cultural materialism, for which the author prefers the term 'neofunctionalism,' and of ecological anthropology, see Orlove 1980: 243–5. The best-known critic of cultural materialism has been Marshall Sahlins (1976), who bemoans the collapse of culture into biology: on Rappaport, see

Sahlins 1976: 77, 87–8, 124, n.51, 168. In response, see Rappaport 1984: 331–6. On the fate of cultural materialism in the wake of the emergence of interpretive anthropology and of postmodernism, see Johnson and Johnson 2001. Rappaport himself distinguishes his position from that of Harris: see Vayda and Rappaport 1968.

3   On Rappaport's indifference to intentions in *Pigs*, see Biersack 1999a: 15, n.3; Gillison 2001: 294–9. For a reinterpretation of Rappaport's pig rituals as effects of individual intentions, see Peoples *et al.* 1982: 291–300. See, as one of the many comments to this article, Rappaport 1982b: 303–4. See, in turn, Peoples' reply: 307–8.

4   For an excellent illustration of Rappaport's thesis to a modern religion, see Leone 1974.

5   Rappaport (1968: 3–4) lists eight functions of the ritual. The first four, which are the more important, are physiological. The last four are social. The eight are a mix of latent with manifest functions.

6   On Rappaport and Durkheim, see Hart 1999; Lambek 2001: 247–51.

7   On holism, see Phillips 1976. Rappaport's brand of holism falls under Phillips' Holism 1. Rappaport himself calls his approach 'holistic': see Rappaport 1971d: 237.

8   On the organic metaphor, see Rousseau 1972.

9   In defense of functionalism, see Rappaport 1977.

10   On what he calls Rappaport's 'eufunctionalism,' see Watson 1969: 528–9.

11   For criticisms of functionalism comparable, though not quite identical, with Hempel's, see Nagel 1961: 520–35.

12   Without identifying the fallacy of affirming the consequent, Sterling Robbins in effect faults Rappaport for committing it: see Robbins 1971: 168. Decades ago, Hans Penner wrote a short essay that simply repeated Hempel's charge that functionalism commits this fallacy: see Penner 1971. In his collected essays he enlarged that essay, oddly never mentioning the original version: see Penner 1989. But his sole point remained the same: that functionalism confuses a merely sufficient condition with a necessary one. That point is simply another way of describing the fallacy of affirming the consequent (and also the fallacy of denying the antecedent).

13   Here Rappaport defends himself not against Hempel or Nagel but against fellow anthropologist Maurice Bloch, who faults Rappaport for following in the erroneous ways of Smith (1889): see Bloch 1973; 1986: 5–7. To be sure, Rappaport does earlier (1977) consider the fallacy of affirming the consequent, but in response to Friedman rather than to Hempel. Rappaport again meets the charge by categorizing his own analysis as one of form rather than of cause: see Rappaport 1979: 74–8. In defense of Rappaport against Hempel's strictures, which are considered too demanding, see Burhenn 1980.

14   Johannes Fabian goes as far as to assert that the divide between the earlier and the later essays in *Ecology, meaning, and religion* constitutes a 'conversion' and a 'gestalt switch' on Rappaport's part from materialism to culturalism: see

Fabian 1982. See, in reply, Rappaport 1982a. See also Biersack 1999a: 7. On the shift from function to form, see Wolf 1999: 21.

15   On myth, see Rappaport 1999: 31, 37–8, 110, 134–6, 151, 168, 233–4; 1986a: 319–29.

16   On the conferring of ritual-like power to myth, see Harrison 1912: 330; Leach 1965 [1954]: 11–12. But where Harrison and Leach thereby want to blur the line between myth and ritual, Rappaport confers myth-like power on ritual to highlight the distinctiveness of ritual vis-à-vis myth.

17   On Rappaport's legacy, see Biersack 1999b; Messer and Lambek 2001.

References

Austin, J.L., 1962. *How to do things with words*, ed. J.O. Urmson. Harvard University Press, Cambridge, MA.

Bellah, R.N., 1979. Review of Rappaport, *Ritual and religion in the making of humanity. Journal for the Scientific Study of Religion* 38 (4), 569–70.

Biersack, A., 1999a. Introduction: from the 'new ecology' to the new ecologies. *American Anthropologist* 101 (1), 5–18.

Biersack, A. (Ed.), 1999b. Ecologies for tomorrow: reading Rappaport today. Symposium. *American Anthropologist* 101 (1), 5–112.

Bloch, M., 1973. Symbols, song, dance and features of articulation: or is religion an extreme form of traditional authority? *Archives Européenes de Sociologie* 15 (1), 55–81.

Bloch, M., 1986. *From blessing to violence*. Cambridge University Press, Cambridge.

Burhenn, H., 1980. Functionalism and the explanation of religion. *Journal for the Scientific Study of Religion* 19 (4), 350–60.

Dalton, D., 2001. Review of Rappaport, *Ritual and religion in the making of humanity. Anthropological Quarterly* 74 (1), 48–9.

Dwyer, P.D., 1985. Review of Rappaport, *Pigs for the ancestors*, enlarged edn. *Oceania* 56 (2), 151–4.

Fabian, J., 1982. On Rappaport's *Ecology, meaning, and religion. Current Anthropology* 23 (2), 205–9.

Freud, S., 1963 [1907]. Obsessive acts and religious practices. In: Rieff, P. (Ed.), *Character and culture*. Collier Books, New York, 17–26.

Friedman, J., 1974. Marxism, structuralism and vulgar materialism. *Man* (n. s.) 9 (3), 444–69.

Gillison, G., 2001. Reflections on *Pigs for the ancestors*. In Messer and Lambek 2001: 291–9.

Harris, M., 1980 [1979]. *Cultural materialism*. Vintage Books, New York.

Harrison, J.E., 1912. *Themis*. Cambridge University Press, Cambridge.

Hart, K., 1999. Foreword to Rappaport 1999: xiv–xix.

Hart, K. and Kottak, C., 1999. Obituary of Roy A. Rappaport. *American Anthropologist* 101 (1), 159–61.

Hays, T.E., 1987. Review of Rappaport, *Pigs for the ancestors*, enlarged edn. *American Anthropologist* 89 (3), 754–5.

Hefner, R., 1983. The culture problem in human ecology: a review article [section III on Rappaport, *Ecology, meaning, and religion*]. *Cambridge Studies in Society and History* 25 (3), 547–56.

Hempel, C.G., 1965. The logic of functional analysis [1959]. In: Hempel, C.G., *Aspects of scientific explanation and other essays in the philosophy of science.* Free Press, New York, 297–330.

Hopgood, J.F., 1982. Review of Rappaport, *Ecology, meaning, and religion. American Ethnologist* 9 (3), 588–9.

Hul, N.V., 1989. On being muddleheaded: 'you can make a living at this.' Faculty profile: Roy Rappaport. *LSAmagazine* 12 (2), 16–17.

Johnson, A. and Johnson, O., 2001. Introduction to reprint of Harris, *Cultural materialism.* AltaMira, Walnut Creek, CA, vi–xiv.

Lambek, M., 2001. Rappaport on religion. In: Messer and Lambek 2001: 244–73.

Leach, E., 1965 [1954]. *Political systems of highland Burma.* Beacon, Boston.

Leone, M.P., 1974. The economic basis for the evolution of Mormon religion. In: Zaretsky, I.I. and Leone, M.P. (Eds.), *Religious movements in contemporary America.* Princeton University Press, Princeton, NJ, 722–66.

McArthur, M., 1974. *Pigs for the ancestors*: a review article. *Oceania* 45 (2), 87–123.

Messer, E., 2001. Thinking and engaging the whole: the anthropology of Roy A. Rappaport. In: Messer and Lambek 2001: 1–38.

Messer, E. and Lambek, M. (Eds.), 2001. *Ecology and the sacred: engaging the anthropology of Roy A. Rappaport.* University of Michigan Press, Ann Arbor.

Nagel, E., 1961. *The structure of science.* Harcourt, Brace, New York.

Orlove, B.S., 1980. Ecological anthropology. *Annual Review of Anthropology* 9, 235–73.

Paul, R.A., 2002. The social act basic to humanity [review of Rappaport, *Ritual and religion in the making of humanity*]. *American Anthropologist* 43 (3), 524–6.

Penner, H., 1971. The poverty of functionalism. *History of Religions* 11 (1), 91–7.

Penner, H., 1989. Functional explanations of religion. In: Penner, H., *Impasse and resolution.* Lang, New York, 103–28.

Peoples, J.G. *et al.*, 1982. Individual or group advantage? A reinterpretation of the Maring ritual cycle. *Current Anthropology* 23 (2), 291–310.

Peterson, G.T., 1980. Growing up with New Guinea: *Pigs for the ancestors* in retrospect. *Dialectical Anthropology* 5 (3), 255–9.

Phillips, D.C., 1976. *Holistic thought in social science.* Stanford University Press, Stanford, CA.

Ploeg, A., 1969. Review of Rappaport, *Pigs for the ancestors. Journal of the Polynesian Society* 78 (2), 271–3.

Rappaport, R.A., 1968. *Pigs for the ancestors*, first edn. Yale University Press, New Haven, CT.

Rappaport, R.A., 1971a. Ritual, sanctity, and cybernetics. *American Anthropologist* 73 (1), 59–76.

Rappaport, R.A., 1971b. The sacred in human evolution. *Annual Review of Ecology and Systematics* 2, 23–44.

Rappaport, R.A., 1971c. The flow of energy in an agricultural society. *Scientific American* 225 (3), 116–32.

Rappaport, R.A., 1971d. Nature, culture, and ecological anthropology. In: Shapiro, H.L. (Ed.), *Man, culture, and society*, rev. edn. Oxford University Press, London, Oxford, New York, 237–67.

Rappaport, R.A., 1974. Obvious aspects of ritual. *Cambridge Anthropology* 2 (1), 3–69. Reprinted in expanded form in Rappaport 1979: 173–221.

Rappaport, R.A., 1976. Liturgies and lies. *International Yearbook for the Sociology of Knowledge and Religion* 10, 75–104. Reprinted in revised form as 'Sanctity and lies in evolution' in Rappaport 1979: 233–46.

Rappaport, R.A., 1977. Ecology, adaptation, and the ills of functionalism (being, among other things, a response to Jonathan Friedman). *Michigan Discussions in Anthropology* 2, 138–90. Reprinted in expanded form in two parts in Rappaport 1979: 43–95 (retitled 'Ecology, adaptation, and the ills of functionalism') and 145–72 (retitled 'Adaptive structure and its disorders').

Rappaport, R.A., 1978. Adaptation and the structure of ritual. In: Jones, N.B. and Reynolds, V. (Eds.), *Human behavior and adaptation.* Taylor and Francis, London, 77–102.

Rappaport, R.A., 1979. *Ecology, meaning, and religion.* North Atlantic Books, Richmond, VA.

Rappaport, R.A., 1982a. Reply to Fabian 1982. *Current Anthropology* 23 (2), 209–11.

Rappaport, R.A., 1982b. Comment. In: Peoples 1982: 303–4.

Rappaport, R.A., 1984. *Pigs for the ancestors*, Enlarged edn. Yale University Press, New Haven, CT.

Rappaport, R.A., 1986a. Desecrating the holy woman: Derek Freeman's attack on Margaret Mead. *American Scholar* 55 (3), 313–47.

Rappaport, R.A., 1986b. The construction of time and eternity in ritual. David Skomp Distinguished Lecture in Anthropology. Indiana University Press, Bloomington.

Rappaport, R.A., 1992. Ritual, time, and eternity. *Zygon* 27 (1), 5–30.

Rappaport, R.A., 1994. On the evolution of morality and religion: a response to Lee Cronk. *Zygon* 29 (3), 331–49.

Rappaport, R.A., 1995. Logos, liturgy, and the evolution of humanity. In: Beck, A.B., Bartelt, A.H., Raabe, P.R., and Franke, C.A. (Eds.), *Fortunate the eyes that see: essays in honor of David Noel Freedman.* Eerdmans, Grand Rapids, MI, 601–32.

Rappaport, R.A., 1999. *Ritual and religion in the making of humanity.* Cambridge University Press, Cambridge.

Robbins, S., 1971. Review of Rappaport, *Pigs for the ancestors. Ethnohistory* 18 (2), 167–8.

Rousseau, G.S. (Ed.), 1972. *Organic form.* Routledge and Kegan Paul, London.

Sahlins, M., 1976. *Culture and practical reason.* University of Chicago Press, Chicago.

Salisbury, R.F., 1968. Review of Rappaport, *Pigs for the ancestors. Annals of the American Academy of Political and Social Science* 380, 202.

Smith, W.R., 1889. *Lectures on the religion of the Semites,* first edn. Black, Edinburgh.

Strathern, A., 1969. Review of Rappaport, *Pigs for the ancestors. Bulletin of the School of Oriental and African Studies* 32 (1), 204–5.

Strathern, A., 1985. Review of Rappaport, *Pigs for the ancestors,* enlarged edn. *American Ethnologist* 12 (2), 374–5.

Strathern, M., 1968. Review of Rappaport, *Pigs for the ancestors. Man* (n. s.) 3 (4), 687–8.

Strathern, A. and Stewart, P.J., 1999. On the theory of stability and change in ritual: the legacy of Roy Rappaport [review essay on Rappaport, *Ritual and religion in the making of humanity*]. *Social Analysis* 43 (3), 116–21.

Tuzin, D.F., 1981. Review of Rappaport, *Ecology, meaning, and religion. American Anthropologist* 83 (2), 403–4.

Vayda, A.J., 1968. Foreword to Rappaport 1968: ix–xiii.

Vayda, A.J. and Rappaport, R.A., 1968. Ecology, cultural and non-cultural. In: Clifton, J. (Ed.), *Introduction to cultural anthropology.* Houghton and Mifflin, Boston, 476–97.

Watson, J. B., 1969. Review of Rappaport, *Pigs for the ancestors. American Anthropologist* 71 (2), 527–9.

Wilson, H.C., 1969. Review of Rappaport, *Pigs for the ancestors. Journal of Asian Studies* 28 (3), 658–9.

Wolf, E.R., 1999. Cognizing 'cognized models'. *American Anthropologist* 101 (1), 19–22.

Yengoyan, A.A., 2000. Review of Rappaport, *Ritual and religion in the making of humanity. American Anthropologist* 102 (2), 404–5.

6

Religious economies and rational choice

On Rodney Stark and Roger Finke,
Acts of faith (2000)

Gregory D. Alles

Rodney Stark is a stereotypically US sociologist of religion. Prior to him, most sociologists of religion treated the United States as an exception to their theories. Stark, along with a group of like-minded scholars, including Roger Finke and Laurence Iannaccone, has taken the United States as his paradigm. In orientation, Stark is not only American but strikingly Reaganesque. His theorizing rests upon a foundation of free-market, supply-side economics that is both dismissive of liberalism, which he simply equates with a lack of religious conviction (Stark and Finke 2000: 276), and triumphalistically Christian, with an especial fondness for American Evangelicalism and Pentecostalism (cf. Carroll 1996). Since the mid-1990s, he has published a series of books (1996, 2001, 2003, 2005, 2006, 2007) that not only present the discovery (rather than the invention, construction, or cognitive emergence) of God as a social-scientific inevitability but also make Christianity responsible for the development of modern science and technology and the 'success of the West.' Islam, he baldly proclaims, was and is a retrograde movement (Stark 2007: 394–5).

However one reacts to these traits, there is good reason to approach Stark's writings with caution. It is simply not possible to write with the breadth that he has embraced in recent years and not make mistakes of the sort sometimes disparaged as howlers, as when Stark claims that the Vulgate refers to translations of the Bible into vernacular European languages (Stark 2005: 226) or when he confuses Bruno Bauer (1809–82), a left-wing Hegelian who denied the existence of Jesus, and Ferdinand Christian Baur (1792–1860), the leader of the quite different Tübingen school of New Testament criticism (Stark 2007: 302). More consequential was a mathematical error in the analysis of a large dataset, undiscovered for ten years, that allowed Stark and his colleagues to insist that these data provided evidence for a positive correlation between religious plurality and religious participation; the correlation was actually inverse.[1] Stark also has an inexplicable fondness for outdated views, such as the theory of *Urmonotheismus* ('primal monotheism') associated with the Viennese anthropologist and priest Wilhelm Schmidt (1868–1954) (Stark 2007: 21–63, esp. 61–2). Even granting the false analogy that Stark draws between contemporary 'primitives' and the earliest human beings, it quickly becomes clear that Stark is himself susceptible to the critique which he so easily aims at earlier anthropologists: he is more than willing to make definitive pronouncements about 'primitive' people and their religious views without, apparently, ever having met any of them. To those of us who have, Stark's characterization of their notions of God as monotheistic is almost as off-base as his use of the word 'primitive' is offensive (cf. Haekel and Tripathi 1966, ch. 8; on Haekel, Pettazzoni 1956, 1958).

Nevertheless, there is also good reason to take Stark seriously. What is most valuable is not his empirical work but the theoretical territory that he stakes out. This territory is important first of all because it provides a strong alternative to many writers whose views are profiled in the rest of this book. Against the entire Kantianesque cognitive-scientific gambit that religion reflects the structures of the mind/brain, Stark persistently pushes the Lockeanesque pawn that, as far as the explanation of religion is concerned, the mind might as well be a *tabula rasa*, a blank slate; all that is needed are rational human beings, that is, people who act in their own self-interest as they understand it. Whether they are correct about that self-interest is, for explanatory purposes, irrelevant (Stark 2007: 43). Stark further calls into question the simple evolutionary scenarios that many naturalists seem to favor; unfortunately, he has not been reticent about expressing his own views on biological evolution, which belong decidedly to the fringe (Stark 2004; cf. 2007: 398). He likewise rejects the Dawkinsian notion that God is a delusion; when people believe in God, he maintains, they are being entirely rational. Most important of all, Stark has been a leading exponent of what some refer to as a 'new paradigm' in the sociology of religion, especially as that sub-discipline is practiced within the United States. As Stark sees it, the heart of this new paradigm is the application of rational-choice theory (think of cost–benefit analysis, the 'law' of supply and demand, and so on) to thought, behavior, and forms of association that we have come to call religious (contrast Chaves and Gorski 2001: 274–5). As a result, many economic ideas, such as ideas about substitute and credence goods, free markets, and the free-rider problem, have been conscripted into the service of explaining religion – and in ways that are at least very suggestive.

Given the current state of knowledge and theory, it may still be possible that religion results from the operation of a specially dedicated mechanism, such as the once-popular 'numinous-detection device' (*sensus numinis*) formulated by Rudolf Otto. It would be scientifically more elegant, however, if it were not. That is, it would be more elegant if we could explain religion as resulting simply from more general processes that make up human beings. Cognitive theorists point to one class of possible explanations: that religion results from the kinds of processing that make up human mentation. Stark points to another: that religion results from the acquisitive tendencies of human beings with desires living in a finite world. What follows explores this second possibility by critically engaging the synthetic theoretical statement that Stark wrote with Roger Finke (2000), *Acts of faith: explaining the human side of religion*. It deliberately focuses on the book's theoretical content.

The 'new paradigm' in the sociology of religion

In *Acts of faith* Stark and Finke aspire to present a comprehensive overview of the new paradigm in the sociology of religion (31). This paradigm involves fundamental shifts in views not only about religion and society but also about human agency and the associations that human beings form.

Stark and Finke introduce this new paradigm through a series of contrasts. If the old paradigm considered religion 'false and harmful' (28), the new paradigm sees it as physically, mentally, and socially beneficial (32). If the old paradigm saw secularization as an inevitable consequence of modernity, the new paradigm sees religion thriving within modernity. According to the old paradigm, the real causes of religion were material; the new paradigm emphasizes religious causes, such as religious doctrines (34). The old paradigm ultimately reduced religion to the psychological, but the new emphasizes the social, especially a social subsystem that it calls the religious economy. Finally, the old paradigm saw religious pluralism as destructive of religious conviction, but the new sees a pluralistic, free religious market as the precondition for religion's thriving.[2]

Underlying all of these shifts is one that is still more fundamental. The old paradigm saw religion as an expression of human irrationality or non-rationality, whether evaluated negatively (e.g., Sigmund Freud) or positively (e.g., Otto). Stark and Finke see religion as a product of rationality. They write (italics removed): 'Within the limits of their information and understanding, restricted by available options, guided by their preferences and tastes, humans attempt to make rational choices' (85 [Proposition 1]). What distinguishes religious from economic activity is neither a peculiar, metaphorical or symbolic way of conceptualizing the world nor a decision-making apparatus that is self-renouncing and emotive rather than self-serving and 'rational' in the cost–benefit sense. Rather, what distinguishes religion is exchange with postulated superhuman agents who constitute 'the only plausible source of certain rewards [such as life after death] for which there is a general and inexhaustible demand' (85). Stark and Finke maintain that this demand is constant. Therefore, any variation in religion must be explained by variation on the supply side.

To be sure, the claim that religion is rational will strike many as counterintuitive. After all, science would seem to epitomize rationality, and conflicts between it and religion are notorious. Stark and Finke insist, however, that science and religion are not incompatible. They point out that natural scientists tend to be considerably more religious than social scientists, especially those who are likely to talk about religion, psychologists, and anthropologists. This claim may well be correct, even if some psychologists have begun to treat religion more positively. Nevertheless, it is difficult to see how it lends much support to the proposition that religion results from rational benefit-seeking.

Even more contentious has been Stark and Finke's claim that secularization is a myth. On their view, what has been called secularization is not the abandonment of religion but the desacralization of society. Over the last two centuries societies have become less publicly religious; nevertheless, the demand for religion among individual human beings has remained unchanged (200). In their eyes the key variability is the degree to which there is a free religious market. In a separate monograph Finke and Stark (1992) have argued that the establishment of a free religious market in the US in the late eighteenth century led to an increase in religious activity. In Europe, where established churches resulted in heavily regulated religious markets, people have abandoned the churches and, they claim, turned instead to religious alternatives.

Although Stark and his co-workers often write as if the evidence for these developments is conclusive and incontrovertible, not everyone agrees. In attempting to assess the competing claims of secularization versus a free market in religion, McCleary and Barro (2006) have found mixed results. Both claims receive some support, but neither succeeds universally. Norris and Inglehart (2004) are bolder. They marshal data from the World Values Surveys, which Inglehart directs, to support an alternate, compound thesis. On the one hand, they maintain, with economic development existential security increases and demand for religion decreases, although a decline is more noticeable in religious practice than religious belief. On the other hand, societies with greater existential insecurity and so greater religious commitment also have higher rates of reproduction. As a result, the world's population is becoming more religious. In addition, Norris and Inglehart (2004: 100, 126) claim to have found, contrary to the free-religious-market thesis, that religious freedom and plurality have actually had an adverse effect on religious practice, beliefs, and values in both Catholic and post-Communist countries.

The micro-, 'meso-,' and macroeconomics of religion

After Part One introduces the new paradigm, the rest of the book develops its implications. It does so on three levels of aggregation, which I will refer to as the micro-, 'meso-,' and macroeconomics of religion.

Microeconomics studies the behavior of individual economic agents, whether these agents are single persons or collectivities such as households or firms. Macroeconomics studies the behavior of entire economic systems. In Part Two, Stark and Finke sketch out a microeconomics of religion; they discuss the behavior of religious people as individuals. In Part Four they sketch out a macroeconomics of religion; they discuss the behavior of entire religious economies. Although it is not a standard term in economics, 'mesoeconomics,' coined from the Greek adjective *mesos, -ē, -on*, meaning 'middle,' seems useful for designating the topic that Stark and Finke address in Part Three. There they talk about religious groups, not as individual agents in a larger economic system but as discrete systems in and of themselves.

The microeconomics of religion

Although Stark and Finke aspire to present a comprehensive account of religion from the perspective of the new paradigm (31), they do not actually do so. On the microeconomic level they address only two topics, 'foundations' and conversion – more precisely, reaffiliation and conversion, but for convenience I will generally write 'conversion.'

In discussing foundations Stark and Finke aim to identify the basic events that generate religion. To do so, they revisit the earlier theory of religion that Stark developed together with William Sims Bainbridge (1987). In that earlier theory religious goods were 'compensators'; they provided objects, such as eternal life, that religious people wanted but could not acquire in any other way. *Acts of faith* abandons talk of substitute goods. It simply notes that people prefer goods from empirical sources, if such sources are available (84, 90 [Proposition 7]). Stark and Finke also try to give greater attention to cognition and emotion than Stark and Bainbridge did, but the results are sometimes jarring. Consider the following definition: 'Religion consists of very general explanations of existence, including the terms of exchange with a god or gods' (91). Never mind that this definition seems to exclude exchanges between the elect and 'hearers' in Manichaeism or between *bhikkhus* or *bhikkhunīs* and laypeople in Buddhism. It also seems to confuse two different categories of concepts, for it is not at all clear that 'terms of exchange' count as 'general explanations of existence.' The tension between the desiderative and the cognitive, however, dissipates quickly, as

Stark and Finke turn their attention almost exclusively to the realm of desire and acquisition, more specifically, to exchanges with gods.

Stark and Finke's starting point is both situationally more specific and mathematically less precise than the starting point in neoclassical microeconomics, which their theory otherwise resembles. Neoclassical microeconomics begins by abstractly modeling the behavior of two-person, two-commodity exchange systems in terms of demand and supply functions (of many shapes) whose interactions identify typical scenarios as markets seek equilibrium. Stark and Finke begin with exchanges between humans and gods, but they then proceed to introduce limiting assumptions. They assume that the demand for religion is constant; it changes neither over time nor from one community to the next. Furthermore, what religious people desire are not specific religious goods but a complete basket of goods labeled religion; compare the basket 'energy' as distinct from individual components such as electricity, natural gas, coal, heating oil, and distilled petroleum. One wonders whether life after death, nirvana, and the sense of community that one acquires, at least potentially, in celebrating the Passover Seder are perfectly interchangeable, as when one switches from natural gas to electricity to heat one's home, so that together they constitute a single, unchanging quantity 'religion.' Stark and Finke propose further: (a) that the supplier (sc. the god) with the broadest powers will command the highest price, because he – perhaps she – can provide the broadest range of religious goods; (b) that in the interests of achieving other-worldly goods people will enter into exchange relations with gods that are both 'extended' and 'exclusive' (they will make repeated, life-long 'payments' to only a single supplier); and (c) that people prefer to enter into religious exchange relations as members of bounded groups defined by religious identity.

These limits seem questionable. First, Stark and Finke conceive of religious exchanges solely in terms of mercantile transactions. They give no attention to gift-giving, although since Marcel Mauss (1925) this has been a classic topic for scholars of religion,[3] and one that economists have studied. Second, a simple thought experiment shows how unconvincing it is to imagine that the god whose benefits cover the widest range receives the most business. (This way of putting it makes more economic sense than 'commands the highest price.') Assume that I am mostly a subsistence agriculturalist. I believe that there is a god whose capacities are particularly wide, but they do not address what is of greatest interest to me, the protection of my crops, domesticated animals, and children. I further believe that this protection falls within the purview of three other gods, each of whose capacities are limited to only one of these areas. It would seem, *contra* Stark and Finke, that I would be much more willing to 'exchange with' the three gods whose range of powers is more limited but of greater interest to me than the god whose powers are more expansive. This presumption is consonant with reports of *dei otiosi*, high gods who have very little specific interaction with people. Finally, Stark and Finke seem incapable of conceiving of religion as occupying any social configuration besides that of bounded, religiously homogeneous groups, defined by religious identity, to which people 'belong.' It seems not to have occurred to them, even as a theoretical possibility, that persons might define their primary social identity in non-religious terms, such as caste membership, and then engage in various religious practices without feeling a need to join a special religious group (see Carroll 1996: 233–4 for another option).

In other words, Stark and Finke stipulate as limits what they should instead derive. At most they make only impressionistic appeals in favor of their limits in order to garner intuitive assent. It is not surprising, then, that in Stark's estimation Christianity would eventually emerge as the supreme religion. That superiority is tacitly built into the model's initial assumptions. (On theoretical if not cultural grounds, it *is* surprising that Islam occupies a lower position.)

The second topic in Stark and Finke's microeconomics of religion high-lights the importance that they attribute to clearly bounded groups defined by religious identity. Drawing upon ground-breaking research that Stark did with John Lofland (Lofland and Stark 1965), Stark and Finke combine a theory of networks with one of social capital to explain why people switch loyalties from one religious group to another. They assert that most people do not convert because they find the new group's teachings attractive; rather, most people tend to find these teachings somewhat odd. They join religious groups primarily because they have 'affective bonds' (Lofland and Stark 1965) with – they are friends or relatives of – people who are already members of the group. Teachings become important later, when people are faced with the decision of whether to stay in the group or leave (137).

Another factor relevant to conversion is 'religious capital,' that is, the store of religious knowledge, abilities, and so on that people accumulate as they go through life. As rational agents, people act in ways that maxi-mize the benefits available from this capital. As a result, Stark and Finke predict that the degree of group-switching will vary in direct proportion to the amount of religious capital that the move allows people to preserve. The more capital a person is able to retain, the more likely that person is to switch affiliation. They also predict that 'the great majority of those raised with a religious affiliation will retain that affiliation' (121).

Stark is fond of claiming that every valid study of conversion confirms his views, but not everyone agrees. For example, James W. Coleman (2001) claims that the majority of American converts to Buddhism whom he studied did not know each other when their interest in Buddhism began; they were attracted instead by Buddhist teachings. Durk Hak (2007) claims to have developed a structural functionalist model of conversion that explains more than Stark and Finke's network and social capital model. In a recent study the Pew Research Center found, contrary to Stark and Finke's predictions, that 28 percent of adult US-Americans convert at least once during their lifetimes; when reaffiliation is added in, the figure jumps to 44 percent (Pew Forum 2008: 22). None of this makes Stark and Finke's analysis untenable. It does create room for reasonable doubt and further investigation.

The mesoeconomics of religion

In Part Three Stark and Finke turn to dynamics within religious groups. In particular, they try to explain why commitment to groups varies and why some groups grow while others do not.

First they distinguish two kinds of religious group, 'church' and 'sect.' This distinction ultimately derives from the German sociology of Christianity and more particularly Max Weber and Ernst Troeltsch. As in the case of Émile Durkheim's (1947: 61) definition of religion – 'a single moral community called a Church' – one wonders why more neutral terminology was not chosen.

According to Stark and Finke a single variable distinguishes sects from churches. Churches have a low degree, sects a high degree of tension with their environments. The term 'tension' refers to 'the degree of distinctiveness, separation, and antagonism between a religious group and the "outside" world' (143). Higher tension requires in turn commitment that is 'more exclusive, extensive, and expensive' (145). As in the case of demand for religion, Stark and Finke treat these characteristics as a single bundle; they allegedly vary together.

This analysis is a little blunt. For example, it seems incapable of making sense of a community like the Katholische Integrierte Gemeinde (Catholic integrated community), with its close, long-term connections to Joseph Ratzinger, now Benedict XVI (Wallbrecher 2005, 2006). At least, however, the categories are formal and analytical. As Stark and Finke proceed, however, tension becomes less a relational quality between a group and its surroundings that must be determined by measurement and more a substantive feature of certain religious beliefs. High-tension groups think of God as dependable, personal, and responsive, while low-tension groups think of God as 'distant, impersonal, and rather unresponsive' (146). 'Even in the most liberal Western divinity schools, many faculty and students affirm some sort of god,' they write. Nevertheless, that god is 'quite unsuitable as an exchange partner' (146).

These claims betray geographical and social limitations as well as religious loyalties that ultimately undermine the theory's usefulness. It is not entirely clear that 'liberals' in the Stark–Finke sense are inevitably in low tension with their surroundings. Consider a congregation of the Metropolitan Community Church in the middle of the so-called Bible belt in the United States. (Church headquarters are, in fact, in Abilene, Texas.) This church bills itself as 'the world's first church group with a primary, positive ministry to gays, lesbians, bisexual, and transgender persons,'[4] a stance that in the United States might be more at home in New England or San Francisco than in central Texas, where, one presumes, antagonism to homosexuality is relatively high. But Stark and Finke are also silent about how to measure tension between a group and its environment and even about which environment is relevant, since tension can vary considerably as the scale changes from neighborhood to municipality, state or province, region, and nation, on up to continent. Instead, they conceive of a group's environment as a unitary, undifferentiated social reality that is inevitably opposed to traditional Christianity. That simply writes a certain Protestant self-understanding into the sociology of religion, namely, the need to see oneself as a righteous community set apart from a sinful world. Such Protestants would need to insist upon this separation even if they made up the vast majority of the earth's population.

The contrast between church and sect frames the main question that Stark and Finke's mesoeconomics of religion addresses: why do some people join high-tension, high-cost groups? Why not buy religion at the cheapest price available? Stark and Finke answer that 'to the extent that one is motivated by religious value, one must prefer a higher-priced supplier' (146). So much for the idea that religious agents are 'guided by their preferences and tastes' (85 [Proposition 1])! To say that people motivated by religious value must prefer a higher-priced supplier is a little like saying that people motivated by culinary value must prefer $1,000-a-dish restaurants, regardless of either their tastes in food or the quality of the cuisine. Some may find more culinary value in a local diner or an all-you-can-eat buffet. A fundamental axiom of contemporary economic analysis is that value is not an absolute property of an object, as in Marx's labor theory of value. It is determined solely by the personal preferences of persons engaged in exchanges. People have different approaches to value – culinary value, musical value, literary value, architectural value, automotive value … and religious value, too.

Nevertheless, to say that people motivated by religious value must prefer a higher-priced supplier is not *exactly* like saying that people motivated by culinary value must prefer $1,000-a-dish restaurants. One important difference is that, unlike restaurants, at least some religious groups do not exist for purposes of consumption. They exist to bring people together for shared activities. This characteristic of religious groups has provided an opening for Laurence Iannaccone (1992) to apply insights derived from the economic analysis of clubs to religious organizations. Stark and Finke adopt Iannaccone's insights.

Groups organized for joint activity inevitably confront a problem: free-riders, that is, people who benefit from belonging to the group but contribute little or nothing to it. In the case of groups that people join voluntarily, higher membership costs tend to discourage free-riders; as a result, people who are looking for a high degree of shared activity may find higher member-ship costs attractive. For example, suppose that I am a passionate weekend mountain climber and that I am looking for a group of experienced people with whom to climb two weekends every month. Given a choice between group A, which requires members to pay a $100 membership fee each year, to own a certain amount of equipment, and to climb at least one weekend a month, and group B, which has no requirements besides a $5.00 membership fee, I am likely to join group A. I will not find its requirements burdensome, provided that I can afford the fee and equipment, because they require only what I actually want to do. I am also much more likely to find climbers who share my passion for climbing in group A than in group B. Now change the setting. Suppose that I am an avid devotee of Lord Krishna and am looking for a group of fellow devotees with whom to sing *bhajans* three or four nights a week. Other things being equal, I will opt for a group in which people are required to be more active. Stark and Finke use this reasoning to explain why religious people are even willing to engage in activities that seem totally bizarre, such as (my example) the toilet-cleaning brigades of Ittōen documented by Winston Davis (1975a: 287–90, 304–5, 316; 1975b: 3–4; disregarding Davis's explanations).

One can imagine several ways to qualify this model. First, people may not locate religious value in group activity. For example, Hinduism provides other avenues for being intensely religious that do not require membership in a group. In addition, people are usually not looking for generic religious value but for religious value of a specific kind. Not just any group will do. Just as an avid mountain climber will choose to join a less intense group of mountain climbers over a more passionate group of swimmers, someone who wants to sing *bhajans* to Lord Krishna will probably not join a local Pentecostal church, even if it is the only intense religious group in town. Even Christians looking for intense group activity might avoid the local Pentecostal church, because it provides them with the wrong kind of group activity. Moreover, people may refuse to pay some membership costs, even if they can afford them, because they seem contrary to the religious values they seek. For example, I once encountered a Christian congregation that required prospective members to pass an examination on the works of major twentieth-century theologians, such as Karl Barth, Emil Brunner, Rudolf Bultmann, and Paul Tillich. Despite such qualifications, however, it is reasonable to assume that higher-cost groups are likely to have a higher aggregate intensity than lower-cost ones.

Stark and Finke use these dynamics to explain a developmental sequence for religious groups that others have noted. Religious groups begin as high-cost sects. Their vitality attracts members, but that is a mixed blessing. Eventually growth in membership leads to free-riding and reduced vitality, and successful sects turn into churches. The churches then lose members as people desert them for groups that provide higher-intensity religion. There can be no question that this sequence describes the trajectory of Methodism in the United States fairly well. I am not yet convinced that it is useful in analyzing, for example, Hinduism in India.

The macroeconomics of religion

In Part Four Stark and Finke shift attention from the religious group to the 'religious economy' as a whole. Once again the fundamental variable is tension, and it remains a hybrid category. On the one hand, it refers to what should be a measurable relation between groups and their surroundings; on the other, it denotes distinct theological positions defined in terms of Christian and Jewish reactions to the European Enlightenment. The problems are easy to foresee.

Stark and Finke identify six niches that religious groups occupy. These are, in order of (allegedly) increasing tension: ultra-liberal, liberal, moderate, conservative, strict, and ultra-strict. They also assert that a standard bell-curve describes the distribution of any given population across these niches. A few people will be attracted to either the ultra-liberal or the ultra-strict extremes, but most people will belong to a religious group that is conservative or moderate. This model not only maps the territory of the religious economy but also charts the route, described in the previous section, according to which religious groups evolve. In Part Four Stark and Finke complete the circuit. They suggest that following a severe decline in membership, a church may become increasingly strict and as a result shift back to being a sect.

In formal terms this is an elegant model. It is also a highly implausible one. For the sake of simplicity, assume a population that is 100 percent Christian, with the distributional shape that Stark and Finke stipulate. Some people belong to ultra-liberal churches and some to ultra-strict churches, but most people are conservatives and moderates. (This is almost by definition the distribution one would find in any homogeneous population, religious or otherwise.) If Stark and Finke are right, this distribution results because most people prefer moderate tension with the surrounding environment, conservatives favoring somewhat more tension than moderates. In our scenario, however, there is no surrounding society for conservatives and moderates to be in tension with. The surrounding society to which they must relate consists mostly of themselves, moderate and conservative Christians. One would presume that in any religiously homogeneous community ultra-liberal and ultra-strict groups would stand in the same degree of tension to the social mean, which is the midpoint between conservatives and moderates. Indeed, that is where one would likely find the social mean among any religiously dominant community, such as Christians in the United States.

This thought experiment points to a very real difficulty. Apparently without realizing it, Stark and Finke push that difficulty virtually to the point of absurdity. In their last chapter they discuss events surrounding activist Methodist clergy who officiated at the marriages of same-sex couples. They note that 'the congregations served by [these] pastors ... experienced substantial declines in attendance, giving, and membership' (270). Given the widespread outcry that the prospect of gay and lesbian marriage has raised in the United States over the last decade in both the political and religious arenas, these losses come as no surprise. What does come as a surprise is Stark and Finke's explanation of them. According to them the clergy concerned were 'pressing for an even lower-tension Methodism' (269), and the people who left wanted to return to a state of higher tension. This account is odd. With precisely what surroundings were these ministers seeking lower tension? According to the World Values Surveys, attitudes toward homosexuality in the United States have become more tolerant since 1982, but in the year of Stark and Finke's incident (1999) 31% of Americans still thought homosexuality was never justifiable, compared to only 13.8% who thought it was always justifiable. More Americans had negative (43.4%) or neutral (15.8%) attitudes toward homosexuality than positive ones (39%), and the US ranked sixteenth of the 21 Western European and North American nations surveyed in terms of tolerance for homosexuality (mean = 4.75 out of 10; standard deviation = 3.254) (www.worldvaluessurvey.org/). One presumes that even many of the respondents who were positively disposed to homosexuality would oppose gay marriage. After all, left-leaning US politicians have preferred to endorse civil unions rather than gay 'marriages,' and that is hardly because they wanted to maintain tension with the American electorate. If people left congregations because their pastors consecrated gay and lesbian marriages, they did so not because they wanted more tension with their environment, but because their pastors created more tension than they could tolerate. If, however, we must abandon Stark and Finke's notion of tension, and I think we must, we have also lost the engine that allegedly explains shifts in religious communities.

Stark and his co-workers are justly well known for their writings on another macroeconomic topic, namely, their emphasis on the role of a religious free market in contributing to religion's vitality. Because that topic was discussed in the treatment of the secularization thesis, we will not return to it here.

A brief assessment

I have already been rather liberal with comments on specific elements of Stark's position. In conclusion I offer brief reflections about the more general theoretical territory.

People who identify with the academic field of religious studies are generally familiar with two classic figures in the area of religion, economics, and society, Karl Marx and Max Weber. They give a third thinker, Adam Smith, much less attention. Stark, however, stands in the tradition of Smith, who in *The wealth of nations* (Book 5, Chapter 1, Part 3, Article 3) anticipates many, although not all, of Stark's most important themes: the competitive advantages of small, new, and strict sectarian groups; the deleterious effect of religious establishment, as well as of excessive remuneration, upon the energy and creativity of religious leaders; the desirability of a free market in religion (although unlike Stark, Smith favors free religious markets because they reduce zeal and fanaticism); the contrast between liberal morality and strict, traditional morality and the association of the latter with religious vitality; and last but not least, the conclusion that structures in one's own nation are the best, as in Smith's praise for Scottish Presbyterianism and Stark's for the religious market in the United States.

Economics is, of course, a highly contested area, especially among humanists. One would hardly expect severe critics of free-market capitalism to embrace Stark's analysis of religion (see Carroll 1996: 227). Conversely, there would seem to be an elective affinity between Stark's rational-choice approach to religion and Evangelical Christian soteriology, which emphasizes human decision-making. One would expect Evangelical Christians to be more favorably disposed to Stark's analysis than, let us say, Shin Buddhists, who, in light of the Buddha's all-encompassing vow, are taught to avoid all calculation in matters of salvation.

Thus, issues of ideological commitment are likely to affect how Stark's theories are received. Rather than engage such ideological debates here, I want instead to make three somewhat abstract comments on the theoretical territory that Stark has staked out. My goal is to identify ways to move the discussion forward.

First, I earlier described economic and cognitive theories of religion as representing a confrontation between two fundamental orientations, one Lockeanesque, the other Kantianesque. That opposition characterizes current practice, but it is, I think, a false one. The two approaches need one another. Cognitive constraints and propensities determine the kinds of postulated beings with whom human beings will attempt to interact; they also determine the decisional calculus that human beings bring to those interactions. Cognitive studies alone, however, cannot predict what happens when people with such propensities and calculative mechanisms aggregate. That is the task of economics. A workable explanatory account of religion requires both approaches, and probably others besides.

Second, Steve Bruce has written, admittedly in a semi-popular review: 'In a nutshell, rational choice does not work for religion because there are enormous constraints on choice and because the information required to make choice rational is not available' (Bruce 2001: 36–7). He is wrong on both counts. Neither constraints nor lack of information impede rational choice in a cost–benefit sense. Constraints simply limit the options among which people must choose, while lack of information simply makes choices less well informed.

An important problem with Stark's theoretical model is just the opposite: it models choice within too many constraints. Although it presents itself as a general theory of religion, it is really only a special theory of religiosity in the United States in the last thirty to forty years. The theory seems to work because it tacitly presumes the characteristics that it seeks to explain. What is needed is a more abstract model of religious exchanges flexible enough to yield results for the wide variety that we encompass with the term 'religion,' and then a sense of the kinds of institutional constraints under which choice operates in specific situations.

Third, although Stark and Finke do not work with the strictest view of rational choice, it probably makes sense to loosen the rational-choice assumption even further. There is rather strong evidence that the *homo economicus* approach does not explain the complexity of actual human behavior. It neglects the role that reciprocity plays in human decision-making in interactive contexts. It also neglects the manner in which the human brain calculates gains and losses. As behavioral economists have shown, human beings negotiate perceived gains and losses differently (Kahneman and Tversky 2000; Thaler 1991). Furthermore, Norris and Inglehart (2004) argue that there is a positive correlation worldwide between degree of religiosity and perceived existential security. Rachel McCleary (2008: 48) has noted, 'We also have some evidence that the stick represented by the fear of damnation is more potent for [the] growth [of religion] than the carrot from the prospect of salvation.' Although Stark and Finke suggest that 'religion is the only plausible source of certain rewards for which there is a general and inexhaustible demand,' I suspect that much of religion results instead from human beings taking cognitive risks to avoid losses. Obviously, this is a view that I cannot develop further here.

Notes

1   The error appeared in Finke and Stark 1989; for further comment on Daniel Breault, cf. Finke, Guest and Stark 1996: 206, n. 4. The error was discovered and Breault vindicated by Daniel Olson 1998. The rebuttal in Finke and Stark 1998 is unconvincing in the light of Chaves and Gorski 2001 and Voas, Olson, and Crockett 2002.

2   The term 'new paradigm' derives from Warner 1993, where it has a somewhat different sense.

3   See the virtual issue, 'Anthropology of the Gift', of the *Journal of the Royal Anthropological Society* (March 2008), online at www.blackwellpublishing.com/vi.asp?ref=1359–0987&site=1#40

4   Online at www.mccchurch.org/AM/Template.cfm?Section=About_Us&Template=/CM/HTMLDisplay.cfm&ContentID=662#Intro (last accessed March 18, 2008).

References

Bruce, S., 2001. All too human. *First Things* (February), 35–7.

Carroll, M. P., 1996. Stark realities and eurocentric/androcentric bias in the sociology of religion. *Sociology of Religion* 57 (3), 225–39.

Chaves, M. and Gorski, P.S., 2001. Religious pluralism and religious participation. *Annual Review of Sociology* 27, 261–81.

Coleman, J.W., 2001. *The new Buddhism: the Western transformation of an ancient tradition*, Oxford University Press, Oxford, New York.

Davis, W., 1975a. Ittōen: the myths and rituals of liminality, parts I–III. *History of Religions* 14 (4), 282–321.

Davis, W., 1975b. Ittōen: the myths and rituals of liminality, parts IV–VI. *History of Religions* 15 (1), 1–33.

Durkheim, É., 1947. *The elementary forms of the religious life: a study in religious sociology*. Free Press, Glencoe, IL.

Finke, R., Guest, A., and Stark, R., 1996. Mobilizing local religious markets: religious pluralism in the empire state, 1855 to 1865. *American Sociological Review* 61 (2), 203–18.

Finke, R. and Stark, R., 1989. Evaluating the evidence: religious economies and sacred canopies. *American Sociological Review*, 54 (6), 1054–6.

Finke, R. and Stark, R., 1992, *The churching of America, 1776–1990: winners and losers in our religious economy*. Rutgers University Press, New Brunswick, NJ.

Finke, R. and Stark, R., 1998. Religious choice and competition. *American Sociological Review* 63 (5), 761–6.

Haekel, J. and Tripathi, C.B., 1966. *Eine Besessenheits-Séance der Rathva-Koli in Gujarat (Indien)*. Hermann Böhlau, Vienna.

Hak, D., 2007. Stark and Finke or Durkheim on conversion and (re-) affiliation: an outline of a structural functionalist rebuttal to Stark and Finke. *Social Compass* 54 (2), 295–312.

98   *Gregory D. Alles*

Iannaccone, L., 1992. Sacrifice and stigma: reducing free-riding in cults, communes, and other collectives. *Journal of Political Economy* 100 (2), 271–91.

Kahneman, D. and Tversky, A., 2000. *Choices, values, and frames*. Russell Sage Foundation, New York.

Lofland, J. and Stark, R., 1965. Becoming a world-saver: a theory of conversion to a deviant perspective. *American Sociological Review* 30 (6), 862–75.

Mauss, M., 1925. *Essai sur le don. Forme et raison de l'échange dans les sociétés archaïques*. Alcan, Paris.

McCleary, R., 2008. Religion and economic development. *Policy Review* 148, 45–57.

McCleary, R. and Barro, R., 2006. Religion and political economy in an international panel. *Journal for the Scientific Study of Religion* 45 (2), 149–75.

Norris, P. and Inglehart, R., 2004. *Sacred and secular: religion and politics worldwide*. Cambridge University Press, Cambridge.

Olson, D.V.A., 1998. Religious pluralism in contemporary U.S. counties. *American Sociological Review* 63 (5), 759–61.

Pettazzoni, R., 1956. Das Ende des Urmonotheismus? *Numen* 3 (2), 156–9.

Pettazzoni, R., 1958. Das Ende des Urmonotheismus. *Numen* 5 (2), 161–3.

Pew Forum on Religion and Public Life, 2008. *U.S. religious landscape survey*. Pew Research Center, New York.

Stark, R., 1996. *The rise of Christianity: a sociologist reconsiders history*. Princeton University Press, Princeton.

Stark, R., 2001. *One true God: historical consequences of monotheism*. Princeton University Press, Princeton.

Stark, R., 2003. *For the glory of God: how monotheism led to reformations, science, witch-hunts, and the end of slavery*. Princeton University Press, Princeton.

Stark, R., 2004. Fact or fable? Digging up the truth in the evolution debate. *The American Enterprise* 15 (6), 40–4.

Stark, R., 2005. *The victory of reason: how Christianity led to freedom, capitalism, and western success*. Random House, New York.

Stark, R., 2006. *Cities of God: Christianizing the urban empire*. HarperSanFrancisco, San Francisco.

Stark, R., 2007. *Discovering God: the origins of the great religions and the evolution of belief*. HarperOne, New York.

Stark, R. and Bainbridge, W.S., 1987. *A theory of religion*. P. Lang, New York.

Stark, R. and Finke, R., 2000. *Acts of faith: explaining the human side of religion*. University of California Press, Berkeley.

Thaler, R.H., 1991. *Quasi rational economics*. Russell Sage Foundation, New York.

Voas, D., Olson, D.V.A., and Crockett, A., 2002. Religious pluralism and participation: why previous research is wrong. *American Sociological Review* 67 (2), 212–30.

Wallbrecher, T., 2005. *Katholische Integrierte Gemeinde: eine Kurzdarstellung*. Urfeld, Bad Tölz.

Wallbrecher, T., 2006. *30 Jahre Wegbegleitung: Joseph Ratzinger, Papst Benedikt XVI. und die Katholische Integrierte Gemeinde*. Urfeld, Bad Tölz.

Warner, R.S., 1993. Work in progress toward a new paradigm for the sociological study of religion in the United States. *American Journal of Sociology* 98 (5), 1044–93.

7

Religion as communication

On Niklas Luhmann, The religion of society (2000)

Peter Beyer

Niklas Luhmann (1927–98) was a German sociologist who spent thirty years at the University of Bielefeld developing a general theory of society, a complex and highly abstract edifice worked out in more than 500 publications over the course of his career. His theory of religion derives from that overall effort, focusing on the analysis of religion as a particular sort of social construction. In spite of significant developments in his theory over the years, the most consistent question that informed all his works was how religion comes to be differentiated within society as a distinct social formation, ultimately as a differentiated societal system, and with what consequences. This was fundamentally an evolutionary question for him, but not in a teleological sense: the differentiation of religion in societies has occurred historically, but it is not a necessary development springing from some *sui generis* nature of religion, let alone from some a priori nature of 'ultimate reality.' Each of Luhmann's major publications on religion – and most of the minor ones – reflect this orientation. In the earliest, *Function of religion* (Luhmann 1977: 26–7),[1] he locates the purpose of religion, its function, in familiar territory:[2] religion grounds the ultimate indeterminability of all meaning; it absorbs the risk of failure inherent in all social representations and determinations. He maintains this understanding into his last major work, the posthumously published *The religion of society* (Luhmann 2000b: 127). This function by itself, however, does not already require the development of differentiated religion. Differentiation is a contingent possibility which historically has taken certain forms, with consequences that vary with the historical development of the societies in which this differentiated religion can be observed to occur. The task for theory then becomes to observe the changing forms and the changing consequences.[3]

In this short essay, it would be impossible even to summarize all that Luhmann had to say on this subject. What follows therefore concentrates on certain key aspects centered on the place of religious communication in his theory. The basis of any differentiation in society – and of society itself – for Luhmann lies in the different ways that communication constructs itself. Such differences are the basis for the formation of different systems. Addressing the question of religious communication in Luhmann's theory is therefore also a way of adumbrating the question of a religious system. There is insufficient space here to make clear all the aspects that constitute a religious system in this theory. Focusing on communication, however, will give an idea of what such differentiation in the larger theory involves.

Communication and ritual

For Luhmann ritual is not the only form of religious communication. His writings do not actually have a great deal to say about ritual. Yet, as will become evident, understanding Luhmann's ideas on ritual is also key to understanding how he saw the particular, differentiable character of religion. It is therefore as well to start the discussion with a look at his vision of the relation between ritual and communication. From his early works, ritual was central to the function of religion and was conceived as a form of communication. Rituals respond to the final indeterminability of human meaning constructions in that they depict and reproduce a range of meanings that are deemed beyond human disposition. In the book-length essay of 1972 (see note 1) we find the following formulation: 'Rituals are processes of important ceremonial communication that control or depict as controlled the risk of all communication: the possible misuse of the symbols' (Luhmann 1984a: 9). It is to the contingency of symbols, the risk that their meanings will distort or lose clarity in the process of using them, that religious ritual responds. It is because of this 'anchoring' function that, even when discursive forms of religiosity such as dogmatic interpretation develop, ritual remains indispensable (Luhmann 1977: 56f.). Moreover, ritual invariably uses human bodies and perceptible objects to effect its restricted, alternativeless character. It is inherently paradoxical: It is communication that is not subject to the risk of all communication, but rather controls that risk; it is communication that symbolizes the indeterminable or ineffable and imperceptible through perceptible objects choreographed into clearly set patterns (Luhmann 2000b: 189). A central question and problem for Luhmann's theory, therefore, is how, as societies develop more complex and thus improbable systems of meaningful communication – including discursive forms of 'spiritual' communication – can and does religion transform into a viable system of such meaningful communication in spite of its peculiar character (cf. Luhmann 1987)? This is essentially the question of the fate of religion under modern conditions. To understand what exactly the issue is for Luhmann, and how he works it out in his theory, requires a step back to look at a key aspect of his overall social theory, the nature of communication as the fundamental social building block.

Communication as selective synthesis

It is probably not going too far to say that one of the most original, indeed daring, aspects of Luhmann's later sociology is his effort to observe society as consisting entirely of communications. The basic building blocks of any society are in his theory not human beings, not human action, and not even something akin to Durkheim's 'collective representations.' Rather, following what is often called the 'autopoetic' (self-generative) turn in his theorizing that began to manifest itself around the early 1980s (e.g. Luhmann 1981: 15–17) and which he elaborates clearly for the first time in the 1984 work, *Soziale Systeme* (Luhmann 1984b: 193–201; Eng. trans. Luhmann 1995b), communications themselves are set forth as the fundamental components of society and sociality. Such communication is not in the first instance to be understood as what people do, as an exchange between actors, for example, so much as a synthesis of three 'selections,' namely information, utterance (*Mitteilung*),[4] and understanding. There is the content of communication, what is being communicated; there is the fact that this information has been given form; and there is the reception of this transaction as the basis of further communication, its connectivity. All three components have to be there and be distinct or else there is nothing being communicated, no communication occurring, or no connection to other and subsequent communication that allows the social to perpetuate itself and thus social systems of communication to form. The abstractness, the passive voice of this formulation, reflects Luhmann's intention of theorizing the social in its own terms. Briefly, human bodies and human consciousness are necessary for society to happen, just as the physical world is necessary for these latter to emerge. Yet, like bodies and consciousnesses, society or sociality is also something additional, an emergent property with its own distinct components and logic. Communications are those components, and society is the autological and recursive network or system of these. Accordingly, 'who' does the communication and 'who' understands it, the attribution of agency, is, socially speaking, only given in the communications themselves. It is not a priori, and therefore communication is inadequately conceived as 'people' or as their 'action.' The riskiness, the fragility of the social is thereby further underscored: communications and the meanings that they carry construct themselves in their own terms; their relation to 'reality' is thereby constructed in them and through them; and if communication ceases, so does society.[5]

Religion as communication

Among the many consequences of this radical reduction of the social to communication was that Luhmann had to adjust the numerous other components of his own complex theory of society to the thus conceived foundation. These included the main function systems (*Funktionssysteme*) of modern society as he had analyzed them since the 1960s. The series of books that began to appear in the late 1980s, each dedicated to one of those function systems, are among the prime locations where one could expect such reformulation to be carried out. The last of these that Luhmann was able to bring to completion to his own satisfaction before his death in 1998 was the one dedicated to the encompassing such system: society (Luhmann 1997). Before that, volumes focusing on the systems for economy (Luhmann 1989b), science (Luhmann 1990), law (Luhmann 1993), and art (Luhmann 1995a) had appeared. Two further volumes have appeared posthumously, one dedicated to the political system (Luhmann 2000a). The other, on religion, is the main focus of this chapter (Luhmann 2000b). Here, as in some of the others, the consequences of observing society as consisting of communications and of analyzing communication as a synthesis of three selections is a major concern, because religion in general and ritual in particular are for Luhmann social constructions that are directly concerned with the riskiness, and indeed improbability, of communication and the meaning that it carries. Accordingly, the main aim of what follows is to examine how and to what extent Luhmann carried out a reformulation of religion as communication, primarily in this final volume, but, because it represents the development of his thinking, also with reference to other publications on this subject that appeared after the early 1980s.

The religion of society does not discuss religion as communication all that much – the significance of this paucity will become evident shortly – but the entire volume is structured around this central notion. It begins by considering the kind of meaning that religious communication embodies. This is followed by an extended discussion of the way that this communication is structured around the core distinction between transcendent and immanent, what Luhmann calls the binary code of religion. In his theory it is essential to the differentiation of religion. This section forms the background for analysis of the function of religion (see above) and of the God-concept in religion (see below), again two critical elements that inform differentiated religion and a religious system. The core chapter focuses specifically on the differentiation of religious communication within society, and each of the remaining ones treats of a different major aspect of this differentiation: religious organization, the evolution of differentiated religion as society changes, secularization as a consequence of functional differentiation becoming the main form of differentiation in modern society, and finally the reflexive factor of self-description, which for Luhmann is a critical aspect of all differentiation. Here cannot be the place for outlining all these aspects further. Instead, it is the central question of religious communication which runs through them that is our specific focus.

As concerns Luhmann's overall theory of society, the question is important from several perspectives. First, since his earliest publications on the subject in the 1970s, Luhmann had shared the sociologically popular notion that, somehow, modern society and religion did not quite resonate with one another, that this society poses critical problems for religion which religion has difficulty facing. Second, as already mentioned, religion for Luhmann has always been something basically paradoxical, and therefore one might expect that the relation between religion and communication would have to reflect this paradoxical character. Religion, for this theory, would have to be communication and, sociologically speaking, could not be anything else; but given that requirement, it should nonetheless maintain its paradoxical quality. Third, however, the fact that religion seems to thrive in contemporary world society suggests that the paradoxical qualities and the seeming difficulties do not amount to maladaptation: whatever peculiarities religion may have as communication, these should not lead to the conclusion that it is destined to disappear or weaken to the point of irrelevance.

In one sense, that conclusion follows from the published book itself. Religion was obviously important enough and systemic enough to warrant a volume in the series dedicated to the most important social domains of modern society. Its status as communication would seem to follow almost automatically. Matters are not that straightforward, however. As it happens, in earlier publications which appeared after the theoretical turn to communication as the basic social element, Luhmann expressed various doubts about religion as communication. These were never unequivocal, but sufficiently clear to raise the question of whether, even in this final volume, Luhmann ever succeeded in observing religion entirely as communication. To clarify this observation and to set the scene for a closer look at this question specifically with regard to *Die Religion der Gesellschaft*, I turn first to these earlier publications.[6]

Religion as communication in earlier publications

In an article from the mid-1990s entitled 'Religion as communication,' Luhmann makes what from the perspective of his theory is the obvious statement: 'It is only as communication ... that religion exists in society. What happens in the heads of countless individuals could never coalesce as "religion" unless through communication' (Luhmann 1998: 137).[7] Having written that, it is just a bit astonishing that nowhere in this or any other of his writings does Luhmann then give one of his characteristically detailed and thorough analyses of what precisely religious communication is. In fact, as we shall see, in certain publications he raises doubts about this very question.

Part of the problem is that Luhmann's most complete previous work on religion (Luhmann 1977) antedates the turn of his theory to communication as the foundational element of society. Not surprisingly, in that earlier volume, Luhmann focused much more on questions of function and meaning than he did on communication. Function especially is what at that time allowed a view of the specifically social in religion (see Pollack 1991); communication did not yet occupy that role. Nonetheless, the status of religious communication as communication did not seem to be in much doubt. The already cited rather positive statement about religious ritual as communication can serve as evidence.

After the early 1980s, that is after the turn to communication, the publications about religion are comparatively infrequent and, with one exception, quite short. Yet it is precisely in these publications that doubts appear about two rather central sorts of 'religious communications,' namely communication by and with gods or spirits and, more generally, ritual. In a 1985 publication, for instance, one reads the following: 'relations between God and man have to be communication ... yet cannot be communication. ... Today this impossibility of communication is not only reinforced by writing, it is reinforced by the structural development of the societal system. ... Moreover, only human beings can support the social networks of communication' (Luhmann 1985: 17). Then, in the context of an article about whether it is still possible to communicate with God in our society we read the following rather unequivocal statement: 'In the final analysis ... this means that neither Revelation nor prayer are to be conceived as communication' (Luhmann 1987: 229). And finally, in the most lengthy article of this period, on the differentiation of religion, we encounter statements to the effect that, as religion develops its peculiar organizing distinction (code) of immanence/ transcendence, communication *with* gods becomes less and less possible 'in the world,' leaving as the only real possibility communication *about* gods (Luhmann 1989a: 336f.) After reading these contributions, one gets the definite impression that religion, for Luhmann, could be 'real' communication in today's world only as communication attributed to human beings; that whatever one imagined the vast panoply of rituals, religious practices, revelations, and the like to be, these seemingly central objects of religion were not communication.

As for the reasons for this unwillingness on Luhmann's part to consider such core religious transactions as communication, the key factors appear to be in the core analysis of what constitutes communication as such. In his longest published work, *Die Gesellschaft der Gesellschaft*, Luhmann characterizes religious ritual as something which allows communication that avoids communication (*Kommunikationsvermeidungskommunikation*; Luhmann 1997: 235).[8] Ritual, in fact, is not communication at all, because it does not differentiate between the informative and performative aspects of communication, between *information* and *utterance* (Luhmann 1997: 236). The utterance *is* the message; the message is that the ritual is being/has been carried out correctly. If one asks why this matters, then the answer is clear: 'normal' communication carries a certain risk, and that is the risk of negation or, what amounts to the same thing, the risk of communicating its own contingency. Given that religion, and religious ritual especially, is about grounding contingency, about rendering the indeterminable determinable, it cannot proceed in such a way as to open itself up to alternatives, to debate, to doing it another way (see also, Luhmann 1997: 584f.). For Luhmann, the difficulty in styling this kind of religious communication as communication thus lies in the paradoxical nature of the enterprise, hence: communication that is not communication.

Religious communication in *The religion of society*

With these discussions as background, we can turn to a more specific consideration of *Die Religion der Gesellschaft*. Here although the question of religion as communication is addressed on more than one occasion and is indeed central to the entire enterprise, overall a certain level of ambiguity remains in spite of a less harsh judgment on the implications for religion in contemporary society.

Although Luhmann refers to the idea of religious communication frequently in his final opus on the subject, only in a very few locations within that volume does he address with any directness the key question that concerns us here, namely that of religion *as* communication. The first of these, in section VII of the opening chapter (39–44), establishes the by now familiar starting point: sociologically, religion can only be communication and not also consciousness, unless the latter becomes a theme of (further) communication. Luhmann here undercuts as clearly as he can the still solidly established modern (and not just Western) notion that religion is primarily an affair of individual consciousness, whether through mystical insight, ritual self-discipline, or the affirmation of belief; that religious communication is at best only the complementary expression of that consciousness (see, for an excellent discussion, Firsching and Schlegel 1998), and perhaps even its inevitable distortion. Significantly in this regard, Luhmann insists that all communication, including religious communication, is an operation of observation (*Beobachtungsoperation*); it is situational, always arising within particular contexts of meaning, always already assuming other/prior/ subsequent communication. In terms of the three selections that together constitute communication, this means that one has to be able to distinguish information, utterance, and understanding (Luhmann 2000b: 42). As Luhmann puts it elsewhere, 'communication is only possible as an observing operation ... [because] it depends on the meaning of the difference between utterance and information being understood and thereby made available for subsequent communication' (Luhmann 1997: 538). In other words, information informs because it introduces something new in relation to previous communication, but it has to be imparted in order to take on the form of communication, and that imparting cannot normally already be the information: 'It was revealed' is an observation, but it has to have content, the 'it' cannot be identical to the revealing. Implicitly, the scene is thus set for asking the question discussed above: to what extent can religion take the form of communication? And, if this is problematic – or better, paradoxical – would one not expect the difficulty to lie in distinguishing the three selections? The connectivity of religion is at stake, its ability to form a distinct (and therefore possibly differentiated) chain and network of communications.

The second, very much related, occasion in which the question of religion as communication arises directly is in a discussion about 'contingency formulae,' in particular about the problem of observing God as unobservable observer (Luhmann 2000b: 155–68, esp. 166–7). The argument is, as usual, quite complex, but for the present purposes, we can express it in simplified form. Contingency formulae are foundational assumptions about reality that, as it were, pre-select from the logically indeterminate range of possibilities for information and thus communication. Examples are scarcity in the realm of economy, legitimacy in the realm of polity/state, justice in the realm of law; thus they are function- or system-specific (Luhmann 1984a: 10). God (or the equivalent[9]) takes on this role in religion. Thus, following from the way that communication and observation are related, imagining God as a kind of super-observer would make it a potential generator of information, if it were not for the fact that this observer is unobservable because its observation subsumes all possible observation. One solution to this problem Luhmann sees in the idea of self-revelation, a kind of gratuitous allowance of restricted observation which itself can be imagined as a kind of communication. The problem, however, is that this communication, as self-revelation, does not allow a very clear differentiation of information and informing (utterance). Implicitly, however, this imaginative construction permits a mysterious communication, which can be fixed, for instance, in a holy book; and which, in spite of taking a paradoxical form, can generate almost endless series of more 'normal' communications about it, such as commentaries, interpretations, sermons, dogmatics, theologies, and so forth.

This discussion, although it is more about the monotheistic god-figure than the overall question of how religion can be communication, does illustrate well how Luhmann sees the problem. The key issue is what one might call the dynamic or performative character of communication. To avoid having 'actors' with their consciousnesses constituting the basic social building block, Luhmann must find another way of expressing their necessary contribution to the fact that communication happens at all. The notion of observation accomplishes this at one level, but in the specific terms of communication, the critical selection in this regard is the informing or utterance. If that selection is not noticeably different from the information involved, then the 'performative' or active aspect of communication is not there: information doesn't just happen; socially speaking it has to be communicated. Indirectly, the question we are dealing with here is the degree to which the anthropomorphic beings of religions can operate as real actors in society.

The section of the book which deals most directly with this issue is also quite short. At the beginning of the fifth chapter, we find a brief but informative discussion of the communicative status of ritual and myth. The core question here, as usual, is how religious communication can become differentiated as religious communication. Although the setting aside of distinct places and times for 'religious communication' is important, we are told (Luhmann 2000b: 189ff.), the communication that takes place there and then still has to take on characteristics that mark it off clearly as religious. It is in this context that Luhmann introduces the idea of ritual. What he means by this is quite clearly not just any sort of religious practice whatsoever, but rather those practices that are more or less formally and strictly prescribed in terms of form, sequence, objects, and words. Presumably, for instance, Hindu *puja*, the Catholic Mass, or Muslim *salat* would count, but not a homily or sermon. Such rituals, he claims, have the characteristic features already adumbrated, including the fact that they depend on bodily involvement, and that they are not subject to discussion, consensus, or disagreement. Most importantly, they actually convey a minimum of information, a feature that Luhmann expresses with the idea that they make a *minimal* (note: not 'no') distinction between information and utterance. The informing is practically the information and vice versa. Religious myths, often but not exclusively tied to rituals, exhibit a similar feature. In Luhmann's words, 'myths relate what one already knows. That is their way of reproducing the unfamiliar within the familiar. Their aim is solidarity, not information' (Luhmann 2000b: 192).

To the extent that communication by and with spiritual beings and communication in the form of ritual and myth are the most widespread forms of what one might call core religious communication, in both instances, Luhmann focuses on the same characteristic as regards his model of communication: in neither case is the information/informing distinction clear. In fact, a minimal differentiation in this regard seems to be typical of these sorts of religious communication. This, as we have seen, is not a noticeable departure from what appears in previous publications, although here the language is somewhat toned down in comparison with the publications of the 1980s.

The final section in which Luhmann pays some concerted attention to the question at hand is in the chapter on self-description. Here again, in two separate places, the same problem of conflation appears, both, in this case, with specific reference to the Christian Holy Spirit. In the first case (Luhmann 2000b: 329f.), Luhmann points out that the information conveyed on the appearance of this figure is always very close to simply the fact that he has manifested himself. Thus, interpolating an example that Luhmann himself does not give, when people 'speak in tongues,' that is interpreted as the presence of the Holy Spirit but also as the speaking of the Holy Ghost. Characteristically enough, however, that speaking is incomprehensible in a normal sense. Like mystical experience, divination, and the trance state (for example, shamanistic voyages), it requires subsequent interpretation to be transformed into such normal (religious) communication. A few pages later (335f.), the same problem appears again with respect to revelation: its status as information is very close to the same thing as its status as divine utterance. Or to put this another way, *what* revelation says is very close to *that* it is revelation. Only subsequent or supplementary communication, one can assume, accomplishes the more solid differentiation between the information and informing selections (what does it mean?) that is at the heart of communication for Luhmann.

Summarizing his pronouncements on religion as communication in this volume, it appears that Luhmann clearly recognized where the core of the issue lies. The kind of communicative event which is at the centre of what makes religion distinctive is precisely the problematic or paradoxical kind, namely occasions where human beings are deemed to have communicative access to whatever it is that represents the transcendent realm, dimension, or reality. Most often, these events involve anthropomorphic symbolization as a way of giving them form as communication. For the most part, the information conveyed in these communications is fairly close to the fact that communication is taking place: information and utterance are not sharply distinguished, and therefore there is little to be understood other than that the communication has occurred. Luhmann also seems to be saying that such ritual, mythic, and revelatory occasions can be and very often are supplemented by additional, interpretative communication that tells people what information has been conveyed, and what its implications are for the conduct of life (other communication). This supplementary communication Luhmann does occasionally discuss in the volume, but he evidently does not consider it problematic as 'normal' communication. We thus have what one might call two types of religious communication: on the one hand there is the paradoxical kind, communication that is also not communication, especially ritual and the various ways that the 'gods are deemed to talk to human beings.' On the other hand, there is the communication about the paradoxical kind, namely interpretation, commentary, speculation, and the like.

Assessing religion as communication

If we can accept such a summary of Luhmann's position on the question of how religion can be communication, there remains the difficult issue of assessing its adequacy, and this in terms of Luhmann's overall theory as well as with respect to empirical observation. Four aspects of this task will occupy us here: how adequate it is to his own overall theory; how adequate it is in terms of its observation of 'religion'; how Luhmann's theory of religion has been received by others; and finally what is missing or how it could be further developed. In all cases, although the foregoing has not dealt to any extent with Luhmann's overall theory of religion, but principally only with one facet, that part is so central to the entire theoretical enterprise that judgments on it will have direct implications for the theory as a whole.

Within Luhmann's overall theory, one of the main purposes in conceiving communication as a three-part synthesis of information, utterance, and understanding is to free it conceptually from the notion that communication is a transmission between two partners. The idea is to formulate the fundamental social element as something other than the action of human individuals (see Luhmann 1984b: 193ff.). Accordingly, if communication is not to be a 'two-person' transmission, but rather a 'three-selection' synthesis (Luhmann 1987: 233f.), then attributing communication, whether as utterance or understanding, *to* God, gods, other non-human partners, or even some sort of impersonal foundational reality should be unproblematic for this theory. And indeed, Luhmann does not locate the problem of religious communication in the existence or non-existence of supra-empirical partners, but rather in the separation or non-separation of two of the selections, information and utterance. It is perhaps just here, however, that the theory is somewhat ambiguous in its own terms. The tendency of much religious communication to make at most a minimal distinction between information and utterance may make it paradoxical communication, and this in turn may lend it a peculiar quality that will play a critical role in the differentiation of religion as religion. Why, in terms of the theory, this should be in any way problematic is not entirely clear, unless the 'real' problem is in the sort of attributions of agency which religion typically makes. What this potential difficulty indicates is that Luhmann may ultimately, even in this last major work, have theorized about religion in terms of the implicit assumptions of the sociologically regnant secularization thesis, and not entirely in terms only of the logic of his own theory.

On a somewhat different note, a feature of Luhmann's work on religion in the past has been its inordinate empirical concentration on Christianity. In this final work as well, the vast majority of the illustrations of various points are still drawn from this religious tradition. The question always was, however, whether this Christian bias was accidental – being, for instance, nothing more than a reflection of Luhmann's own level of familiarity with different religions – or whether it pointed to a general limitation of his theory of religion. In this regard, two features of *The religion of society* stand out. First, the number of examples from other religions, notably Judaism, Islam, Buddhism, and African religions, has increased somewhat, although not all that much. Second, however, and more importantly, Luhmann's analysis of the somewhat paradoxical features of core religious communication is, if anything, more suitable to non-Christian religions than it is to Christianity itself. The emphasis which the latter religion (especially Protestant versions) has put on correct *belief*, which is to say correct information, in combination with its high degree of 'theologization' or reflective interpretation, has perhaps tended to obscure the degree to which this tradition has also always rested on the kind of core religious communication that has been our primary focus here. One might be able to make a similar observation about Islam, given its similarly complex traditions of interpretation and elaboration of the fundamental revelation. Other religions, however, including the less intellectualized and more popular forms of Christianity and Islam, have historically stressed what is often called 'orthopraxis' over 'orthodoxy.' That is to say, in most religious traditions around the world and historically, what matters most is correct performance of religious practices, especially rituals, and this with a minimum emphasis on what information is conveyed through them – although that is certainly not excluded – and a much greater weight on the fact that they are being executed correctly. In this respect, the focal point of Luhmann's analysis of religion as communication corresponds well to religions more broadly. That said, the emphasis on elite, Western (usually European), and institutional Christianity remains in his work, as well as the sense that this religion in particular faces 'secularizing' challenges in modern and contemporary society. Had Luhmann been able to pay more attention to religion outside the institutional Western Christian sphere, his analysis might have taken on different emphases, above all as concerns the effectiveness of religious communication in modern society, which is to say the ability of religious communication to perpetuate itself and even increase its societal presence; in terms of the three selections, its capacity for being understood.

Flowing from these considerations is the impact of Luhmann's theory of religion. Here another peculiarity manifests itself: the intellectual sector in which it has had the clearest and most extensive reception is specifically among European, even mostly German, theologians (see e.g. Welker 1985; Dahlmann 1994; Thomas and Schüle 2006). While German sociology of religion has also registered a certain impact (see e.g. Tyrell *et al.* 1998; Tyrell 2002), outside these spheres, Luhmann's theories on religion are comparatively little known, and this applies also to the English-speaking world.[10] While the difficulty and abstractness of Luhmann's theories are possibly one factor in this restricted effect, another could be the degree to which his actual development of the theory seems implicitly to have so much the situation of European Christianity in mind.

What these observations on adequacy and reception indicate is that Luhmann's theory of religion may have potential, but it is a potential that requires some development. In terms of *The religion of society*, this means that one would have to judge it somewhat disappointing. On close reading, the answers to such questions as the status of religion as communication are contained in the analyses offered. But barely so. It would seem that such a fundamental theoretical question might have received much more elaborate attention than it did, especially given the degree of attention which Luhmann usually paid to foundational questions. To be sure, Luhmann did not have the opportunity to complete this volume to his own satisfaction; but it appears unlikely that eventual additions would have filled in all the gaps that we his readers might find important. In the final analysis, Luhmann's overall work was a vast exercise in macro-theory construction, and this book is but one plank in that effort. Inevitably perhaps, for those looking for a useable theory as well as one that is elegant and complete in its own terms, the proof or lack thereof will be in others' ability to program the general theory for specific applications. In that regard, it bears just a tiny resemblance to the revelations that are occasionally discussed in this book: its status as communication depends to a large degree on the possibilities for subsequent communication on its basis.

Acknowledgement

This chapter is a substantially revised revision of Beyer 2001.

Notes

1   An earlier major work, *Religious dogmatics and the evolution of societies* (Luhmann 1972; Eng. trans. Luhmann 1984a) was republished in revised form as chapter 2 of this 1977 publication. Already in this title, one notes the evolutionary concern.

2   Luhmann's formulation is very much in the tradition of functional conceptions of religion in sociology. See, as representative examples, the renditions of three of his contemporaries, Robert Bellah (1964), Peter Berger (1967), and Thomas Luckmann (1967).

3   And, indeed, Luhmann's only other major publication on religion is entitled *The differentiation of religion* (Luhmann 1989a).

4   Translating *Mitteilung* into English is not easy, because the words that come closest to the sense in which Luhmann uses it are 'information' and 'communication.' To get at the explicitly performative connotation, words like 'utterance' or 'informing' suggest themselves.

5   For the developed presentation of this basic conceptualization, see Luhmann 1984b: ch. 4.

6   The exact sequence of the various publications is of course not entirely certain since Luhmann had a habit of working on manuscripts for a long time, in the meantime publishing other things. I am therefore not claiming that this last volume was necessarily written last. The editor of the posthumous volume, André Kieserling, in fact asserts that Luhmann began writing it in the early 1990s (Luhmann 2000b: 357). As his final (and only second) book-length work on the subject, however, it does take on the function of a final word.

7   All translations from the German in cases where the publication quoted is published in German are by the author.

8   In this regard, Luhmann's references are instructive because they appear relatively often in his discussions of the ritual core of religion. The three authors he cites here, as elsewhere, are Mary Douglas, Anthony F.W. Wallace, and Roy Rappaport. Michel Serres's notion of 'quasi-objects' also appears in this context, helping to make the point about ritual's exceptional status as communication. A more precise analysis of this intriguing relation has to await another occasion. To anticipate, see also Luhmann 2000b: 190f. The same three authors, along with Serres, are cited.

9   On the degree to which Luhmann's work on religion implicitly uses Christianity as its model, see below.

10   The present author is somewhat of an exception in his regard. See Beyer 1994, 2006.

References

Bellah, R.N., 1964. Religious evolution. *American Sociological Review*, 29 (3), 358–74.

Berger, P., 1967. *The sacred canopy: elements of a sociological theory of religion.* Doubleday Anchor, New York.

Beyer, P., 1994. *Religion and globalization.* Sage, London.

——, 2001. Religion as communication in Niklas Lumann's *Die Religion der Gesellschaft. Soziale Systeme* 7 (1), 46–55.

——, 2006. *Religions in global society.* Routledge, London.

Dahlmann, H-U., 1994. *Die Systemtheorie Niklas Luhmanns und ihre theologische Rezeption.* Kohlhammer, Stuttgart, Berlin, Cologne.

Firsching, H. and M. Schlegel., 1998. Religiöse Innerlichkeit und Geselligkeit. Zum Verhältnis von Erfahrung, Kommunikabilität und Sozialität – unter besonderer Berücksichtigung des Religionsverständnisses Friedrich Schleiermachers. In: Tyrell, H., V. Krech and Hubert Knoblauch (Eds.), *Religion als Kommunikation.* Ergon, Würzburg, 31–82.

Luckmann, T.,1967. *The invisible religion: the problem of religion in modern societies.* Macmillan, New York.

Luhmann, N., 1972. Religiöse Dogmatik und gesellschaftliche Evolution. In: Dahm, K-W., N. Luhmann and D. Stoodt, *Religion – System und Sozialisation.* Luchterhand, Darmstadt, Neuwied, 15–132.

——, 1977. *Funktion der Religion.* Suhrkamp, Frankfurt am Main.

——, 1981. Vorbemerkungen zu einer Theorie sozialer Systeme. In: *Soziologische Aufklärung 3: Soziales System, Gesellschaft, Organisation.* Westdeutscher Verlag, Opladen, 11–24.

——, 1984a. *Religious dogmatics and the evolution of societies.* Translated by P. Beyer. Edwin Mellen Press, Lewiston, NY.

——, 1984b. *Soziale Systeme: Grundriß einer allgemeinen Theorie.* Suhrkamp, Frankfurt am Main.

——, 1985. Society, meaning, religion: based on self-reference. *Sociological Analysis* 46 (1), 1–20.

——, 1987. Läßt unsere Gesellschaft Kommunikation mit Gott zu? In: *Soziologische Aufklärung 4: Beiträge zur funktionalen Differenzierung der Gesellschaft.* Westdeutscher Verlag, Opladen, 227–35.

——, 1989a. Die Ausdifferenzierung der Religion. In: *Gesellschaftsstruktur und Semantik: Studien zur Wissenssoziologie der modernen Gesellschaft,* vol. 3. Suhrkamp, Frankfurt am Main, 259–357.

——, 1989b. *Die Wirtschaft der Gesellschaft.* Suhrkamp, Frankfurt am Main.

——, 1990. *Die Wissenschaft der Gesellschaft.* Suhrkamp, Frankfurt am Main.

——, 1993. *Das Recht der Gesellschaft.* Suhrkamp, Frankfurt am Main.

——, 1995a. *Die Kunst der Gesellschaft.* Suhrkamp, Frankfurt am Main.

——, 1995b. *Social systems.* Translated by J. Bednarz, Jr. and D. Baecker. Stanford University Press, Stanford.

——, 1997. *Die Gesellschaft der Gesellschaft.* Suhrkamp, Frankfurt am Main.

——, 1998. Religion als Kommunikation. In: Tyrell, H., V. Krech and Hubert Knoblauch (Eds.), *Religion als Kommunikation.* Ergon, Würzburg, 135–45.

——, 2000a. *Die Politik der Gesellschaft.* Suhrkamp, Frankfurt am Main.

Luhmann, N., 2000b. *Die Religion der Gesellschaft.* Edited by André Kieserling. Suhrkamp, Franfkurt am Main.

Pollack, D., 1991. Möglichkeiten und Grenzen einer funktionalen Religionsanalyse: Zum religionssoziologischen Ansatz Niklas Luhmanns. *Deutsche Zeitschrift für Philosophie 39,* 957–75.

Thomas, G. and A. Schüle (Eds.), 2006. *Luhmann und die Theologie.* Wissenschaftliche Buchgesellschaft, Darmstadt.

Tyrell, H., 2002. Religiöse Kommunikation. In: Schreiner, K. (Ed.), *Frömmigkeit im Mittelalter: Politisch-soziale Kontexte, visuelle Praxis, körperliche Ausdrucksformen.* Wilhelm Fink Verlag, Munich, 41–93.

Tyrell, H., V. Krech and H. Knoblauch (Eds.), 1998. *Religion als Kommunikation.* Ergon Verlag, Würzburg.

Welker, M. (Ed.), 1985. *Theologie und funktionale Systemtheorie: Luhmanns Religionssoziologie in theologischer Diskussion.* Suhrkamp, Frankfurt am Main.

8

Exotic experience and ordinary life

On Andrew Newberg, Eugene D'Aquili, and Vince Rause, Why God won't go away: brain science and the biology of belief (2001)

Matthew Day

I shall begin with a handful of extremely general points that most – if not all – theorists engaged in the contemporary academic study of religion would be willing to take for granted. First, the anthropological record reveals a fairly robust pattern of human communities dedicating time, energy, and resources to thinking about and interacting with a class of beings that includes gods, ghosts, ancestors, and spirits. Second, human beings are the result of the same Darwinian evolutionary process of descent with modification that has produced every other living organism on the planet. Third, regardless of how one parses the murky relationship between culture and biology, the human capacity for engaging in complex behaviors – including our penchant for trafficking with non-obvious creatures – would be strictly impossible without the various motor and cognitive abilities of the fragile human brain.

What happens when we add these three principles together? Not much, actually. At best, we arrive at soggy generalizations like *we could never have our kinds of gods if we did not first have our kind of brain*. Part of the problem is that at this level of theoretical abstraction, nearly all of the most interesting questions – like how deeply evolution shapes the content of human cognition, or whether biology 'holds culture on a leash' (Wilson 1978: 167) – are obscured. Another contributing factor is that since the cognitive neurosciences are still quite young, we are unable to tell a very detailed story about the evolutionary and neurological roots of religion. Nevertheless, over the last quarter century or so, two different camps of scholars have concluded on the basis of these three principles that there is something unmistakably 'natural' about religion.

One camp – which goes by the name of the *cognitive science of religion* – attempts to explain how apparently universal properties of human cognitive architecture shape, constrain, and generate religious systems (Barrett 2000). In general, their case is that the anthropological pattern of religious thought and behavior should be seen as a relatively meaningless by-product of the evolved structures of the human mind. The other camp – which has christened itself *neurotheology* – embraces the 'naturalness' thesis wholeheartedly, but insists that a well-informed neuroscientific perspective of the brain demonstrates that there is something 'real,' 'authentic,' or 'true' about religion. In what follows I want to use one of the most popular neurotheological treatments of religion – Andrew Newberg, Eugene D'Aquili, and Vince Rause's *Why God won't go away: brain science and the biology of belief* (2001) – as an entry point for examining what this approach has to offer scholars of religion. Before turning to the book, however, it only seems proper to first introduce its authors.

Eugene D'Aquili trained as psychiatrist after completing his MD in 1968 at the University of Pennsylvania. However, he was apparently never content with the limitations of psychiatric practice, and went on to earn a PhD in anthropology from the University of Pennsylvania in 1979. Throughout his professional career, D'Aquili was particularly interested in overcoming the notion that religion and science are intrinsically at war with one another. The non-reductive style of D'Aquili's scientific interest in religion can be seen in early works such as *The spectrum of ritual* (1979), which attempts to apply the principles of biogenetical structuralism – a school of 'neuroanthropology' which D'Aquili founded along with Charles D. Laughlin – to the evolution and function of ritual activity. In addition to searching for scientific approaches to religion that avoided the hostility towards 'spirituality' that he found in a figure such as Sigmund Freud, he also was an active participant in the Institute for Religion in an Age of Science (IRAS) and the project of establishing a positive cultural and philosophical relationship between religion and science in general.

Andrew Newberg earned his MD from the University of Pennsylvania in 1993 and went on to train in Internal Medicine at the Graduate Hospital in Philadelphia. In addition to *Why God won't go away*, his collaboration with D'Aquili on the neurological foundations of religion produced numerous articles and, most notably, *The mystical mind: probing the biology of religious experience* (1999), which won the 1999 award for Outstanding Book in Theology and the Natural Sciences from the Center for Theology and the Natural Sciences. Since D'Aquili's death in 2001, Newberg has continued to probe the neurobiological roots of the religious life. This work has resulted in the recent publication of *Why we believe what we believe: uncovering our biological need for meaning, spirituality, and truth* (2006) and *Born to believe: God, science, and the origin of ordinary and extraordinary beliefs* (2007).

With the demands of academic good manners now met, it is time to turn our attention to the book itself. To provide readers with a sense of where they are being taken, here is an outline of what is to come. In the first section I will present a summary of the main arguments in *Why God won't go away* and highlight the evolutionary rationale that structures its agenda. In the second section I will briefly review the critical responses to this book, and add a few observations of my own. In the third and final section, I will suggest why the program of neurotheology – or at least the neurotheological program established in *Why God won't go away* – isn't likely to advance our understanding of religion very far down field.

High tech machinery and Stone Age existentialism

Why God won't go away begins with a riddle that has attracted the attention of philosophers, theologians, and historians of religion since the nineteenth century. Why is it that members of geographically isolated and culturally distinct communities report similar-sounding 'mystical' or 'religious' experiences? Phrased a bit less delicately, what in the world is going on when we find Meister Eckhart, a medieval European Catholic, and Lao-tzu, a Chinese Taoist, making comparable-looking claims about the experience of divine 'emptiness' and 'nothingness' (Suzuki 1957)?

In the past, scholars such as W.T. Stace (1960) were content to respond to this puzzle by establishing phenomenological typologies of mystical experience which explicitly bracketed any interest in identifying the underlying physiological causes. Traditionally, the primary reason given for tabling any causal discussion about religious experience has been that this approach fails to reckon with the idiosyncratic content of first-person experiential reports. As William James makes the point in *Varieties of religious experience*: 'The plain truth is that to interpret religion one must in the end look at the immediate content of the religious consciousness' (James 2002: 15). One consequence of this strategy is that discussions of mystical experience tend to wobble between two pivot points. At one pole scholars discount the physiology of an experience in order to take the reported cognitive content seriously; at the other pole scholars discount the cognitive content in order to take the relevant physiology seriously. Broadly speaking, the aim of *Why God won't go away* is to convince the reader that these two positions can and should be synthesized. Indeed, the book's fundamental contention is that the content of religious experience is made more secure when we take the neurophysiology into account.

The empirical centerpiece of this project is the use of single photon emission computed tomography (SPECT) cameras to produce neurological 'snapshots' of the brain's behavior during meditative states or contemplative prayer (i.e., 'religious experience'). Using both Tibetan Buddhists and Catholic Franciscan nuns as their experimental subjects, Newberg *et al.* detected common activation patterns within the SPECT scans. In both groups a discrete area in the left posterior superior parietal lobe reliably indicated surprisingly low levels of neuronal activity at the peaks of these meditative or contemplative states. This finding is noteworthy because the area in question – which the authors call the 'Orientation Association Area' (OAA) – is thought to regulate our awareness of our surroundings. Specifically, the SPECT scans seemed to be revealing a connection between the subjective experience of union with a transcendent reality or god and the objective neurological state in which the OAA, for lack of a better term, goes 'off-line' for a bit. The predictable consequence of this is that our ability to distinguish between *self* and *non-self* is momentarily impaired. On the basis of the apparent link between cognitive content and physiological foundation, Newberg *et al.* conclude that 'the mystical experiences of our subjects – the altered states of mind they described as the absorption of self into something larger – were not the result of emotional mistakes or simple wishful thinking, but were associated instead with a series of observable neurological events' (7).

In principle, this discovery about the neurological substrate of a 'religious experience' could be an intriguing but isolated finding that is akin to Olaf Blanke's enticing discovery that the subjective qualities of 'near-death' or 'out-of-body' experiences can be artificially and dependably induced (Blanke and Thut 2006). That is to say, knowing the neural mechanisms that generate an 'out-of-body experience' fails to provide enough empirical or conceptual ammunition to build a comprehensive theory of religion in the round – much less a substantive theory of 'religious experience.' So too, even if we are generous and concede that the ability to tell a detailed story about how 'x' happens in the brain of person 'p' when they have experience 'e' allows us to say something about 'religious experience,' it doesn't even come close to a robust theory of religion – something more is required. This is where the ambitions of *Why God won't go away* begin to break the surface. The book begins with an overview of the brain's neural architecture and its physiological relationship with motor and cognitive function. From there, it fans out to build a full-fledged neurobiological explanation of religion on the back of the notion that 'mystical experience is biologically, observably, and scientifically real' (7).

Thanks in part to the popularity of evolutionary psychology, it is now commonplace to see references to the 'Stone Age mind' that is said to be housed in our anatomically modern skulls. The rationale behind this claim is that given the stately pace at which evolutionary change typically occurs, there simply hasn't been enough time for natural selection to rewire human neural machinery that was originally adapted to address the demands of paleolithic life. *Why God won't go away* turns this evolutionary psychological formula inside out. According to Newberg *et al.*, the earliest humans were already struggling with profoundly philosophical questions about death and the meaning of life. Their evidence for this assertion is that Neanderthal communities went to the trouble of deliberately burying their dead – suggesting that these communities had working concepts of death and the afterlife. 'By comprehending their own mortality,' we are told, our prehistoric ancestors 'had stumbled onto a new dimension of metaphysical worries, and their questioning minds must have presented them with difficult and unanswerable questions at every turn: Why were we born only eventually to die? What happens to us after we die? What is our place in the universe? Why is there suffering?' (61).

Newberg *et al.* argue that the weight of this Pleistocene metaphysical despair would have prompted early humans to search for solutions through myth-making. The structure of mythological thinking is everywhere and always the same, we are told:

> [A]ll myths can be reduced to a simple framework. First, they focus upon a crucial existential concern – the creation of the world, for example, or how evil came to be. Next, they frame that concern as a pair of apparently irreconcilable opposites – heroes and monsters, gods and humans, life and death, heaven and hell. Finally, and most important, myths reconcile those opposites, often through the actions of gods or other spiritual powers, in a way that relieves our existential concerns. (62)

Their argument is that these structural features of myth are universal because they reflect the universal machinery of human cognition (i.e., the 'causal' and 'binary' cognitive operators [63]). Thus, the same mechanisms which allow us to frame these existential puzzles in a form that invites a resolution are also responsible for making these solutions compelling. This is how I understand the claim that while 'culture and psychology may influence them significantly, it's the neurological grounding of mythic stories that gives them their staying power, as well as the authority through which they resolve our existential fears' (76). Yet, in order for this conceptual work to count as a genuine solution to these existential dilemmas it has to feel like it resolves the anxiety. This, according to Newberg *et al.*, is where ritual enters the picture.

On their account, rituals are responsible for enacting myth in such a way that the wispy abstractions of cosmological tales are made to look eminently local and feel uniquely real. The 'neurobiological effects of ritualized behavior give ceremonial substance to the stories of myth and scripture,' we are told:

'This is the primary function of religious ritual – to turn spiritual *stories* into spiritual *experiences*, to turn something you can believe into something you can feel' (91). *Why God won't go away* proposes that the primary ritual strategy for achieving this end – selecting some arbitrary sequence of repetitive or rhythmic movements which draws attention to itself – generates increasing levels of arousal within the limbic system. In response to this highly charged state, the hippocampus begins to regulate neural activity with an eye towards maintaining some degree of functioning equilibrium by selectively creating blockades around particular brain structures. One of the structures likely to be affected by this neurological embargo or deafferentation, they submit, is the 'Orientation Association Area.' They write: 'The likely result of this deafferentation is a softer, less precise definition of the boundaries of the self. This softening of the self, we believe, is responsible for the unitary experiences practitioners of ritual often describe' (87).

Even the most ferocious critic of religion could agree with much of what Newberg *et al.* have to say about the neural foundations of 'religious' experience. In fact, it is easy to imagine how the Freud of *Civilization and its discontents* – who begins the book by explicitly reflecting on the somatic foundations of the 'oceanic feeling' encountered during religious experiences – might approve of this bid to apply the brain sciences to the study of religion (Freud 1961: 64–73). However, because *Why God won't go away* wishes to take both the physiology of religious experience and the first-person reports of those experiences seriously, it cannot stop here; otherwise it gives ammunition to those who, like Freud, would prefer to discredit the mystic's metaphysical 'insights' as nothing but the side-effects of a frenzied limbic system. The reductive naturalist might accept Newberg *et al.*'s perspective and still view religious rituals as little more than a shrewd form of neurological technology that particular communities have invented for constructing religious selves: do this, chant that, and soon you'll experience 'union with the transcendent.' According to Newberg *et al.*, James gets it just about right when he complains about the medical materialists who 'criticize our more exalted soul-flights by calling them "nothing but" expressions of our organic disposition.' We 'feel outraged and hurt,' James continues, 'for we know that whatever be our organism's peculiarities, our mental states have their substantive value as revelations of the living truth' (James 2000: 15–16). To address this outrage, the book presents a neurological defense of religion in addition to a naturalistic explanation.

In general Newberg *et al.* adopt the tactic of arguing that the content of religious experiences does not arise out of these peculiar brain states but only by means of them (cf. Otto 1923: 113). They articulate this point by translating it into an evolutionary analogy. Even though wings appear to have first evolved for the purposes of thermoregulation rather than flight, through successive generations of cumulative natural selection the result was a class of organisms that really can fly. As they put it, 'The potential for flight always existed. When evolution finally stumbled in the right direction, this potential was realized and the wonder of flight became real' (126). So too, while the evolution of the human brain was driven by the Darwinian imperatives of survival, reproduction and offspring preservation, successive generations of cumulative natural selection ultimately fashioned a brain that really can perceive the divine. Indeed, they are prepared to hypothesize that 'the very structures and pathways involved in transcendent experience – involving the arousal, quiescent, and limbic systems – evolved primarily to link sexual climax to the powerful sensations of orgasm' (125). This line of thought culminates in the contention that a neurobiological approach to religion 'suggests that God is not the product of a cognitive, deductive process, but was instead "discovered" in a mystical or spiritual encounter made known to human consciousnesses through the transcendent machinery in the mind' (133). So, while a hippocampus prodded into action by neural over-stimulation may be a necessary precondition for a religious experience, Newberg *et al.* treat this neurobiological requirement as nothing more than a mere condition of possibility. Neural circuitry doesn't cause our perceptions of the transcendent, they insist, it only provides the machinery necessary for us to be able to perceive it. 'As long as our brains are arranged the way they are,' we read, 'as long as our minds are capable of sensing this deeper reality, spirituality will continue to shape the human experience, and God, however we define that majestic, mysterious concept, will not go away' (172).

How much work can a SPECT scan do if a SPECT scan can do work?

At times, *Why God won't go away* can be surprisingly comfortable talking about 'the neurological machinery of transcendence' (125), 'the transcendent machinery of the mind' (133), the brain's 'neurological mechanism for self-transcendence' (146), or 'the neurology of transcendence' (168). This satisfaction grows out of the book's confidence that since SPECT reveals objective neurological activity that can be correlated with first-person reports of 'union with the transcendent' there is something real going on during mystical states. For lack of a better term, Newberg *et al.* are *neurological realists* when it comes to the reported content of religious experience. As a case in point, we are told that mystics don't suffer from pathological delusions but 'rather, their experiences are based in *observable functions* of the brain. The neurological roots of these experiences would render them as *convincingly real* as any other of the brain's perceptions. In this sense, the mystics are not talking nonsense; they are reporting *genuine, neurobiological events*' (143; italics added). The breed of neurological realism that inspires this assertion also motivates the evolutionarily informed neurobiological theory of religion that Newberg *et al.* put forward. Although it is the metaphysical weight of existential anxiety that pushes human beings into myth-making and ritual practice, it is the genuine reality of religious experiences which guarantees that religion will endure. 'Evidence suggests that the deepest origins of religion are based in mystical experience,' Newberg *et al.* judge, 'and that religions persist because the wiring of the human brain continues to provide believers with a range of unitary experiences that are often interpreted as assurances that God exists' (129).

Given the promise of using cutting-edge brain science to both explain and defend religion, *Why God won't go away* predictably turned heads and sold copies. Yet, despite its popularity, the book received very little attention from professional scholars of religion. The science journalist Michael Shermer (2001a,b) published two separate assessments of the book in *Science* and *Psychology Today*, and while his reviews were politely critical they failed to address whether Newberg *et al.* had something important to teach the academic study of religion. The simple truth of the matter is that this indifference is partially deserved, because *Why God won't go away* is fatally compromised by conceptual confusions, obsolete scholarship, clumsy sleights of hand and untethered speculation. For example, beyond some middling professional agreement that Neanderthals treated their dead differentially, there is currently no anthropological consensus on what that differential treatment really means – and a brief survey of the relevant literature would have revealed this (Gargett 1989). As a result of the academic silence that greeted their book, any general survey of the critical reception that Newberg *et al.* received threatens to be embarrassingly brief. To counterbalance this, I want to highlight the most substantive evaluation of the book – written by the psychologist Kelly Bulkeley for *Religious Studies Review* (2003) – and then offer a couple of my own comments.

According to Bulkeley, *Why God won't go away* suffers from at least two fundamental faults. The first is that Newberg *et al.* fail to consider how the laboratory setting is an artificial environment with the potential to produce artificial results. In his own area of expertise and research, for example, Bulkeley notes that 'people who serve as subjects in sleep laboratories tend to have dreams with less fear, aggression, and sexuality than people who sleep in a home setting – the lab evidently has a homogenizing effect on people's dreams, making it less likely they will have rare or unusual types of dreaming experience' (2003: 128). When we apply this lesson to the case at hand, it means that what Newberg *et al.* discovered in the clinical environment of SPECT machines, intravenous lines, and radioactive dyes might not occur anywhere else except a lab. Now that they have studied the neurological nature of domesticated mystical experience, Bulkeley would have them stalk religious experience in the wild.

The second issue that Bulkeley identifies is the book's 'runaway universalism' (2003: 128). On my reading of *Why God won't go away*, this is putting things politely. Throughout their project, Newberg *et al.* consistently discount the messy reality of empirical religious heterogeneity in favor of an ecumenical portrait of universal religious homogeneity. For example, we are told that:

> Each religion may find its own definition of truth and chart a different course toward union with the divine. A hundred human variables – history, geography, ethnicity, even politics – may help shape its final form. In every case, however, the authority of that religion and its essential relation to God are rooted in transcendent experiences of mystical union, whether mild or extremely powerful. (139)

That is, the particular empirical traits that distinguish one religious community from another are little more than charming local details that can be safely ignored.

This studied indifference to manifest variety is what allows *Why God won't go away* to synthesize the first-person reports of Tibetan Buddhists and Franciscan nuns despite that fact that these accounts do not say the same things. On the one hand, the Tibetans typically described a meditative experience in which they discover that the self is not an 'isolated entity' (for criticism of the notion that meditation is about producing 'experience' see Sharf 1998). On the other hand, the Franciscan nuns depicted an experience that is distinguished by a sense of the immediacy or closeness of God. Why must we pay attention to what these test subjects say? For one simple reason. 'There is no intelligible way that anyone can legitimately argue that a "no-self" experience of "empty" calm is the same experience as the experience of intense, loving, intimate relationship between two substantial selves, one of whom is conceived of as the personal God of western religion,' Steven Katz writes. 'If none of the mystics' utterances carry any literal meaning then they cannot serve as the data for any position' (Katz 1978: 39–40). As a result, the problem isn't that 'Newberg and D'Aquili seem blissfully unaware of the past half-century of critical scholarship questioning universalistic claims about human nature and experience' (Bulkeley 2003). In principle, this could be forgiven.

The real concern should be that in their attempt to defend the reality of religious experience they discount the specific content of the mystics' reports and then replace it with homogenized redescriptions of their own making. In this way, *Why God won't go away* suffers from the same problem that any attempt to locate the trans-cultural and trans-historical essence of religious experience bumps into. By separating out an invariant core from its varied and various expressions, perennialist theories of mysticism lose the thing they are trying to examine (Proudfoot 1985: 121). Yet, this isn't the only conceptual hurdle that the book fails to clear.

One of the most vexing features of the book is that there is never any attempt to cash out what 'neurobiological realism' about religious experience actually means. As far as I can tell, it often amounts to the claim that during periods of meditation and prayer something is really going on in the brain. This, at least, is how I understand them when they insist that SPECT photography demonstrates that the experiences of their human subjects 'were not the result of emotional mistakes or simple wishful thinking, but were associated instead with observable neurological events' (7). Now, if this is what Newberg *et al.* mean by neurobiological realism, at least two questions must be answered before we go much farther.

One, why aren't wishful thinking or emotional mistakes legitimate candidates for neurobiological realism? The contrast between 'mystical experience' and 'wishful thinking' or 'emotional mistake' that they construct seems to imply that whereas the first has some observable neural correlate the latter does not. However, is there a compelling reason for not supposing that if we asked a human subject to concentrate on a particular scene of wishful thinking – for me this would involve a remote Caribbean island, white sandy beaches and plenty of surf – and then applied the same SPECT research protocol that we would find some observable pattern of neurological activity? Try as I might, I can't find one. Phrased a bit more pointedly, unless and until one is prepared to argue the quixotic premise that only true beliefs or true representations have neurological correlates, the fact that a given brain state is made 'observable' or 'real' by means of SPECT scans means almost nothing.

Two, has anyone except a hard-core dualist ever doubted that something is going on inside the brain during the kinds of experiences that interest *Why God won't go away*? If one looks carefully at the history of scholarly debates about mysticism and religious experience, the point of contention has been the epistemic status of the noetic content of these experiences rather than their neurobiological foundations. In other words, the salient issue isn't whether the brain state is 'real,' or whether the mystic believes she is telling the truth. Rather, the question is whether the experience and its reported content have any value as justifications for a particular philosophical or theological claim. Although the bid to combine the somatic and epistemic questions is what makes *Why God won't go away* interesting, the way in which Newberg *et al.* advance their case is conceptually confused or philosophically underhanded. In either case, it results in the book's most obvious theoretical misstep: the move from an excessively vague claim about *neurobiological* realism and the neural mechanisms of a given brain state to a curious claim about *epistemic* realism and the reported content of the associated brain states. The fact that mystics really believe their own mystical reports (i.e., are being 'genuine' when they describe them), and that there appear to be 'real' neural events which correlate with a particular kind of religious experience is neither here nor there. When it comes to figuring out the truth, 'genuineness' is not a relevant epistemic consideration.

The key philosophical question that I'm trying to highlight here is whether, to call upon Robert Brandom's (1994) inferentialist idiom, a given mystic is *entitled* to her specific propositional commitments. That is to say, does the mystic have any good reasons to offer why her claims about the 'nature of reality' or the 'transcendent' are warranted? No doubt, Newberg *et al.* would have us treat their SPECT scans as a particularly strong form of justification for the mystic's beliefs; after all, they might add, these images reveal that something is really happening in the brain (174). Yet, this move cannot settle the issue if for no other reason than this: *Why God won't go away* offers its readers no reason for thinking that the human perceptual mechanisms we count on in our day-to-day lives are also reliable in these situations. Given that Olaf Blanke and his colleagues have established that the human perceptual system can be easily fooled into producing an 'out-of-body' experience, the challenge is not a merely philosophical one. A 'genuine' report about a 'real' brain state can, in principle, make the unfortunate mistake of taking a neurological *trompe-l'oeil* a bit too seriously.

Brandom helpfully draws attention to the role that the dependability of human perception plays in this context when he notes that a causal relation can 'underwrite a justification just because and insofar as those assessing knowledge claims *take* it as making a good kind of *inference*. Non-normative causal relations between worldly facts and someone's claims do not exclude normative epistemic justificatory relations between them, since others can *take* the causal relations *as* reasons for belief, by endorsing reliability inferences' (Brandom 2000: 166). Thus, if Newberg *et al.* want the relationship between worldly facts about brain states revealed in SPECT scans and first-person accounts which report the content of religious experiences to justify the mystics' commitments, they have some work left to accomplish. The limitations of the human perceptual systems are well known. Dogs are able to discern smell far better than we can. Hawks can see better than we can. Owls can hear better than we can. Thus, Newberg *et al.* must persuade us that the same perceptual systems that we rely on to successfully navigate the relatively obvious world of rush-hour traffic, grocery stores, and crying babies should also be relied on to 'transcend the limited self and perceive a larger, more fundamental reality' (Newberg *et al.* 2001: 175). God knows we miss plenty of things in other, far less mysterious corners of our lives.

In praise of shallowness

Daniel Dennett has commended Gilbert Ryle's *The concept of mind* as an 'importantly shallow' philosophical exercise which teaches 'us how some of the deepest waters in philosophy could be made to evaporate' (Dennett 2000: xvi–xvii). Turning this ironic praise on its head, I would say that in spite of its general clumsiness *Why God won't go away* is nevertheless an 'importantly wrong' book that can teach us something about how the brain sciences should *not* be utilized in contemporary religious studies.

As I read the book, the theoretically significant misstep is not the modified natural theological case for the neurological authenticity of mystical experience, nor the slippery philosophical transition from talking about the neurobiological foundations of religious experience to discussing the noetic content of these experiences. Unfortunately, there is no interesting tale to tell about these traits. The feature of *Why God won't go away* that I believe is *importantly* wrong is the assumption that religious thought, behavior, and 'experience' represent spheres of life so utterly unique that they must depend on something equally unique happening in the brain. In *Why God won't go away*, this hunch appears as the notion that religion is sustained by 'a neurological process that has evolved to allow us humans to transcend material existence' (9). Thus, Newberg *et al.* insist on constructing *religion* as a domain that is 'profoundly differentiated' or 'radically opposed' to the workaday world in which we live our lives and thus requires distinctive neurological machinery (Durkheim 1995: 36).

The trouble with adopting this strategy is that religion quickly becomes an unintelligible activity when we divorce it from ordinary life. This isn't because one of the classical features of mystical experience is its alleged 'ineffability' – although that certainly doesn't help matters. Rather, it is due to the fact that in order to make sense of *anything* we must be able to treat it as 'an instance of something known, of something we have seen before' (Smith 1982: 112; see also Smith 2004). As a case in point, the enduring genius of Freud's essay on 'Obsessive actions and religious practices' is the way in which it domesticates the structure and motivation behind religious rituals by transferring insights about the structure and motivation behind mundane 'neurotic ceremonials' (1959: 116–27). If contemporary social psychology happens to indicate that Freud may have actually been on to something, so much the better (cf. Zhong and Liljenquist 2006); but the theoretically significant aspect of Freud's case remains the method by which he makes it.

The conviction that religion is so exceptional that it must be cordoned off from the merely quotidian leads *Why God won't go away* to ignore vast stretches of prosaic social life. For example, we are told that ritual activity consists of 'distinctive behaviors – bows, slow processions, portentous gestures of the hands and arms – that serve no practical purpose in everyday life' (82–3). The idea that these sorts of 'distinctive behaviors' could have no 'practical purpose' is only compelling if we turn our backs on the diplomatic requirements of everyday life. Despite what Newberg *et al.* might think, etiquette is inescapably practical behavior, whether we are interviewing for a job, courting a lover, appeasing the whims of a dictator, or interacting with the gods. After all, if 'sacred spaces' are distinguished from 'profane spaces' by the restrictions a community imposes on the kinds of behavior that is appropriate in these contexts, isn't religion a kind of etiquette at the end of the day?

Thus, in its bid to make a privileged 'neurobiological' space for religion, *Why God won't go away* must snub much of what constitutes a human life. In one sense, this is one area where neurotheology's academic rival – the cognitive science of religion – has gotten things right. Instead of perpetuating the Jamesian proclivity for the ecstatic and eccentric, the cognitive scientific approach has helped to 'domesticate' religion by drawing attention to the ways in which religious thought, behavior, and experience rely on the normal operations of human cognition. As Pascal Boyer notes, if we wish to make the brain sciences relevant to the study of religion we 'do not need to assume that there is a *special* way of functioning that occurs only when processing religious thoughts' (Boyer 2001: 311). Accordingly, if neurotheology is to usefully inform our scholarly interests in religion, it will have to turn away from its Romantic fixation on exotic experiences and plumb the superficial depths of the neurobiological scaffolding that supports our ordinary lives.

References

Barrett, J., 2000. Exploring the natural foundations of religion. *Trends in Cognitive Sciences* 4, 29–34.

Blanke, O. and Thut, G., 2006. Inducing out of body experiences. In: Della Salla, S. (Ed.), *Tall tales about the mind and brain*. Oxford University Press, Oxford, 429–39.

Boyer, P., 2001. *Religion explained: the evolutionary origins of religious thought.* Basic Books, New York.

Brandom, R., 1994. *Making it explicit: reasoning, representing, and discursive commitment.* Harvard University Press, Cambridge, MA.

Brandom, R., 2000. Vocabularies of pragmatism. In: Brandom, R. (Ed.), *Rorty and his critics*. Blackwell, Malden, 156–82.

Bulkeley, K., 2003. The gospel according to Darwin: the relevance of cognitive neuroscience to religious studies. *Religious Studies Review* 29 (2), 123–9, online at www.kellybulkeley.com/articles/article_RSR_cognitive_neurosci_review.htm

D'Aquili, E., McLaughlin, C., and McManus, J. (Eds.), 1979. *The spectrum of ritual: a biogenetic structural analysis.* Columbia University Press, New York.

Dennett, D., 2000. Re-introducing *The concept of mind.* In: Ryle, G. *The concept of mind.* University of Chicago Press, Chicago, xii–xvii.

Durkheim, E., 1995. *The elementary forms of the religious life,* trans. Karen Fields. Free Press, New York.

Freud, S., 1959. Obsessive actions and religious practices. In: Freud, S., *The standard edition of the complete psychological works of Sigmund Freud,* volume IX, ed. J. Strachey. London: Hogarth Press and the Institute of Psychoanalysis, 115–28.

Freud, S., 1961. Civilization and its discontents, In: Freud, S., *The standard edition of the complete psychological works of Sigmund Freud,* volume XXI, ed. J. Strachey. London: Hogarth Press and the Institute of Psychoanalysis, 59–146.

Gargett, R., 1989. Grave shortcomings. *Current Anthropology* 30 (2), 157–90.

James, W., 2000. *The varieties of religious experience.* Modern Library, New York.

Katz, S., 1978. Language, epistemology and mysticism. In: Katz, S. (Ed.), *Mysticism and philosophical analysis.* Oxford University Press, Oxford, 22–74.

Newberg, A. and D'Aquili, E., 1999. *The mystical mind: probing the biology of religious experience.* Augsberg Fortress, Minneapolis.

Newberg, A., D'Aquili, E., and Rause, V., 2001. *Why God won't go away.* Ballantine Books, New York.

Newberg, A. and Waldman, R., 2006. *Why we believe what we believe: uncovering our biological need for meaning, spirituality, and truth.* Free Press, New York.

Newberg, A. and Waldman, R., 2007. *Born to believe: God, science and the origin of ordinary and extraordinary beliefs.* Free Press, New York.

Otto, R., 1923. *The idea of the holy.* Oxford University Press, Oxford

Proudfoot, W., 1985. *Religious experience.* University of California Press, Berkeley.

Sharf, R., 1998. Experience. In: Taylor, M. (Ed.), *Critical terms in religious studies.* University of Chicago Press, Chicago, London, 94–115.

Shermer, M., 2001a. Is God all in the mind? *Science* 293 (5527), 54.

Shermer, M., 2001b. God on the brain. *Psychology Today* (November/December), online at www.psychologytoday.com/articles/pto-20011101–000030.html

Smith, J.Z., 1982. *Imagining religion.* University of Chicago Press, Chicago, London.

Smith, J.Z., 2004. The domestication of sacrifice. In: Smith, J.Z., *Relating religion.* University of Chicago Press, Chicago, London, 145–59.

Stace, W.T., 1960. *Mysticism and philosophy.* Lippincott, Philadelphia.

Suzuki, D.T., 1957. *Mysticism: Christian and Buddhist.* Harper, New York.

Wilson, E.O., 1978. *On human nature.* Harvard University Press, Cambridge, MA.

Zhong, C.-B. and Liljenquist, K., 2006. Washing away your sins: threatened morality and physical cleansing. *Science* 313 (5792), 1451–2.

9

Religion as the unintended product of brain functions in the 'standard cognitive science of religion model'

On Pascal Boyer, Religion explained (2001) and Ilkka Pyysiäinen, How religion works (2003)

Jeppe Sinding Jensen

The cognitive science of religion is a new field of inquiry, and there can be no doubt that it *is* a major breakthrough in the study of religion. The present contribution is a critical review of the approach advocated by two prominent theoreticians, Pascal Boyer and Ilkka Pyysiäinen. I call their version of the cognitive science of religion the 'standard cognitive science of religion model' as it has so far been the dominant model. The basic tenets of the model have been succinctly presented by Ilkka Pyysiäinen:

> One of the basic ideas in the *cognitive science of religion* is that religious thought and behavior are made possible by evolved cognitive capacities which are the same for all humans and which thus can explain certain recurrent patterns in religious representations. One important point is that the human mind is understood not as an all-purpose problem-solver but as a collection of sub-systems carrying out content-specific operations. The mind operates differently in such domains as folk biology, folk psychology and naïve physics. Religion is based on cognitive processes in which the boundaries between these ontological domains are violated. (2002: 1)[1]

This is a very different way of thinking about religion. It does not resemble anything from my student days. So, if religion is to be described and analyzed as a 'violator of ontological domains,' as I rephrase it, then this is certainly a critical view of religion, now 'explained' as a widespread case of mental disorder. Or maybe just as a result of a natural order, for as Pascal Boyer says:

> Religious believers and sceptics generally agree that religion is a dramatic phenomenon that requires a dramatic explanation, either as

a spectacular revelation of truth or as fundamental error of reasoning. Cognitive science and neuroscience suggests a less dramatic but perhaps more empirically grounded picture of religion as a probable, although by no means inevitable by-product of the normal operation of human cognition. (2003: 123)

That is why Boyer has repeatedly promoted the notion of the 'naturalness of religious ideas.'

Cognitive theorizing is one more tool at our disposal in our work with that most complicated human marvel: religion. In *How religion works: towards a new cognitive science of religion* Ilkka Pyysiäinen proclaimed, in quoting Lawson and McCauley (1990), that '[w]e should study minds rather than symbol systems themselves, and see how ritual structures are mentally represented by people' (2003: 86). This kind of proclamation will of course arouse the suspicions of scholars of religion (and culture, for that matter), for what is, for instance, the supposed benefit of studying individual minds reading Shakespeare, instead of studying the works of Shakespeare himself? Yes, minds *do* process the Qur'an, the Bible, the Zen Koans – but what about the 'meaning of the texts'? The study of individual minds is rarely conceived as a major purpose in the history of religions or in anthropology. The new 'cognitive science of religion' has also come up with a completely different idea about what constitutes 'data' for the study of religion: what counts is hard 'scientific' evidence such as brains, neurons, labs, statistics, monkeys, toddlers, and what have you. But is it *really* about religion?

'Subject matter' and 'theoretical object'

In order to understand the cognitive science of religion and decide upon its usefulness one should keep in mind the fundamental distinction enunciated in the philosophy of science between 'subject matter' and 'theoretical object.' Healing rituals could be the subject matter in a cognitive science analysis, whereas the actual interest of the analyst, her 'theoretical object', is the function of innate cognitive mechanisms. Likewise, to give a few examples, Carl G. Jung studied myths (subject matter) to learn about archetypes (theoretical object), whereas Claude Lévi-Strauss looked for universal features of 'l'ésprit humain' (the human mind). What is relevant to one's own study has to be decided in each case, but it is an effect of the theory: when Bronislaw Malinowski studied myth he was theoretically concerned with the *function* of tradition in society. In Boyer's *Religion explained* we see that what *has* been explained are certain mental mechanisms without which there probably would not be religion. When told by Pyysiäinen *How religion works* we are not so much on the way 'Towards a new science of religion' as we are in the realm of psychological explanation. That is, however, not simply to be rejected as irrelevant to the study of religion, for it is also through the explanations of the workings of these mental mechanisms that we may understand 'past minds' or the similarities across religions.

It should also be noted that the cognitive science of religion is reductionist, both thoroughly and on purpose, because the ambition is not interpreting but 'explaining' (which some see as 'explaining away'). Boyer, for instance, both begins and ends his explanation of religion by referring to it as 'airy nothing' (2001: 2, 330) and it would be difficult to be more reductionist than that. 'Airy nothing' is in every sense (and in my opinion) a silly way of describing religion and totally in contrast to the immense power religion has had over minds ever since its 'invention.' Religion is so many things that it defies any one explanation; you can explain some aspects of religion in cognitive terms, others demand other kinds of explanation. However, it is the task of all science to be reductionist, and so the issue is rather one of deciding what kind of reduction is useful or makes sense in a given task (e.g., Jensen 2003: 134–9).

'E-religion' and 'i-religion'

The apparent 'great divide' between cognitive science of religion proponents and other research traditions could be elegantly solved, I think, by applying a very simple distinction between 'i-religion' and 'e-religion,' where 'i-' stands for 'internal' and 'e-' for 'external' (a distinction imported from linguistics).[2] Most historians, archaeologists, anthropologists, and sociologists of religion have studied 'e-religion', that is, religion 'outside-the-head': in texts, in social practices (rituals, purity systems, etc.), in monuments, in material culture, in all that which is symbolic and available to newcomers in a given society. The general consensus in the study of religion has been to study 'e-religion,' while 'i-religion' has remained the province of the psychology of religion. The cognitive study of religion has become a 'new' psychology of religion, but not so much in the established psychology of religion circles. The cognitive study of religion is carried out by a wholly different group of scholars, with very diverse backgrounds: anthropologists, philosophers, psychologists, theologians, and, of course, some scholars ('historians') of religion. We are also now better equipped to move back and forth between 'i-religion' and 'e-religion.' For instance, we may look into the mental mechanisms that enable the social constructionism that Berger and Luckmann described decades ago (1967).

It also turns out that some of the earlier ideas in the cognitive study of religion have become increasingly better validated, that the scientific evidence is growing, e.g. with advances in brain-imaging techniques. New insights are due to one very fundamental characteristic of the cognitive study of religion: that it is entirely naturalistic and non-religious. This means that any scientific advance in the study of mind in general also has potential consequences for the study of religious minds, the main principle being that they are 'just minds,' and that religious beliefs are 'just beliefs.' There is no transcendence, nothing ineffable, nothing awe-inspiring, nothing 'sacred' in the cognitive study of religion, at least not as *explanans*, but merely as *explanandum* – it is all about human minds and what they do. Thus, any addition to our knowledge of the working of minds can in principle be applied in the cognitive study of religion. And that makes it very interesting and attractive as a scholarly project.

Introducing Boyer and Pyysiäinen

Why choose these two scholars as proponents? For Boyer's part, it is the result of his importance in the development of the field from a mainly anthropological perspective. Pyysiäinen's contribution takes off from a more history-of-religions-oriented basis, and he has also keenly kept on including and referring to philosophical as well as psychological issues in cognitive analyses of religious phenomena. Their biographies are different. Boyer began in anthropology with fieldwork in francophone Africa and studies of oral transmission of tradition and knowledge, moved to cognitive analyses of religious thought, and now works in experimental psychology, mainly on memory and ritual. Pyysiäinen studied the history of religions, specializing in Buddhist studies, turned cognitivist, studied belief and religion in general, and has since been researching the cognitive foundations of the human propensity to conceive of supernatural agents. Their bibliographies demonstrate their development from two different traditions, how they have converged and then gone in separate, but somehow parallel directions. Both Boyer and Pyysiäinen have been proponents of what I term the 'standard cognitive science of religion model.' It is based largely on the theories of Dan Sperber (see below) and evolutionary psychology (Barkow *et al.* 1992). Boyer comes out of a French rationalist tradition, with an interest in the workings and the products of the human mind ('*ratio*') in general, and Pyysiäinen contributes a relation to the history of religions and philosophical issues. Boyer has fieldwork experience in a non-literate society (the Fang), and Pyysiäinen is philologically trained in a highly literate tradition (Buddhism), and so they complement each other within the confines of the same theoretical stance.

The cognitive turn in the study of religion can be fairly reliably dated to 1990, when Lawson and McCauley published their first book on cognitive ritual theory.[3] In the following years Pascal Boyer was one of the first to promote cognitive theory in the study of religion, and he did so noticeably with a series of publications (see References) in his Cambridge years (the 1990s). Pyysiäinen joined the field some years later. Boyer was probably *the* major herald of this new approach to the study of religion, not least with the seminal article (1992) which presented a new 'psychology of religion' in a framework based on cognitive and neuroscience approaches.

Theoretical background and inspirations

The cognitive study of culture and religion can be said to have a long history, including such prominent figures as Hume, Kant, Feuerbach, and many more, but here I shall limit the focus to just one scholar who features prominently in both Boyer's and Pyysiäinen's work. Dan Sperber, a French anthropologist, formerly of a structuralist persuasion, is undoubtedly the main inspiration for both scholars and for the 'standard cognitive science of religion.' He is a pioneering figure in devising cognitive approaches to the study of culture and religion, and in the 1970s he initiated a rethinking of anthropology in a markedly psychological or cognitive direction. In his early work on symbolism (1975) he attempted to redefine this not as a cultural phenomenon but as a mental mechanism. This proved to be a starting point for a reconception of the task of anthropology as explanatory rather than interpretive. The ambition was scientific and based on a thoroughly individualistic methodology, that is, cultural phenomena were to be studied as mental, individual processes, made possible by universal psychological mechanisms. However interesting that theory was in its day, in my view it suffered from a deficient and philosophically inadequate referentialist theory of meaning. The main work, *Explaining culture: a naturalistic approach* (1996), consists of essays written during the 1980s and 1990s. Here, Sperber introduces the notion of an 'epidemiology of representations': culture consists of 'contagious ideas,' representations that are distributed and propagated so effectively that they invade whole populations. These representations are transmitted between individuals, they are externalized as public representations, and then internalized as mental representations by individuals. Some representations become widely spread and last for generations, so that they become 'paradigmatic cases of cultural representations' (1996: 25). Any new representation of a representation is always an interpretation, and so they are not like, for example, viruses that copy themselves in a population (1996: 58). Culture, then, consists of representations that 'play an essential role in defining cultural phenomena' (24). Sperber claims that 'beliefs, intentions and preferences are mental representations. Until the cognitive revolution, the ontological status of mental representations was obscure.' But now, he says, they are clearly seen as material: 'in psychology, the material character of mental representations has changed from a mystery to that of an intelligible problem' (25). Thus, as his ambition is stated, 'a truly materialist programme in the social sciences becomes conceivable' (ibid.). He continues:

> In spite of its heterogeneity, the ontology of an epidemiology of representations is strictly materialist: mental representations are brain states described in functional terms, and it is the material interaction between brains, organisms and environment which explains the distribution of these representations. (1996: 26)

Many will wish that he was right, because then all would be really simple, but the philosophically inclined reader will notice quite a few problems in the argument. One of the main problems, in Sperber's own view, is that of the *distribution* of representations. It seems probable that humans prefer content that is easy to remember and has 'greater cognitive effects,' that is, new content that is relevant because it is in tune with what is otherwise known or important in a society. This is important, because otherwise socio-cultural differences would be very difficult to explain. Cognitive factors are at play because of the 'mental modules' that handle cultural contents in the cognitive domains they 'specialize in.' Interestingly, Sperber distinguishes between the cultural domains of modules from 'both their proper and their actual domains' (1996: 139). Sperber writes that 'cultural transmission causes, in the actual domain of any cognitive module, a proliferation of parasitic information that mimics the module's proper domain' (1996: 141). Music is a very telling example of this. There is no evolutionarily evolved cognitive module for music – 'it' uses a combination of other modules, and so music is found in all societies around the globe. In brief, it has been Sperber's aim to reform anthropology so that it will be able to account for both human social universals as well as cultural variation, but without the snares of relativism and in a manner that is more scientifically valid than the customary modes of presenting anthropological knowledge. One example of his turn from socio-cultural interpretations to cognitive explanations is found in his proposal for 'Rethinking symbolism' (1975). Sperber stated that an interpretation of a symbol is nothing but an extension of the interpretive range of the meaning of the symbol, and so an interpretation was really not an explanation. Instead, symbolism should be explained in terms of the causal mental mechanisms that produce it. The shift is a very profound one from the domain of the social to that (or those) of mental properties and functions.[4] His program is also a prescriptive one, for as Armin W. Geertz and Joseph Bulbulia have noted:

He [Sperber] repeatedly speaks of the epidemiological approach in proscriptive terms, i.e. what the 'proper' objects for anthropological theorizing are, what kinds of questions the approach 'should' be able to ask and answer, etc. He encourages colleagues to identify types of causal chains, be they ecological or psychological, whose features are essential to their emergence and maintenance. Thus until such features are fully identified, his approach remains more promising than useful. (Geertz and Bulbulia forthcoming: 49)

We need to stay with Sperber for yet a brief moment in order to better understand some of the arguments of our two scholars. He introduced a very useful distinction between two analytic kinds of beliefs.[5] 'Intuitive beliefs are derived, or derivable from perception ... on the whole concrete and reliable in ordinary circumstances' (1996: 89). On the other hand, reflective beliefs are beliefs that we acquire from others, from tradition, etc.: 'They cause belief behaviors because, one way or another, the beliefs in which they are embedded validate them' – that is, we believe in ancestors and so act on those beliefs – 'from loosely held assumptions to fundamental creeds' (89–90). Importantly, although they may be mysterious (as in theological dogma), 'that does not make these beliefs irrational: they are rationally held if there are rational grounds to trust the source of belief (e.g. the parent, the teacher, or the scientist)' (91). As a consequence, and here Sperber deserves to be quoted at full:

[t]here are two classes of beliefs and they achieve rationality in different ways. Intuitive beliefs owe their rationality to essentially innate, hence universal, perceptual and inferential mechanisms; as a result they do not vary dramatically, and are essentially mutually consistent across culture. Those beliefs which vary across cultures to the extent of seeming irrational from another culture's point of view are typically reflective beliefs with a content that is partly mysterious to the believers themselves. Such beliefs are rationally held, not in virtue of their content, but in virtue of their source. (Sperber 1996: 92)

It is difficult to decide whether Sperber's hypothesis about the 'epidemiology of representations' qualifies as 'cultural eliminativism'. He does not say that 'culture does not exist,' but as he explains:

An epidemiology of representations would establish a relationship of mutual relevance between the cognitive and the social sciences, similar to that between pathology and epidemiology. This relationship would in no way be one of reduction of the social to the psychological.

Social-cultural phenomena are, on this approach, ecological patterns of psychological phenomena. Sociological facts are defined in terms of psychological facts, but do not reduce to them. (Sperber 1996: 31)

Typical of the standard cognitive science of religion model is the predilection for 'inside-out' explanations, that is, explanations of how cognitive mechanisms and properties in individual minds produce social and cultural matters. It is in that sense also a typical 'bottom-up' explanatory procedure, where matters at 'lower levels' give rise to phenomena at 'higher levels.'[6] This upwards explanation method poses the problem of epiphenomenalism in the sense that higher-order levels are not considered relevant or to have explanatory potential, there is no 'downward causation' (Jensen 2002: 219–20). Sperber's idea of 'epiphenomenalism' is generally accepted among scholars in the standard cognitive science of religion, and here is how he explains it in a critique of structural analysis:

[C]omplex objects, such as cultural phenomena, display all kinds of properties. Most of these properties are epiphenomenal: they result from the fundamental properties of the phenomenon, but are not among those fundamental properties. In particular, they play no causal role in the emergence and development of the phenomenon, and are not, therefore, explanatory. (Sperber 1996: 47)

If they were allowed to be explanatory, on his view, they would then be circular. But I do think that a measure of circularity is allowed in the explanation of social affairs, where actors do act on reasons.[7] A further problem in the ontology of the 'true materialism' in cultural studies, as Sperber advocates, is the problem – or rather absence – of (semantic) meaning (which is not an entry in Sperber's 1996 book, nor in Boyer 2001). If humans navigate in universes of semantic meaning, as many of us think they do, then that should be a concern for cognitive theorizing. It could be in the future.

Against 'the blank slate' in the 'standard social science model'

In Sperber's model, culture is constantly re-created by human mental machinery, where cognitive models with rich inferential potential work together, and where the main features of all culture are constrained by our cognitive constitution. Human minds are not 'blank slates' on which just anything can be written. Human 'nature' is to a large extent driven by species-specific traits that are the product of a long trail of evolution, and therefore in conflict with the basic assumptions of what John Tooby and Lea

Cosmides called the 'standard social science model' (Barkow *et al.* 1992). In spite of superficial cultural differences there *are* limits to which products of the mind become represented and reproduced, and there are cognitive constraints on why anything does *not* 'go.' Boyer originally set out from a thesis about strong cultural memory in non-literate society, questioning why some representations become more widespread and better remembered than others (Boyer 1990). This pointed in the direction of both cognitive salience and constraints of cultural 'materials': distributed representations. The next step was to inquire why certain types of religious representations seem to be both exceptionally well distributed and preserved, and this in turn led to the observation that religious representation about, typically, superhuman agents were not at all as mysterious as the scholarly tradition presumed. Ideas about gods and ancestors (the entire superhuman cata- logue) are very similar to the ideas we have about humans, only that there is a little 'tweak' in the qualities and properties of the superhuman agents: they are, e.g., immortal or all-knowing. Such ideas then go against the grain of our 'natural' perceptions, our 'intuitive ontology,' and so they are 'counter- intuitive' in that they violate our expectations about things in the world, such as statues that weep or trees that remember. Thus, superhuman agents have many 'natural' qualities, and hence Boyer's idea about the 'naturalness' of religious thought: it is and has been very easy for humans to entertain certain ideas about the superhuman agents and their 'world' (Boyer 1994a). This idea he expressed briefly in another context, where he criticized anthro- pology and the philosophy of religion (!) as trying to explain the origin of religion with implausible answers because:

> They are all untestable, as they generally refer to historical scenarios for which there is no conceivable evidence … Progress in our knowledge of evolved human capacities provides a better account that is testable, based on what we find in the anthropological record rather than in familiar settings, and that predicts only the narrow range of concepts observed rather than a variety of other possible concepts. Religious concepts are not around because they are good for people or good for society or because of an inherent need or desire to have them. They are around because they are more likely to be acquired than other variants. (Boyer 2000a: 211)

Thus, religious concepts are here simply because they are easy to pick up and to remember. And further, there seems in fact to be a rather limited catalogue of possible religious phenomena when the apparent plethora of religious ideas is boiled down to a finite list of possible combinations (see below; and Boyer 2000a, 2001). Religious thought (and what comes with it) is the result of a mixing of quite ordinary human mental capacities that have been selected for during evolution. There is no specific 'religious organ,' but when mental mechanisms coordinate in certain ways the result is a set of cognitively salient representations. Religious conceptualization activates discrete mental systems that were 'made' for other things, and so religious thought becomes a by-product of brain function (Boyer 2003). Religion becomes a 'spandrel' – an unforeseen result of brains running 'amok,' but at the same time this opens up the possibility that religious thought and beliefs may be turned into empirically tractable objects for experiments in a cognitive neuroscience. And that is a new turn in the study of religion.[8]

New methodological 'turns' in the analysis of culture

There are so many new steps and turns in the cognitive perspective that both Boyer and Pyysiäinen (and others) work on, but they also seem to discard almost all research that is 'pre-1990.' At best it stands to be refuted by them. A few examples should suffice to display the most salient twists in method. So, on the influence of Durkheim, Pyysiäinen tries to 'show that although religion has important social functions, these functions cannot be the cause of religion. In giving social functions too central a place, the Durkheimian approach fails to deal with what is specific about religion, i.e. counter-intuitive representations.' (2003: ix–x). Durkheim does not explain what he means by 'collective consciousness' or 'how it emerges from individual consciousnesses. Nor is there any compelling evidence for the existence of any such entity' (2003: 74).[9] Durkheim's theory provides, however, a useful perspective on what makes counter-intuitiveness religious, i.e. that some beliefs are serious and they have prominent position in social life (75). On Geertz, Pyysiäinen states that his views on culture and symbolism have 'turned out to be too vague to offer any sure ground for theories about religion' (2003: 53). '"Cultures" are merely abstract summaries of the thoughts and behaviors of individuals, not identifiable wholes that can be empirically explored' (ibid.). The main cause of confusion is Geertz's 'dogmatic anti-psychologism.'[10] The cure, then, is to apply Sperber's approach, according to Pyysiäinen.[11] This statement also indicates the often strained relations between anthropology and psychology, relations that Boyer has also faced. Few anthropologists are convinced that Boyer's approach holds much promise for anthropology and anthropologists.

Such doubts may be justified, for Pascal Boyer's view of culture is also 'eliminativist.' That is, culture does not have a 'robust ontology' and so it is 'confusing to say that people share a culture, as if culture were common property. We may have strictly identical amounts of money in our respective wallets without sharing any of it' (2001: 35–6). Seemingly a compelling argument, but it merely demonstrates how Boyer's individualism makes him blind to the fact that we must share an economy to have money in our wallets in the first place! Culture cannot cause anything as it is just 'a similarity between people's ideas' and 'How could a similarity cause anything?' (ibid.). Is it possible, however, to do without the concept? Here is how it works, along the lines of Sperber's epidemiology (46): 'Religion is cultural. People get it from other people' (47). That is probably the simplest explanation possible, but it is also more profound than Sperber and his followers would want to admit, for it requires the cultural intervention of language and symbolism in order to be transmittable. Any understanding of such intervention is beyond individualist explanations, because they leave culture out of the picture.

Boyer and Pyysiäinen are sincere proponents of psychological universalism: 'The explanation for religious beliefs and behaviors is to be found in the way all human minds work. I really mean all human minds, not just the minds of religious people or of some of them. I am talking about human minds, because what matters here are properties of minds that are found in all members of our species with normal brains' (2001: 2). Boyer's basic question is: 'How could we explain a phenomenon (religion) that is so *variable* in terms of something (the brain) that is the *same* everywhere?' Psychological universalism warrants methodological individualism, that is, what applies to the individual applies universally to all humans, and vice versa. And, very often, what is individual is judged innate, at least in Boyer's psychological anthropology. And most of the time we are not aware of what is innate in us and what works subconsciously. That goes for religious ideas as well: 'When people have thoughts about gods or spirits or ancestors, a whole machinery of complex mental devices is engaged, most of which is completely outside conscious access' (2001: 49). There is no 'magic bullet' explanation of religion. It is much more complex, as religion triggers 'important social, cognitive, emotional effects' (50). Thus there *are* connections and relations between the mental and the socio-cultural. So, for instance, science may change our conscious views and explanations of things, but the underlying mental machinery remains the same. As Boyer says:

> To sum up, then: during human history and across cultures, people have been and are faced with very diverse environments (social and natural) as well as different, culturally transmitted explicit accounts of what makes things solid, what making living things live, what constitutes a mind and so on. These differences provide substantial evidence for the 'plasticity' of mind, understood as the capacity to entertain a wide variety of concepts and beliefs. However, it is also striking that

we find no corresponding differences in intuitive ontology. Cultural input seems to build upon intuitive ontology, to challenge it sometimes, even to build a more powerful ontology in the case of science. But it does not eliminate the intuitive expectations. (2000b: 288)

Thus, we have cultural and social knowledge, and we also have science, but most importantly for us as a species, we have 'intuitive ontology,' that is, an inherited set of intuitions about the world that result from our evolutionary history. This is one of the key notions that Boyer and Pyysiäinen employ in order to explain the complexity.

Key notions

As noted above in discussing Sperber's theory, the idea of 'mental modules' and the 'modularity of mind' has been prominent. The idea should perhaps not be taken at face value, for critics have long held that such modules do not exist. 'Module' is at best an analytic construct with heuristic value (Karmiloff-Smith 1992).[12]

A fundamental notion with both authors is that of 'intuitive ontology,' by which we understand that humanity is genetically predetermined to think and perceive about certain entities in the perceived world in specific ways and to have specific expectations of items belonging to various domains. The evidence for this is mostly derived from experiments with infants (Pyysiäinen 2003: 199–208; Boyer and Barrett 2005).[13] Even small children have different expectations of the behavior of humans, plants, animals, and material objects, and so we as humans have 'built-in' primitive, intuitive physics (about the material world), intuitive psychology (about conspecifics), and intuitive biology (about plants and animals). These 'objects' have different properties and belong to different ontological domains. Interesting aspects of the domain specificity of objects and concepts is their relation to 'templates,' the models on which we form our intuitive expectations. For instance, tell a child that a 'morg' drinks milk and instantly the child will know that 'it' lives, eats, has offspring, etc. This is a rational way for the mind to work on minimal information. As Boyer says, 'the human mind is constantly trying to solve domain-specific problems with a minimum of cognitive fuss' (Boyer 2001: 201). How innate this knowledge is remains a matter to be explored. Boyer's working hypothesis about innateness and domain is dependent on Frank Keil's work in developmental psychology on the ways in which children acquire knowledge of the world.[14] For the study of religion, the most interesting consequences of this theory occur when properties from different domains are mixed and expectations are violated. In such cases we detect 'counter-intuitive ideas' and these are the basic building blocks of religious ontologies, cosmologies, institutions, and behavioral patterns and, not least, rituals (e.g. Pyysiäinen 2001: 215–34).

Counter-intuitiveness had been seen as the basis of religion before Boyer produced his theory. Recall for instance David Hume's view on miracles. But it is Boyer who coined the term and has demonstrated its utility in the study of religion. Counter-intuitiveness is, however, not a specific trait of religion only.[15] It is the fundamental basis of human imagination in general, but along lines that are in accord with cognitive science findings generally. For instance that humans imagine alternatives to actions rather than to inaction and counterfactual imagination can be seen to be quite rational. Imaginative thought is not merely irrational, it is imaginative along certain lines (Byrne 2007). The ontology of Mickey Mouse illustrates this.

Now, armed with the concepts of ontologies, domains and, counter-intuitiveness we are better able to grasp the utility of Boyer's cross-religion 'catalogue.' As there seem to be an infinite number of religious ideas in the world it is Boyer's long-lasting contribution to the study of religion that he can show how there is in fact only a limited number of combinations. The basic ontological categories he works with are *person*, *animal*, *plant*, *artifact*, and *inanimate natural object*. Certain expectations and inferences are triggered subconsciously for objects in these categories when we perceive them. Now, religious concepts are interesting, 'cognitively salient,' or 'attention grabbing' precisely because they violate some of our intuitive expectations while they simultaneously take for granted standard expectations: gods, ancestors, and spirits are very much like humans – except for their superhuman capacities. And, most importantly, this holds all over the globe (Boyer and Ramble 2001)

In Boyer's catalogue, any religious concept is built on the following: templates (models, as above) that (1) point to a particular domain, (2) violate intuitive expectations (either a breach of expectation or a transfer of properties from another domain), and (3) link to default (normal) expectations for the category. As templates are very general, religious *concepts* add a further two elements: (1) a 'slot' for additional encyclopedic information and (2) a lexical label (Boyer and Ramble 2001: 537). For instance, a god has a cognitive 'tag' that points to the domain 'person,' but one that has counter-intuitive properties such as living forever, knowing all, being all over the place at one time, etc. Consequently, there seem to be no more than 15 possible varieties of counter-intuitive assumptions, based on five ontological domains or categories (the terminology varies) and three possible actions: default cognitive activation, violation of expectation, and transfer of properties. As Boyer says: 'In other words, there are not that many ways of "tweaking" intuitive ontology so as to produce supernatural concepts, so that a "general catalogue of the supernatural" should be rather short' (2000a: 198–9). The catalogue of the templates can be represented as in Figure 9.1.

(1) Person	+ breach of physical expectations
(2) Person	+ breach of biological expectations
(3) Person	+ breach of psychological expectations
(4) Animal	+ breach of physical expectations
(5) Animal	+ breach of biological expectations
(6) Animal	+ breach of psychological expectations
(7) Plant	+ breach of physical expectations
(8) Plant	+ breach of biological expectations
(9) Plant	+ transfer of psychological expectations
(10) Natural object	+ breach of physical expectations
(11) Natural object	+ transfer of biological expectations
(12) Natural object	+ transfer of psychological expectations
(13) Artifact	+ breach of physical expectations
(14) Artifact	+ transfer of biological expectations
(15) Artifact	+ transfer psychological expectations

Figure 9.1 Boyer's 'catalogue of the supernatural' as resulting from permutations and transformations of intuitive ontological categories, transfer of properties and violation of domain specificity.

After Boyer 2000a: 198–9.

As an illustration of how this works, Boyer gives the following example:

> For instance, this is the template for the concepts of 'spirit' that we find in so many cultures: (1) an ontological category: PERSON; (2) a violation of intuitive physics, e.g. spirits are invisible; (3) activation of non-violated expectations: being persons, spirits have a mind, they can perceive events, forms beliefs, have intentions, etc.; (4) place-holder for additional (local) detail. (Boyer 2000a: 198)

Obviously, specific religious traditions may not use all of these combinations of categories and templates for ordering them, but a more rigorous, empirical description could be given as evidence of their frequency and distribution. The validation of the universality of their presence consists not so much in the actual finding of them everywhere as in the universality of the mechanisms behind their operation. There is no doubt that Boyer's catalogue, as a cross-cultural model, is a radical contribution to the classificatory phenomenology of religion. A fundamental axiom is that religious thought and behavior do not demand any special cognitive system, mentality, or psychology as all religious cognition and emotion is performed by mental systems that work for other 'mundane' activities. On a final note Boyer says on the ubiquity of 'attention-grabbing' religious concepts:

To understand why we find these recurrent themes, we do not have to imagine that they are particularly good or useful or that the human mind needs them in any particular way. There is a simpler explanation. They are such that acquiring them activates some mental systems, produces some inferences in the mind, *a little* more than other possible concepts. (2001: 325)

This is a very (and probably the most) undramatic theory of the origin of religion. It is also the main reason why religion is so 'natural' (Boyer 1994a). It is the outcome of quite ordinary, this-worldly human cognitive capacities, not least for 'decoupling' and imagining. Does this also mean that we then know when religion appeared? Not quite, for as Boyer says near the end of his book:

So it would seem that we now know when people 'invented' religion: when such representations could occur in people's minds and exert enough fascination to be painstakingly translated into material symbols. Things are a little more complicated, however, because religion as we know it is not just a matter of counterintuitive concepts. Religion is not just about flying mountains, talking trees and biological monsters but also about agents whose mental states matter a lot, about connections with predation and death, about links with mortality and fortune. (2001: 324)

After this presentation of some of the basics of the 'standard cognitive science of religion model' as presented by Boyer and Pyysiäinen we are better equipped to evaluate their contributions on a range of related themes.

Related themes

In Boyer's project of 'explaining religion,' he delves into the questions of why religions are so preoccupied with death and hypothesizes that it is because corpses trigger complex and conflicting inferences from various cognitive systems; they seem like the people we knew and yet they are not (2001: 222–8). On rituals, Boyer presents a whole catalogue of bizarre instances of behavior, and (reasonably) asks what could possibly be behind such strange kinds of formal and rigid behavior. There are striking similarities, he ventures, with pathological modes of behavior such as can be found in patients with obsessive-compulsive disorders (OCD) (2001: 238–9; Boyer and Liénard 2008). Rituals are about (among other things) 'management of precaution against undetectable hazards' (2001: 240) and the formation and maintenance of coalitions, where it is of the utmost importance that all members signal their loyalty. This is done in ritual, especially so in initiations. In Boyer's analysis of fundamentalist behavior this is used to explain how and why the violence that is apparently aimed against outsiders is mainly used to discipline members of the 'in'-group.[16] An important theme that builds up during the course of the book is that of the links between ideas concerning superhuman agents and morality. Now, what a monkey does not see, it does not know, but humans are different, very different, because we want to know as much as we possibly can – also vicariously. And quite often we know what we cannot see, because of our social intelligence. And so it happens that imagined super-human agents can acquire and share 'strategic information' with us (164–7), and that we therefore may use such information as we can retrieve from ancestors, gods, or oracles in the social processes of 'policing' the morality of our social partners (e.g., 190–1). All of these things happen because they are driven by relevance in our social environment, and because our brains and minds have evolved as they have. Boyer's book is certainly worth a read, if one has an interest not only in religion, but also in human cognition as such, because 'we can highlight and better understand many fascinating features of our mental architecture by studying the human propensity towards religious thoughts' (2001: 330). Here, again, we see that the subject matter relates to religion, whereas the theoretical object is 'our mental architecture.'

Generally working from the same theoretical principles, i.e. the legacy of Sperber, Pyysiäinen tells a somewhat different story with a focus on beliefs, worldviews, and ethics. He goes into the neurophysiology of religious expe-rience and uses the theories of Antonio Damasio (e.g., 2000) to explain the role of emotions in religious belief and ritual, for as he says: 'The persist-ence of religion as a "symbolic cultural" phenomenon cannot be explained without taking into account the emotional basis of religious belief and truth claims' (2003: 139). His methodological individualism renders him skeptical of the utility of 'worldview' as a characterization of religion: 'I merely want to emphasize that in reality these "worldviews" are abstract summaries, not actually existing structures in people's minds, and that as such they cannot be causal factors in social development' (150). This convic-tion further causes a lack of focus on the more systemic aspects of religion, for these aspects do not really 'explain' anything scientifically interesting, though they do perhaps provide information on the statistical frequency of distribution of beliefs, as in the 'epidemiology of representations.' It remains, I would say, to be proven that socio-cultural matters become more 'real' by being in somebody's mind, but that is how psychologism works. Pyysiäinen offers a discussion of morality and ethics on a naturalistic basis, where, as it turns out, even small children are able to perform social evaluations which are then expanded through experience. All humans have moral intuitions, and he considers this to be purely natural. The intuitions 'are the outcome of continual readjustment of our convictions and practices in the light of our unfolding experience of the real world' (194). Recent developments in moral psychology suggest that there is much to commend Pyysiäinen's view, and that there may in fact be a place for naturalized morality and ethics. In a discussion of the relational nature of such notions as 'self' and 'world,' Pyysiäinen notes the unforeseen concurrence between postmodernism and cognitive science. This coincidence deserves to be quoted as evidence of the underlying ontological commitments of cognitive science:

> Neither concept [self, world] can provide an ultimate ground for ethics or for anything else, both of them being conditioned by the natural drift of evolution. The difference between postmodernism and cognitive science is that cognitive scientists accept the process of evolution as a truly explanatory factor. Neither the external world nor cognition is taken as a fixed given, both being viewed as co-evolving systems without any ultimate ground. The human cognitive system is an emergent outcome of the self-organization of matter; external reality is perceived in the way it is because evolution has shaped the human perceptual system to be such as it is. Organisms and environment enfold into each other and unfold from each other. (2003: 164)

Criticism

Criticism has been abundant, of Boyer and Pyysiäinen as well as other proponents of the standard science of religion model. As might be expected, some of the criticisms seem to have failed to notice just *what* the cognitive approaches are about. Also the cognitive science of religion has been dismissed as simply 'reductionist,' as 'stuff about the brain,' or as a kind of psychology that has no importance for the (real?) historical study of religion. This is quite understandable, for if the occupation with religion as subject matter is in fact applied to say something about our evolved 'mental architecture,' then the 'cognitive science of religion' is not so much about religion as it is about how humans interact with imagined agents. Then, to the voiced criticism, we may add the 'silent criticism' which consists in simply ignoring the cognitive approaches. It has taken quite a while for the cognitive approaches to become integrated in established international congress programs, for instance.

On the note of positive criticism it is fairly obvious that the study of religion will never be the same again. The 'evolution' of the field is irreversible, and in my opinion we face a 'cognitive turn' that will have lasting consequences similar to those of the 'social turn' (the legacy of Durkheim) and the 'linguistic turn' (the legacy of Saussure). However, as has happened with other 'turns,' this new 'cognitive turn' will also need modifications and refinement, and perhaps even rather drastic reformulations, but the basic move has been made. Inspiration from the cognitive study of religion can be used in many ways, from political science to archaeology. One of the most radical additions to the study of religion that is offered by the cognitive approach is the contribution to a solution of the 'insider / outsider problem' (Day 2004: 241–4). The 'insiders,' or believers, no longer have privileged epistemic authority in explaining their behavior, because cognitive science has demonstrated that introspection does not reveal to us how the mind works: we do not know why we think the way we do (Day 2004: 242). Religious representations are not 'transparent' to the mind: the complex mental machinery that produces and activates ideas about gods, ancestors, etc. is completely outside access by the conscious mind (Boyer 2004: 431).[17] So, this is one major achievement of the cognitive science of religion.

As for negative criticism and what is 'wrong', needs correction, and amplification, it turns out that what Sperber, Boyer, Pyysiäinen, and other proponents of the standard cognitive science of religion model have produced is based on a rather narrow spectrum of what the cognitive sciences can offer. As an example we may question their 'distaste' for culture and their very marked opposition to, for example, more conventional anthropology. This may partly be explained as a strong reaction to existing paradigms, reactions that other 'folks' in the cognitive science have taken part in, simply because they came from other academic quarters and directions. Cognitive psychologists, for instance, have recently 'embraced' culture as an area of great interest (e.g. Tomasello 1999; Donald 2001; LeDoux 2002; Frith 2007). As early as 1991, Bradd Shore remarked: 'Yet we lack a comprehensive understanding of mental representations that incorporates both cognitive and sociological dimensions of meaning' (1991: 9). That is still true: the social and cultural dimensions must be included, not least if we want to understand religion.

So, there is much more that can be included in a more comprehensive cognitive science of religion, not only from the cognitive sciences, but, for example, from philosophy on the problems of ontology and epistemology, from moral psychology, and not least from neuroscience and neurobiology on the neural correlates of all the hypothesized cognitive modules, mechanisms, and properties of human minds. There is also a lot of cognition that does not solely happen in brains but, even more importantly, between them (e.g. Hutchins 1995). Thus I agree with Armin Geertz when he says:

> One of the main problems with Boyer's work is that in his attempts to get beyond the variability of cultural detail, he restricts himself to what is going on inside the brain. This heuristic device, as already mentioned, is self-defeating because the story of cognition and the manipulation

of symbols is not restricted to the brain. It is not that Pascal Boyer is unaware of the significance of the social context (2001: 27–8), but he is more concerned with internal cognitive processes. (2004b: 361)

That is certainly correct, as it seems that Boyer and those who are of the same persuasion are indeed concentrating on finding and analyzing a range of cognitive mechanisms ('inferential systems') that *are* located in the human brain. In so doing they provide extremely valuable insights, but there is more to the story that what is located inside the skull. Recently, James Laidlaw, who is otherwise positive towards the cognitive approach to religion, has pointed out some weaknesses of the cognitive approach as it is practiced in the standard cognitive science of religion model. Some of his criticism deserves to be quoted at length. He sees as especially problematic the disregard for the importance of self-interpretation involved in social practices:

> The reflective process of understanding and articulating one's experience in terms of these emotions, motivations, and qualities of character is never just to describe but always also evaluate, and thus to affect. In understanding and articulating our experience in such terms, we necessarily act upon the self, because we ascribe not only content but *import* to the emotions or motivations or qualities of character so described. Such self-interpretations are constitutive. (Laidlaw 2007: 224)[18]

We are often mistaken about the workings of our own mental mechanisms, as the standard cognitive science of religion model so forcefully has demonstrated, but there is another side of psychology that deserves due recognition:

> It follows that, while we may in important ways be mistaken about our own thoughts, emotions, and motivations, our self-understandings are never *merely* mistakes, for they are part of the fact of the matter, part of what they seek to articulate. The articulation, even if partly mistaken or even actively self-deluding, is nevertheless part of its object. But further, it is important not to think of this constitutive self-interpretation as a merely psychological process, in the sense of it being internal to the individual. It takes place within institutions and relationships, and through instituted practices and language. (Laidlaw 2007: 224)

Laidlaw rightly (in my opinion) emphasizes the effect of 'tradition' on emotions in a manner very different from what Pyysiäinen stated above about beliefs and truth claims in the individualist perspective. For Laidlaw (as for most of us), language is highly important for self-interpretations and for the existence of specific emotions:

> [S]o the language and the emotion could not exist without the tradition and the institutions and practices through which it is cultivated and experienced. And because these emotions and motivations are historical products, invented and developed contingently in particular times and places, and sustained by particular practices and institutions, they cannot be adequately described purely in terms of cognitive mechanisms, internal to individual minds. (Laidlaw 2007: 225)

Language, meaning, thought, and experience are inter-subjective in this account. Minds are not just in brains and bodies, they are also in society, in culture, in language. The first steps in the cognitive science of religion have been to study the workings of 'inferential systems' in individual minds, but they are the first steps in what seems a long journey. This is also expressed by Matthew Day:

> At times, the mainstream cognitive program has displayed an ill-advised penchant for treating social structures, cultural practices, and material artifacts as extraneous features of a biologically fixed cognitive system. From my perspective, the bid to capture the contours of the human mind cut loose from the cognitive scaffolding provided by our physical embodiment and socio-cultural embeddedness seems 'as misguided as seeking to investigate the true nature of an ant by removing the distorting influence of the nest.' (Day 2007: 49)[19]

Consequently, in order to move forward in theorizing religion in relation to cognition, we need to pay more attention to extended cognition, distributed cognition, social and cultural cognition and normative cognition, to the roles of intentionality and language, and – probably – to a greater extent than we can currently imagine.[20] So far we have had a good dose of naturalist cognitive theory of religion, and so we may expect the antidote to be something like radical enculturation of cognition. There is growing 'hard' empirical and experimental evidence that cultural learning literally changes the brain, and there is thus much more to be said for culture than we have heard so far. Maybe brains not only do something for religion – invent it, for example – but maybe religion also does something to and for brains. We do not really know yet, but we are on the way to finding out.[21] We may therefore concur with Boyer's expectations: 'Much remains to be done, but progress in our understanding of the mind is gradually transforming many mysteries of culture into mere problems, including that of the origins of religion' (2000a: 211). Against this optimism, Matthew Day has expressed doubt as to the ambitious task of explaining religion and – in closing – his argument deserves to be quoted:

> [I]t may be the case that a comprehensive, genuinely explanatory theory of religion is simply out of our reach. Mind you, if this is so, it would not be because such a theory is *prima facie* impossible, or because religion represents a *sui generis* fact about the world, or because religion is an irreducibly 'spiritual' phenomenon. In fact, a philosophical naturalist should reject these conclusions out of hand. Rather, an explanatory theory of religion would be beyond *our* grasp because the disjunctive empirical complexities that such a theory must track – be they social, cognitive, neurological or all of the above – would far exceed our restricted computational powers. (Day 2007: 63)

So, no matter how convincing certain research results may appear, there is a lot more to be done. Religion has so far not been 'explained,' but we do know more and more. And now it also seems that the study of religion is beginning to look more like a 'normal science,' with the possibility of accumulating *some* knowledge. Rival paradigms will continue to be with us, but that is simply a function of the complexity of the object of study. Whatever else religion is, it is 'many things.'

Notes

1 References are omitted here. The selection in Slone 2006 is representative of the 'standard cognitive science of religion model.'

2 I am indebted to my friend and colleague Joseph Bulbulia for directing my attention to this distinction. See also Bulbulia's chapter on Scott Atran's theory in this volume for this distinction.

3 See the chapter by Steven Engler and Mark Gardiner in this volume.

4 How profound a shift can be illustrated by making an analogy with music: from studying music as a cultural entity to a study of the mental mechanisms that enable humans to make music. That would be a completely different enterprise.

5 By 'analytic' I indicate a distinction that is made for the purpose of analysis without necessarily corresponding directly to 'reality' – analytic concepts are theoretically informed. A well-known example is Max Weber's notion of 'ideal type.' See, e.g., Jensen 2003.

6 Higher and lower according to convention. Most likely this echoes earlier Hegelian and 'scala perfectionis' motifs in the history of the Western 'mind.'

7 More importantly, but an entirely different story, explanations are not only about causality (on the role of explanation in the study of religion, see e.g. Jensen 2003: 223–41).

8   See Pyysiäinen 2003: 224 for '[t]he belief box', a 3-D figure that 'illustrates the mutual relationships between various types of mental representations using a spatial analogy.'

9   This illustrates Pyysiäinen's empiricism and methodological individualism. What would count as 'evidence for the existence' of a general abstract concept such as 'collective consciousness'? His critique of Durkheim seems beside the point.

10 This characterization of Geertz has become a pseudo-truism in many commentaries on his work, but it is simply wrong.

11 Geertz's contribution (in the 1960s) of the linguistic turn in philosophy into anthropology goes unnoticed by Pyysiäinen and many others. See Armin W. Geertz's discussion of Clifford Geertz's relevance for cognitive theory in 2004a: 7–9.

12 In Frith 2007, a very able exposition, there is no mention whatsoever of 'modularity' or 'modules.' Most current textbooks on cognitive neuroscience and cognitive psychology do not contain entries on 'modules.'

13 This is not 'ontology' in any philosophical, metaphysical, or epistemological sense, it is simply 'the world' as we have evolved to intuit it with our bodies and brains. So, in philosophical terms, it is 'naïve realism' and not 'metaphysical realism.' 'Domain' is not an entry in Boyer 2001, but see pp. 40–6 on 'templates.' Boyer changes his terminology in successive publications.

14 Strangely, Keil (e.g. 1992) is not listed in the Boyer 2001 bibliography. Keil builds on the philosophy of Fred Sommers (who is not in the index of Keil 1992). Why hide inspirations?

15 McCauley (forthcoming) notes: 'By itself, though, the counter-intuitiveness of representations is an extremely weak condition on the "religious," since so many other sorts of representations – from those in cartoons to those in science – also fit the bill. But noting *that* fact need not stymie subsequent theorizing. Rather it is a provocation to formulate proposals about additional necessary conditions for something to count as religious, which, in turn, will stimulate further empirical research' (11).

16 Boyer's ingenious explanation of fundamentalist behavior should be required reading for anyone with an interest in these matters (2001: 287–96).

17 Day also notes: 'It was once a given in the philosophy of mind that each of us has privileged, unmediated first-person access to the contents and workings of our minds' (2004: 242). However, this phenomenological stance is now challenged: 'Based on the extensive clinical and experimental evidence regarding the idiosyncrasies of human cognition and perception, there is now widespread consensus that any rigorous science of the mind must be conducted from the outsider's third-person perspective ... although first-person phenomenological reports may be treated as incorrigible when it comes to how things appear from the inside they are no more (and no less) than another set of empirical data for the third-person heterophenomenological project of scientific explanation' (ibid.).

18 Here, Laidlaw refers to the philosopher Charles Taylor (1985: 45–76). (As an anthropologist, Laidlaw has worked on Jain and Buddhist traditions as well as ritual theory.)

19 Day quotes Griffiths and Stolz 2000: 44–5.

20 It is not possible to go into details here, but see the references for contributions by e.g. Clark 1997; Day 2007; Deacon 1997; Donald 2001; Hutchins 1995; Rowlands 2003; Siegel 2001; Tomasello 1999; Wexler 2006.

21 Recent findings by Shinkareva *et al.* (2008) provide striking evidence for the effects of cultural learning.

References

Atran, S., 1990. *Cognitive foundations of natural history*. Cambridge University Press, Cambridge.

Atran, S., 2002. *In gods we trust: the evolutionary landscape of religion*. Oxford University Press, Oxford, New York.

Barkow, J.H., Cosmides, L., and Tooby, J. (Eds.), 1992. *The adapted mind: evolutionary psychology and the generation of culture*. Oxford University Press, Oxford, New York.

Berger, P.L., Luckmann, T., 1967. *The social construction of reality*. Penguin, Harmondsworth.

Boyer, P., 1990. *Tradition as truth and communication: a cognitive description of traditional discourse*. Cambridge University Press, Cambridge.

Boyer, P., 1991. Review of *Rethinking religion*. *American Anthropologist* 93, 984–5.

Boyer, P., 1992. Explaining religious ideas: elements of a cognitive approach. *Numen* 39 (1), 27–57.

Boyer, P. (Ed.), 1993. *Cognitive aspects of religious symbolism*. Cambridge University Press, Cambridge.

Boyer, P., 1994a. *The naturalness of religious ideas: a cognitive theory of religion*. University of California Press, Berkeley, Los Angeles, London.

Boyer, P., 1994b. Cognitive constraints on cultural representations: natural ontologies and religious ideas. In: Hirschfeld, L.A. and Gelman, S. (Eds.), *Mapping the mind: domain-specificity in culture and cognition*. Cambridge University Press, New York, 39–67.

Boyer, P., 1998. *Creation of the sacred*: a cognitivist view. *Method & Theory in the Study of Religion* 10 (1), 88–92.

Boyer, P., 1999. Cognitive tracks of cultural inheritance: how evolved intuitive ontology governs cultural transmission. *American Anthropologist* 100 (4), 876–89.

Boyer, P., 2000a. Functional origins of religious concepts: conceptual and strategic selection in evolved minds. *Journal of the Royal Anthropological Institute* 6, 195–214.

Boyer, P., 2000b. Natural epistemology or evolved metaphysics? Developmental evidence for early-developed, intuitive, category-specific, incomplete and stubborn metaphysical presumptions. *Philosophical Psychology* 13 (3), 277–97.

Boyer, P., 2001. *Religion explained: the evolutionary origins of religious thought.* Basic Books, New York.

Boyer, P., 2003. Religious thought and behaviour as by-products of brain function. *Trends in Cognitive Sciences* 7 (3), 119–24.

Boyer, P., 2004. Religion, evolution and culture (Atran's *In gods we trust*, Wilson's *Darwin's cathedral*). *Current Anthropology* 45 (3), 430–3.

Boyer, P. 2008. Evolutionary economics of mental time-travel. *Trends in Cognitive Science* 12 (6), 219–23.

Boyer, P. and Bergstrom, B., 2008. Evolutionary perspectives on religion. *Annual Review of Anthropology* 37, 111–30.

Boyer, P. and Ramble, C., 2001. Cognitive templates for religious concepts: cross-cultural evidence for recall of counter-intuitive representations. *Cognitive Science* 25, 535–64.

Boyer, P. and H.C. Barrett, 2005. Evolved intuitive ontology: integrating neural, behavioral and developmental aspects of domain-specificity. In: Buss, D. (Ed.), *Handbook of evolutionary psychology.* Wiley, New York, 96–118.

Boyer, P. and Liénard, P., 2006. Why ritualized behavior? Precaution systems and action-parsing in developmental, pathological and cultural rituals. *Behavioral and Brain Sciences* 29, 1–56.

Boyer, P. and Liénard, P., 2008. Ritual behavior in obsessive and normal individuals: moderating anxiety and reorganizing the flow of behavior. *Current Directions in Psychological Science* 17(4), 291–4.

Byrne, R.M.J., 2007. *The rational imagination: how people create alternatives to reality.* The MIT Press, Cambridge, MA.

Clark, A., 1997. *Being there: putting brain, body, and world together again.* The MIT Press, Cambridge, MA.

Damasio, A., 2000. *The feeling of what happens: body, emotion and the making of consciousness.* Vintage, London.

Day, M., 2004. The ins and outs of religious cognition. *Method & Theory in the Study of Religion* 16 (3), 241–55.

Day, M., 2007. Let's be realistic: evolutionary complexity, epistemic probabilism, and the cognitive science of religion. *Harvard Theological Review* 100 (1), 47–64.

Deacon, T., 1997. *The symbolic species: the co-evolution of language and the human brain.* Penguin: Harmondsworth.

Donald, M., 1991. *Origins of the modern mind: three states in the evolution of culture and cognition.* Harvard University Press, Cambridge, London.

Donald, M., 2001. *A mind so rare: the evolution of human consciousness.* W. W. Norton & Company, New York.

Frith, C., 2007. *Making up the mind: how the brain creates our mental world.* Blackwell, Oxford.

Geertz, A.W., 2004a. What is religion for? Theoretical perspectives. In: Bulbulia, J.A. and Morris, P. (Eds.), *What is religion for?* University of Wellington, Victoria, 1–12.

Geertz, A.W., 2004b. Cognitive approaches to the study of religion. In: Antes, P., Geertz, A.W., and Warne, R.R., *New approaches to the study of religion*, vol. 2. Walter de Gruyter, Berlin, New York, 347–99.

Geertz, A.W. and Bulbulia, J., forthcoming. *An introduction to cognition and religion.* Ashgate Publishing, Aldershot.

Geertz, C., 1973. The impact of the concept of culture on the concept of man (orig. 1966). In: Geertz, C., *The interpretation of cultures: selected essays,* New York: Basic Books, 33–54.

Griffiths, P. and Stolz, K., 2000. How the mind grows: a developmental perspective on the biology of perception. *Synthese* 122 (1–2), 29–51.

Guthrie, S.E., 2002. Animal animism: evolutionary roots of religious cognition. In: Pyysiäinen, I. and Anttonen, V. (Eds.), *Current approaches in the cognitive science of religion.* Continuum, London, New York, 38–67.

Hutchins, E., 1995. *Cognition in the wild.* The MIT Press, Cambridge, MA.

Jensen, J.S., 2000. Structure. In: Braun, W. and McCutcheon, R. (Eds.), *Guide to the study of religion.* Cassell, London, 314–33.

Jensen, J.S., 2002. The complex worlds of religion: connecting cultural and cognitive analysis. In: Pyysiäinen, I. and Anttonen, V. (Eds.), *Current approaches in the cognitive science of religion.* Continuum, London, New York, 203–28.

Jensen, J.S., 2003. *The study of religion in a new key: theoretical and philosophical soundings in the comparative and general study of religion.* Aarhus University Press, Aarhus.

Jensen, J.S., 2004. Meaning and religion: semantics in the study of religion. In: Antes, P., Geertz, A.W., and Warne, R.R., *New approaches to the study of religion,* vol. 1. Walter de Gruyter, Berlin, New York, 219–52.

Jensen, J.S., forthcoming. Normative cognition – the case of religion: cognition and culture in interaction. *Journal of Anthropological Psychology.*

Karmiloff-Smith, A., 1992. *Beyond modularity: a developmental perspective on cognitive science.* The MIT Press, Cambridge, MA, London.

Keil, F.C., 1992. *Concepts, kinds and cognitive development.* The MIT Press, Cambridge, MA.

Laidlaw, J., 2007. A well-disposed social anthropologist's problems with the 'cognitive science of religion'. In: Whitehouse, H. and Laidlaw, J., *Religion, anthropology and cognitive science.* Carolina Academic Press, Durham, NC, 211–46.

Lawson, E.T. and McCauley, R.N., 1990. *Rethinking religion: connecting cognition and culture.* Cambridge University Press, Cambridge.

LeDoux, J., 2002. *The synaptic self: how our brains become who we are.* New York: Viking.

McCauley, R.N., forthcoming. Is religion a Rube Goldberg device? Or oh, what a difference a theory makes? Department of Philosophy, Emory University, available online at www.emory.edu.

McCauley, R.N., 2006. How far will an account of ritualized behavior go in explaining cultural rituals? *Behavioral and Brain Sciences,* 29 (6), 623–4.

McCauley, R.N. and Lawson, E.T., 2002. *Bringing ritual to mind: psychological foundations of cultural forms.* Cambridge University Press, Cambridge.

Pyysiäinen, I., 1996. *Belief and beyond: religious categorization of reality.* Åbo Akademi, Åbo.

Pyysiäinen, I., 2002. Introduction: cognition and culture in the construction of religion. In: Pyysiänen, I. and Anttonen, V. (Eds), *Current approaches in the cognitive science of religion*. Continuum, London, New York, 1–13.

Pyysiäinen, I., 2003. *How religion works: towards a new cognitive science of religion*. Brill, Leiden.

Pyysiäinen, I., 2004. *Magic, miracles, and religion: a scientist's perspective*. AltaMira Press, Walnut Creek.

Pyysiäinen, I., 2005. *Synti – Ajatuksin, sanoin ja töin (Sin in thought, word and deeds)*. WSOY, Helsinki.

Pyysiäinen, I., 2006. *Jumalten keinu: Kiertoajelu uskontotieteessä (The swing of the gods: A guided tour in the study of religion)*. Gaudeamus: Helsinki.

Pyysiäinen, I. and Anttonen, V. (Eds.), 2002. *Current approaches to the cognitive science of religion*. Continuum, London, New York.

Rappaport, R.A., 1999. *Ritual and religion in the making of humanity*. Cambridge University Press, Cambridge.

Rowlands, M., 2003. *Externalism: putting mind and world back together again*. Acumen, Chesham.

Shinkareva, S.V. *et al.*, 2008. Using fMRI brain activation to identify cognitive states associated with perception of tools and dwellings. *PLoS ONE* 1, e1394, 1–9.

Shore, B., 1991. Twice-born, once conceived: meaning construction and cultural cognition. *American Anthropologist* 93, 9–27.

Siegel, D.J., 1999. *The developing mind: how relationships and the brain interact to shape who we are*. The Guilford Press, New York.

Siegel, D.J., 2001. Toward an interpersonal neurobiology of the developing mind: attachment relationships, 'mindsight,' and neural integration. *Infant Mental Health Journal* 22 (1–2), 67–94.

Slone, J. (Ed.), 2006. *Religion and cognition: a reader*. London: Equinox.

Sperber, D., 1975. *Rethinking symbolism*. Cambridge University Press, Cambridge.

Sperber, D., 1980. Is symbolic thought prerational? In: LeCron Foster, M. and Brandes, S.H. (Eds.), *Symbol as sense: new approaches to the analysis of meaning*. New York, Academic Press, 25–44.

Sperber, D., 1982. Apparently irrational beliefs. In: Hollis, M. and Lukes, S. (Eds.), *Rationality and relativism*. Basil Blackwell, Oxford, 149–80.

Sperber, D., 1985. Anthropology and psychology: towards an epidemiology of representations. *Man* 20 (1), 73–89.

Sperber, D., 1990. The epidemiology of beliefs. In: Fraser, C. and Gaskell, G. (Eds.), *The social psychological study of widespread beliefs*. Clarendon Press, Oxford, 25–44.

Sperber, D., 1994. The modularity of thought and the epidemiology of representations. In: Hirschfeld, L.A. and Gelman, S. (Eds.), *Mapping the mind: domain-specificity in culture and cognition*. Cambridge University Press, New York, 39–67.

Sperber, D., 1996. *Explaining culture: a naturalistic approach*. Basil Blackwell, Oxford.

Taylor, C., 1985. *Human agency and language: philosophical papers 1*. Cambridge University Press, Cambridge.

Tomasello, M., 1999. *The cultural origins of human cognition*. Harvard University Press, Cambridge, MA.

Tooby, J. and Cosmides, L., 1992. The psychological foundation of culture. In: Barkow, J.H., Tooby, J., and Cosmides, L. (Eds.), *The adapted mind: evolutionary psychology and the generation of culture*. Oxford University Press, New York, 19–136.

Wexler, B., 2006. *Brain and culture: neurobiology, ideology, and social change*. The MIT Press, Cambridge, MA.

Whitehouse, H., 1995. *Inside the cult: religious innovation and transmission in Papua New Guinea*. Oxford University Press, Oxford.

Whitehouse, H., 2000. *Arguments and icons: divergent modes of religiosity*. Oxford University Press, London, New York.

10

Religion as evolutionary cascade

On Scott Atran, In gods we trust (2002)

Joseph Bulbulia

Darwin teaches us that given (1) variation, (2) high-fidelity inheritance, and (3) constraints on reproduction, organization in nature will gradually accumulate. Opposable thumbs, echolocation, zebra stripes, and colour vision manifest striking design. But they do not require architects. Many have considered the elimination of designer gods to be evolutionary biology's most important contribution to the study of religion. Scott Atran thinks differently. For Atran, naturalists after Darwin should avoid theology. We should instead study theologians. That is, we should use evolutionary biology to shed light on religious minds. Here I present, motivate, and evaluate (Atran 2002).

Biographical sketch

Scott Atran rates among the several most respected cognitive psychologists in the world. He is a director of research in anthropology (tenured) at the National Center for Scientific Research, and works with the Jean-Nicod Institute (now part of the École Normale Supérieure) in Paris. He is visiting professor of psychology and public policy at the University of Michigan and is presidential scholar in sociology at the John Jay College of Criminal Justice in New York City. He commands the attention of policy-makers at the highest levels of government. He has addressed the National Security Council on the role of religion in political conflict, more than once, and much of his influence remains classified. Atran combines a modern-day William James with James Bond.

Scott Atran was born in New York City in 1952 and received his PhD in anthropology from Columbia in 1984. In 1974 (at the ripe age of 22) he organized one of the most important debates in twentieth-century psychology on the topic of 'Human Universals' at the Abbaye de Royaumont in France. The debate featured Noam Chomsky, Jean Piaget, Jacques Monod, Claude Lévi-Strauss, and others. 'Human Universals' subsequently provided the focus of Atran's dissertation on the cognitive basis of science, and has informed most of his subsequent research. In the late 80s Atran's reputation as an outstanding cognitive scientist was firmly established through his original work on human folk categorizations of nature. His surveys of distinct and causally unrelated cultures (North American university students and the Itzaj Maya) demonstrated that in spite of rich cultural variance, we all think about nature according to a common plan. In the 1990s Atran shifted his attention to human reasoning and political decision-making.

But it is religiosity that has bothered Atran throughout his life, like a sore tooth. In a recent interview Atran describes his 10-year-old self writing on a wall: 'God exists: or we're all in trouble.'[1] As a young anthropologist he encountered deeply entrenched religious commitments among the Druze people of the Middle East. 'As I went on to study and live with other peoples, the structural outline of Druze religious beliefs and practices appeared to crop up everywhere I sojourned: among forest Maya, desert Bedouin, steppe-roaming Pashtuns, Indian farmers, Tibetan mountaineers' (Atran 2002: ix) – human universals again, in wild religions.

The generality of common religious elements interests Atran the anthropologist, but to the biologist, it is the persistence of religious commitment that raises the interesting questions. For religious commitment presents a *cost problem*. Cutting oneself, leaping from heights, paying priests, bowing before icons, etc. do not appear sensible methods for increasing fertility. Over time, selection eliminates inefficiency. So the fact that we remain – indeed could ever have been – religious ranks among biology's most interesting riddles.

In gods we trust weaves together many distinctive research programmes in cognitive, social, and historical sciences, with literally hundreds of empirical studies cited. The book, like the man, is an intellectual *tour de force*. Yet we've come a long way since 2002, or so I shall claim at the end. But before considering that book, let me motivate Atran's approach. Why should we use evolutionary cognitive science to make sense of religion, rather than any other of the many approaches on offer?

Background: cognitive science and evolutionary psychology

Let's begin with a more fundamental question: what is cognition? Stripped to its basics, all thought involves the transformation of data structures through the application of rules. (Thought is more than this, but it is at least this.) Brains are metabolically expensive tissue. Naturalists suppose that they evolved to monitor and control bodily and worldly change.

Because thought transforms information, we can analyze cognition computationally. Of course, our meaty brains do not compute like a desktop PC. Nevertheless, like ordinary computers, brains register and manipulate information. (Compare: birds fly, airplanes fly – *both* differently *and* according to Bernoulli's principles, which we can use to explain each.) Cognitive psychology approaches thinking through the formal analysis of the informational processing capacities of the human mind. It is a science in search of algorithms.

Let's assume thought is, in some basic respect, computational. Importantly, information processing *takes time*. But the problems we solve are complex. Indeed, *very complex*. It is therefore puzzling how we manage to think as we do.

Consider a simple example. Suppose Peter has only 10 behavioral options in his repertoire. He can stand, site, bit, leap, utter 'TRULY,' etc. Suppose further that Peter can initiate at most only 10 behaviors each minute. This means that after one minute the sequence of behaviors available to Peter is 10^{10} (a hundred billion.) After two minutes there are 10^{20} possibilities, and after a mere 10 minutes there are 10^{100} possibilities – a number exceeding the number of electrons in the universe (see Cosmides and Tooby 1992: 102). Even small data sets give rise to what computer scientists call 'NP-hard' problems (nondeterministic polynomial-time hard) – by which they mean: *very complex*.

Our minds, then, are confronted with a 'combinatorial explosion' (Cosmides and Tooby 1992). Search spaces need to be dramatically narrowed. Likely answers need to be anticipated. Yet the world we encounter is never the same twice. We cannot fully anticipate what remains unknown. How, then, do we manage?

The modular theory of mind emerged in the 1970s as the leading candidate architecture to describe the psychological organization of the human mind (Fodor 1985) (though not without recent controversy, see: Sterelny 2003; Barsalou, Niedenthal, Barbey, and Ruppert 2003). It is this theory that Atran (2002) and most other cognitive scientists of religion embrace.[2] Modular designs consist of a number of smaller computational subsystems organized to process information over specific task domains. Large unsolvable problems are decomposed into smaller, discrete, and so tractable problems. And cognitive scientists suppose that much of these modular designs are innate, and developmentally entrenched. Selection forges the modules over evolutionary deep time.

Let us suppose that our minds are modular. How does this fact bear on our explanation of religion? For Atran, religious cognition must substantially *cause* religious culture, rather than vice versa. External culture provides only a triggering and shaping function.

[W]e have seen that religion in general – and gods, ghosts, devils, and demons in particular – are culturally ubiquitous because they invariably meet or systematically manipulate modular input conditions of the human mind/brain ... Without such biologically poised competencies – the products of millions of years of biological and cognitive evolution – a child's acquisition of such a wide range of cultural knowledge in only a few short years would be miraculous. (Atran 2002: 211)

The implications are Copernican, for the standard view of religious acquisition becomes inverted.[3]

In gods we trust is dedicated to understanding the biological and informational organization of component systems that give rise to religious commitment. We might have guessed that Atran would have used evolutionary reasoning to reverse-engineer religiosity's adaptive benefits. Quite the opposite.

Religiosity as a spandrel

Atran does not posit a dedicated 'religion faculty' because he does not perceive any design to religiosity per se. '*Religions are not adaptations and they have no evolutionary functions as such*' (12) (emphasis original). Instead, he urges that we best explain religion as a by-product of systems that have evolved for other purposes. Religion is best explained as what Gould and Lewontin call a 'spandrel' – a phenotypic feature that does not exhibit biological design, but which rather emerges as an after-effect of design (Gould and Lewontin 1979). Our eyes did not evolve for reading nor

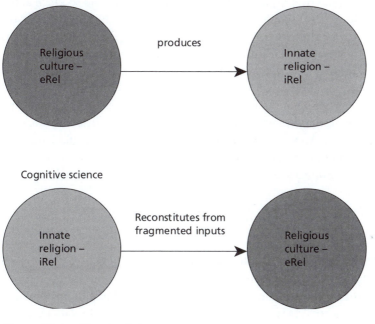

Figure 10. 1   Standard view

did our chins evolve as pillow hooks. They are *adaptive to* these purposes but are *not adaptations for* them. Similarly, 'religio[n] may be adaptive in some contexts without being an adaptation in an evolutionary sense' (24).

To explain religion as a spandrel, Atran invokes the image of a river flowing through a varied landscape. 'The class of humanly plausible religions is one such set of paths in the landscape's drainage basin' (11). We can imagine the topography of the land as composed of peaks representing the numerous functionally designed systems of the mind – language, vision, memory, theory of mind, folk biology, emotion, and others. The river is the flow of conceptual information that wends its way through the valleys and vales of human intelligence. Topography (plus the weather – think 'inputs') causes the river to flow as it does. We can accurately explain and predict the river's properties by characterizing of the geology that feeds and supports it. 'Religion is not an evolutionary adaptation, but it does more or less describe a natural space of possibilities, – a set of paths' (280).

Atran discusses many relevant systems; we shall explore the several most important.

Minimally counterintuitive concepts

In the early 90s, the cognitive anthropologist Pascal Boyer[4] urged that we approach religious concepts as ordinary concepts slightly adjusted to compel attention. Boyer argues that we are able to understand so much about religious culture because religious concepts resemble ordinary concepts, the inferential features of which are largely innate. But crucially, religious agents are also distinctive and uncanny. Religion is the *familiar*, made *strange*.

Indeed, the idea was that religion might have something to do with the violation of expectation was first elaborated by Dan Sperber and Atran in the early 1980s in a course at the École des hautes études en sciences sociales, and is discussed in his *Fondements de l'histoire naturelle* (Atran 1986; Atran, pers. comm.). However, Atran points to two areas of trouble in the familiar-made-strange version of the model. First, to *remember* a concept is one thing, to (1) *believe* and (2) *commit to* it, another. We can illustrate this point with a story.

Once upon a time there was a dragon. The end.

Memorable, but you will not believe it, or modify your life. Boyer's explanation faces what Atran calls 'the Mickey Mouse' problem. We easily recall Mickey Mouse (and Zeus, Santa Claus, or my dragon) but find it difficult as adults to believe in them. Moreover such memorable 'minimally counterintuitive concepts' (MCI-concepts) are insufficient to motivate powerful commitments and costly behaviors. From an evolutionary stance we need to explain not only religious beliefs, but also selection's tolerance for the real costs these bring. Why do we get so worked up about the gods?

Atran seeks to modify Boyer's account through an anomaly he finds in Boyer's data. I gave the example of the memorable MCI dragon. Yet Atran demonstrates that contrary to Boyer and Ramble (2001) and Barrett and Nyhof (2001), we do not, in fact, remember MCI concepts better than we do ordinary intuitive concepts. Atran and Ara Norenzayan tested the claim experimentally, finding that: '[u]nlike other recent studies, intuitive beliefs showed better recall rates than minimally counterintuitive beliefs' (103). Atran attributes this finding to the contextual expectations of participants. Agents are attentive to features they take to be important to the memory studies. They were not expecting to be quizzed about MCI concepts, so did not focus on them (much as we might find it hard to remember all the details of a Greek mythology lecture, unless we expect a test). Yet 'importance' varies according to interests and purposes.

To explain this discrepancy in the data, Atran develops the concept of a 'belief set' which he takes to be the minimal unit of cultural transmission. When concepts are presented through narratives, the salience of MCI concepts does yield the MCI memory effect. More precisely, when delayed recall and rates of memory degradation are considered over time, belief sets that are composed of mostly intuitive notions combined with a few minimally counterintuitive notions do best. 'Minimally counterintuitive beliefs … [a]lthough … themselves are not as memorable as intuitive beliefs, … draw attention to the entire belief set in which they are embedded' (106). Atran points out that his explanation squares better with the historical and anthropological data. It is the stories in which MCI concepts are imbedded that survive.

But how are 'belief sets' represented? Atran points to our robust metarepresentational capacities. Humans are distinctive for our ability to produce rich offline representations of worlds, real and actual. We can remember our first bike ride, imagine Fiji, plan a trip, place life events in an autobiographical time line, and contemplate Shakespeare's characters. Human thought may be intricately decoupled from its immediate surroundings.

This capacity to generate and examine imagined worlds equips us for many tasks – to plot, remember, and plan. But it also enables us to entertain 'belief sets' peppered with MCI concepts. For Atran, 'the meaning of an act of faith is not an inference to a specific proposition or set of propositions, but to an emotionally charged network of partial and changeable descriptions of counterfactual and counterintuitive worlds' (100). Yet why do we believe in these strange narratives? The answer is complex.

Part of the story lies in the cultural context. Because religious narratives are backed with traditional or institutional authority, religious believers accord them truth and significance. Religions are believed in because they are presented as true. But they are also believed in because they enable us to better cope. Through them we deal with aspects of the actual world that 'people wish were otherwise' (113). Religious narratives 'provide the hope and promise of eternal and open-ended solutions through representations of counterintuitive super-natural worlds. This enables people to imagine minimally impossible worlds that appear to solve existential problems, including death and deception' (113). We will come back to this hypothesis about meaning and solace in a moment.

Agency detection

It has long been known that anthropomorphism can be activated with impoverished exposures. In their classic experiment Heider and Simmel (1944) found that participants invent anthropomorphic stories to explain the movements of two-dimensional triangles and squares, items that in their physical properties only marginally resemble ordinary persons. We are incessant animators.

Beginning in 1980, and crystallizing in his 1993 *Faces in the clouds*, Stewart Guthrie developed what may be the first cognitive theory of religion (Guthrie 1993).[5] Guthrie noticed that where the costs of false positives are lower than the cost of true negatives, organisms will tend to evolve agent-projective tenden-cies (see also Barrett 2000). This remains true even where the probability of an agent in the world is low.[6] Perfect perceptual capacities need not evolve.

Atran integrates *Guthrie's* view with Boyer's by considering both lines of research as describing adaptive peaks in an evolutionary landscape. Part of the explanation for *why* we believe, according to Atran, comes through an understanding of *how* we perceive. We are wired to find agents everywhere as a low-cost, high-benefit cognitive strategy. These anthropomorphic algorithms also provide an *evidential basis* for religious belief-sets. Given adaptive anthropomorphism, it is no wonder that we sense MCI agents in the world. We not only *remember* supernatural agents, we also *discover* them. MCI agents become available to our experience of reality.

	agent p	empty $1 - p$
see	A	$-C$
blind	B	0

Average payoffs for action appropriate for agent response where:
p = probability that an agent is there.
$1 - p$ = probability that an agent is not there.
A, B, C, 0 = returns on conditional interactions
Average payoff = $p(A) - (1-p) C > p(B)$

Figure 10.2   Guthrie's wager

In melding Boyer to Guthrie, Atran identifies two important systems that contribute to religious cognition. But there must be others. For it remains unclear why we become so emotionally invested in supernatural reality, and why, so often, religious differences define moral exchange groups.

Costly signaling

Humans are exceptionally cooperative primates. Yet for cooperation to evolve, organisms must be able to reliably estimate trustworthy exchange partners. In a chapter on religion, ritual, and solidarity, Atran describes what has since come to be known[7] as 'the costly signaling theory of religion.'[8] The theory turns on the idea that religions flourish because (1) religions are associated with (in-group) moral principles, and (2) religious agents possess non-arbitrary signaling devices. Costly religious practice functions much as a lie detector. It vets the pious from those who might imitate them for gain.

Consider an analogous problem. Two peacocks have a vested biological interest in persuading a peahen to mate. The hen's preference is for the biologically superior male. Considering arbitrary peacock signals will not further her discernment, for both males would submit: 'I am better.' But signals that clearly co-vary with target properties will solve the hen's dilemma. A bird fit enough to produce and survive gaudy displays proves his endowment. Over time, display competition sets off an evolutionary cascade that elaborates birds with Spielberg-like capacities for spectacle.[9] Signals do not need to be infallible to evolve. They just need to be reliable enough to justify the risks (see Frank 1988, 2001).

Atran documents some egregiously expensive ritual behavior – teeth punching, penis cutting, house burning, pyramid building, and the like (6). However the benefits to cooperation that religion brings are capable of paying for these costs (see Bulbulia 2004; Irons 2001; Sosis 2003). Costs, as signals, are investments. Piety to the gods also motivates and certifies respect for the pious. Yet Atran chides commitment theories for being 'mindblind.' The theories largely emerged from *behavioral* sciences (notably economics and ethology). And of course, these sciences seek to explain behavior. But they do not in general seek to explain behavior's proximate psychological mechanisms. According to Atran, without understanding how religious minds work we cannot explain why religions become especially effective in their special use of supernatural agents to promote in-group morality.[10] Notice that by feeling powerful emotional commitments to the gods, with whom we interact through anthropomorphic experience, we have *added* incentive to cooperate beyond what we might find in purely secular commitments (146). Supernatural eyes see all. And we sense those eyes upon us.

We have considered how cognitive psychology explains the *incidental* attractiveness of religious concepts. Religions, once invented, will often help us. But remember, for Atran religion is no more a biological adaptation for group solidarity than is the Tour de France, the Communist Party, or Alcoholics Anonymous. We are wired to seek and signal common cause, but we are not wired to seek and signal religious causes.

Ritual emotion

Having explained religious morality, we have still not explained religious solidarity – the emotionally powerful identifications of religious persons to their gods and each other. One of the most influential cognitive theories of ritual emotion comes from Harvey Whitehouse. According to Whitehouse's 'modes theory' religious rituals tend to cluster towards one of two basins of attraction (Whitehouse 2000).

Rituals in the 'imagistic mode' are rare but emotion-saturated events that furnish participants with powerful existential purposes. They also (and relatedly) support vivid episodic memories. Imagistic rituals enter into our autobiographical imagination. Because we remember and like those who partake of these rituals with us, social bonds are welded. Imagistic rituals provide what might be called a solidarity of the heart.

On the other hand, rituals in the 'doctrinal mode' happen by way of frequently repeated behaviors that are unsupported by powerful emotions and rich episodic memories. They are tedious. But the repetitions of messages explicitly conveyed by the doctrinal mode facilitate the high-fidelity transmission of specific cultural information – rules of conduct, knowledge of scriptures, interpretations and explanations for the world. Doctrinal rituals activate semantic memory. They furnish permanent knowledge like 'do not cook goats in milk,' 'Prakriti is opposed to Purusha,' 'God is triune,' and other items that can be recorded on a list. Such knowledge retains little autobiographical detail. (Once we learned our names, that apples were edible, and that the earth is round, but we cannot remember when.) Doctrinal rituals provide what might be called a solidarity of laws.

Atran disagrees with Whitehouse's modes theory, for he can find no evidential support. He replaces it with a theory according to which rituals of both varieties activate jointly felt emotions and entrain behavior. He first points out that that stressful experience enhances cohesion directly in complex ways (not merely through the memory of friends or laws). Indeed the data suggest this tendency is stronger when the adversity comes from a known source. 'Intense religious episodes – severe initiations, sudden conversions, mystical revelations – combine aspects of personal memory for stressful events … and socially widespread schema … to ensure lifelong effect' (173).[11]

More interestingly, Atran points to a social dynamic achieved through the use of music and other forms of ritual entraining to coordinate social emotions in what might appear on the face of it to be tedious, repetitive, rituals: 'Humans, it appears are the only animals that spontaneously engage in creative, rhythmic bodily coordination to enhance possibilities for cooperation (e.g., when hammering with a stranger, swaying in a crowd)' (171). What Whitehouse views as boring doctrinal imprinting, Atran views as emotional coordination: 'religious rituals involve sequential, socially interactive movement and gesture (chant, dance, murmur, etc.) and formulaic utterances (liturgies, canonical texts, etc.) that synchronize affective states among group members in displays of cooperative commitment' (172). Indeed: 'Even more frequent, less emotionally intense rituals – daily prayer, weekly services, yearly festivals – affectively manipulate and rhythmically coordinate actors' minds and bodies into convergent expressions of public sentiment: a sort of N-person courtship' (173). For Atran both rare and repetitive rituals cause, as well as signal, solidarity and commitment.

The Tragedy of Cognition

So far Atran's solution to the cost problem may strike readers as a hodge-podge of cognitive and biological theories. Yet combining distinct bodies of research is not as easy as raking leaves. Showing how to reconcile that which is correct in Boyer, Guthrie, Whitehouse, and hundreds of empirical studies is no mean feat, for the theories make different and sometimes incompatible claims. And we have seen that Atran frequently introduces novel research of his own.

One particular novelty that finds little reflection in other cognitive theories of religion relates to existential concern (though see Bering 2003). If we do not require *specifically* religious concepts to fuel success, why do supernatural concepts remain incorrigible? Atran departs from the modular view of mind to consider facts about our global rationality. He notices that unlike other organisms, we are smart enough to richly represent ourselves as individuals with futures. And so we are able to appreciate the inevitability of death. The emotional fallout from this knowledge dramatically enhances religion's appeal. To lose religion amounts to losing life.

[P]eople cannot avoid overwhelming inductive evidence predicting their own death and that of persons to whom they are emotionally tied, such as relatives, friends, and leaders. The emotions compel such inductions and make them salient and terrifying. This is 'the Tragedy of Cognition'. (66)

Supernatural belief is profoundly appealing, our only avenue of escape. In support of this view, Atran reports an experiment demonstrating that making mortality awareness explicit (imagining one's death) leads to substantial increases in religious conviction (see Norenzayan and Atran 2002). Merely thinking about death strengthens belief in life eternal.

Adaptationism revisited

In my view, the strength of Atran's book lies in its attempt to bridge two important literatures – cognitive theories of mind and commitment theories of solidarity, while addressing weaknesses in each.

> The criterion of costly commitment appears to rule out purely cognitive theories of religion as sufficient. Such theories are motiveless … The criterion of belief in the supernatural rules out commitment theories of religion as sufficient, such theories are mindblind, in that they ignore the cognitive structure of the mind and its causal role … such theories can't distinguish strong secular ideologies from religious belief. (264)

Resulting from this combination is a subtle theory according to which religion emerges through multiple cognitive resources. Religion is information flowing to cognitive sinks created by numerous, discrete psychological systems – a kind of mental Alpine range. Atran's explanation is complicated, but so too is the mind. And while the explanation is complex, it minimizes the attribution of design to these cognitive systems. For it dispenses with a special 'religion' faculty. This minimalism is laudable because it leaves less about the mind to be explained.

To me, however, the marriage of commitment theory to cognitive psychology suggests rather strongly that religiosity is the product of a biologically adapted system – that there is a religion faculty. Religious commitments not only respond to various cognitive systems, they *activate* some of the most powerful emotions and motivations of which we are capable, reliably affecting behavior (see Johnson and Bering 2006; Norenzayan and Shariff 2007; Sosis, Kress, and Boster 2007). In religion, selection has mixed the nitrogen of error with the glycerin of desire. Yet these activations are finely articulated to avoid harm and support success. For though powerful and unrelated to natural utilities, religious commitments tend to cause inference only to specific behaviors. Religious persons may believe in peaceful after-worlds, but nevertheless fear and avoid death. They may believe in supernatural justice but still punish scoundrels. They may believe that God will provide, yet still provide for themselves. They may hate tyrants, but love a god who demands worship – that is, a tyrant. So religion looks peculiarly encapsulated. Religious inferences tend *not* to be globally damaging. To my mind this subtle articulation looks like design, and ever since Darwin, our best explanation for design has been selection. Moreover we should want to know whether religion is the product, rather than by-product of selective forces, because with this knowledge we can better reverse-engineer religious minds, revealing further complexity. The question remains methodologically relevant (see Bulbulia 2007a).

There is another, more serious deficit in Atran's position, one that centers on an issue that has become increasingly important to evolutionary and cognitive scientists. Recall that Atran urges that cultures influence mind design only minimally and at the margins. Substantially all religious minds are the same and religion emerges as a 'human universal.'

This idea that minds organize cultural complexity works well for language. A child knows vastly more about language than she learns. Yet evolutionary psychologists now recognize that language may be exceptional. Selection acts on phenotypes in populations, but it need not manipulate *genes* to do so. Children receive beneficial information from their parents (and others) epigenetically through the transmission of ideas. We appear to have *evolved* the capacity for culture as an epigenetic developmental system, one capable of building more functionally adapted brains. Indeed many competencies are assembled through cultural inputs and structured social learning. The knowledge and skill required for Inuit sled-making does not spring from our genome. Indeed many skills have been around long enough to predate humans. Stone industries, foraging techniques, the control of fire, and other capacities vastly enriched the lives of our ancestors. Many – like fire – were universals. But they were transmitted outside the genome. Fire has been with us for at least 600,000 years (probably for over a million), but there has never been a fire combustion gene (see Sterelny 2003). Moreover, the importance of externally stored design has produced a dramatic life-history effect. Maturation in our lineage is slow. Children and adolescents do not begin to repay their resource debts until their late teens (see Richerson and Boyd 2005; Sterelny 2003). The gains made possible through this long period of learning come at a cost.

Figure 10.3 Religious culture as cognitive noise

Indeed the emerging consensus view among evolutionary psychologists is that learning environments matter to the development of adaptive systems. As Tooby and Cosmides write:

> Genes underlying adaptations are selected so that, in development, genes and specific aspects of the world interact to cause the reliable development of a well-designed adaptation ... This means that information and structure necessary for the proper development of an adaptation may be stored in the world as well as in the genome, and that selection will shape developmental programs to exploit information-rich features of the world. (Tooby and Cosmides 2001: 15)

And we should not be surprised that this is so. Selection, the great economizer, will shift the informational burden from a genome to an external resource wherever it can do so reliably. As Dennett anthropomorphizes: 'Mother Nature is not gene centrist!' (Dennett 2006: 127).

So culture provides an efficient evolutionary vehicle for the transmission of potentially adaptive information. Through it, adaptations may bypass slow and wasteful genetic tinkering. And because cultural information is copied with reasonably high fidelity, culture evolves. The methods of evolutionary biology, then, may be marshaled to the task of its explanation (Boyd and Richerson 1985). In the cognitive study of religion, we poorly describe the cognitive organization of the mind by focusing *only* on its entrenched modular features (Geertz 2008; Jensen 2004). Much work in the cognitive study of religion since Atran has pursued co-evolutionary themes, seeking precise explanations for how eReligions evolve to matter to religious cognition (see Bulbulia 2008; Day 2004).[12]

Of course, none of these relatively recent horizons in the study of cognition and religion support 'general learning.' Nor (to my mind) do they undermine the motivations for approaching thought computationally. It is insufficient to notice that thought crucially depends on the world. Atran is right to notice that such locutions only dignify mystery with a slogan. The trick is to precisely explain the dynamics of that dependence. This work lies ahead of us.

Final comment

Earlier I mentioned that one of Atran's most important contributions comes through his integration of wide-ranging literatures drawn from a large number of distinct empirical subfields. Though I have focused on Atran's use of evolutionary and experimental literatures, the book is interfused with empirical materials drawn from the work of anthropologists, historians,

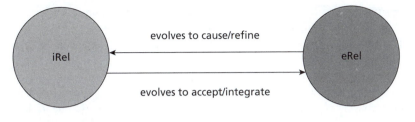

Figure 10.4 Reformed model

and scholars of religion. Theories and evidence do not come pre-fitted, as pieces of a jigsaw. Figuring out how to relate the results of disparate scientific and social scientific projects requires understanding the implications of work not originally conceived for partnership. But conceptual integration is not merely difficult; it is an absolute intellectual obligation. Consistency is *not merely* a scientific virtue, it is a norm regulating all scholarly (indeed rational) exchange. Whether or not we are accountable for another's beliefs and commitments, we are certainly accountable for our own.

Most of us accept Darwinian evolution. And most accept that thought cannot depend on miracles. Atran shows us how much follows from these widely held assumptions. Whatever the relevance of culturally supplied information to religious thinking, religious thought would not be possible were the architecture of the mind not already richly elaborated to support it. We can know that selection forges this design. (Though I have suggested that *In gods we trust* underestimated the degree to which selection exploits epigenetic resources – culture – to support adaptive cognitive design.) And we can rule out any explanation based on general learning or general intelligence as hopeless. Moreover, we can know that our subjective experience, taken in isolation, is probably a poor guide to scientific discovery. The theologian's chair is an imprecise instrument. The care with which Atran used the best available science of his day to follow the implications of these reminders set a new standard of excellence. It has yet to be matched.

Notes

1   www.nytimes.com/2007/03/04/magazine/04evolution.t.html?pagewanted=1
2   For alternatives, see Day 2004; Geertz 2009; Schjodt 2007.
3   Call these biologically entrenched computational features of a religious person's mind (Atrans's *explanandum*): iReligion (i = innate). Call those extra-skeletal material and informational elements that precede and survive an agent's life eReligion (e = cultural). This follows a common distinction in linguistics, between iLanguage and eLanguage, see Chomsky 2000; Bulbulia, 2005. The distinction applied to religion emerged through interchanges with Armin Geertz.

4   See Jeppe Sinding Jensen's chapter on Pascal Boyer in this volume.
5   See Benson Saler's chapter on Stewart Guthrie in this volume.
6   More precisely: $p(A) - (1 - p)C > p(B)$, where p = probability of encounter and $p-1$ = probability of no encounter.
7   For better or worse, see Bulbulia, 2007b.
8   The ideas originate in Schelling 1960 and Frank 1988 and are developed in Iannaccone 1992 and especially Irons 1996, 2001. Moreover, the theory has been empirically tested in Sosis 2000; Sosis and Bressler 2003; and more recently by Soler 2007.
9   Any reader interested in the generality of costly signaling systems should read the work of Zahavi and Zahavi (1997), who observe the rampancy of costly signaling in nature. Moreover rigorous mathematical models demonstrate their adequacy for solving cooperative dilemmas (Grafen 1990; Johnstone 2000).
10 Irons himself would agree, for he does not think religious affiliation is especially motivating, see Irons 2007.
11 I am unsure Whitehouse would see differences worth any distinction to the imagistic theory here.
12 We return to this position in the chapter on David Sloan Wilson's work.

References

Atran, S., 1986. *Fondements de l'histoire naturelle. Pour une anthropologie de la science*. Editions Complexe, Brussels.

Atran, S., 2002. *In gods we trust: the evolutionary landscape of religion*. Oxford University Press, New York.

Barrett, J.L., 2000. Exploring the natural foundations of religion. *Trends in Cognitive Sciences* 4 (1), 29–34.

Barrett, J.L. and Nyhof, M., 2001. Spreading nonnatural concepts. *Journal of Cognition and Culture* 1, 183–201.

Barsalou, L.W., Niedenthal, P.M., Barbey, A., and Ruppert, J., 2003. Social embodiment. In: Ross, B. (Ed.), *The psychology of learning and motivation*, vol. 43. Academic Press, San Diego, 43–92.

Bering, J., 2003. Towards a cognitive theory of existential meaning. *New Ideas in Psychology* 21, 101–20.

Boyd, R. and Richerson, P., 1985. *Culture and the evolutionary process*. University of Chicago Press, Chicago.

Boyer, P. and Ramble, C., 2001. Cognitive templates for religious concepts: cross-cultural evidence for recall of counter-intuitive representations. *Cognitive Science* 25, 535–64.

Bulbulia, J., 2004. Religious costs as adaptations that signal altruistic intention. *Evolution and Cognition* 10 (1), 19–38.

Bulbulia, J., 2005. Are there any religions? *Method & Theory in the Study of Religion* 17 (2), 71–100.

Bulbulia, J., 2007a. Evolution and religion. In: Dunbar, R.I. and Barrett, L. (Eds.), *Oxford handbook of evolutionary psychology*. Oxford University Press, New York, 621–36.

Bulbulia, J., 2007b. Free love: religious solidarity on the cheap. In: Bulbulia, J., Sosis, R., Genet, R., Harris, E., Wyman, K., and Genet, C. (Eds.), *The evolution of religion: studies, theories, and critiques*. Collins Foundation Press, Santa Margarita, 153–60.

Bulbulia, J., 2008. Meme infection or religious niche construction? An adaptationist alternative to the cultural maladaptationist hypothesis. *Method & Theory in the Study of Religion* 20, 1–42.

Chomsky, N., 2000. *New horizons in the study of language and mind*. Cambridge University Press, New York.

Cosmides, L. and Tooby, J., 1992. The psychological foundations of culture. In: Barkow, J.H., Cosmides, L., and Tooby, J. (Eds.), *The adapted mind: evolutionary psychology and the generation of culture*. Oxford University Press, New York, 19–36.

Day, M., 2004. Religion, off-line cognition and the extended mind. *Journal of Cognition and Culture* 4 (1), 101–21.

Dennett, D., 2006. *Breaking the spell: religion as a natural phenomenon*. Viking Adult, New York.

Fodor, J.A., 1985. Precis of 'The Modularity of Mind'. *Behavioral and Brain Sciences* 8, 1–42.

Frank, R., 1988. *Passions within reason: the strategic role of the emotions*. W.W. Norton & Company, New York.

Frank, R., 2001. Cooperation through emotional commitment. In: Nesse, P. (Ed.), *Evolution and the capacity for commitment*. Russell Sage Foundation, New York, 57–77.

Geertz, A., 2008. From apes to devils and angels. In: Bulbulia, J., Sosis, R., Genet, R., Harris, E., Wyman, K., and Genet, C. (Eds.), *The evolution of religion: studies, theories, and critiques*. Collins Foundation Press, Santa Margarita, 43–9.

Geertz, A., 2009. Gossip as religious narrative: cognitive and psychological perspectives. In: Geertz, A. and Jensen, J. (Eds.), *Fantastic re-collection: cultural vs. autobiographical memory in the exodus narrative*. Equinox, London.

Gould, S.J. and Lewontin, R. C., 1979. The spandrels of San Marco and the Panglossian program: A critique of the adaptationist programme. *Proceedings of the Royal Society of London* 250, 281–8.

Grafen, A., 1990. Biological signals as handicaps. *Journal of Theoretical Biology* 144, 517–46.

Guthrie, S., 1993. *Faces in the clouds: a new theory of religion*. Oxford University Press, New York.

Heider, F. and Simmel, M., 1944. An experimental study of apparent behavior. *American Journal of Psychology* 57, 243–9.

Iannaccone, L.R., 1992. Sacrifice and stigma: reducing free-riding in cults, communes, and other collectives. *Journal of Political Economy* 100, 271–91.

Irons, W., 1996. Morality, religion, and evolution. In: Richardson, W.M. (Ed.), *Religion and science: history, method, and dialogue*. Routledge, New York, 375–99.

Irons, W., 2001. Religion as hard-to-fake sign of commitment. In: Nesse, R. (Ed.), *Evolution and the capacity for commitment*. Russell Sage Foundation, New York.

Irons, W., 2007. Why people believe (what other people see as) crazy ideas. In: Bulbulia, J., Sosis, R., Genet, R., Harris, E., Wyman, K., and Genet, C. (Eds.), *The evolution of religion: studies, theories, and critiques*. Collins Foundation Press, Santa Margarita, 51–60.

Jensen, J., 2004. *The study of religion in a new key*. Aarhus University Press, Aarhus.

Johnson, D. and Bering, J., 2006. Hand of God, mind of man: punishment and cognition in the evolution of cooperation. *Human Nature* 4, 219–33.

Johnstone, R.A., 2000. Models of reproductive skew: a review and synthesis. *Ethology* 106, 5–26.

Norenzayan, A. and Atran, S., 2002. Cognitive and emotional processes in the cultural transmission of natural and nonnatural beliefs. In: Schaller, M. and Crandall, C. (Eds.), *The psychological foundations of culture*. Erlbaum, Hillsdale, NJ, 149–69.

Norenzayan, A. and Shariff, A., 2007. God is watching you: priming god concepts increases prosocial behavior in an anonymous economic game. *Psychological Science* 18, 803–9.

Richerson, P. and Boyd, R., 2005. *Not by genes alone: how culture transformed human evolution*. University of Chicago Press, Chicago.

Schelling, T., 1960. *The strategy of conflict*. Oxford University Press, New York.

Schjodt, U., 2007. Homeostasis and religious behaviour. *Journal of Cognition and Culture* 7 (3–4), 313–40.

Soler, M., 2007. Commitment costs and cooperation: evidence from Candomble and Afro-Brazilian religion. In: Bulbulia, J., Sosis, R., Genet, R., Harris, E., Wyman, K., and Genet, C. (Eds.), *The evolution of religion: studies, theories, and critiques*. Collins Foundation Press, Santa Margarita, 167–74.

Sosis, R., 2000. Religion and intragroup cooperation: preliminary results of a comparative analysis of utopian communities. *Cross-Cultural Research* 34 (1), 77–88.

Sosis, R., 2003. Why aren't we all Hutterites? *Human Nature* 14 (2), 91–127.

Sosis, R. and Bressler, E., 2003. Co-operation and commune longevity: a test of the costly signaling theory of religion. *Cross-Cultural Research* 37 (2), 11–39.

Sosis, R., Kress, H., and Boster, J., 2007. Scars for war. *Evolution and Human Behavior* 28, 234–47.

Sterelny, K., 2003. *Thought in a hostile world: the evolution of human cognition*. Blackwell, Oxford.

Tooby, J. and Cosmides, L., 2001. Does beauty build adapted minds? Toward an evolutionary theory of aesthetics, fiction and the arts. *Substance* 95, 6–27.

Whitehouse, H., 2000. *Arguments and icons*. Oxford University Press, Oxford.

Zahavi, A. and Zahavi, A., 1997. *The handicap principle: a missing piece of Darwin's puzzle*. Oxford University Press, New York, Oxford.

11

Religion as superorganism

On David Sloan Wilson, Darwin's cathedral (2002)

Joseph Bulbulia and Marcus Frean

One of the most important biological theories of religion is also the most controversial. Here we describe and partially defend David Sloan Wilson's group selectionist model. According to Wilson, religions are best explained as 'superorganisms' adapted to succeed in competition against others. The evolutionary history of religion is a battle of these titans.

Background

Biographical sketch

Wilson was born in 1949 in Norwalk, Connecticut. He is the son of the late novelist Sloan Wilson, author of fifteen books including *The man in the gray flannel suit* (1955) and *The ice brothers* (1979). David Wilson received his PhD in evolutionary biology from Michigan State in 1975. He soon became notorious among biologists as a zealous defender of group selection, the theory that evolution operates at multiple levels of biological organization, not just on genes. Sticking up for group selection in the 1970s was a bit like wearing a flashing neon 'kick me' sign. This was the era of the 'selfish gene' – phenotypes were considered vehicles of benefit for perennial DNA, and selection's targets were thought to be limited to genetic substrates. In 1966 the eminent evolutionary biologist George Williams published *Adaptation and natural selection*, which most took to be a knock-down refutation of group selection (Williams 1966). Within ten years Richard Dawkins's enormously popular book *The selfish gene* hit the presses, taking the gene's-eye view to the masses (Dawkins 1989 [1976]). Apart from Wilson, almost no credible biologist at the time believed in group selection. Now, thanks to Wilson and friends, nearly everyone does, though under the less threatening slogan: 'multilevel selection.' This version integrates a mathematically correct account of group selection to Williams's and Dawkins's selfish gene perspective. Our genes, it turns out, can eat their cake and share it too.[1]

Wilson's latest battle lies on the methodological frontiers of religious studies. *Darwin's cathedral* (hereafter *DC*) promotes an 'organismic concept of religious groups' as a 'serious scientific hypothesis' (1). For Wilson, the testing and development of this hypothesis relies on the collaborative efforts of both scientists and traditionally trained scholars of religion. His shibboleth: without biological theory, religious studies is blind; lacking scholarly data, biological speculation is empty.

Individualism and holism in evolutionary studies

Standard cognitive models explain religiosity in terms of biological endowment – a mental *Bauplan*. A child requires only minimal cultural inputs to grow her religion. Religions are modeled as body parts: we do not learn to build our kidneys, fabricate our jaws, or color our bones white.[2] Nor do we learn most features of our religions. Learning triggers an already entrenched design.

Cognitive theories have their rivals. An increasingly popular alternative views religion as an adaptation, though not ours. According to meme theorists, exogenously transmitted religious ideas are best conceived as replicators that infect religious minds, much like viruses. Becoming religious is like catching a cold.[3]

Wilson urges that both naturalistic pictures are misconceived: they telescope to the wrong level of selection. To understand the evolution of religious traits we need to appreciate the evolutionary forces acting on religious groups. For Wilson, religious adaptations are group-level adaptations. A 'group' is made up of those members sharing traits that impact on how members relate to each other. Religions evolve to promote and secure traits for solidarity.

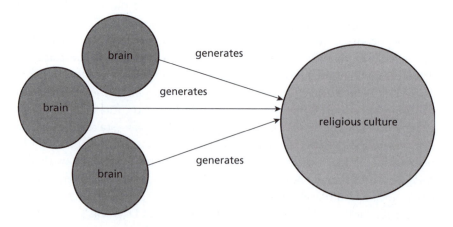

Figure 11.1 The standard cognitive picture

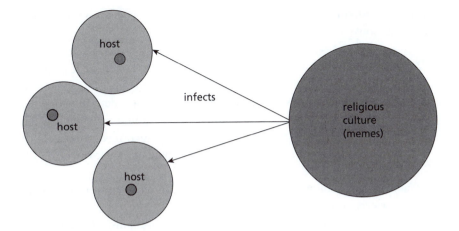

Figure 11.2   Religion as cognovirus

DC defends three theses about group selection and the evolution of religion.

Thesis 1: Beyond genes in human evolution

'This book is about evolution but it is not restricted to genetic evolution' (11).

The averaging fallacy

From the anti-group selection perspective, biological fitness is averaged across populations. Wilson argues that this method commits an 'averaging fallacy' (14) (see also Sober and Wilson 1998). Suppose we identify a 'group' in virtue of some trait shared by its members.[4] If a selfish action increases the fitness of an individual but decreases the fitness of her trait group, then over time we expect that the selfish trait will diminish in absolute frequency. Individuals in groups lacking group-demoting

Figure 11.3   Darwin's cathedral

selfishness will do better than will selfish individuals going it alone. Wilson reasons:

> When the trait is a non-social behaviour that alters the fitness of the individual alone, we needn't concern ourselves with groups. But when the trait is a social behaviour, the fitness of an individual is determined by its own trait and the traits of the individuals with whom it interacts. These individuals constitute the group, which must be identified accurately to calculate the fitnesses that determine the outcome of evolution. (15)

Averaging across groups rules out group selection by definition. But there are no a prioris in science.

If we consider altruism to be an evolutionary mechanism for *collective* benefit, then another layer of evolutionary adaptation emerges: the functional properties of groups. These properties are invisible when we limit our perspective to relations between individuals. To perceive relevant design we need to look a level up (see below).

Culture matters to development

There has been enough migration between human populations to make it implausible to think that human groups are organisms in the way that Mr. P is an organism. In humans, the germ-line is segregated early in development. The interests of those genes that build Mr. P's brain are intimately bound to the fate of his sex cells, which (if all goes well for P) make genetic copies in offspring. However, if P finds better opportunities in another group he can always try to cut and run. So the analogy of groups to organisms must be qualified.

Wilson argues that cultural transmission holds the key to understanding the evolutionary dynamics of human groups. Children resemble their parents because children share parental genes. But children also learn from their parents. Adaptive structure is often exported from the genome to the environment. Social transmission provides a crucial information channel for replicating adaptive traits. Wilson writes: 'it is important to think of heritability as a correlation between parents and offspring, caused by any mechanism. This definition will enable us to go beyond genes in our analysis of human evolution' (7).

Wilson observes that minds are genetically designed for developmental flexibility. This position is most assuredly warranted for many skills and capacities. A !Kung child is not born with an innate knowledge of bow manufacture or the seasonality of *mongongo* nuts. She is rather born to absorb and improve information supplied by family and peers. 'Far from marginalizing culture, innate psychology provides the building blocks from which innumerable cultural structures have been built' (198–9).

Our minds have co-evolved preferences and capacities to keep up with the latest development. The flexibility has enabled our lineage to master (and degrade) nearly every terrestrial habitat, without having to anticipate every habitat in our genes. Most importantly, flexibility holds an important key to unpacking the evolutionary dynamics of group selection without relying on genetic substrates.

Cultural evolution

Suppose that social learning provides a vehicle for the transmission of functionally adaptive traits. Selection will then act in two directions. First it will modify the genetic substrates that facilitate social learning. Benefiting culture will select for genes that support its acquisition. Selection will also act on the information itself. As with genetic information, useful cultural inventions will tend to be transmitted, and harmful information will tend to go extinct. Cultural products themselves will evolve.[5]

Suppose there arises some culturally transmissible information effective at combating defection. The individuals who are prone to the 'altruistic traits' this information builds will tend to form larger functional units that enable members to survive better than they would going through the world alone.[6] The trait may spread vertically from parent to child, or horizontally and obliquely among unrelated agents. Through social learning, mean fitness within the group will rise.

Notice, as the trait-group increases, perhaps to a limiting threshold, the total number of individuals in the population nevertheless remains fixed. Cultural evolution need not lead to population expansion or decline if individuals merely 'change hats.' Competition will drive the evolution of information that better facilitates altruistic learning, as cultural selection ratifies cooperation technologies. Innovations that increase group-size thresholds may also arise and spread.

In this scenario, cultural transmission enables the evolution of effective groups without requiring that genetic adaptations do all the work. Culturally encoded group selection can thus operate in genetically well-mixed populations. Through cultural transmission we find the evolutionary resources for evolving human superorganisms.[7]

Wilson observes:

Darwin's solution to the fundamental problem of social life is elegant and perhaps even obvious in retrospect. After all, if adaptations evolve by differential survival and reproduction, it makes sense that group-level adaptations evolve by the differential survival and reproduction of groups. (9)

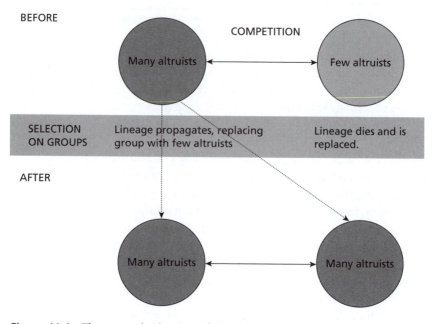

Figure 11.4   The natural selection of altruistic groups

So in short, cultural transmission appears to give rise to a new species of hopeful monsters. God-fearing evolves Godzilla.

So what?

Wilson's evolutionary model is supposed to enable us to reverse-engineer group-level design. 'We fail to see the evidence, not because it is obscure or requires sophisticated measuring devices, but because we are employing the wrong theories' (125). A better theory focuses observation to epigenetic systems of heritable variation. It also attends to the evolution of the information transmitted by these systems, over historical timescales, in the face of specific cultural-selective pressures. In the next section, we shall consider how the model mines for culturally acquired traits capable of binding individuals into efficient, competitive exchange groups and directs attention to the role of institutions in monitoring and enforcing social norms. But the model's importance extends beyond the refinement of observation. It is also meant to teach us an important lesson about ourselves: our traditions constitute our natures.

Wilson thinks that it is in our culturally evolved natures to be cooperative. Religion's role in the evolution of human sociality leads to the second major thesis of his book.

Thesis 2: Religion is a group-level adaptation to enhance in-group cooperation

'Evolutionary theory explains how social groups can be like individuals in the harmony and coordination of their parts' (2).

The evolution of cooperation

Throughout nature, cooperation abounds. Genes work together to create chromosomes, which combine to fashion cells. Cells cooperate in the tissues of organs. These aggregate to form bodies. Organisms team up with other organisms. Cooperation exists at every level of the biological hierarchy. From the slime mould *Dictyostelium*[8] to UNESCO, creatures unite in larger functional units. In our own lineage no one survives alone. Our partnerships are many, complex, and obligatory.

Cooperation is surprising. Evolution by natural selection is a theory of success through competition: 'from the war of nature, from famine and death, the most exalted object which we are capable of conceiving ... directly follows' (Darwin 1988/1859: 649). The image suggests combat. Yet we observe much harmony: 'endless forms most beautiful and most wonderful' (ibid.). Why?

Cooperation and coordination as evolutionary problems

Cooperation may appear inevitable where the average benefits of transactions exceed their average costs. However, selection is shortsighted. Tax-supported society beats the state of nature. But we do better by avoiding our taxes, irrespective of whether others pay theirs. The problem iterates and generalizes. We do better letting others fight the war. We could earn money, though unpunished crime pays better.

The efforts of one often make little difference to a cooperative outcome. Cooperative benefits compile over many transactions. Best-response dynamics frequently doom cooperation. Mutually beneficial trade requires mechanisms that suppress defection.

Matters, indeed, are worse. Even among those who share common cause with *no defection incentives*, cooperation faces significant evolutionary obstacles. 'Even when [defection problems] can be solved ... formidable problems of coordination remain' (109).

A coordination problem arises where individuals can benefit from joint action, with no threat of cheating. Here uncertainty rather than cheating threatens cooperation, ratifying sub-optimal patterns of interaction. Indeed risk-averse strategies dominate optimal exchange over time (see Young 1998).

Rousseau poses the problem through a story about a hunt (Rousseau 1984/1754). Suppose that hunting stags brings a higher average payoff (more meat) than hunting hares. However, suppose a team of hunters is required to bring down a stag, whereas solitary hunters can capture hares. Solitary hunting pays less, but the payoff is assured. Suppose further that as each hunter opts out of a stag hunt, the probability of capturing the big meat parcel falls. Suppose further that the probability of success if all hunt is 1; 'defection' does not pay better than cooperation. The maximally bene-fiting equilibrium is available, then, but the risk not all will choose it brings incentive to the sub-optimal choice. Benefits of additional winnings may not be worth the risk of starvation. Hunters require motivating conventions.

Coordination problems also iterate and generalize (see Bicchieri 2006; Harsanyi and Selton 1988; Skyrms 2004). Here, too, a mechanism securing exchange is required. Coordinated action is far from fated.[9]

Selfish genes or cooperative teams?

From the selfish-gene perspective, altruism remains evolvable only where average returns exceed average costs (or the cost-to-benefit ratio > likelihood of gain) (Nowak 2006).[10] The relevant literatures explain how altruism is possible, but on their own do not explain any particular mechanism that assures it. For this we need to consider specific cases and systems. We do not *discover* the functions of a white blood cell by looking at how its actions help the cell itself to survive. Leukocytes are typically suicidal. Instead we examine cellular activity in the context of a larger functional system. So too for the explanation of human behaviors arising through multilevel selection.

Wilson hypothesizes that religious traits evolve to functionally integrate the behaviors of persons who share them. Religions evolve as superorgan-isms. And the behavior of religious individuals can only be properly framed as part to these wholes.

	others hunt stag	one or more hunt alone*
you hunt stag	eat well	starve
* you hunt hare	eat poorly	eat poorly

* = risk-averse (evolutionarily stable)

Figure 11.5 Coordination problem

Subversion from within

While groups may behave like 'organisms,' group selection is not evolutionarily fated: 'the days of axiomatically thinking of groups as adaptive units are gone forever. Special conditions are required that may or may not be satisfied in the real world. Opposing forces exist that may or may not be overcome' (10).

The most damaging of these is internal subversion. Where group selection is weak, and where migration remains possible, unpunished defectors in cooperation dilemmas will out-compete cooperators. Defection undermines functional evolution at a higher level of organization (see Sterelny 2007).

Similarly, group selection predicts culturally evolved mechanisms for diminishing selfish individualism within groups. These include systems of internal monitoring, censure, punishment, and exile. 'Social control, rather than highly self-sacrificial altruism, appears to solve the fundamental problem of social life at the individual level' (19).

We shall shortly see that Wilson considers religious beliefs to be exquisite devices for generating altruistic motivation. But he thinks they are insufficient to prevent social breakdown. Instead, groups require specific policing institutions:

> No matter how powerful, a belief system by itself is probably insufficient to turn a group into a societal organism. A social organization is also required to enforce [norms] ... all adaptive units, including individual organisms, require mechanisms to prevent subversion from within (105).

We think Wilson underestimates the efficiency and power of religious belief in preventing outlaws. Where believers are able to find each other's cooperation does not require an institution. The problem turns on the effectiveness of mechanisms for distinguishing the genuinely god-fearing from defecting frauds. We agree with those who notice that the emotional and ritual activity of a religious group produces reliable signaling, enabling the relevant correlation (for example Alcorta and Sosis 2005; Irons 2001; Schloss 2007). Institutions matter to ritual signaling, for there are few rituals without institutions. Moreover institutions teach, disseminate, and maintain marking conventions. But they need not punish the uncooperative, at least not straightforwardly. For example, individuals can punish by withholding cooperation to those who do not follow a convention. To be fair, Wilson observes the prospects for effective signaling in a discussion of Iannaccone 1992 (*DC*: 81–3). But he does not identify signaling practices as a core feature of religious altruism, as Sosis (2003) laments. Though we cannot pursue the issue here, we think this oversight leads to an incorrect view of religious institutions as *primarily* vigilance and punishment machines.

Signaling aside, there nevertheless remains much institutional policing. The heresy trials, witch-hunts, and inquisitions of the past suggest that groups will tolerate much intra-group viciousness in the service of wider group benefits. Indeed the prospect of violence looms large for any group threatened by internal subversion, not merely for religious groups.

Conflict

The prospects for brutality become more apparent when we consider inter-group competition. 'Group selection does not eliminate conflict, but rather elevates it up the biological hierarchy, from among individuals within groups to among groups within a larger population' (10).

Observe that internal violence is constrained by selection at the level of groups. At the limit, a group cannot harm all its members and remain viable. This is not true of group aggression. Where resources remain limited, so that not all groups can peacefully coexist, competition between groups of altruists will produce hostility. Wilson sees no prescription for universal love. There is no assurance whatsoever that a successful group will act with moral goodness, towards its members and towards others.

One form of particularly dangerous altruism is sacrificial violence on behalf of god or country (for evidence see Bulbulia and Mahoney 2008). Wilson's model predicts that strong selection will evolve groups of suspicion, anger, and spite.

So what?

Let's consider Wilson's evolutionary picture more carefully. It might appear that cultural evolution brings wide scope to religious variation. 'Applying these insights to the study of religion, we should think of religious groups as rapidly evolving entities adapted to their current environments' (35). If religion is solidarity technology, then religions should differ over place and time – much as the subsistence and extraction practices of Siberian foragers, Navaho desert peoples, and posh New Yorkers vary. We think it worth considering whether the opposite is true.

No one is as well aware of religious change as are historians of religion. Overwhelming scholarly evidence suggests that religions are not eternal monoliths but rather creatures of time in constant flux. Nevertheless some core features of religious culture resist change over millennia. For example, the gods and scriptures, and many of the arcane rites, of ancient pastoral peoples remain dominant to this day. When we compare this localized conservation to other domains of civilization we find important contrasts. Technological change appears exponential. Political systems, too, are in

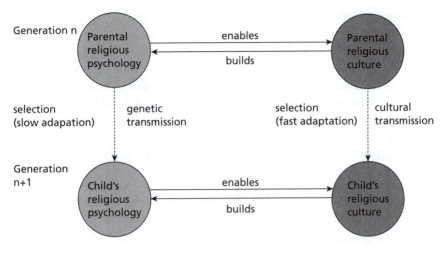

Figure 11.6 Developmental processes

flux, as are the relations among nations. Language pronunciation shifts gradually. Shakespeare's English is difficult and Chaucer's baffles. Gradually, over generations of mutually intelligible language speakers, the vocabulary, phonetics, and grammar of English drifted. By contrast, the rate of religious change for some core traditional features appears comparatively slow. A quick glance at the dominant world religions reveals the gods and scriptures of modern peoples were fixed many centuries or even millennia ago. This suggests a strong principle of localized conservation. Whatever the explanation for this conservation,[11] rates of variation within religious culture are patchy, and in some of its central features, religious culture appears surprisingly resistant to evolutionary change.

What about variation among different traditions? If religion were language-like, we could make a case for biologically fixed 'religious grammars' that develop along entrenched developmental pathways. Yet cultural transmission *in principle* allows for rapid evolution, thus expanding the universe of potential religions. So entrenchment cannot be assumed on developmental grounds alone.

There are, however, further grounds for predicting constraints. If Wilson's evolutionary hypothesis is correct, religious variation will be inhibited by the functions for which religions are selected: the demands of community-building. The *means* by which humans forge religious solidarity may be narrowly circumscribed. The *outputs* of religious solidarity may be narrower still. These demands may well over-determine the functional architectures embedded in human religions. Not just any design will work. Loving thy co-religionist and converting/abusing others look like candidates for invariant properties. In short, diversity may be limited, not by a mental *Bauplan*, but rather by the optimization of interaction.

Finally, solidarity theory predicts similarity will be difficult to perceive. Overlooking what we have in common will often be functionally (if not morally) desirable. It is tough shelling persons whose religion appears, branding aside, virtually identical to our own (Bulbulia 2005).

The functionality of religious beliefs forms the subject of Wilson's third thesis, which we shall presently explore. For now, we maintain that the bandwidth of religious variation remains an open question.

Thesis 3: Religious outlooks enhance solidarity through 'practical realism'

'The fog – if that is what it deserves to be called – only descends in some contexts' (41).

Wilson distinguishes between what he calls 'factual realism' and 'practical realism.' The terms designate two distinct modes of dealing with the world. Factual realism refers to beliefs that accurately describe the world, regardless of their practical value. Practical realism refers to beliefs that are useful, regardless of their factual basis. Evolutionary reasoning suggests that we will affirm propositions that are useful, regardless of whether they are true. Roughly, where the benefit of believing is greater than the cost of holding the belief, selection will favor belief (for a formal treatment see Foster and Kokko 2009).[12] The veracity of a belief will often play a role in its utility, but not always. For example, it may be adaptive to think of myself as competent, to better fool others into helping me. Evolution predicts a bias, whether I am or not (see Trivers 2001). Wilson writes: 'There are many, many other situations in which it can be adaptive to distort reality. Even massively fictitious beliefs can be adaptive, as long as they motivate behaviours that are adaptive in the real world' (41). On Wilson's model, religions do not evolve for accuracy. They evolve to secure harmony. Notice, the question of whether the gods exist is left open. Importantly, religious beliefs may be true or false. But whether or not we believe in them has to do with their evolutionary effects. Factual reason, on the other hand, is the product of the self-correcting process exemplified by scientific inquiry. Here, the aim is to determine how the world is, irrespective of whether beliefs help us to make more babies or build stronger communities.

The means by which practical realism generates solidarity, Wilson hypothesizes, is through the compelling manipulation of expectation and affect:

> We might therefore expect moral systems to be designed to trigger powerful emotional impulses, linking joy with right, fear with wrong,

	Selected for	True	False
Practical realism	Biological utility effect of belief > cost/benefit of holding belief	Mother bears are dangerous.	I am a trustworthy politician.
Factual realism	Accuracy	Our universe is expanding.	Whales are fish.

Figure 11.7   Evolution: utility versus accuracy

anger with transgressions. We might expect stories, music, and rituals to be at least as important as logical arguments in orchestrating the behaviour of groups. Supernatural agents and events that never happened can provide blueprints for action that far surpass factual accounts of the natural world in clarity and motivating power. (42)

An important prediction of Wilson's hypothesis about practical realism is that religious cognition will be functionally encapsulated (see Bulbulia 2006). Religion will be considered all-important to social domains, but virtually ignored elsewhere (compare Malinowski 1935). Believing that Zeus will punish our enemies will not be evolutionarily useful if we leave Zeus to punish them (Zeus' non-existence means he cannot help). But the belief may be useful, perhaps to comfort or motivate additional harm ('heaping coals of fire on their heads').

Wilson does not disparage religious persons for their fictions: 'religion is often portrayed as stupid, but it is the observer who is stupid' (217). Those who condemn religion do not understand its benefit. Religion is not bad science. Its aims differ. Indeed Wilson closes *Darwin's cathedral* with a most unusual locution: 'Like a Nuer tribesman and a Balinese farmer, let us know exactly what our unifying systems are for, and then pay them homage with overflowing belief' (233).

Wilson justifies this kind of enthusiasm by appealing to the functional insights that biology brings: 'Evolution causes us to think about the subject in a completely different way. Adaptation becomes the gold standard against which rational thought must be measured alongside other modes of thought' (123).

We, however, would have preferred Wilson to avoid any evaluation of religion, positive or negative. As Wilson himself understands, selection brings no moral assurances. Where group selection is strong, religions will evolve as killing machines. To pay fictional monsters homage with overflowing belief seems doubly perverse.

Practical realism and altruism

Wilson suggests: 'A fictional belief system can be more motivating than a realistic belief system ... [it] can perform the same functions as externally imposed rewards and punishments, often at a much lower cost' (99).

His idea can be made more precise. Consider Harry deciding whether to flee as the opposing army approaches. Suppose he can do so anonymously (averting punishment). Harry does his best to flee, no matter what others do. Harry's effort will not win the war. His retreat will not lose it. But his decision criteria generalize: all may well have the same incentive to run. If so, Harry's society may fall prisoner to a socially destructive rationality. Notice, however, that believing Harry and his religious cohort perceive a different problem. For believing Harry, cooperation is supernaturally motivated. His problem is one of coordination: to find like-minded believers while avoiding others.

This and other coordination problems, too, find simple solutions through the confidence and authority religion brings (see Bulbulia 2004). Religious belief alters perceived payoffs. The anointed decide and broadcast exchange conventions, which are motivated because they are considered sacred ('Woe unto thee who fails to hunt stags'). Visible symbols provide assurance of mutual knowledge of and commitment to the conventions ('By their signs ye shall know they are stag hunters'). Religiosity places optimal equilibria within evolutionary reach.

So what? Rational choice theorists miss the benefits of fictional beliefs

Wilson's most persistent target throughout *DC* is rational choice theory.[13] This conceives of religion as misdirected economic practice. Individuals are rational. But we work from imperfect information. And we sometimes reason badly. Religion is our method for seeking goods that we cannot acquire through natural means. We want the rain, can't make it rain, so ask the cloud god, offering virgins in exchange.

	others fight	others run
believing Harry fights	Heaven	death
believing Harry runs	Hell	OK

NB: this game has two equilibria – pay if others pay, not otherwise.

Figure 11.8   Zeus commands: 'Woe unto ye who run instead of fight!'

	others hunt stags	others hunt hare
* you hunt stags	* *WIN*	*Risky*
you hunt hare	*Hell*	*OK*

* Coordination overcomes risk when a recognition problem is solved:
We each judge ourselves to be godfearing, and predict the other will act
on this judgment

Figure 11.9 Zeus commands: 'Hunt stags with thy brethren!'

Rational choice theory, like Wilson's evolutionary model, also predicts two modes of engagement: natural and supernatural. Yet because rational choice theory lacks the appropriate biological framework, Wilson argues that it overlooks the benefits of irrationality: 'Missing entirely from [rational choice theory] is the category of goods that can be procured by human action, but only by coordinated human action, and the role of religion in achieving the required coordination' (49). Moreover, Wilson's model predicts that the mechanisms supporting group benefit will frequently suppress utility-maximizing rationality. Group-evolutionary dynamics will favor the graceful over the greedy.

Perhaps, however, the differences between Wilson and the rational choice economists are not too stark (so to speak). If practical realism furnishes agents with new utilities, then means–end rationality remains possible. Perhaps believers value pleasing God. For all we know their actions are best explained as motivated to this end. Moreover, practical realism suggests practical rationality, for the realism is not inert. It would seem, then, that rational choice and group selection are compatible. Whether rational choice enriches understanding or merely presents a new gloss remains an open question.

Evaluating the theory

If the environment changes over time and space, and if religions adapt human groups to their environments, we should be able to predict the properties of religion at a fine spatial and temporal scale as surely as we can predict the properties of upstream and downstream guppies. (98)

A call to arms

DC presents a dozen or so historical and ethnographic examples to illustrate religion's group-enhancing power. Among the religious systems he considers are Calvinism (Chapter 3), Balinese water temple systems (126–33), Judaism (133–47) and the early Christian Church (147–57). Wilson does not claim that his discussion adds new empirical facts to existing scholarship, so we shall not review these examples in detail. He describes his studies as 'a refinement of what careful scholars of religion have been doing all along' (117). With respect to Christianity:

> I cannot claim too much credit for the evolutionary perspective because Pagels (1995) and her colleagues have already grasped the functional and locally adapted nature of the Gospels without ever breathing the word 'evolution.' Many evolutionary biologists got it wrong when they rejected group selection and at least one branch of religious scholarship got it right. (218)

Traditionally trained scholars might worry that Wilson's model contributes little besides impressive jargon. We think Wilson's Chapter 7: 'Forgiveness as a complex adaptation' helps to allay scholarly worries.

The discussion begins with a review of defection management strategies. In the early 80s the political scientist Robert Axelrod ran a competition for the best cooperative strategy for pair-wise exchange in a mixed population of altruists. Of all the strategies submitted, the most powerful was also the simplest: 'Tit-for-tat' (Axelrod 1984). Here, an agent starts by cooperating but defects in any subsequent encounter with a defector. Eventually the strategy interacting with itself leads to teams of cooperators who succeed in competition with defectors. The shadow of the future polices their behavior.

Wilson notes, however, that while 'Tit-for-tat' is effective in supporting cooperation, the strategy breeds disaster in fallible populations (see Axelrod 1997). Occasionally a trembling hand or misplaced judgment will lead to mistakes, which in turn lead to cooperation-wrecking cascades of retribution. Error, too, must be factored into the shadow of the future. Optimal strategies turn out to be more complex, requiring contrition and forgiveness.

Wilson uses the evolutionary game literature to reinterpret ethnographic accounts of densely knit, small-scale societies such as the Mtubi (195–8) and Nuer (199–202) and dispersed, larger-scale societies like the early American frontier (198), exposing the central role of 'practical realism' in promoting optimal group formation and maintenance. In a discussion of Christianity, Wilson explores isolating mechanisms, entry barriers and other institutional arrangements that orchestrate behavior to maximize collective benefits (204–14). He also predicts rules for a differential forgiveness sensitive to group-functional demands. 'Even without knowing the details, we can be certain that the instructions for behaving adaptively, which somehow are encoded in the beliefs and practices of a religion, must be complex' (205.) He scours the writings and practices of early Christian authors for evidencing this complexity, citing Paul's doctrine of punishing sins not sinners, Mark's struggle for coherence in the face of the Temple destruction, Matthew's desire to deflate rival Pharisees, and Luke's attempt to attract Gentile audiences. In each case, Wilson reads the scholarship as describing something close to the local cooperative maxima that game theory predicts: 'Forgiveness has many faces in the Christian beliefs that survived, as it must for Christians to behave adaptively in their complex social environments' (215).

Of course, more precise quantitative models are needed to test Wilson's conjecture, along with careful historical research into the social effects of these writings on actual communal organizations. Nevertheless, Wilson's point is not to produce a robust game-theoretic analysis of Christian forgiveness. It is rather to suggest a method for enriching and deepening current explanatory projects. His is a voice crying out in a desert.

Perhaps a more pressing worry arises from the potential for sampling biases. Wilson assures us that a randomized sample would work equally well (157–60).[14] But no matter how careful the protocols, should we not be surprised to find adaptations in successful traditions? If so, then so what?

In defence of Wilson, data may well evaluate specific hypotheses. If group selection is not a powerful evolutionary engine of adaptive change then we should expect selfishness to overwhelm most groups. Non-reciprocal altruism should quickly extinguish. Well-calibrated evidence-based models are within reach. Moreover experiments can test for the presence of non-reciprocal altruistic tendencies among specific groups, the lack of which would signal the importance of non-group selective factors (see Bulbulia and Mahoney 2008). Of course, evolution is a messy and wasteful process. It need not perfect society: 'Unfortunately, dysfunction can be as complex and locally stable as function' (69). Models do not stand or fall with data points. Much data are needed, hence Wilson's rallying cry.

In our view Wilson would have improved his advertising by more carefully modeling features specifically predicted by his theory. For example, it would have been interesting to consider the trade-offs between practical and factual realism among specific religious communities – how particular religious groups alternate between religious and non-religious perspectives to optimize benefits, comparing model to data. Further, a rigorous comparative analysis of several religious traditions, or of one tradition considered across place and time, might have better supported Wilson's prediction that religions will be contextually adaptive. If Wilson is right, we might, for example, discover that the Islam in the Kashmir has more in common with Northern Irish Catholicism than it does with the Islam of South

Africa. For violent group competition yields different strategic values to peace. Still another interesting avenue opens from Wilson's prediction that: '[a] large society is robust to the extent that its structure fulfils the spirit of communitas' (224). This prediction contrasts with, say, Marxist perceptions of increasing alienation in industrial mass society (Marx 1867/1992).

In short, Wilson's book has yet to show scholars of religion the elephant he thinks they are missing, even if he notices its smell. *DC* remains largely programmatic.

Wilson is mindful of the book's limitations:

> Let me be the first to admit that the adaptationist program has not yet proven itself for the subject of religion. On the other hand, this book represents a three-year effort by one person. By comparison, the litera-ture on guppies, which demonstrates the full power of adaptationism, represents hundreds of person-years of effort. When religious groups are studied this well from an adaptationist perspective, by social scientists and religious scholars who learn about evolution in addition to evolution-ists such as myself who learn about religion, the hypothesis that religious groups function as adaptive units will either self-destruct – a virtue in science – or stand on very firm ground. (188)

It is worth observing here that the collaborative project Wilson has in mind differs from the 'functionalist' campaigns many scholars of religion oppose. Wilson does not take functionalism to be axiomatically true. Multilevel selection hypotheses can be tested and compared with other models.[15] We can identify features of religion that do not count as functional at the group level. Considering elements of religion on a case-by-case basis may well expose alternative dynamics. Evolutionary theories are compelling precisely because the models can be tested. We can expect that science to 'be a major undertaking requiring many scholar-decades of work' (11).

Since its publication in 2002, many have objected to Wilson's book because they reject group selection or cultural evolution (for example Atran 2002; Boyer 2004; Sosis 2003). We hope to have cast some doubt on these doubters. To others, Wilson's project will appear to be a kind of methodolog-ical futurism. Wilson's reply: 'Rather than complaining about the difficulty of testing functionalist hypotheses, we need to roll up our sleeves and start using our proven tools on the material at hand' (73).[16]

Acknowledgments

Thanks to Caitlin Dalzell and David Sloan Wilson for their helpful comments.

Notes

1 For a clear, accessible overview of the issues see Wilson and Wilson 2007.

2 The latter two of these features are evolutionary by-products of development; the first is an explicitly targeted design. In evolutionary studies of religion we find both by-product and adaptationist theories of religion. For discussion see Boyer and Bergstrom 2008; Bulbulia 2007.

3 See Armin Geertz's chapter on Richard Dawkins and Daniel Dennett in this volume.

4 'The reason that the definition of groups is so closely tied to the details of the trait is because we are trying to predict the evolution of the trait' (15).

5 If this position seems similar to selfish-meme theory, it is! Selfish-meme theorists, however, urge that socially transmitted information evolves for its own benefit, whereas Wilson emphasizes the importance of host success. Where group selection is strong, we expect maladaptive information to perish, and group-enhancing information to spread. Symbiosis will reign over parasitism (Dennett 2006). These differences of view are empirically testable. The animosity between Wilson and Dawkins is overstated, in the first instance, by Wilson and Dawkins, see Dawkins 2007; Wilson 2007; 2008.

6 How altruistic traits become common when rare poses difficult problems, though these are orthogonal to the question of *how possibly* group selection can emerge from mechanisms of cultural transmission.

7 In fact, the evolutionary dynamics are more complex. Wilson's treatment of cultural evolution does not distinguish between three types of relevant information. There may be competition between institutions – say corporations – leading to structural adaptations that better equip these for success. IBM may change its organization without modifying the phenotypes of its employees (at least in the relevant sense). Design here does not emerge from the blind operation of chance laws. It is instead the result of intelligent planning. Variation is directed. For this reason, the 'natural selection' of culture must be qualified. Moreover, different types of cultural information may combine to become more competitive against other types of cultural information for social transmission. Memes can form teams. Dawkins urges that the threat of hellfire combines with a valuing of blind faith to produce a potent 'memeplex' capable of defying even the most carefully reasoned argument (Dawkins 2006: 196–200). Finally, information may replicate without causing *competitive* 'trait groups.' The trait group whose members consist of those who have telephones that are simultaneously video cameras presumably does not compete against other trait groups, even if their manufacturers compete. These distinctions are obscured in Wilson's treatment – perhaps sensibly. If his project is to forge a new methodology for the study of religion, it is perhaps best to steer clear of the many thorny paths surrounding it, even if these must eventually be traveled.

8 In which a single gene causes individuals to produce an adhesive that literally sticks them together into a fruiting multi-cellular body.

9   Though Wilson describes the problem he does not formally explain how religion solves it (see Frean and Bulbulia, in preparation).
10   The biologist William Hamilton showed that giving may evolve towards kin, where the cost-to-benefit ratio exceeds degree of relatedness (c/b > r) (Hamilton 1964). Direct and indirect reciprocity are also available to non-kin, though only where the likelihood of gain (in kind, through reputation enhancement, or by downstream benefits to kin) exceeds the cost-to-benefit ratio of the gift (see Alexander 1987; Nowak and Sigmund 1998; Trivers 1971).
11   We suspect it relates to the solution to coordination dilemmas, though will not explore the argument here.
12   See Benson Saler's chapter on Stewart Guthrie in this volume.
13   On Rodney Stark's theory, see the chapter by Gregory Alles in this volume.
14   He pursues randomization in subsequent work (see Wilson 2005).
15   Wilson lists six possible evolutionary hypotheses on his evolutionary studies website. Each of these is in principle capable of usurping multilevel selection: http://evolution.binghamton.edu/evos/index.html.
16   Those interested in Wilson's collaborate project, complete with a 'Beginner's Guide to Evolutionary Religious Studies,' should see: http://evolution.binghamton.edu/religion/guide.html.

References

Alcorta, C. and Sosis, R., 2005. Ritual, emotion, and sacred symbols: the evolution of religion as an adaptive complex. *Human Nature* 16 (4), 323–59.
Alexander, R., 1987. *The biology of moral systems*. Aldine de Gruyter, New York.
Atran, S., 2002. *In gods we trust: the evolutionary landscape of religion*. Oxford University Press, New York.
Axelrod, R., 1984. *The evolution of cooperation*. Basic Books, New York.
Axelrod, R., 1997. *The complexity of cooperation*. Princeton University Press, Princeton.
Bicchieri, C., 2006. *The grammar of society: the nature and dynamics of social norms*. Cambridge University Press, Cambridge.
Boyer, P., 2004., Religion, evolution, and cognition. *Current Anthropology* 45 (3), 430–2.
Boyer, P. and Bergstrom, B., 2008. Evolutionary perspectives on religion. *Annual Review of Anthropology* 37, 111–30.
Bulbulia, J., 2004. Religious costs as adaptations that signal altruistic intention. *Evolution and Cognition* 10 (1), 19–38.
Bulbulia, J., 2005. Are there any religions? *Method and Theory in the Study of Religion* 17 (2), 71–100.
Bulbulia, J., 2006. Nature's medicine: empirical constraint and the evolution of religious healing. In: MacNamara, P. (Ed.), *Where man and god meet: the new sciences of religion and brain*. Greenwood Publishers, Westwood, CT, 87–121.

Bulbulia, J., 2007. Evolution and religion. In: Dunbar, R.I. and Barrett, L. (Eds.), *Oxford handbook of evolutionary psychology*. Oxford University Press, Oxford, New York, 621–36.

Bulbulia, J. and Mahoney, A., 2008. Religious solidarity: the hand grenade experiment. *Journal of Cognition and Culture* 8 (3–4), 295–320.

Darwin, C., 1988/1859. *The origin of species*. William Pickering, London.

Dawkins, R., 1989/1976. *The selfish gene*. Oxford University Press, New York, Oxford.

Dawkins, R., 2006. *The god delusion*. Houghton Mifflin, Boston, MA.

Dawkins, R., 2007. Richard Dawkins replies to David Sloan Wilson. *eSkeptic: the email newsletter of the Skeptics Society*, July 11, online at www.skeptic.com/eskeptic/07–07–11.html#reply

Dennett, D., 2006. *Breaking the spell: religion as a natural phenomenon*. Viking Adult, New York.

Foster, K.R. and Kokko, H., 2009. The evolution of superstitious and superstition-like behaviour. *Proceedings of the Royal Society of London (Series B)* 276, 31–7.

Frean, M. and Bulbulia, J., in preparation. Fight club: religion and coordination.

Hamilton, W., 1964. The evolution of altruistic behavior. *American Naturalist* 97, 354–6.

Harsanyi, J. and Selton, R., 1988. *A general theory of equilibrium selection in games*. The MIT Press, Cambridge, MA.

Iannaccone, L.R., 1992. Sacrifice and stigma: reducing free-riding in cults, communes, and other collectives. *Journal of Political Economy* 100, 271–91.

Irons, W., 2001. Religion as hard-to-fake sign of commitment. In: Nesse, R. (Ed.), *Evolution and the capacity for commitment*. Russell Sage Foundation, New York, 292–309.

Malinowski, B., 1935. *The foundations of faith and morals: an anthropological analysis of primitive beliefs and conduct with special reference to the fundamental problem of religion and ethics*. Oxford University Press, London.

Marx, K., 1867/1992. *Capital: a critique of the political economy*. Penguin Books, New York.

Nowak, M., 2006. Five rules for the evolution of cooperation. *Science* 31 (4), 1560–3.

Nowak, M. and Sigmund, K., 1998. Evolution of indirect reciprocity by image scoring. *Nature* 393, 573–7.

Pagels, E.H., 1995. *The origin of Satan*. Random House, New York.

Rousseau, J., 1984/1754. *A discourse on inequality*. Trans. M. Cranston. Penguin Books, New York.

Schloss, J., 2007. He who laughs best: involuntary religious affect as a solution to recursive cooperative defection. In: Bulbulia, J., Sosis, R., Harris, E., Genet, R., Genet, C., and Wyman, K. (Eds.), *The evolution of religion: studies, theories, and critiques*. Collins Foundation Press, Santa Margarita, 197–207.

Skyrms, B., 2004. *The stag hunt and the evolution of social structure*. Cambridge University Press, Cambridge.

Sober, E. and Wilson, D.S., 1998. *Unto others: the evolution and psychology of unselfish behavior*. Harvard University Press, Cambridge, MA.

Sosis, R., 2003. Book review: *Darwin's cathedral: evolution, religion, and the nature of society*. *Evolution and Human Behavior* 24, 137–43.

Sterelny, K., 2007. Social intelligence: from brain to culture. *Proceedings of the Royal Society of London (Series B)* 362 (1480), 719–30.

Trivers, R., 1971. The evolution of reciprocal altruism. *Quarterly Review of Biology* 46, 35–57.

Trivers, R., 2001. *Natural selection and social theory*. Oxford University Press, New York.

Williams, G.C., 1966. *Adaptation and natural selection: a critique of some current evolutionary thought*. Princeton University Press, Princeton.

Wilson, D.S., 2002. *Darwin's cathedral: evolution, religion, and the nature of society*. University of Chicago Press, Chicago.

Wilson, D.S., 2005. Testing major evolutionary hypotheses about religion with a random sample. *Human Nature* 16 (4), 419–46.

Wilson, D.S., 2007. Beyond demonic memes: why Richard Dawkins is wrong about religion. *eSkeptic: the email newsletter of the Skeptics Society*, July 4, online at www.skeptic.com/eskeptic/07–07–04.html#feature

Wilson, D.S., 2008. Evolution and religion: the transformation of the obvious. In: Bulbulia, J., Sosis, R., Harris, E., Genet, R., Genet, C., and Wyman K. (Eds.), *The evolution of religion: studies, theories, and critiques*. Collins Foundation Press, Santa Margarita, 197–210.

Wilson, E.O. and Wilson, D.S., 2007. Rethinking the theoretical foundation of socio-biology. *Quarterly Review of Biology* 82 (4), 327–48.

Young, P., 1998. *Individual strategy and social structure: an evolutionary theory of social institutions*. Princeton University Press, Princeton.

12

Roots in the brain

On David Lewis-Williams and David Pearce, Inside the Neolithic mind (2005)

Donald Wiebe

Introduction

It is in an attempt to make sense of the rock paintings and engravings of the San of South Africa that David Lewis-Williams, then Professor of Cognitive Archaeology at the University of Witwatersrand, adumbrated a theory of religion that accounts for its origin and nature (though not the particularities of content) in wholly neuropsychological terms. Presented first in his *Believing and seeing* (1981), the theory has been elaborated in successive works in collaboration with several other scholars: especially with Thomas A. Dowson (a colleague in the Rock Art Research Institute in the University of Witwatersrand) in 'The signs of all times: entoptic phenomena in Upper Palaeolithic art' (1988); Jean Clottes (a scholar of prehistoric rock art in France) in their book on *The shamans of prehistory* (1998 [1996]); and David Pearce (a researcher in the Rock Art Institute), in their co-authored *Inside the Neolithic mind* (2005).

In the most recent elaboration of the theory in *Inside the Neolithic mind* Lewis-Williams and Pearce complain that neither historians of religions, archaeologists, nor anthropologists have been able to provide a persuasive theory of religion. Laurence Sullivan, they point out, for example, presents a theological reading of South American religions that simply ignores the issue of explanation and theory (2005: 25). Archaeologists in general, they insist, tend to see the notion of the uniqueness of cultures as telling the whole story about culture and are, therefore, reluctant to seek general explanations of any cultural phenomenon (8). Anthropologists, in their judgment, fare no better: Clifford Geertz's account of religion, they write, 'does not adequately explain *how* ... what he calls "conceptions of a general order of existence" acquire "an aura of factuality"' (25). And Harvey Whitehouse's categorization of religions as either imagistic or doctrinal, they argue, 'does not explain why people anywhere ... believe in gods, spirits and another realm of existence different from the one of

daily life but interacting with it' (25). As they put the matter: 'Categorizing religions is not the same as explaining why they exist' (25). The
theory of religion they present here in the context of the Neolithic revolution draws on Lewis-Williams's earlier *The mind in the cave* (2002a),
and on Jacques Cauvin's account of the essential causes of the Neolithic
revolution found in his *The birth of the gods* (2000 [1994]). Central
to their theory is the claim that religion is ultimately embedded in the
brain, but they also insist that they do not espouse a neurological or
even neuropsychological reductionism. Like Cauvin, they place significant emphasis on the role of the symbolic in the 'construction' of religion (2005: 285) – what Cauvin calls the psycho-cultural initiative that
cannot be reduced to the materialistic level (2000: 208) – and reject naïve
materialism and reductive positivism. A review of earlier developments
in Lewis-Williams's theory, and a brief account of Cauvin's views on the
religion of the Neolithic, will be helpful in assessing the character and
import of what Lewis-Williams and his various collaborators call their
neuropsychological theory of religion.

A theory of religion in the making

In *Believing and seeing* Lewis-Williams establishes that the San rock paintings
of animals such as the hartebeest and eland are not merely representations of
everyday animals made available to be admired or contemplated. Rather, he
argues, the paintings and engravings depict 'realities' that belong to a spirit
realm of supernatural potency and therefore have special significance for the
San (1981: 75); their paintings, that is, were essentially expressions of their
deep thoughts regarding values and meaning. He further maintains that trance
experience is the source of those thoughts, and that it is trance experience
that facilitates contact between the terrestrial world in which the San live
their daily lives and the alternate spirit world of special power on which they
also relied. The paintings, therefore, are in effect 'reified visions of the spirit
world,' as he and Pearce put it in their later work on *San spirituality* (2004).
Consequently, they insist that there is no understanding of San spirituality
and religion without an understanding of the neuropsychology from which
it derives for, according to them, San spirituality/religion is 'a way of coming
to terms with [and making use of] the electro-chemical functioning of the
brain' (xxiv). Their spirituality is identical to the experience of altered states
of consciousness (19) and their religious beliefs and ritual practices are
derived from those spiritual experiences by way of interpretation; that is,
by way of a 'negotiation of consciousness' (25) that also involves a process
of socialization and social differentiation. With respect to the former they
write: 'All attempts to make sense of the products of our brains ... must

necessarily be social, not simply personal and individual; they must be fashioned in and accepted by the community' (34). As for the latter, Lewis-Williams had already dealt with the matter in *The shamans of prehistory*: 'By drawing on this [electro-chemical] resource, some people were able to lay claim to special knowledge and special insights that set them apart from and probably above others' (1998: 114).

In *The mind in the cave* (2002a) Lewis-Williams argues that the earliest form of religion is to be found in association with cave paintings of Upper Palaeolithic peoples which he thinks were reified visions of spirit worlds in the same manner as the rock art of the San. He argues here that there are few, if any, indications of a rich set of experiences and beliefs in the Middle Palaeolithic or among the Neanderthal; abstract and representational art, that is, were essentially absent from these contexts. Such artistic capacities, he argues, are the result of the neural potential of the anatomically modern Upper Palaeolithic mind/brain which produces a different kind of conscious-ness that is capable of image-making and other symbolic activity and which made possible a revolution in experience and belief. Since the people of Upper Palaeolithic Europe are anatomically and behaviourally modern, their neuronal potential is the same as ours, and the brain/mind, therefore, constitutes a bridge by which we can gain an understanding of their spiritual and religious experience – especially 'the visual imagery of the intensified spectrum' of consciousness connected with trance experiences (2002a: 126). It is here, they maintain, that what we call religious experiences are generated and from which, therefore, religions are ultimately derived.

Despite the whiff of reductionism that surrounds their argument, Lewis-Williams and Pearce nevertheless accept Cauvin's account of Neolithic religion, which eschews reductionism. Cauvin's central argument is that 'the birth of the gods' is not the result of changes in subsistence practices of the Neolithic brought on by natural or economic disasters, but rather that changes in subsistence practices among the Neolithic were the result of a change in symbolic consciousness. At the beginning of the period of Neolithization the people of the Near East, he maintains, were provided a 'benevolent environment'; one 'able to accommodate the human population for a long time yet' (2000: 65). Thus, Cauvin argues, the descendants of the pre-Neolithic societies (the Natufians) 'might not have been satisfied with their ancestral systems of survival, and these reasons may have been quite simply of a cultural nature' (65); 'they must have "wanted" to change [and] [s]uch a wish could only come from the area of collective psychology, where our dissatisfactions emerge and transformations of culture which do not necessarily have economic reasons as their foundation are elaborated' (66). Thus for Cauvin the Neolithic revolution is due essentially to dissatisfaction with traditional life in the pre-Neolithic societies; and therefore is essentially a symbolic development, an imaginative or psychological initiative that made possible 'an internal expansion of consciousness' (208). For Cauvin, therefore, the symbolic revolution was also a religious revolution that 'had generated a general theory of a self-regulating world, which extended to the role that he [man] had given himself in it' (209).

Although Lewis-Williams and Pearce agree with Cauvin's claims regarding the symbolic revolution in the life of the Neolithic, they do not respond to his suggestion that this development might be satisfactorily explained by reference to a collective psychology or that perhaps psychoanalysis can help us to understand the links between their psychic energy and the symbolic thought underlying their behaviour. They are suspicious, moreover, of what they consider Cauvin's commitment to a form of functionalism in his suggestion that mythology and rituals were created by the Neolithic in order to achieve solidarity (Lewis-Williams and Pearce 2005: 78–9).

Lewis-Williams and Pearce proceed with the development of their own theory, then, both espousing Cauvin's central claim about the primacy of the symbolic in human life, but also indirectly critical of Cauvin in so far as he, like other archaeologists, is reluctant to seek generalities about human behaviour; 'about innate human commonalities' (2005: 8). In dealing with the Neolithic, they recognize that there are both significant differences between the Near East and Atlantic Europe but also something common to both that 'held the Neolithic together and gave it its essential flow' (7). Thus they ask whether there might have been 'an underlying, not easily detected bedrock of belief that expressed itself in contrasting ways' (8). This question is much the same as that raised by Lewis-Williams in attempting to account for the similarities he detected between San rock art and the cave paintings of the Upper Palaeolithic. Given the vast differences in time and space between these two bodies of data, Lewis-Williams sought an explanation for them in terms of the human brain/mind, the only human universal that in his judgment could bridge the gap between these cultures. Lewis-Williams and Pearce, therefore, suggest that accounting for the unity and flow of the Neolithic culture, despite its various cultural specificities, can only be achieved by reference to this same human universal. As they put it: the 'generality' that characterizes the Neolithic is likely 'founded on the working of the human brain that, in all its electro-chemical complexity, creates what we call our minds. The neurological functioning of the brain, like the structure and functioning of other parts of the body, is a human universal' (6). They suggest, therefore, that principles of human behaviour that are derived from the functioning of the brain can account for those aspects of behaviour that turn up in a wide diversity of cultures – that is, for the commonalities of culture. With respect to religion, for example, they maintain that all religions have an ecstatic component and all involve altering human consciousness, despite local variations in the substance of the beliefs involved. They state their thesis as follows:

> [T]he human mind is an experience that is created by the working of the brain. The enormously complex neurology of the brain, its lobes, synapses and electro-chemical functioning, facilitates our thinking and our consciousness – in short, our minds. Now here is the pivotal point: the neurology and functioning of the brain creates a mercurial type of human consciousness that is universal. And the ways in which the consciousness can be accommodated in daily life by human beings are not infinite, as world ethnography, spanning a multitude of cultures, indeed shows ... We [therefore] propose certain principles that we derive from the universal function of the human brain. We then use ethnographic instances as *illustrations* of the ways in which that universal functioning can find expression ... [and draw attention to how] the diverse ways in which communities come to terms with shifting human consciousness are sometimes recognizable in the archaeological record ... [Thus] [i]n emphasizing the interaction between neurologically generated universals and cultural specifics we are not 'dragging in' an unnecessary factor – human consciousness – as some archeologists may be inclined to think. (9, 10)

For Lewis-Williams and Pearce, then, the key to understanding the unity and the flow of Neolithic culture is the 'neurologically generated and emotionally charged cosmology inhabited by supernatural beings and forces that influenced human life' (12). Neolithic peoples, that is, made use of a kind of thinking different from that employed in their daily round of activities, grounded in the complexity of a mercurial, shifting consciousness. As they put it, echoing Cauvin, '[t]o invoke a biblical trope, we may say that they show that people do not live by bread alone' (14); rather, they exist within 'a web spun by their own minds' (12).

A theory of religion: its neuropsychological core

Given that persons do not live alone but in communities, explaining religion will require more than just understanding the brain and its mercurial behaviour. Lewis-Williams and Pearce acknowledge that there must have been a kind of 'social contract' that allowed Neolithic societies to function smoothly and that can account for their particularities. But they also quickly point out that this cannot be the whole story (2005: 39). As they see it, there must have been a concomitant contract – what they call 'the consciousness contract' – that allowed the Neolithic to cope with daily mental experiences. As they point out: '*Whatever influence the material environment may have*

on human behaviour, and we do not underestimate its power, all people have
to live with and to accommodate the products of their brains in a society of
other brains and bodies' (36; emphasis added). Thus, in anticipation of their
study of the Neolithic, they point out that the generality of the claims they
make about Neolithic experience and belief

> [i]s founded on the working of the human brain that, in all its electro-
> chemical complexity creates what we call our minds. The neurological
> functioning of the brain, like the structure and functioning of other parts
> of the body, is a human universal. The specific content of individual
> minds, their thought, images and memories, are another matter alto-
> gether; content is largely, but not entirely, provided by cultures as they
> are, or were, at a specific time in human history. Content is therefore
> always changing. The way in which brain structure and content interact
> to produce unique life-patterns and belief systems is a key issue that we
> explore. (6–7)
>
> It is, therefore, the altered states of consciousness, hard-wired into
> the human brain, that constitute the foundation for religious experience
> [of the ineffable] and, subsequently, by way of cultural interpretation of
> these experiences, religious beliefs that in turn provide the foundation for
> religious practice. (39)

According to Lewis-Williams and Pearce, the spectrum of human
consciousness ranges along a continuum moving from what they call the
consciousness of rationality or 'alert consciousness' to 'deep trance'; a spectrum that moves from outward-looking states of mind to inward-directed
states of mind that can give rise to felt encounters of an alternate reality.
The outward-looking states of mind include both the waking state as well
as 'light' altered states such as daydreaming, lucid dreaming (and dreaming
states), while the inward-directed states are generated wholly in and by the
brain. The inward-directed trance states are all similar, despite how they are
effected or caused (that is, whether they are induced by migraines, dancing,
chanting, rhythmic clapping of hands, drums, meditation, sensory deprivation,
hunger, fatigue, flickering light, extreme pain, near-death experiences, drugs,
temporal lobe epilepsy, or schizophrenia), and pass through three stages
from light to deep trance that are not discrete but rather shade into one
another. The potential for human nervous systems to enter into such altered
states of consciousness and to generate hallucinations is of great antiquity,
not only wired into the human nervous system but the mammalian nervous
system more generally.

Although Lewis-Williams is aware that many archaeologists are uneasy
about invoking theories of human consciousness in attempting to account

for the thought-life and beliefs of prehistoric human communities, he is nevertheless convinced that it is only through the adoption of such new approaches to interpreting the data that research in the discipline can be advanced, and particularly so 'for piecing together humankind's first "religious" concepts and experiences' (2002b [1988]: 189). Using a neurological model of the kind he proposes – one that focuses attention less on human intelligence and more on the marginalized elements of human consciousness – Lewis-Williams argues, is a reasonable avenue of research in seeking an understanding of both the ancient human mind and, for example, the mind of the San. It is reasonable because all anatomically modern human beings have brains that function in scientifically discoverable ways, and modern neuropsychological research involving laboratory subjects has provided us with information about the ways human consciousness affects us and, therefore, how it could have influenced people's minds in prehistoric times. He admits that we do not know how the functioning of the brain produces consciousness, but he also points out that this is not the stumbling-block some might consider it to be, because all that is necessary in this context is that we are able to describe some aspects of consciousness. And on the basis of the results of modern neurological and neuropsychological research (referred to in his 2002b [1988] and 2004) he points out that there exists a broad range of human psychological experiences beyond what has been called the 'consciousness of rationality' – that is, of 'waking problem-oriented thought' – upon which he can construct a neuropsychological model of human experience that he believes will better account for both San rock art paintings and the art of Upper Palaeolithic and Neolithic peoples. Such a model, he maintains, will show the brain to be the root of all (at least) archaic spirituality/religion, which, given the ethnographic evidence, is best described as shamanistic.

Neuropsychological research, as Lewis-Williams and his colleagues point out, reveals three stages in trance experience among human beings. The first stage in this trajectory involves only what he refers to as 'light trance' and includes experiences that are common to all (or at least most) human beings across all cultures. This level includes hypnagogic experiences – states of consciousness intermediate between wakefulness and sleep – that include vivid mental imagery generated by the optic system (entoptic phenomena) and a transfer of sensation from one sensory modality to another (synesthesia). The entoptic phenomena generally consist of geometric mental images that include a diversity of forms such as grid or lattice designs, sets of parallel lines, bright dots and short flecks, zigzag lines, nested catenary curves, filigrees and thin meandering lines, and spirals. Given their ubiquity it is surmised that they are hard-wired into brains and therefore inescapable and must be dealt with by individuals and the communities they constitute.

Given the particularities of the social and cultural settings involved, some of these basic experiences may be ignored and others valued and cultivated, and may even be transformed into systems of symbols.

A second, deeper, stage of altered consciousness involves attempting 'to make sense of the entoptic forms by construing them as objects with emotional or religious significance' (2005: 50). This is often connected with an experience of passage through a vortex, descent into an underworld, entering a portal into another world, and something like a near-death experience. These experiences are clearly hallucinatory.

Lewis-Williams and Pearce describe the third and deepest level of trance state as follows: 'Emerging from the vortex, subjects enter a bizarre, ever-changing world of hallucinations' (54). The individual's experience here is 'autistic'; wholly closed-off from the outside world. Hallucinations have an increased vividness, are experienced in all senses, are associated with powerful emotions and feelings, and involve processes of fragmentation and integration that produce compound images in which the subjects participate in their own imagery. Such deep trances also create the illusion of dissociation from one's body that produces sensations of possession or a sense of extra-corporeal travels in an alternate world, and puts one in touch with spirits and other supernatural powers, giving one control of the weather, or of spirit-animals (and actually feeling oneself becoming an animal), or power to heal the sick.

Religion: rooted in the brain, sedimented in society

The power of the neuropsychological theory of religion, and particularly of its central core that takes into account the full range of human consciousness including the various levels of altered states of consciousness, lies in its ability to account for the ultimate source of religion and its social developments and, in the process, its capacity to unearth humankind's hypothetical original religion (ur-religion). Early *Homo sapiens sapiens*, individually and collectively, had to make sense of the full range of 'products' of their brains, including the spiritual experiences – that is, experiences of what seemed to them to be alternate realities to those of everyday living – generated in altered states of consciousness. Interpretation of those non-ordinary psychological and somatic experiences as non-natural and out-of-this-world, both by individuals and the communities of which they were members, constituted what we now call religious experience. That is, the meanings attached to those experiences – to the relatively uninterpreted electro-chemical firings in the brain – both individual and social, amount to the construction and institutionalization of religious experience which grounds religious belief and practice. In light of such an account of the imaginative mental capacities of our hominid forebears, interpreting the cave paintings of Upper Palaeolithic peoples as the expression of such individual and collective experience of alternative 'supernatural' realities, gives us the most coherent account of that data that we possess. And given the character of those out-of-the-ordinary experiences and the role they played in the lives of individuals and communities (expressed in the cave paintings and later rock art), it would seem that the ur-religion of humankind is some form of hunter-gatherer shamanism.

Lewis-Williams and Jean Clottes point out that the hypothetical original religion of humankind could extend to our earliest hominid forebears. They suggest, that is, that those early ancestors may well have considered the world around them as more than simply a source of food and shelter. There is no way of knowing, of course, because there are insufficient archaeological remains to provide evidence 'that the thought of these species went beyond the satisfaction of their immediate bodily needs' (2007: 7). However, this does not mean, they write, 'that they were no more than brutish animals' (7). The best evidence for the existence of religion that we have, they insist, is in the cave art of our fully modern ancestors in the Upper Palaeolithic. They acknowledge that not all Upper Palaeolithic art is necessarily religious, but they see much of it as providing 'illuminating clues about its authors' beliefs' (11). Thus they also acknowledge that the quest for humankind's ur-religion is 'inevitably intertwined with the origins of art' (9).

The uniformity of the complex imagery of Upper Palaeolithic art, and therefore of the beliefs underlying the paintings, suggests that the hypothetical original religion of our species 'was in some sense shamanistic' (31). And given the nature of those early communities they argue that the widespread occurrence of this form of religion cannot be accounted for by simple diffusion but is more persuasively explained in terms of a 'universal neurological inheritance that includes the capacity of the nervous system to enter altered states of consciousness and the need to make sense of the resulting experiences and hallucinations within a foraging community' (33). And that clearly requires consideration of both 'the behaviour of the nervous system and the social contexts in which the behaviour takes place' (34).

Evaluation: criticism and promise

Lewis-Williams's work has stirred up considerable controversy, with questions raised not only about appropriate standard procedure in rock art research and other more general methodological issues but also about how much of the cave painting and other rock art is religious; about how much of it is actually susceptible of a shamanic interpretation. Other issues include concern over the claim that shamanism is characteristic of all hunter-gatherer societies and questions as to whether the neuropsychological theory can actually account for the social transmission of the religious beliefs of the shaman. The most serious criticism, however, concerns the correctness of the neuropsychological claims upon which he relies for his interpretation of the Upper Palaeolithic and Neolithic art and religion, and I therefore focus attention on it first.

Patricia A. Helvenston (a neuropsychologist) and Paul G. Bahn (an archaeologist specializing in prehistoric art) first raised their concern about the scientific adequacy of Lewis-Williams's neuropsychological theory of religion in a privately published pamphlet titled *Desperately seeking trance plants: testing the 'three stages of trance' model* (2002). In fact, their review of the model there and in 'Testing the "three stages of trance" model' (2003) amounted to an all-out attack on the theory as presented by Lewis-Williams and Dowson in their 1988 paper 'The signs of all the times.' Helvenston and Bahn state their claim succinctly and bluntly in the latter essay. They claim that 'the only trance states that are consistent with those described in the TST [Three Stages of Trance] model are drug-induced trances caused by plants containing mescaline, lysergic acid dietheylamid, or psilocybins' (2003: 213), and that there is no evidence to show that such plants were readily available in Upper Palaeolithic Europe or that they were used in the vicinity of the painted caves (215). They conclude, therefore, that the 'neuropsychological research regarding drug-induced and natural trance states ... does not support the TST model' (220) and 'one can only conclude that anyone who continues henceforth to cite or apply the TST model is either ignorant of the facts or has little respect for truth in scholarship' (223). Under fire from other scholars published in *Reaction*, which also appeared in the *Cambridge Archaeological Journal* a year later, they admit that some issues (namely, altered states of consciousness as motivating factors in Upper Palaeolithic art and the possibility that hypnagogic and hypnapompic states might well produce the kinds of images to which Lewis-Williams and Dowson refer) were raised that merit further consideration. Nevertheless, they still insist, somewhat inexplicably, that attempts to understand rock art and cave painting data can, at best, be simply 'more or less well-informed speculation' (Clottes *et al.* 2004: 95).

In his response to this critique Lewis-Williams points out first of all that he did not base his theory exclusively on drug-induced altered states of consciousness as his critics imply, and that, furthermore, there is a considerable 'neuropsychological literature that destroys their contention that psychoactive substances are essential for the induction of the three stages of altered consciousness (2004: 107). After setting out the evidence for this claim Lewis-Williams concludes that his rejection of the Helvenston/ Bahn critique is not simply a matter of interpretation or opinion. 'On the contrary,' he writes, 'it is an empirical issue: the literature reports research showing that the full range of hallucinations, as encompassed by the three stage model, can be experienced in circumstances that do not include drug ingestion and, moreover, that the experiences derive from the structure of the human cortex' (110).

Archaeologists Miranda and Stephen Aldhouse-Green claim in their book *The quest for the shaman* that the 'archaeological community has yet to reach a definitive view on this matter' (2005:30). Clearly, there are still important issues that must be settled to achieve a general convergence of scientific judgment on this matter across the various disciplinary communities on whose work these issues impinge. However, just as clearly, there is no complaint here that the theory is inconsistent with the neurobiological data about how the brain functions. Furthermore, as Lewis-Williams points out, his theory does not contradict the empirical data of rock art studies and the agreed characterization of shamanic religious belief and practice. In his earlier treatment of the San he points out, for example, 'that human neurology ... explains the ubiquity of the tiered cosmos [of shamanism]' and that '[c]osmological travel [by shamans] is paralleled by mental travel along the spectrum of consciousness and its attendant transformations' (Lewis-Williams and Pearce 2004: 35). Comparing the San material to the similarities found elsewhere in the world, as well as to the art of the Upper Palaeolithic, he writes: 'I can think of no other way to explain the similarities: they are the product of the universal human nervous system in altered states of consciousness, culturally processed but none the less still recognizably deriving from the structure and electro-chemical functioning of the nervous system' (2002a: 170). Thus, again, it is clear that the theory makes good sense of the cave paintings as 'reified visions of the spirit [that is, the electro-chemically produced] world' experienced by the shaman. As he notes, he and Dowson found evidence in the cave paintings of all three stages of altered consciousness (2002b [1988]: 181).

The other criticisms mentioned above can be treated more succinctly. As for the problem of the cultural transmission of the shaman's vision, Lewis-Williams shows that hypnagogic hallucinations, dreams, and reveries are experienced by most everyone in these contexts and provide the people with 'glimpses' of the 'transcendent realms' of 'supernatural powers' revealed by the shamans. This in turn provides an obvious basis on which transmission of the beliefs of the shaman occurs with relative ease. Lewis-Williams is justified, therefore, in claiming that people were not simply being gulled by the shamans, but rather that they based their acceptance of beliefs, at least partially, on their own internal experiences generated by the electro-chemical functioning of their brains (2003: 276). With respect to the claims about his unjustified assumption about all ancient cave paintings and rock art being religious in nature, he points out that the claim isn't true. He agrees that it is unlikely that all rock art is the expression of shamanic visions, but he also points out that it is not always possible to distinguish between what was secular and what religious, and that in spite of this it is clearly the case that 'the quest for ur-religion [is] inevitably intertwined with the origins of art' (Lewis-Williams and Clottes 2007: 9). As for the claim about the universal presence of shamanism in hunter-gatherer societies, he writes: 'There have been and still are many other researchers who believe that some form of shamanism was the first to attempt to deal with functions of the brain, humankind's ur-religion; by no means do I stand alone. We must not become so obsessed by differences between communities and their beliefs that we do not see fundamental continuities' (2002b: 190).

Lewis-Williams has also responded to the methodological critiques. On the matter of the most appropriate methods in the study of rock art, for example, he shows that earlier empiricist approaches to the field can at best provide one only with descriptive inventories of the data, not explanations of it. As for the matter of 'proving' the correctness of his theory, he points out that such a goal is only appropriate in logic and mathematics. His aim in the study of cave and rock art, he notes, is rather to develop an explanation of that data that is more empirically adequate than existing accounts (Lewis-Williams and Pearce 2004 [1988]: 235).

Lewis-Williams is fully aware that he has not responded to all the criticisms raised against his theory and that he has not answered all the questions that can be asked of it. Nevertheless, I think he is right in his claim that he is under no obligation to explain everything in order to have explained something (2003: 276), and that partial insight is better than no insight at all (2003: 278).

The 'extended' neuropsychological theory, then, including both the social and consciousness contracts, provides us with a plausible theoretical account of what we today call religious experience, belief, and practice; of religion's first institutionalization in the form of shamanism; of its relevance to the formation of stratified societies in so far as deep trance experiences were likely restricted to limited numbers of people, thus investing them with greater social relevance and therefore greater social power; of its continuing influence on early historical religions in the Near East and, later, Europe; and of the immunity of religion to any logic but its own. Nevertheless questions about its utility in accounting for the religious traditions that seem to have replaced shamanism in later Neolithic societies and in early historical civilizations, or in the explanation of contemporary religious developments, still require attention. The first matter to bear in mind here is that the theory involves not only what Lewis-Williams and his various collaborators call the 'consciousness contract' – the core element of the three stages of trance experience – but also the 'social contract'; accounting for later developments in religious thought and practice may well focus greater attention on cultural and socio-political factors involved in '(re-) interpreting' the meaning and significance of their spiritual experience and how that process contributes to the transformation of original shamanistic forms of religion. As Lewis-Williams and Dowson point out, for example, the emergence of anthropomorphic deities in the Neolithic period is in some sense a continuation (reinterpretation) of the element of ancestor worship in shamanic religion. The birth of the gods in the Neolithic and the elaboration of their worship in early Near Eastern civilizations, that is, are not wholly *de novo* developments. Continuities are also to be found in later historical developments, as well as differences. What is significant, however, is the similarity of interior experience among devotees across these divisions. Understanding the similarity underlying the developments is precisely what the central core of the theory can help to explain, for it has once again made possible an explanatory role for 'religious experience.' The broader value of the theory, therefore, will also be shown in exploration of the possible connection of contemporary religious experience (and the apparent immunity of that experience, and its interpretation, to scientific explanation) to what Lewis-Williams and Dowson call the introspected end of the consciousness spectrum, whether in direct intimations of tran-scendent realities or in sympathetic resonance to them in the mythic and ritual thought and practice of organized religions.

References

Aldhouse-Green, Miranda and Stephen Aldhouse-Green, 2005. *The quest for the shaman: shape-shifters, sorcerers, and spirit-healers of ancient Europe.* Thames and Hudson, London.

Cauvin, Jacques, 2000 [1994]. *The birth of the gods and the origins of agriculture.* Cambridge University Press, Cambridge.

Clottes, Jean, 2006. Spirituality and religion in Paleolithic times. In: Shults, F. LeRon (Ed.), *The evolution of rationality: interdisciplinary essays in honor of J. Wentzel van Huyssteen.* Eerdmans, Grand Rapids, 133–48.

Clottes, Jean and Lewis-Williams, J. David, 1998. *The shamans of prehistory: trance, and magic in the painted caves.* Harry N. Abrams, Inc., New York.

Clottes, Jean, David Pearce, David Wilson, and Patricia Helvenston and Paul Bahn, 2004. Reactions. *Cambridge Archaeological Journal* 14 (1), 81–100.

Helvenston, Patricia A. and Paul G. Bahn, 2002. *Desperately seeking trance plants: testing the 'three stages of trance' model.* RJ Communications, New York.

Helvenston, Patricia A. and Paul G. Bahn, 2003. Testing the 'three stages of trance' model (with comments by John L. Bradshaw and Christopher Chippendale). *Cambridge Archaeological Journal* 13 (2), 213–24.

Lewis-Williams, J. David, 1981. *Believing and seeing: symbolic meanings in southern San rock paintings*. Academic Press, London, New York.

Lewis-Williams, J. David, 2002a. *The mind in the cave: consciousness and the origins of art*. Thames and Hudson, London.

Lewis-Williams, J. David, 2002b. *A cosmos in stone: interpreting religion and society through rock art*. Rowman and Littlefield Publishers, New York, Oxford.

Lewis-Williams, J. David, 2003. Review feature: *The mind in the cave: consciousness and the origins of art*. *Cambridge Archaeological Journal* 13 (2), 263–79.

Lewis-Williams, J. David, 2004. Neuropsychology and Upper Palaeolithic art: observations on the progress of altered states of consciousness. *Cambridge Archaeological Journal* 14 (1), 107–11.

Lewis-Williams, J. David, 2006. Building bridges to the deep human past: consciousness, religion, and art. In: Shults, F. LeRon (Ed.), *The evolution of rationality: interdisciplinary essays in honor of J. Wentzel van Huyssteen*. Eerdmans, Grand Rapids, 149–66.

Lewis-Williams, J. David and Jean Clottes, 2007. Palaeolithic art and religion. In: Hinnells, John R. (Ed.), *A handbook of ancient religions*, Cambridge University Press, Cambridge, 7–45.

Lewis-Williams, J. David and T. Dowson, 1988. The signs of all times: entoptic phenomena in Upper Palaeolithic art. *Current Anthropology* 29 (2), 201–17 (with Comments and Reply, 217–45).

Lewis-Williams, J. David and D. Pearce, 2004. *San spirituality: roots, expression, and social consequences*. Rowman and Littlefield Publishers, New York, Oxford.

Lewis-Williams, J. David and D. Pearce, 2005. *Inside the Neolithic mind: consciousness, cosmos and the realm of the gods*. Thames and Hudson, London.

13

Boundary maintenance: religions as organic-cultural flows

On Thomas Tweed, Crossing and dwelling (2006)

Aaron W. Hughes

This chapter critically examines Thomas A. Tweed's *Crossing and dwelling*, which presents an account of religion based on the themes of motion and home building. More specifically, Tweed defines religion as responsible for positioning religious practitioners temporally and spatially – in the body, the home, the homeland, and ultimately the cosmos. Tweed also focuses on the many ways in which religions both enable and constrain corporeal, terrestrial, and cosmic crossings. Drawing upon insights from a variety of natural and social sciences, Tweed surveys data gleaned from the world's religions in order to develop cross-cultural patterns. The assumptions behind his theory, however, revolve around the actual work 'religion' does, and how this work is conceptualized as different from cognate terms such as culture and ideology. There also exists an inherent tension in Tweed's works between local, observed religious idioms and the search for universal trends that tend to level the particular.

Biographical sketch

Thomas A. Tweed, who received his PhD from Stanford University in 1989, currently hold the Gwyn Shive, Anita Nordan Lindsay, and Joe and Cherry Gray Professorship in the History of Christianity in the Department of Religious Studies at the University of Texas, Austin. Tweed teaches and researches religion in the United States, with particular emphases on ethnography and theory and method. His publications reflect his manifold interests in the historical, ethnographic, and theoretical study of religion in America. For instance, he has edited *Retelling U.S. religious history* (1997b), which contains essays by leading scholars that examine traditionally marginalized topics such as sexual pleasure, colonization, gender, and inter-religious exchange. This volume is interested in taking seriously religious groups, in addition to geographical sites of difference. He has also co-edited, with Stephen Prothero, *Asian religions in America: a documentary history* (1999), a collection of essays devoted to examining the breadth and depth of American encounters with Asian religions and their place within the American religious landscape and imagination.

Tweed's authored monographs include *The American encounter with Buddhism, 1844–1912: Victorian culture and the limits of dissent* (1992, 2000), which examines the manifold ways in which American interpreters, many of whom considered themselves to be dissenters from mainstream American culture, imagined Buddhism using precisely the same Victorian values and categories from which they wished to escape. Most significant for the discussion here is his *Our Lady of the Exile: diasporic religion at a Cuban shrine in Miami* (1997a), which won the 1998 American Academy of Religion's Award for Excellence in the Historical Studies category. In this book, Tweed examines the religious lives, motivations, and hopes of Cuban exiles. He argues that the pilgrims to this shrine construct their collective identity through it and thereby transport themselves to a Cuba of 'memory and desire'. In this work, Tweed moves beyond the local context of Cuban-American Catholicism and begins to think more generally about place, migration, and the interconnected relationship between crossing and dwelling.

Many of the themes, then, that we encounter in *Crossing and dwelling* – ethnographic and historic analyses, home and not-home, migration and movement – have preoccupied Tweed for much of the past fifteen years. It is in the latter book, however, that he gives these subjects a full theoretical elaboration and, in the process, seeks to show their utility as heuristic categories.

Crossing and dwelling: argument and structure

Crossing and dwelling, in essence, extrapolates a universal theory of religion from a specific and local context, the Cuban diasporic community of South Florida. To succeed, Tweed must articulate a critical vocabulary and set of categories that not only account for his own data with this community, but will also be of use to those working with other data in different geographical and temporal contexts. It is this delicate balance between the local and the global, the culturally specific and the cross-cultural, that any theory of religion must ideally address. However, there is a tension between the local and the global, and a focus on one necessarily involves certain sacrifices made with the other. It is this juggling act, as the problems that have plagued previous accounts that rely on the context-less and cross-cultural use of data have well shown, that makes the development of a universal theory difficult if not outright impossible.

At the heart of Tweed's work, as his title makes explicit, is an attempt to articulate a theory of religion that adequately addresses and accounts for the themes of movement, relation, and position. Tweed puts such weight on these that he structures his book thematically around them, dividing its chapters into the following themes: (1) Itineraries, (2) Boundaries, (3) Confluences, (4) Dwelling, and (5) Crossing. His presentation, although having as its point of departure the devotees of Our Lady of Charity, moves quickly from the historical and specific to the ahistorical and the thematic.

In chapter one, 'Itineraries', Tweed provides a 'map' and a 'compass' for what is to follow. He is particularly interested in emphasizing the positionality, or location, of the theorist, the person who gazes at something from somewhere. Reflecting the larger theme of the book, Tweed's invocation of 'map' and 'compass' metaphors signals his desire to construct a theory that, not static, accounts for movements and relations – of the data, of the theorist, and of the theorist's relationship to the data. Tweed, thus, makes much of the term 'itinerary':

> I suggest that theories are embodied travels ('a line or course of travel; a route'), positioned representations ('a record or journal of travel, an account of a journey'), and proposed routes ('a sketch of a proposed route; a plan or scheme of travel'). Theories are simultaneously proposals for a journey, representations of a journey, and the journey itself. (9)

Having articulated the notion of theory as itinerary and itinerary as theory, Tweed proceeds to take, what he calls, a 'locative' approach,[1] which both acknowledges and accounts for the situatedness of theorists and their theories within specific social and intellectual contexts. He defines his own context as that of 'a middle-aged, middle-class, Philadelphia-born white guy of Irish Catholic descent' (18) trying to 'find a new language that might make more sense of the movement, relation, and positionality I noticed at the annual festival in Miami' (26).

In chapter two, 'Boundaries', Tweed discusses 'constitutive terms', i.e., those that mark the boundaries of a field of study, mastery of which are necessary for defining and understanding the field in question. For religious studies, this term, not surprisingly, is 'religion'. Tweed argues that scholars of religion must take this term seriously and that they should accordingly invest considerable time and energy in understanding this term so that they are able to master the discourses that travel in its wake.

Because Tweed invests so much in constitutive terms, he is critical of those who make the case for abandoning the term 'religion' as a Western construct, and thus of little heuristic value, and who argue that it should be replaced with some less imperialistic alternative. He takes issue with, for example, McCutcheon (1997), Fitzgerald (2000), and Dubuisson (2003), all of whom have suggested, in one way or another, that the term 'religion' does not do any real work in helping us to understand better various cultural and ideological phenomena. Taking the opposite approach, Tweed contends that '*religion* has been the primary category used by scholars in [our] professional conversation since the mid-nineteenth century and cannot be easily replaced' (38; his italics). He argues that, instead of abandoning 'religion', we must constantly refine the term and continually revise our understanding of it.

Since he invests quite a lot in constitutive terms, Tweed must ultimately propose his own definition. His prerequisites for an adequate definition of religion include clarity of purpose and transparency concerning the orientating tropes that inform it. At the beginning of chapter three, 'Confluences', Tweed gives us his own definition:

> Religions are confluences of organic-cultural flows that intensify joy and confront suffering by drawing on human and suprahuman forces to make homes and cross boundaries. (54)

This definition further underscores the twin notions of movement and relation, which Tweed emphasizes by calling religions (note the plural) 'confluences of organic-cultural flows'. His employment of the aquatic trope 'confluences' is meant to suggest further that religions are dynamic and relational; that religions are not univocal and monolithic substances, but complex processes.

Tweed makes much of the trope of 'flows' or 'flowing' because it enables him to argue that religions move and morph through both time and space, interacting with a series of cultural and organic processes. In other words, religions move through time (e.g., as one generation passes on religious gestures to the next), and space (e.g., through missionary activity or dislocation); yet, they also develop and metamorphose based on a number of organic (e.g., neural, physiological, emotional, and cognitive) and cultural (e.g., linguistic, tropic, and ritualistic) constraints.

Presumably what makes these organic-cultural flows 'religious' is, to paraphrase the other part of his definition, the intensification of joy and the confrontation of suffering. Tweed argues that although such emotions have biological bases they are nonetheless constructed differently among cultures. So, even though religious traditions give names to similar emotions, each ultimately encodes them differently.

In the final clause of his definition – 'to make homes and cross boundaries' – he switches from aquatic to domestic and spatial tropes. Tweed now hopes to convey something of the ways religions orientate and help devotees locate themselves individually, communally, and cosmically. These features, 'dwelling' and 'crossing', will subsequently form the constituent parts of the remaining chapters of the book.

In chapter four, 'Dwelling: the kinetics of homemaking', Tweed focuses his theoretical lens on the concept of dwelling. He understands this term as 'the confluence of organic-cultural flows' that enable devotees to map, build, and inhabit. In particular, his goal here is to

> discuss how religion as dwelling orients devotees in time and space and, so, functions as watch and compass. Second, I note that this spatial and temporal orientation involves both organic processes and cultural practices. Finally, I argue that the 'autocentric' and 'allocentric' reference frames that emerge from these processes and practices allow the religious to map, construct, and inhabit ever-widening spaces: the body, the home, the homeland, and the cosmos. (83–4)

As 'watch and compass', Tweed contends that religions provide their members with a sense of belonging, a reminder whence they have come, and a prelude to what the future (corporeal and non-corporeal) holds. At this point he invokes what he calls 'autocentric' and 'allocentric' frames of reference: the former is responsible for orienting humans within their bodies and their immediate environment, whereas the latter orients them beyond these.

Based on these nuances and distinctions, Tweed argues that religions orient by means of the intersection of four 'chronotypes': the body, the home, the homeland, and the cosmos. He claims that religions code the body *qua* organic-cultural form by imagining it in a number of ways (e.g., biologically, gendered, sexually). By home, Tweed refers to everything from a hut to a nation-state to the universe, all of which, once again, are constructed using a variety of organic and cultural hierarchies, which inform and are informed by religion. Both of these autocentric frames of references have their allocentric counterparts in the homeland and the cosmos, which are in turn signified by numerous and overlapping tropes, forms, and social organizations. The importance of religions in the concept of dwelling resides in their ability to anchor these 'chronotypes' in a variety of artifacts and in transmitting them, culturally and generationally, in rituals.

Tweed devotes chapter five to 'Crossing', which he subtitles 'The kinetics of itinerancy'. Here his goal is to demonstrate how religions are not simply about the situation of practitioners in time and space, but that they also facilitate movement across a variety of borders and boundaries. He subsequently subdivides these crossings into subtypes: terrestrial, corporeal, and cosmic. Tweed explains these as follows:

> *Terrestrial crossings*, as devotees traverse natural terrain and social space beyond the home and across the homeland; *corporeal crossings*, as the

religious fix their attention on the limits of embodied existence; and *cosmic crossings*, as the pious imagine and cross the ultimate horizon of human life. (123; his italics)

The principle behind all of these crossings is that religions are responsible for, on the one hand, setting various limits and, on the other, the promotion of crossing these limits. Such limits – whether embodied, life-cyclical, pilgrimatic – are all potentially restrictive and thus fraught with confusion. Where religions come into play, Tweed wants to suggest, is in their uncanny ability to provide the mechanisms that facilitate these crossings.

Tweed concludes his monograph by returning to the concept of 'itinerary'. Here he comes back to his own data, that of Cuban migrants in South Florida, having spent several chapters surveying various cross-cultural materials to test his thesis. He claims that his previous discussion has successfully met his criteria for what is required of a new theory of religion.

Tweed's theoretical assumptions

Despite Tweed's optimistic conclusion that he has successfully fulfilled his professional duty as a religionist and met his role-specific obligation to reflect on the field's constitutive term, we have to ask if Tweed has really succeeded in doing this. Towards this end, I shall now examine some of the theoretical assumptions and rhetorical moves that Tweed has made in order to construct his theory.

Tweed works on the assumption that there exists naturally in the world something called 'religion' and that this can be neatly isolated in such a manner that it is distinct from other cultural and/or ideological trajectories. For instance, he argues that 'religions cannot be reduced to economic forces, social relations, or political interests' (60). Tweed here implies that religion is irreducible, and it is for this reason that he can isolate it as *the* constitutive disciplinary term. Yet such a claim is problematic owing to (1) recent interrogations of the term 'religion' as a viable category; (2) all of the baggage that the term 'religion' carries in its wake; and (3) the very existence of a discipline, often called 'religious studies', which circularly claims for itself the possession of analytical tools to uncover something amorphously referred to as 'religion' in the first place.

Within this context, Tweed too easily dismisses the wills to power that have been responsible for the discourses used to create religion as a category and that subsequently manufactured specific religions (e.g., Buddhism, Hinduism, Islam) as valid objects of study. For instance, he ignores the ways in which a Western scholarly discourse invented a number of global, cross-cultural objects of study, each of which was seen to possess an essence regarded as not inherently different from that found in the others. More often than not, this essence was based on something internal to the individual and reflected Protestant sensibilities, such as experience over liturgy, creaturely feeling over the messiness of culture, and metaphysical beliefs over the embodiedness of ritual (see, e.g., the comments in Orsi 2005: 186–92). If it were simply a matter of recognizing this oversight today all might well be fine; however, such is not the case. The repercussions of this antiquated model of an essentialized, irreducible, and *sui generis* thing called religion remain at the heart of the discipline and do not seem to be going anywhere quickly. Indeed, it is a model to which Tweed implicitly subscribes.

Tweed does not interrogate these issues. As a result, he reifies religion, which, in turn, informs and influences how he approaches data. Since he assumes that religion is an adequate descriptive category and that it can be neatly extracted from other cultural forms, he is able to survey copious amounts of data that have been removed from their specific social, historical, and ideological contexts. In many ways Tweed has to do this since his chief aim is to demonstrate that his theory does not simply explain his own local data at the shrine of Our Lady of Charity, but that it can, ideally, also be of use in accounting for other data:

> Toward that end, I select examples from varied cultures and multiple periods as I try to persuade readers by being amply illustrative rather than propositionally argumentative. After all, it would be difficult to convince anyone that this theory has some interpretive reach if I restricted myself to examples from the Miami shrine. (84)

Unlike many earlier theorists who surveyed data from the world's religions, Tweed makes a point of being conscious that he is selective and ahistorical. This seems to make him quite comfortable in gathering and situating data gleaned from reading, not ethnography, from which he originally began to develop his theory. Tweed, to use his own words, relies 'on histories, translations, and ethnographies from many colleagues, who offer interpretations of the sites along the way' (85).

If Tweed moves seemingly effortlessly among data derived from his reading of secondary literature, itself responsible for maintaining the existence of world religions, he also draws freely from a number of different academic disciplines. Perhaps the discipline from which he draws most is geography (for a favourable review of the work in this discipline, see Prorok 2007). For instance, he refers to religions as 'sacroscapes' (61), 'glocalities' (62), and as that which 'position women and men in natural terrain and social space' (74). As I shall discuss in greater detail below, Tweed also draws upon the disciplines or sub-disciplines of fluid mechanics, hydrodynamics, and geophysics in order to 'follow a flow in a vectorial field' (171). Tweed, however, rarely makes consistent use of these disciplines; the result is that we are often left with a series of sound bites from them, yet rarely do we encounter a full-scale elaboration of how precisely such disciplines can contribute positively to the academic study of religion.

All of these disciplines, including the metaphors and other tropes that they presuppose, enable Tweed to argue that 'religions are not reified substances but complex processes' (59). This is why Tweed is most interested in using aquatic metaphors in his definition. By claiming that religions function as 'organic-cultural flows', he seeks to avoid 'essentializing religious traditions as static, isolated, and immutable substance' (60). Each religion, thus, represents

> a flowing together of currents – some enforced as 'orthodox' by institutions – traversing multiple fields, where other religions, other transverse confluences, also cross, thereby creating new spiritual streams. (60)

The question arises, however, as to what exactly Tweed means by 'flows', and how this conceptual metaphor can be adequately and coherently applied to the study of religion (cf. further the critiques in Paden 2007 and Reader 2007). If religion is a flow, for example, then how can it, as Tweed seems to imply, maintain its uniformity in terms of related metaphors such as velocity, volume, and direction? Moreover, following the semantic field of the metaphor a little, what is the source from which religions flow and, alternatively, into what are they channeled? If religion is but one flow, then how does it overlap with presumably competing flows such as politics, economics, and culture?

Tweed is certainly correct to envision religions as unstable, non-static, and fluctuating entities; however, the repercussions of his aquatic metaphors potentially take him in directions in which he might not be comfortable. In addition, Tweed also assumes that religions are not simply flows, but, more specifically, organic-cultural ones that involve 'both neural pathways in brains and ritual performances in festival' (62). Here Tweed seems to want to reach out to work done in cultural studies and cognitive science simultaneously. Whether or not he does, or does so effectively, will be for those working in these cognate fields to determine.

Internal and external coherence

In his often cited *Adde parvum parvo magnus acervus erit* (1978a), Jonathan Z. Smith names and categorizes four comparative models that have driven the academic study of religion, only two of which necessarily interest me here. I refer primarily to the 'ethnographic' and the 'encyclopedic', both of which derive from specific encounters with others and which, accordingly, possess distinctive presuppositions and methods of presentation. The hallmark of the ethnographic model, to use Smith's words, is when 'something other has been encountered, and it is surprising either in its similarity or dissimilarity to what is familiar "back home"' (246). The encyclopedic model, on the contrary, offers 'a topical arrangement of cross-cultural material (arranged either by subject matter or alphabetically) culled from reading' (250). Here the tendency is to give a certain epic quality to lists, in which depth is frequently forfeited in favor of the seemingly endless enumeration of data.

I want to suggest that what Tweed does is conflate – whether intentionally or unintentionally, consciously or unconsciously, is not my concern here – the encyclopedic and the ethnographic modes of comparison. Although I do not want to imply that there necessarily exist airtight borders separating these models, their genealogies present aims and purposes that are, potentially at least, at cross-purposes with one another. Moreover, I certainly do not want to intimate that Tweed is guilty of the categorical mistakes that have traditionally plagued these classical models; I want only to highlight that his development of a theory is ethnographic (i.e., that developed out of his own work on Cuban immigrant communities in South Florida), and that his method of making this into a universal category is encyclopedic. As such, I raise the possibility that perhaps the encyclopedic presentation of data may not be the most useful method to give support to that encountered ethnographically.

It is precisely in Tweed's presentation of data, the accumulation and invocation of increasing number of relatively context-less examples, that the nuances of the local ethnographic insights are potentially lost. For example, in his discussion of the body in a chapter devoted to 'Dwelling', Tweed writes:

One famous Buddhist text, for example, imagined the body as a chariot. In *The Questions of King Melinda*, the Buddhist Nâgasena explains the nature of the embodied person ... Some passages in the Hebrew Bible propose that embodied humans resemble the divine ... Other narratives, from the Zoroastrian tradition, use martial images to imagine the body as battleground between cosmic forces of good and evil. (99)

Too much occurs too quickly in this one paragraph. Sure Tweed can point to Genesis 1:26–27 and 5:1–3 as supporting his general claim of divine embodiedness, but these are widely considered to come from the theological school of the so-called J (or Y) level of the Torah, a school that had an ideological ax to grind with other competing schools or ideologies, some of which also made their way into the final redaction of the Torah. What about all those places where strict lines are drawn between humanity and God (e.g., Genesis 1:1–3)? It is the manner in which all of the data sits univocally in passages such as this that, for me, potentially limits the utility of Tweed's book (this is also a criticism found in Paden 2007). This is potentially compounded once we remember that the genealogy of this mode of comparison takes us back to Herodotus via the likes of Tylor and Frazer.

Where Tweed is at his best is in working with his own data. The further he strays from this, however, the less certain he is and, as such, the more he is forced to rely upon the secondary work of others, operating on the assumption that such work accurately images or reflects reality 'on the ground'. Yet, as J.Z. Smith's essays have so poignantly demonstrated with respect to Eliade's sources, we cannot always read the reports of others at face value. Much of chapters three and four are awash with example after example, becoming a set of lists. Here Tweed moves from Buddhism to Islam to Judaism to Hinduism and back again. One always hates to criticize an important generalist work like this, one with potential wide appeal, through recourse to area studies or one's own area of specialization. Yet, when one either fails to recognize the tradition that one studies in such a theory or it is presented very generally and context-less, a number of problems ensue.

Related to Tweed's presentation of data is, potentially, the inability to recognize the nuances of one's own tradition.[2] Let me use as an example Judaism. Tweed mentions 'Judaism' in his index sixteen times; of these sixteen instances, ten are simply generic (e.g., Judaism does or Jews do 'x' or 'y'), and three reduce Judaism to the teachings found in the Hebrew Bible. Only twice do we encounter real Jews: on pp. 108–9, Tweed tells us about 'Orthodox Jews' in Toronto who have constructed an *eruv* around their neighborhood so that they can perform certain acts on Shabbat. In fact the only individual Jew we meet in the work is Arthur Hertzburg, who, speaking in the context of the *Shoah*, writes 'I have never found a way to absolve God' (140).

This, to me, is a real problem. What about real flesh and blood Jews, whether now in the present or who lived in other times and places? It is precisely real people that Tweed lived with, talked with, ate with, and with whom he worked in South Florida; moreover, it is precisely such people that become lost in *Crossing and dwelling*'s movement between the ethnographic and the encyclopedic.

Aside from Tweed's presentation of data, another important constituent of his definition concerns religion's ability to 'intensify joy and confront suffering'. Tweed once again situates the emotive quality of religions against the backdrop of organic-cultural processes: 'neurological and physiological processes set certain constraints, but cultural practices

– including religious practices – generate emotional idioms and rules that frame affective life' (69–70).

The problem here is not so much that emotions are biologically based but interpreted culturally; rather it is that religion is somehow responsible for framing such emotions. This returns us to some of the problems that circulate around Tweed's operating assumption that 'religion' is a valid category that adequately or better explains phenomena than other, more quotidian categories (e.g., culture, ideology). As I intimated above, Tweed taps into, whether he wants to or not is not the issue, the genealogy that privileges the uniqueness of religion, as that which adequately explains other data, but which, in turn, cannot be explained by or reduced to such data.

In this regard, it is unclear how religion 'intensifies joy' or 'confronts suffering' in ways that are different from other cultural forms. On one level, Tweed may certainly be correct in that whenever people get together in a variety of ritualistic or liturgical settings, they involve their emotions by the very fact that they interact with other humans. Yet, is this not what virtually every inter-human encounter does? Every time humans get together of their own volition – to go for dinner, to a movie, to a concert – surely they 'intensify joy and confront suffering'?

Tweed attempts to differentiate between the religious and cultural framing of emotions by adding that religions do this by drawing not only on human forces, but also suprahuman ones. Again, however, the fact that devotees may well think that they are appealing to forces larger than themselves does not alter the fact that the emotions that they perceive, feel, and confront are culturally, not religiously, constructed. In fact, one could very well argue the opposite of what Tweed implies by stating that emotions organize so-called religious responses, as opposed to claiming that religions 'provide the lexicon, rules, and expression for many different sorts of emotion, including those framed as most positive and most negative, most cherished and most condemned' (70).

These aforementioned critiques all lead to what may well be one of the most difficult challenges which Tweed's theory must face: Are the categories of 'crossing' and 'dwelling' so broad and all-inclusive that they are unhelpful in understanding religions (cf. the criticisms in Reader 2007)? In other words, basic to all human cultural forms is the desire or need to move, to cross, to cohabit, and to dwell. Religions may well sanction such phenomena and they may even be appealed to, *post factum*, as a way to justify, legitimate, or otherwise ameliorate the potential dangers and traumas associated with such phenomena.

Tweed might well come back and argue that the beauty of his theory is its simplicity, its ability to point out the obvious, and that this theory closely resembles reality and the historical record that presumably documents it. However, his privileging of religion in all of these cultural movements, migrations, artifacts, and emotions is potentially obfuscatory. Tweed must convince us that religion is actually doing the work that he claims that it is doing; that the term 'religion' is not hiding under it a more complex and helix-like set of other cultural, ideological, economic, cultural, and social phenomena. I am not entirely convinced that he has.

Again, let me take as an example Judaism, especially the concept of a *minyan* (a quorum of ten individuals), which is needed to carry out a complete prayer service, including that of the mourner's *qaddish*. On the one hand a *minyan* is a provisional Jewish center, one founded on the loss of the Temple in 70 CE. However, the qualification for being part of a *minyan* is genealogical, and not necessarily 'religious'.

One shows up to a *minyan*, then, not to cross some boundary, but to help someone have enough Jewish bodies to say, more often than not, *qaddish* for the dead. Certainly one crosses a threshold, signaled by a *mezuzah* on a front door, but once inside there is little fondness for either recollecting or crossing towards Jerusalem (or anywhere else), nor is there any attempt to move, migrate, flow, or travel across anything. Moreover, if one arrives at the house and finds that there are already enough people to form a *minyan*, one might well go home. And once over there are usually arguments about recent discussions of same-sex unions in the Conservative movement or complaints about this or that. Obligation to Jewish community –'I've worked all day, I'm tired, but David might need an extra body so he can say the mourner's prayer for his mother' – thus trumps any generic terms that imply 'crossing' or 'dwelling'.

Further theorizing

Tweed's earlier work is based on keeping 'close to the ground' (85). In other words, his main concern has been with providing close and contextual thick descriptions of particular case studies (e.g., Victorian America, Cuban Americans) in order to illumine a larger problem. In *Crossing and dwelling*, however, he takes the opposite approach by attempting to establish a general theory and then presenting copious amounts of context-less data in order to back it up.

The question emerges: What exactly are we supposed to do with a new theory of religion? I, for one, am not entirely sure. Will Tweed's theory help us understand the form of cultural work that scholars rather lazily call 'religion' any better? Parts of this work certainly will. In this context, Tweed is at his most lucid and most sophisticated when he is working with the data that he knows well (e.g., the religious forms and idioms of Cuban immigrants).

Yet, it is precisely when Tweed moves beyond the data with which he is familiar that categorical problems arise. His movement from the local to the global, from the ethnographic to the encyclopedic, creates a number of tensions within the book, but that also, more broadly, are indicative of the tensions that have traditionally plagued the academic study of religion. To just what extent, for instance, is it useful to take the nuances and particularities of specific micro-traditions and attempt to subsume them within larger categories? Does what is gained (e.g., a universal theory) outweigh what is lost (i.e., local religious idioms)? Or is the case the opposite: that we level the particular by forcing it to fit into a larger theory that is often not interested in the particular to begin with?

An interesting counterpoint to the work of Tweed is that of Robert A. Orsi. Both count as their data religion in America and, more specifically, that of 'lived religion'. Yet, Orsi takes a very different approach. He prefers to show how the dynamics of lived religion – for him, primarily post-industrial Italian-American Catholicism in New York and Chicago – cannot be subsumed into larger categories precisely because this activity edits out the particularities that are inherent to their specific religious idioms. For Orsi:

> [R]eligious cultures are local and to study religion is to study local worlds. There is no such thing as a 'Methodist' or a 'Southern Baptist' who can be neatly summarized by an account of the denomination's history or theology. There are Methodists in Tennessee in the 1930s struggling with particular realities of work and home, politics and gender, with children leaving, old people dying, work closing, and so on ... What exists are histories of people working in their worlds in specific ways at specific times and places. (2005: 167–8)

Tweed, in his earlier work, might well have agreed with such a statement. However, in *Crossing and dwelling* he has relinquished the local and the contextual for the sake of establishing a universal paradigm that can ideally be applied to any religious datum, irrespective of time or geography. And while he is certainly to be congratulated for his boldness and his vision, it must be realized that both of these virtues are not without their fair share of problems.

It is precisely this problem or tension, that between the specific and the universal, that I have tried to isolate here. Tweed has a tendency to conflate the ethnographic and encyclopedic modes of encountering, juxtaposing, and understanding data. In short, the ethnographic model demands that we observe, on a local level, those that are 'not us' in order to understand another culture and ultimately ourselves. In the case of earlier scholars this involved travelers' accounts, but in the case of Tweed's earlier work it involved disciplined and sensitive participant observation. Precisely because of this, it involves listening to these subjects, trying to understand their hopes, fears, desires, and imaginings.

Yet, juxtaposed against this is the encyclopedic model presented in most of *Crossing and dwelling*. This model is not interested in hearing the voices of others. On the contrary it is obsessed with the collection of more and more data. This necessarily involves moving away from fleshy humans and into the activity of presenting and processing cross-cultural data, often once, twice, or even thrice removed from real people. Individuals are now 'Jews' or 'Muslims' who, deprived of their singularity, become shadows or ideal essences of themselves. As such, they are easier to fit into a discourse with which their concrete manifestations may well disagree.

Notes

1   Tweed does not employ the term 'locative' in the perhaps more customary theoretical way suggested by Jonathan Z. Smith, who argues that it represents a worldview preoccupied with boundaries, especially their maintenance and control (see Smith 1978b: 147–51).

2   This certainly need not be the sole or, even, a valid criterion for evaluating a theory of religion. However, I think it important that a theory such as Tweed's, which developed from examining particular bodies in a particular situation, ought to be translatable to other particular bodies in other particular situations.

References

Dubuisson, D., 2003. *The Western construction of religion: myths, knowledge, and ideology*. Johns Hopkins University Press, Baltimore.

Fitzgerald, T., 2000. *The ideology of religious studies*. Oxford University Press, Oxford, New York.

McCutcheon, R. M., 1997. *Manufacturing religion: the discourse on sui generis religion and the politics of nostalgia*. Oxford University Press, Oxford, New York.

Orsi, R.A., 2005. *Between heaven and earth: the religious worlds people make and the scholars who study them*. Princeton University Press, Princeton.

Paden, W., 2007. Review of *Crossing and dwelling: a theory of religion* by Thomas A. Tweed. *Religion* 37 (1), 101–3.

Prorok, C.V., 2007. Review of *Crossing and dwelling: a theory of religion* by Thomas A. Tweed. *Annals of the Association of American Geographers* 97 (1), 226–7.

Reader, I., 2007. Review of *Crossing and dwelling: a theory of religion* by Thomas A. Tweed. *Nova Religio* 11 (1), 126–9.

Smith, J.Z., 1978a. *Adde parvum parvo magnus acervus erit*. In: Smith, J.Z., *Map is not territory: studies in the history of religions*. University of Chicago Press, Chicago, 240–64.

Smith, J.Z., 1978b. Birth upside down or right side up? In: Smith, J.Z., *Map is not territory: studies in the history of religions*. University of Chicago Press, Chicago, 147–71.

Tweed, T.A., 1992 [2000]. *The American encounter with Buddhism, 1844–1912: Victorian culture and the limits of dissent*. North Carolina University Press, Chapel Hill.

Tweed, T.A., 1997a. *Our Lady of the Exile: diasporic religion at a Cuban Catholic shrine in Miami*. Oxford University Press, Oxford, New York.

Tweed, T.A. (Ed.), 1997b. *Retelling U.S. religious history*. University of California Press, Berkeley.

Tweed, T.A., 2006. *Crossing and dwelling: a theory of religion*. Harvard University Press, Cambridge, MA.

Tweed, T.A. and Stephen Prothero (Eds), 1999. *Asian religions in America: a documentary history*. Oxford University Press, Oxford, New York.

14

Theory of religion as myth

On Loyal Rue, Religion is not about God (2005)

Hubert Seiwert

For most of the twentieth century, theory in the study of religion was marked by two main approaches – theologically or philosophically informed phenomenology and social-scientific theories of religion. It was only in the last decade of the century that theories inspired by the natural sciences, particularly evolutionary biology and cognitive psychology, became popular. The book to be considered in this chapter – Loyal Rue's *Religion is not about God* (Rue 2005) – in some respects combines all three of these approaches, although at first sight it appears to be attributable to the natural-scientific faction. This is due to the fact that its starting point and core argument is the biological evolution of the human species and its vocabulary makes heavy use of the terminology of cognitive psychology.

Contemporary evolutionary theories of religion oscillate between two opposing interpretations. One of them – exemplified by the works of Pascal Boyer (Boyer 1994, 2001)[1] and apparently to date the majority – considers religion a natural phenomenon that is a by-product of the evolution of the human brain without adaptive functions. The other one – represented by David Wilson (Wilson 2002)[2] – sees religion as a product of biological and cultural evolution with immense adaptive value for group survival. Rue's position belongs to the latter school of thought, although his theoretical and methodological approach is different from Wilson's. For Rue, religion is of utmost importance for the survival and well-being of the human species. His theory may thus be seen as the extreme opposite to Richard Dawkins's biological interpretation of religion (Dawkins 2006), who – while equally using evolutionary theory and cognitive psychology for his argument – concludes that religion is one of the major obstacles to human well-being.[3]

The sympathetic attitude Rue takes towards religion may partly be due to his academic background. He is Professor of Philosophy and Religion at Luther College in Decorah, Iowa. A two-time Templeton Award winner, he has published several philosophical books on natural history, including *By the grace of guile: the role of deception in natural history and human affairs* (Rue 1994) and *Everybody's story: wising up to the epic of evolution* (Rue 1999). *Religion is not about God* takes up again many thoughts of these earlier works to use them for his theory of religion.

The purpose of this book is 'to show how the ideas, images, symbols, and rituals of religious traditions have been designed to engage and to organize human neural systems for the sake of human survival, and then to examine the contemporary conditions that have compromised their adaptive utility' (1).[4] To this end, Rue proposes a 'general and naturalistic theory of religion' (2), whose core argument is that there is a universal human nature that can be known by examining the evolutionary history of humankind. In this context, religion is seen as fulfilling vital functions in influencing the cognitive and emotional systems of humans in a way that allows for the achievement of personal and social well-being.

This chapter summarizes and critically comments on the main arguments of Rue's book, following roughly the sequence of its three parts: 1. On human nature; 2. On spiritual traditions; and 3. On the future of religion. The focus is on the theory of religion and its evolutionary and psychological background. I will conclude with some methodological comments on Rue's theoretical approach.

The evolution of behaviour

The theory of religion is presented in the first part, 'On human nature'. It starts with a narrative account of evolution that begins with the 'creation of matter from energy' (22), reviews the emergence of life, and continues with the evolution of behaviour. Humans are part of this natural process and at the same time unique in the combination of their traits, which evolved 'for doing what every life form must do – that is to endure and to reproduce' (26). To the extent that humans are living beings, their nature can be described as fitness-maximizing biochemical systems. But what makes them unique? It is the astonishing range and complexity of behaviour that makes the species stand apart from all the others.

Consequently, Rue's discussion of human nature turns to the evolution of behaviour, beginning with the biochemistry of bacteria up to complex emotional and cognitive systems. The behaviour of higher animals is controlled by the brain, which processes information about the environment and steers motor responses of the organism. In the course of evolution, the architecture of the brain became increasingly complex, comprising quite a number of different neural systems (or neural modules) that handle various tasks including perception, memory, emotion, and cognition. The evolution of neural modules, according to Rue, was largely determined by the sequence in which animals faced challenges as new environmental circumstances selected for abilities to process new forms of information (32). Here, as elsewhere in the book, Rue suggests that natural selection works as a goal-directed process to respond to environmental 'challenges'. He ignores the fact that evolutionary changes have no direction such as increasing complexity. For some reason, his otherwise fairly comprehensive evolutionary narrative does not mention the mechanisms of genetic evolution. Perhaps the idea of pure chance being a driving force of evolutionary change would have spoiled his narrative, which depicts evolution as a meaningful process.

However, it may also be that Rue pays no attention to the genetic mechanisms of evolution because what he is really interested in is not genetic but cultural evolution. For Rue, evolution – while being a natural process – is more than biological evolution that can be explained by genetic variations and natural selection. His theory of human behaviour is naturalist in that he stresses the fact that the capacities of the brain are a result of biological evolution. However, he does not ignore the fact that human behaviour is also influenced by social and cultural factors. The brain is 'almost literally, a social artifact' (45). To explain how the working of the brain depends on both innate cognitive algorithms acquired through genetic evolution and culturally shaped algorithms acquired through social interaction, Rue presents a hypothetical model of different types of mental operators.

Mental operators

As Rue describes it, human behaviour is regulated by two sets of brain functions or 'operators'. On the one hand, there are *primary operators* of the cognitive system, which are innate modules that process information and produce an intuitive worldview. On the other hand, there are *secondary operators* that compete with the primary operators. The 'intuitive worldview' includes both 'intuitive science' – that is, information about which things exist and what they are like – and 'intuitive morality' – that is, information about the value of things. Intuitive morality is the result of the functioning of primary valence operators that evaluate the significance of external facts relative to the biological *teloi* of the species, which are survival and reproduction. Rue makes a strong point that humans come into the world equipped with a biological value system – an intuitive morality embedded in the goal-directed workings of their basic drives and emotional systems (56).

The concept of primary mental operators producing an intuitive worldview is based on Steven Pinker's theory that the human mind is a naturally selected system of organs of computation (Pinker 1997). Rue develops this theory further by hypothesizing that the human brain also constructs '*secondary operators* that compete with our primary operators in ways that inevitably and differentially override our intuitive worldviews' (61). Were there only primary operators, all humans would share more or less their ways of feeling, thinking, and behaving, guided by the same intuitive science and morality. It is the secondary operators, which are shaped in the course of one's individual life, that are responsible for the behavioural patterns of different individuals. To the extent that they share a common social and cultural environment, these patterns exhibit certain similarities. As behaviour is controlled by neural processes, we can conclude that the brain's behaviour mediation systems are influenced by cultural factors that may overrule the algorithms of intuitive science and morality (60–3).

The working of secondary operators is illustrated with the formation of self-esteem, which Rue sees as the most dominant of all our behaviour mediation systems. He explains self-esteem as being dependent on a process of self-monitoring that observes the outcome of one's own behaviour (63f.). Now, it is not only the primary valence operators that evaluate one's behaviour but also secondary valence operators. While the primary valence operators evaluate the significance of external facts relative to the *biological* goals or *teloi* of the species, the secondary valence operators evaluate according to culture-specific values. What is regarded as good or bad behaviour depends on socially induced standards. The reactions of others will influence the subject's evaluation. Positive reactions will induce positive feelings and reinforce behaviour that provokes positive reactions. At the same time, this will increase one's self-esteem and link it with values that are in conformity with social standards. These secondary values may diverge from the biological *teloi* pursued by the primary valence operators. The secondary valence operators are not part of our biological heritage but of our socio-cultural heritage. They operate by extra-genetic rules in that they are objectified and transmitted across generations through symbols (63–6).

Symbol systems and cultural evolution

The use of symbols marks the passage from genetic to cultural evolution. Symbol systems contain information on the world and the value of things that give orientation to human behaviour. Intuitive science and intuitive morality are no longer the sole form of guidance. '[S]ymbol systems are both extra-genetic and extra-somatic: They exist outside the body, in the objective social domain, a sort of commons where their elements are negotiated and modified in relation to other elements' (70). While the evolution of behaviour governed by genetically transmitted information was slow, the use of symbols enabled it to reach an unprecedented dynamism tied to the dynamics of cultural evolution. Rue borrows the term *memes* from Richard Dawkins (cf. Dawkins 1976: 203–15) for the units of symbolic variation, transmission, and selection in the course of cultural evolution. 'A cultural tradition is the sum of its memes' (70). I doubt that this concept helps much to clarify the mechanism of cultural evolution, but as it is not central to Rue's argument we may leave it at that.

The meaning of life

More important is the final paragraph of the chapter on the evolution of behaviour, which is presented as a kind of conclusion. Its heading, 'Human nature and the meaning of life', indicates that the focus is suddenly shifting from questions of biology and psychology to the big questions of philosophy. Unfortunately, Rue is not very precise in his argumentation – at least, so it appears to me. We read that 'the point of pursuing a view of human nature is to discern the point of human existence, the meaning of life' (74). This seems to imply that the meaning of life is the same as 'the point of human existence', but what does 'point' mean in this context? Apparently it means 'purpose' or '*telos*'. As Rue explains: 'The meaning of human life should be expressed in terms of how our particular species pursues the ultimate telos of reproductive fitness' (75). Moreover, he claims

> that these immediate pursuits are about a pair of mutually depending yet mutually contending intermediate goals: *personal wholeness* and *social coherence*. Everything we do at the behest of our behavior mediation systems can be seen to contribute toward, or detract from, an achievement of one or both of these twin teloi. (75; italics in original)

The last sentence is logically true under any circumstances, because everything we do can be seen as either contributing to or detracting from these goals. But what reasons can be given to support the claim that the meaning of human life is to pursue personal wholeness and social coherence? The argument seems to be that these two goals are essential for reaching the ultimate *telos* of human existence – reproductive fitness. This may be the case or not; that is an empirical question. It is my impression that most individuals fail to meet the standards of 'whole persons' as described by Rue:

> Whole persons are those who are fully engaged with the world, and whose motivational systems are robust yet efficiently managed – persons who are able to construct agendas of sequential tasks, to anticipate outcomes, to assign priorities, and then attend to the most important matters while

> momentarily suppressing the demands of competing impulses. By such
> means the whole person is able to achieve a state of functional unity
> against the odds inherent in a plurality of motivational systems. (76)

Although such whole persons appear to resemble more a superman than
ordinary humans, the reproductive fitness of the species does not seem to
have been significantly impaired by the fact that this ideal is seldom realized.
Thus, empirical evidence hardly supports the claim that personal wholeness
is the ultimate *telos* of human existence. There are, however, also theoretical
objections to Rue's conclusions.

Central to his argument is the idea that human nature can be detected by
understanding the meaning and purpose of evolution. In his grand 'Epic of
evolution' humans emerge 'for doing what every life form must do – that is to
endure and to reproduce' (26). This, for him, is the purpose of existence, the
ultimate *telos* of evolution. Yet, we also could narrate the epic of evolution
from a different perspective. Then it would be the story of countless forms of
living that have been extinguished. It would appear that it is not survival and
reproduction that are the essence of natural selection but elimination. What
could be the ultimate *telos* of those life forms that have disappeared? Is it
to drive forward the process of evolution by allowing their more successful
competitors to survive? In any case, their *telos* could not have been to endure
and to reproduce, for then there would have been no selection and no evolution. To look for a *telos* – an ultimate purpose – of existence with evolutionary
theory is to misunderstand the theory. Biological evolution has no *telos*,
it is not a teleological process (Mayr 2005: 154). We can, of course, with
Rue narrate evolution as an epic. In this epic, every chapter has a meaning
in that it is a prelude to the following. But meaning is not inherent in the
evolutionary process; it is constructed by the narrator. If some individuals or
species survive and others don't, it is not due to the purpose of their nature.
It just happens because some are better adapted than others. It is no more the
ultimate *telos* of a species to reproduce than it is the ultimate *telos* of rivers
to carry water. If they cease to do so, they will disappear like so many other
things that have disappeared over the millennia. Natural selection is basically
a process of elimination (Mayr 2005: 150). Evolutionary theory may explain
the causes of what happens in nature – of survival and elimination – but for
its meaning and purpose we have to look somewhere else.

I do not think, therefore, that Rue's suggestion of defining the meaning
of human life in terms of its ultimate *telos* can be grounded in evolutionary
theory – at least not in its prevalent biological variant. This is not to say that
it cannot be grounded in other theories such as philosophical anthropology.
We may ignore this question here and proceed to the subsequent chapters of
his book, which lead to his theory of religion.

Religion and the education of emotions

Before he comes to this, Rue further explains the role of emotions in human behaviour. In his view, which is informed mainly by the works of Richard Lazarus (Lazarus 1991) and Antonio Damasio (Damasio 1999), emotions arise when inputs from the environment are appraised by the cognitive system as either contributing to or distracting from the subject's goals. They vary according to the goals of a subject. Emotional states have a central position in Rue's theory of human behaviour as they trigger behavioural responses; they are 'powerful forces' that hold potentials for danger as well as good; they can be conducive or threatening to the achievement of the ultimate *telos* of personal wholeness and social coherence. 'For this reason, humans have always found it necessary to develop various strategies for managing the emotional process' (107). Managing emotions is seen as an essential function of culture. Cultures moralize the emotional life by defining rules specifying the conditions under which the display of certain emotions is considered appropriate or inappropriate. In this sense, they can be said to play a crucial role in 'the education of emotions', as the third chapter is entitled.

The education of emotions is mediated by the symbol systems that every culture provides and which contain information about what is real and what is important. This symbolically expressed cosmology and morality competes with the intuitive science and morality shared by all humans. However, to the extent that the culturally transmitted morality is internalized by individuals, its values dominate the appraisal process of emotions and stimulates behaviour. In this way, human behaviour can overcome the constraints of our biological nature and is free to develop a variability of adaptive strategies that far surpasses all other species. 'In short, we have in our nature the means to manipulate our nature' (122).

At this point, Rue finally shifts his attention from human nature to spiritual traditions, which for him seem to be the core of 'the conventional meanings inherent in cultural systems' (123). Rue summarizes their 'consilience' with the 'adaptive meanings inherent in biological and psychological systems' by the 'principle of reduction', which is expressed in five points:

1   The myths, symbols, and practices in a religious tradition will have a decisive influence on the mental objects featured in the working memory of individuals.
2   The mental objects (neural imaging) featured in the working memory will have a decisive influence on the cortico-limbic interactions taking place during appraisal and coping events.

3 Patterns of cortico-limbic interaction will have a decisive influence on the mediation of human behaviour.
4 The mediation of behaviour will have a decisive influence on the prospects for achieving personal wholeness and social coherence.
5 It is by the achievement of personal wholeness and social coherence that members of our species influence the odds favouring reproductive fitness. (123ff.)

In short, religious myths, symbols, and practices are devices for producing certain patterns of neural stimulation. The theory of religion, which Rue elaborates in the following chapter, holds that the neural stimulation produced by religions works in such a way as to provoke emotions and behaviour that contribute to the achievement of personal wholeness and social coherence – that is, to the ultimate purpose and meaning of human existence.

The structure of religions

The chapter entitled 'The nature of religion' starts with the thesis that all religions have a common structure. Rue develops a structural model of religions that describes 'all particular religions as narrative traditions or myths, which are formulated and revitalized by a set of ancillary strategies. These strategies (intellectual, experiential, ritual, aesthetic, institutional) may be seen as overlapping dimensions that collectively shape the religious life' (143). The core of every cultural tradition is a story, a myth, which is a narrative integrating ideas about how things ultimately are and which things ultimately matter – that is, it includes cosmology and morality (126).

As Rue sees it, every myth is centred on a 'root metaphor' – a concept that is not further explained but illustrated by examples. The root metaphor of the Abrahamic traditions is God-as-person, in the Greek tradition it is *logos*, in Chinese myth it is the Tao. Later in the book, we also learn that the root metaphor of the Indian traditions is *dharma* (215). The root metaphor of a religious tradition links cosmology to morality, it integrates facts and values, and 'renders the real sacred and the sacred real' (127). The root metaphor is, as it were, what keeps the mythic narrative together and gives meaning both to cosmology and morality.

The origin of religion

Having identified myth as the core of religion and the various dimensions of religious life that explain, confirm, perform, express, and control the mythic narrative, Rue turns to the origins of religion. He gives a highly speculative account of what might have happened during the last 200,000 years of human history. It is a story narrating how small bands of hunter-gatherers that in many respects resembled groups of chimpanzees gradually developed intellectual competencies that allowed them to form larger social units (149–59). The theoretical background of this story is Rue's assumption that between 200,000 and 40,000 years ago two great cultural transitions must have happened. During this development, the intuitive science and intuitive morality were partly replaced by '*ad hoc* science' and '*ad hoc* morality', that is, culturally constructed worldviews ruled by secondary mental operators (149). Rue believes that the first of these transitions was gradual – lasting for about 120,000 years – and saw the development of an anthropomorphic interpretation of nature similar to what Edward Tylor describes as an animistic worldview. However, for Rue such ideas of gods and immortality were not religious, but rather proto-scientific (152).

The second transition was not gradual but a great leap forward occurring about 40,000 years ago. It was the step from intuitive morality to *ad hoc* morality, that is, the invention of social rules that allowed for the formation of larger social units that are too complex to function on the basis of the innate valence operators. Rue believes that new patterns of social organization developed as small groups of hunter-gatherers established episodic yet stable coalitions. These changes were analogous to the emergence of multicellularity from unicellular forms of life (156). The sheer novelty of these emerging forms of sociality generated a crisis of self-understanding which left individuals confused and perplexed about fundamental personal and social realities:

> Our ancestors found themselves in a state of desperate need for a story that could tell them who they were, where they came from, what the group was, how it came to be, and why they should follow the new rules. (159)

To this need responded the early thinkers who borrowed the anthropomorphic language of *ad hoc* cosmology and expanded it to include the nature of self and society, thus unifying the cosmic and moral orders. Religion emerged when storytellers imagined the first myths that brought together cosmological and moral ideas in a coherent narrative of gods and spirits. 'The first religious traditions arose as these stories found their distinctive strategies for carrying on' (159).

The strong point in Rue's account of the evolutionary origins of religion is that it is a fairly plausible if invented story of how things could have happened. It is a narrative that mixes up facts and fiction, and in this way makes fiction appear as facts. It cannot be denied that somehow and at some time in the past humans must have developed the ability to produce systems of symbols representing cosmological and moral ideas guiding behaviour in a way that goes beyond the intuitive orientations of innate responses to external stimuli. Rue's theory is an attempt to explain how, when and why this happened by proposing a possible scenario.

The weak point is that it is a just-so story and not a scientific theory that could in any way be confirmed or falsified on the basis of available evidence. One can, however, ask some questions. What is the foundation of the claim that socially constructed morality (*'ad hoc* morality') emerged in a 'great leap forward' about 40,000 years ago (152)? If it is true that the human brain developed the ability to form secondary valence operators that can overrule the intuitive values of the primary operators, why should this ability have remained unused for more than 100,000 years in the history of *homo sapiens*? How could this ability of the human brain have been naturally selected if it was without function? Why should the small bands of hunter-gatherers not have had cultural traditions and rules adapted to their diverse natural environments? As Rue does not address or resolve these questions, his account of the origins of religion is pure speculation. Given his understanding of religion, all we can say about the origin of religion is that it emerged when humans started to invent and transmit myths.

The function of religion

More central to the main argument of the book is Rue's description of the function of religions, which he sees in the achievement of personal wholeness and social coherence. It should be clear by now how he thinks religion fulfils this function. The mythic narratives and the ancillary strategies of religions shape the emotions and motivations of individuals in a way that allows them to overrule the innate intuitive morality of their biological heritage in favour of the culturally defined values encoded in the myths. Of course, this is premised upon the notion that religious myths actually do promote a morality that induces behaviour leading to personal wholeness and social cohesion. One may ask whether there is empirical evidence for this claim. Rue's answer is rather general:

> For example, whenever solidarity, cooperation, security, and harmony appear to be decreasing, or whenever social animosity, discrimination, injustice, and conflict appear to be increasing, we may begin to suspect a failure of religious function. And likewise, whenever happiness, toler-ance, generosity, and forgiveness appear to be giving way to depression, aggression, obsession and repression, we may wonder about the religious life. (160)

To suspect and to wonder are certainly good reasons to ask questions and possibly also to formulate hypotheses. But there is neither a logical nor a theoretical connection between the decline of social harmony and the decline of 'religious function'. At best, there could be an empirical correlation – although even this may be doubted given the unprecedented prosperous and harmonious developments in Western Europe after the Second World War. As is well known, it is a period that is also marked by a singular decline of religious commitment and belief in the core myth of the prevailing Christian religion. Which empirical cases could Rue have in mind? In the second part of his book he gives a survey of major religious traditions (Judaism, Christianity, Islam, Hinduism, Buddhism) to support his claim by empirical evidence. He tries to show that each of these religions centres on a core myth and uses the ancillary strategies mentioned to support it. He also argues that the meaning of this core myth and in particular its inherent morality enhanced personal wholeness and social coherence – if they were properly understood and practised. What he does not discuss, however, is the question of the extent to which these religious traditions really contribute to the achievement of personal wholeness and social coherence in the cultures under consideration.

Rue shows a certain sensitivity to this question when he deals with Christianity and reveals that he is quite aware of the gap between possibility and reality:

> One wonders what psychological and social consequences might follow if something close to a majority of self-professed Christians practiced their religion in the manner envisioned by its principal architects. …
>
> If Christians seriously apply themselves to resolving intellectual problems of the myth; if they seek personal validations of the myth in extraordinary experiences; if they saturate themselves with aesthetic expressions of the myth, making every effort to apprehend their multivalent meanings; … if they observe the sacraments; if they prompt themselves to ask what Jesus would do in situations they face – if they do all these things with regularity and consistency, then we may expect harmony with the Christian vision of how things ultimately are and which things ultimately matter. (222)

Obviously, there are many ifs. Religions might promote personal wholeness and social coherence if they functioned according to Rue's theory. But do they function in this way? Is it possible to give empirical evidence? Has this function of religion ever been fulfilled? If it is true that there were times when humans lived a religious life, believing their religious myths, participating in religious rituals and consuming religious art, then we must suppose that these were times of whole persons living in harmonious societies. When and where was it? I would guess that it was *in illo tempore*, in the mythic time when things were as they ought to be. What Rue presents as the functions of religion is a normative theory that describes how religions *should* work to serve their intended purpose.

Functions or effects?

There is nothing wrong with designing normative theories that explain how things should work if all interfering factors were eliminated. Economists do it all the time. If we remove the normative element, we arrive at what could be called 'pure theory' – that is, a theory that constructs an abstract model to understand the effects of some factors of the real world without denying that the real world is far more complex and the calculated effects may be distorted by countless other factors ignored by the theory. Would it be possible to interpret Rue's theory in this way? I think some of its aspects have considerable heuristic value. In my view, the most important contribution of Rue's theory to the study of religions is to emphasize the role of emotions in human behaviour and to show that religions have a significant share in the cultural shaping of emotions. Rue makes it clear that religious myths, rituals, and aesthetic perceptions can influence attitudes, moods, and motivations that shape the emotions of everyday life and not only religious experiences. This perspective allows us to understand better the psychological mechanisms that connect religious symbol systems with human behaviour.

A famous definition of religion given by Clifford Geertz starts with the phrase:

> [A] *religion* is (1) a system of symbols which acts (2) to establish powerful, pervasive, long-lasting moods and motivations in men by (3) formulating conceptions of a general order of existence... (Geertz 1966: 4)

Here, we have some ideas similar to Rue's theory: symbol systems (e.g., myths) that act to influence moods and motivations (and thereby emotions) by formulating conceptions of a general order of existence (i.e., cosmology and morality). Of course, Rue's theory comprises much more than these elements, but it is enlightening to consider a significant difference between these two theories: Geertz leaves open the question what kind of moods and motivations are established by religions. His theory does not exclude that the mood induced by a religion may be aggression and the feeling hatred. I would argue that this indefiniteness is more in accord with empirical evidence than the idea that religions generally promote emotions that enhance personal wholeness and social coherence. In contrast to Rue, Geertz describes in his definition of religion not its *functions* but its *effects*. The difference should not be ignored. The notion of *function* contains a normative component in that it evaluates the effect positively (Searle 2006: 17). We may say that the *effect* of a certain religious myth is to foster intolerance; if we say that the *function* of a certain religious myth is to foster intolerance, we imply that intolerance is a desired effect, at least for some observers or participants.

When Rue explains that it is the 'ultimate function' of a religion to enhance personal and social well-being, he means that they *should* do so. He is aware that religions do not really work in this way. Thus, he mentions that the 'exploitative aspects of Aryan-Indian religious life might erode the conditions for personal wholeness and social coherence' because 'the sacrificial system encouraged psychological dependency and fatalism' (255). We must conclude that this religion did not fulfil its ultimate function. Rue would probably agree and could argue that the function of the heart is to pump blood, but not all hearts function properly, which may eventually cause the death of an organism. Similarly, a culture or society whose religious function is impaired would have difficulty surviving.

Religious naturalism

It is this view that forms the background of the last part of the book, entitled 'On the future of religion'. What will happen if religions fail to fulfil their function to adapt human emotions and behaviours to the challenges of a changing environment? Rue sees the present situation of humankind as facing nearly unsolvable problems marked by a global environmental crisis that has been induced by excessive human impact on the life-supporting natural systems. He depicts this global crisis in the darkest possible colours. There are just two options: either humans quickly and thoroughly change their modes of behaviour that undermine the natural fundament of their survival; or they continue to increasingly overstrain the life-supporting systems, which will eventually result in a massive reduction of the human population caused by natural disasters.

Rue has little hope that there is time enough to avoid an environmental catastrophe, for this would call for a new morality that gives high priority to the protection of nature. He is convinced that such a change in value systems, which would demand personal sacrifices for the sake of saving natural resources, could only be accomplished by religion. However, the received religions do not seem to be able to respond appropriately to this challenge. There are two reasons for this: First, their traditional morality does not accord nature a high rank in the hierarchy of values, and this may change too slowly. Second, the traditional religions are undergoing a 'crisis of influence' in the contemporary world. The ultimate cause of this crisis is the dwindling belief in the reality of their root metaphors effected by the rise of modern science and the awareness of religious diversity. Another factor is consumerism, which Rue describes as sharing the basic structure of a religion, including a myth and ancillary strategies to support and maintain the myth. He even concedes that consumerism fulfils the functions of a religion as '[p]ersonal wholeness and social coherence are both maximized by a growing market, with no discernible sacrifices for anyone' (339). Though consumerism does not undermine belief in traditional religions intellectually, it simply drives them out of the mind and replaces religious values by its own goal hierarchies. However, the side-effects of consumerism are to increase the exploitation of natural resources. It will therefore only speed up the coming environmental catastrophe.

Rue is rather concrete in depicting possible doomsday scenarios, which would see humankind 'descending into hell' (358–60). He also envisions the aftermath of a global collapse, when the human population will be greatly reduced. Then, 'the remnant will clamor for ways to make their experience intelligible and restore the conditions for personal wholeness and social coherence' (361). In other words, they will need a new religion – a religion that gives meaning to their experience and provides a morality shaped by it. Rue guesses that the central myth of this religion would seek to integrate a naturalist cosmology with an 'eco-centric morality, the imperative to sustain human life on the planet by addressing the needs for personal wholeness and social coherence within the limits of natural systems' (363). It would be *religious naturalism*. As he says, prophets of the myth of religious naturalism have already started to appear, and we may suppose that he is one of them.

Seen from this perspective, many traits of this book that on first reading are irritating make sense. Rue's description of natural history and evolution is presented as a narrative, a story to be told – the 'epic of evolution'. *Epic* is a literary genre common to myths. Rue proposes a myth of religious naturalism that starts with the creation of matter and primordial chaos and ends with apocalyptic events preceding redemption. It is a myth informed by science and natural history, but unlike science it includes morality. In this myth, nature has meaning and life has a purpose.

The book has been extensively discussed in four articles published in the journal *Zygon* (Braxton 2007; Klemm 2007; Marsh 2007; Rottschaefer 2007). Significantly, none of them pays particular attention to Rue's theory of religion, but they all concentrate on the theological and philosophical implications of his prophesied religious naturalism. They are possibly right in taking the last, if shortest part of the work as being the *telos* of Rue's argument, but after all he starts with the promise to propose 'a general and naturalistic theory of religion' (2). For the study of religions, it is the first part of the book that deserves discussion.

A general and naturalistic theory of religion?

Rue proposes a general and naturalistic theory of religion. For him, a *general theory* is one 'that tells us what religion is, where it comes from, and how it functions' (2). We may ask to what extent his book answers these questions. Rue deals with the first question by describing the structure of religion, which consists of a central myth and ancillary strategies to transmit the myth and make it appear plausible. However, he finds the same structure in consumerism. Is consumerism a religion? Given the fact the Rue also states that consumerism fulfils the 'religious function' we must suppose that it meets his criteria for being a religion. We can go further and note that any cultural tradition could be described as comprising a core myth and ancillary means of making the myth appear real. Rue does not explain the difference between religion and other cultural traditions, if there should be any.

Rue obviously does not agree with most cognitive scientists of religion, who would maintain that religion is different because it implies ideas of counterintuitive supernatural agents. 'Religion is not about God' is the first sentence of the book (1). In Rue's view, religion 'is about *us*. It is about manipulating our brains so that we think, feel, and act in ways that are good for us, both individually and collectively' (1; italics in original). This sounds a bit like addressing a congregation. It seems to imply that a cultural tradition is a religion if and only if it is good for *us*, or perhaps its followers. Do Judaism, Christianity, Islam, Hinduism and Buddhism cease to be religions when they legitimate war and violence? Rue's description of these religions, which is intended to provide empirical evidence for the central religious functions of personal wholeness and social coherence, ignores the fact that these traditions have also been sources of individual suffering and social conflicts. His theory does not tell us what a religion is and how it functions; it rather appears to be an idealized vision of what religion should be and how it should function.

As to the question where religion comes from, the theory offers two kinds of answer. One is a story telling us how and when paleolithic man started to invent myths that integrated socially constructed cosmological and moral ideas into narratives. It is a plausible story but no scientific theory. The other answer is more theoretical, in that it uses the language of neuropsychology in explaining why human behaviour is not completely determined by the cognitive algorithms developed through genetic evolution, but instead guided by culturally transmitted cosmological and moral concepts. The explanation postulates a set of secondary mental operators that enable the human brain to overrule the impulses of the innate primary operators. Religion, then, is based on these secondary operators and may be said 'to come from' the brain's ability to construct them.

One could object that the theory of secondary operators just expresses in other language what was known before, that is, that human behaviour is influenced by genetic as well as by cultural factors. However, it should be recognized that his translation of insights of the cultural sciences into the terminology of neuropsychology and biological evolutionary theory is a valuable attempt to overcome the lack of communication between cultural and natural sciences. Rue subscribes to Edward O. Wilson's programme of consilience (Wilson 1998) – the unity of science based on scientific materialism. His theory of religion is intended to integrate the social sciences and the humanistic sciences into the consilience programme designed in the natural sciences (16). To develop a common terminology certainly is an important step to this end. In this respect, Rue's theory of religion can be seen as a significant contribution that may open new paths of cooperation and mutual stimulation of the natural and social sciences.

It is in view of the consilient unity of science that Rue is advocating not only a general but also a *naturalist* theory of religion. However, if by 'naturalism' he should mean *scientific* naturalism, there are some problems with his approach.[5] Rue sees evolution as a teleological and meaningful process. If we understand the 'epic of evolution', we can find out what the meaning and purpose of human nature is. Yet evolution is no epic composed to make us understand the meaning of life, but a natural process. Unless we subscribe to the theory of intelligent design, there is no goal, purpose, *telos*, or meaning in natural evolution. *Scientific* naturalism is a major agent of what Max Weber has called the 'disenchantment of the world'. It deprives the world of the meaning it had when religious and other myths described it as a cosmos full of mysteries. What Rue proposes is a *religious* naturalism engaged in the re-enchantment of the world to nurture an 'acquired sense for the mystery and sanctity of nature itself' (17). His theory of religion drafts the myth of religious naturalism.[6]

As a postscript and to do justice to Rue, it should be added that he is without doubt well aware that he is offering a myth camouflaged as scientific theory. In one of his earlier books he argues for the necessity of inventing a 'noble lie ... to reenchant the universe' as an adaptive strategy 'for opposing the maladaptive truth of nihilism' (Rue 1994: 279). To this end he envisions the creation of a 'biocentric myth' that 'takes its basic vocabulary from the sciences, adding only a narrative dimension to them' (Rue 1994: 304). This is what he has done in the book under scrutiny here. He may be right in thinking that deception can be more adaptive than truth and mythmaking more necessary than scientific argument. I doubt, however, that we should assign the task of inventing myths to the study of religion.

Notes

1 On Boyer's theory see Jeppe Sinding Jensen in this volume.
2 On David Sloan Wilson's theory see Joseph Bulbulia in this volume.
3 On Dawkins's theory see Armin Geertz and Marcus Frean in this volume.
4 Unless further specified, numbers in brackets refer to the pages in Rue 2005.
5 'Naturalism' is a diffuse concept that cannot be discussed here. It includes both ontological naturalism and methodological naturalism. Rue oscillates between them. He apparently is an ontological naturalist ('the natural is real and the real is natural' [12]), which implies that he is also a methodological naturalist ('reducing religious experiences and expressions to the status of natural events having natural causes' [2]). *Scientific* naturalism would be methodological naturalism based on the theoretical concepts and methodological principles of the natural sciences.
6 For a more explicit description of his understanding of the 'spiritual' dimensions of evolution see Rue 1997.

References

Boyer, P., 1994. *The naturalness of religious ideas: a cognitive theory of religion.* University of California Press, Berkeley.

Boyer, P., 2001. *Religion explained: the evolutionary origins of religious thought.* Basic Books, New York.

Braxton, D.M., 2007. 'Religion is not about God' – Responding to Loyal Rue. *Zygon* 42 (2), 317–41.

Damasio, A., 1999. *The feeling of what happens.* Harcourt, Brace & Co., New York.

Dawkins, R., 1976. *The selfish gene.* Oxford University Press, New York and Oxford.

Dawkins, R., 2006. *The God delusion.* Houghton Mifflin, Boston.

Geertz, C., 1966. Religion as a cultural system. In: Banton, M. (Ed.), *Anthropological approaches to the study of religion.* Tavistock Publications, London, 1–46.

Klemm, D.E., 2007. Religious naturalism or theological humanism? *Zygon* 42 (2), 357–66.

Lazarus, R., 1991. *Emotion and adaptation.* Oxford University Press, New York.

Marsh, L., 2007. Taking the *super* out of the supernatural. *Zygon* 42 (2), 343–55.

Mayr, E., 2005. *Das ist Evolution.* Goldmann, Munich (English trans., *What Evolution Is.* Basic Books, New York, 2001).

Pinker, S., 1997. *How the mind works.* W.W. Norton & Co., New York.

Rottschaefer, W.A., 2007. Mythic religious naturalism. *Zygon* 42 (2), 369–408.

Rue, L., 1994. *By the grace of guile: the role of deception in natural history and human affairs.* Oxford University Press, New York, Oxford.

Rue, L., 1997. Going deeper: spiritual dimensions of the epic of evolution. *Earth-Light Magazine* 26, 12–13, online at www.earthlight.org/personal26.html, accessed 18.8.2008.

Rue, L., 1999. *Everybody's story: wising up to the epic of evolution.* State University Press of New York, Albany.

Rue, L., 2005. *Religion is not about God: how spiritual traditions nurture our biological nature and what to expect when they fail.* Rutgers University Press, New Brunswick, London.

Rue, L., 2007. Religious naturalism – where does it lead? *Zygon* 42 (2), 409–22.

Searle, J.R., 2006. Social ontology. Some basic principles. *Anthropological Theory* 6 (1), 12–29.

Wilson, D.S., 2002. *Darwin's cathedral: evolution, religion, and the nature of society.* University of Chicago Press, Chicago, London.

Wilson, E.O., 1998. *Consilience: the unity of knowledge.* Alfred A. Knopf, New York.

15

New Atheistic approaches in the cognitive science of religion

On Daniel Dennett, Breaking the spell (2006) and Richard Dawkins, The God delusion (2006)

Armin W. Geertz

The growth of New Atheism in the United States during the last 20 years has closely paralleled the increase of religious extremism in the world. New Atheists are organizing themselves and are conducting systematic campaigns to reduce the influence of religious fundamentalism in all aspects of public society, ranging from anti-Darwinian school curricula to anti-abortion measures and foreign affairs decisions by the US government. An important part of New Atheist activities is the publication of popular books on religion, its origins, and its horrors. Peter Berkowitz reports in the *Wall Street Journal* (2007) on impressive book sales by New Atheist writers. In less than 12 months over a million books were sold. As of 2007, 500,000 hardcover copies are in print of Richard Dawkins's *The God delusion* (2006), 296,000 copies of Christopher Hitchens's *God is not great* (2007), 185,000 copies of Sam Harris's *Letter to a Christian nation* (2006),[1] 64,100 copies of Daniel Dennett's *Breaking the spell* (2006), and 60,000 copies of Victor J. Stenger's *God: the failed hypothesis* (2007). These are the main New Atheist authors, but there are also other recent publications which follow suit.[2]

The fact that authors Daniel Dennett and Richard Dawkins are included in this collection indicates that their impact is worth noting. The problem is that they are not scholars who have produced scientific books and articles arguing their particular theories of religion in the peer review contexts of the academic study of religion.[3] Both books are popular books with clearly formulated ideological, apologetical, and polemical agendas. There is no doubt in the reader's mind that religion in their view is bad and should be removed from the human race in the name of world peace and sanity.

Dennett's and Dawkins's books have no regard for, nor are written to, other scholars of religion. Their knowledge of religion is woefully limited and spotty, they reference comparative religionists from more than a half century ago, and they ignore the highly relevant and theoretically sophisticated scholars of religion who have been active since the 1970s. When they do refer to scholars of religion, it is only to the pioneers of the cognitive science of religion, especially Pascal Boyer.

Why, then, if Dennett and Dawkins have not contributed to the scientific study of religion, are more interested in atheistic crusades than in scholarship, and know very little about religion, are they included in this book? Have they contributed anything original to theories of religion? If not, why not just enjoy their entertaining books and leave them out of serious theoretical discourse about religion? My answer becomes clear if we take a look at the curious lineage of ideas before us. Put simply and highly generalized: Dawkins builds on Dennett, who builds on Boyer, who refers to Dawkins. All three build on Darwin.

What might a Darwinian theory of religion look like?

The last point is highly relevant to theorizing on religion. How can the principle of natural selection throw light on theories of religion? All three authors, and also many cognitive scientists of religion, have grappled with this problem in interesting and creative ways.

A Darwinian theory of religion, however, raises the important issue of reduction; of reducing cultural phenomena to levels of lower magnitude. I fully agree that all science, even human science, consists of reduction. We reduce complexity to basic fundamentals in order to better understand complex worlds. Narrative, for instance, consists of many levels of magnitude: narratological, receptive psychological, pragmatic contextual, social psychological, and neurobiological.

But how do Darwinians reduce complexity? The problem is that the main principles involved in modern evolutionary theory are very unwieldy in terms of cultural evolution: natural selection, adaptation, genetic drift, gene flow, mutation, and speciation. Richard Dawkins formulated his particular interpretation that genes are the true unit of selection. In his book *The selfish gene* (1976), he argued that Darwinian principles are also exhibited in non-biological phenomena like culture and computer viruses, thus his now famous meme theory. The problem is not that he has developed a meme theory of religion, but that the analogies he and Dennett and others use to explain this and other evolutionary theories are banal, even to the point of being silly.[4] One might counter that this is only a question of less elegant forms of discourse and exemplification, but perhaps the problem is more fundamental. Perhaps in the reductive process some central phenomena are lost sight of.

An often used example of natural selection in cultural phenomena is language. Both Dennett and Dawkins use the example to show how languages and dialects evolve without conscious design. But the problem that many who use the language analogy ignore is that language is more than lexical combinations and grammatical variations. Other theories approach language in different ways. Language, Merlin Donald (2001) argues, is first and foremost the servant of semantics in the service of cognitive networks. Language, Rukmini Bhaya Nair (2002) argues, is first and foremost co-created narrative in social contexts. Language, Elinor Ochs and Lisa Capps (1996, 2001) argue, is first and foremost the narrative (co-)creation of selves and group identities. Language, Daniel Siegel (1999, 2001) argues, is first and foremost narrative that produces resonance and integration in the bicameral brain. From such perspectives, how useful is the Darwinian language analogy, except to show the rather trivial principle that languages presumably develop without conscious design?

On the other hand, one might rightly ask whether they actually *do* develop without conscious design. We know that peoples and governments have language policies. In Denmark there is a Language Commission which decides on disagreements on spelling, grammar, semantics, and foreign loan-words. Their decisions are enforced by the Danish government, for instance by demanding that all state institutions (which in Denmark, as many people know, encompass almost every aspect of Danish social life) must use the rules set up by the Language Commission in all written documents.[5] Similar policies are found in Iceland, where all loan-words are translated into Icelandic words[6] or in France, where Francophone policies are legion. The ancient history of language policies, for instance in China, is also a fascinating topic. So how much of the development of language is the result of natural selection and how much is the result of ideological design?

The second point of my little history of ideas is that all three authors (Dawkins, Dennett, and Boyer) draw inspiration from Dawkins's own meme theory. If anything, this is the core theory that deserves a chapter in this book, and therefore I will describe his theory in more detail below. Dennett's more or less cohesive discussion of the evolution of religion can, secondarily, be viewed as a synthesis of scientific theories on various aspects of the evolution of religion and thus also a relevant subject of this book. His synthesis, therefore, will be described in the following section.

Daniel Dennett – the philosopher spellbreaker[7]

Daniel Dennett, a former student of philosophers Willard van Orman Quine at Harvard and Gilbert Ryle at Oxford, is a philosopher of science and biology and is Co-Director (with Ray Jackendoff) of the Center for Cognitive Studies and the Austin B. Fletcher Professor of Philosophy at

Tufts University in Medford, Massachusetts. Dennett is well known for his philosophy of mind and for his book *Consciousness explained* (1991), which is the culmination and synthesis of his earlier publications on the subject. His work on consciousness caused public interest in his widely publicized polemical debates with philosopher John E. Searle. With his book *Darwin's dangerous idea* (1995), Dennett moved prominently into the field of Darwinian evolution and readdressed earlier topics in his later books, such as *Kinds of minds* (1996) and *Freedom evolves* (2003). Dennett became a prominent atheist and with the publication of *Breaking the spell* (2006), he applied evolutionary and memetic theory to religion together with an uninhibited polemical attack on religion.

The title *Breaking the spell* refers to how an exhaustive and invasive examination of religion may lead to breaking its spell or enchantment. In fact, Dennett says in several places that if your religion can't withstand such examination, then it is not worth holding: 'I for one am not in awe of your faith. I am appalled by your arrogance, by your unreasonable certainty that you have all the answers' (51).

The point of the book is: 'What is this phenomenon or set of phenomena that means so much to so many people, and why – and how – does it command allegiance and shape so many lives so strongly?' (27). After a chapter on the obstacles confronting the scientific study of religion, Dennett takes the reader through several chapters on the evolutionary aspects of religion, and a number of chapters charting the evolutionary history of religion. Chapter 9 ('Towards a buyer's guide to religions') works its way through several barriers to answering the question of whether religion is a good thing. These barriers are love, academic territoriality, and loyalty to God. Chapter 10 on 'Morality and religion' is a moral tirade on religious moralists. The more sober argument in the chapter is that moral cognition research has indicated that religion does not necessarily create or ensure moral behavior. On the contrary, belief in heaven and hell can cause people to perform monstrous acts justified, as it were, with a license to kill (280). The book ends with Dennett's answer to whether religion is a good thing. The answer is a resounding 'No!'

> We need to secure our democratic society, the home base for this research, against the subversions of those who would use democracy as a ladder to theocracy and then throw it away, and we need to spread the knowledge that is the fruit of free inquiry. (307)

The most interesting part, and the most relevant for this chapter, of *Breaking the spell* is Dennett's evolutionary theory of religion. Dennett's central claim is that religion in actual fact has little to do with what people claim it does. Religion is about believing in belief and, more importantly, avowing it to be so. The rest of religion is more or less illusory. Some people may get better lives out of being religious, but, Dennett insists, we need to test such claims (56). And, furthermore, we need to decide whether the side-effects of religious belief are worth the price, the side-effects being bigotry, murderous fanaticism, oppression, cruelty, and enforced ignorance (56).

Religion is, according to Dennett, a product of the accumulation of memes. This term was coined by Richard Dawkins, and since I will dwell on meme theory in the next section, I will simply paraphrase Dennett's understanding of the term in his essay in Appendix A.[8] A meme is 'any culturally based replicator,' such as words, songs, and artefacts, which blindly compete with other memes for residence and retention in human brains. Even though the process is mindless, the goal, as with genes, is the replication of information. All of these mindless, competing information vessels crowd into our memory and overload it. Drawing on Pascal Boyer, Dennett says that counterintuitive anomalies are a kind of 'fiction-generating contraption' which triggers a sort of 'curiosity startle' that starts 'churning out "hypotheses" of sorts' (119–20). Many such thoughts are forgotten almost immediately, others stick around and sometimes a 'lineage of ideas' is born and becomes self-replicative. It only becomes a meme when it escapes the individual mind and spreads through culture. It is a kind of proto-meme, understood as being a 'slightly obsessional – that is, oft-recurring, oft-rehearsed – little hobbyhorse of an idea' (120). Rehearsal, Dennett reminds us, is replication. And then he provocatively claims that 'this is probably the source … of *episodic memory*, our ability to recollect events in our lives' (121). This, I believe, is a good start, better perhaps than Dennett's theory of narrative gravity in his book *Consciousness explained* (1991).

Dennett's evolutionary theory begins at this point. Much of religious tradition, he claims, consists of the more or less automatic, unquestioning copying of designs passed on by our mothers and fathers, grandmothers and grandfathers. Sometimes it is simply passed on as mindless 'tradition.' This mindless copying is similar to genes, but human copying produces many more variations or errors in the copying process than in gene replication. Whole new traditions can arise through variations in the copying process. 'A culturally transmitted design can, in this way,' Dennett argues, 'have a free-floating rationale in exactly the same way a genetically transmitted design does' (78). This differential replication process where 'copies are made with variation, and some variations are in some tiny way "better" … will lead inexorably to the ratcheting process of design improvement Darwin called evolution by natural selection' (78).

Thus, Dennett's claim is that 'cultural transmission can *sometimes* mimic genetic transmission' since the revisions have '*no deliberate, foresighted authors*' (78). His best example of this is how languages develop branches and dialects: 'The gradual transformations that turned Latin into French and Portuguese and other offspring languages were not intended, planned, foreseen, desired, commanded by anyone' (79). The same with folk art, folk music, folk medicine, folklore, superstition, and so on. Sometimes there are deliberate improvements, but most often a mechanical 'sifting-and-duplicating process.' This is not yet religion. We get religion when systems get developed by specialists.

Following Boyer (2001), Dennett discusses briefly the evolution of mind through the use of 'cultural gadgets' (2006: 107ff.) They are neat, attention-demanding tricks that thrive on salience in order to help the mind grasp and retain information. Furthermore, Boyer claims that there are six distinctive cognitive systems designed for salience cues, namely agent-detector, memory-manager, cheater-detector, moral-intuition-generator, sweet tooth for stories, and various alarm systems (Boyer 2001: 101–35). Dennett adds one other system which he calls 'the intentional stance' (108). Any mind with these tools, Dennett says, will eventually have religion.

After discussing Justin Barrett's (2000, 2004) hyperactive agent detection device (HADD), which is nature's way of providing humans and other animals with too much of a good thing, thus improving their chances of survival (better to be jumpy than to end up in a tiger's jaws), Dennett argues that humans and animals share the adoption of the intentional stance. This stance assumes that other agents have limited beliefs about the world, specific desires, and more or less rational behavior, thus allowing for prediction, ploy, and counterploy (109–10). This is the basis of folk psychology. Since we cannot delete our files on other 'intentional systems' (meaning here people who have passed away), we indulge in remembering them, using reminders, preserving relics, or stories about them. Dennett refers to Boyer's discussion on death, where burial rituals solve the crisis of the simultaneous need to bury the corpse and preserve the virtual person or spirit (112–13). Thus, we are on our way, although not quite there, to religion.

Dennett needs first to account for other supernatural agents. Our dead relatives have become virtual agents who are free to evolve in our minds and become ancestors. They became more and more social, more and more linguistic, more deeply involved in the everyday lives of their living heirs. Add the human tendency to animism (Guthrie 1993),[9] Boyer's claims of counterintuitive anomalies, and behavioral psychologist B.F. Skinner's (1948) experiments with pigeons which seem to show how a 'superstition effect' with concomitant ritual behavior can be generated even among animals, and suddenly you have a fantastic world of supernatural beings narrated in mythologies that enthrall, puzzle, and frighten us:

> This mindlessly generates a vast overpopulation of agent-ideas, most of which are too stupid to hold our attention for an instant; only a well-designed few make it through the rehearsal tournament, mutating and improving as they go. The ones that get shared and remembered are the souped-up winners of billions of competitions for rehearsal time in the brains of our ancestors. (123–4)

The end result is superstition – not yet religion.

A key facet in religion, as Boyer argues, is that gods are interested parties. They keep track of human affairs and are full-access agents with strategic knowledge. Dennett argues that such ideas may be the result of prolonged parental care and training, during which the 'imprinting effect' or the baby's bias to obey its parents is a primary factor (127ff.) Drawing on Dawkins (2004: 12ff.), this infantile bias is translated into adult obedience to tribal elders. In fact, Dennett claims that a direct psychological transference is witnessed by the common habit of calling religious leaders 'fathers' (131).

A primary concern for humans is to get hold of the strategic knowledge that gods have. This is the source of divination. Dennett makes use of Julian Jaynes's formulation 'exopsychic methods of thought or decision-making,' commonly known in American idiom as 'passing the buck.'[10] Divination helps people to make strategic and timely decisions in predicament situations. Further to the evolution of ritual, Dennett argues that people have discovered over and over again the placebo effect. They have noticed how ritual, medicinal herbs, and other factors stimulate this life-saving mechanism. Dennett also argues that the evolution of treatment styles – which is cultural – goes hand in hand with the susceptibility to treatment – which is genetic: 'Just as lactose tolerance has evolved in peoples who had the culture of dairy-herding, hypnotizability could have evolved in peoples who had the culture of healing rituals' (137).

Again, this is a seductive argument which is, however, perhaps irrelevant, because healing rituals are found in every known culture in human history. At any rate, the argument runs that the culture of shamanic healing could have created the selective pressure for response to such rituals (140). This is still folk religion, not organized religion.

One last element that may have contributed to the evolution of ritual is the use of ritual as a memory-engineering device in oral cultures. The idea is that bringing a group of people together helps improve 'copying fidelity' during meme transmission because there is a good chance that a handful of participants can catch errors and help others adjust without recourse to extraordinary memory (147).[11]

Dennett asks further questions about why people are motivated to perform ritual. He suggests that some of the factors might be shamanic-advertising, innate curiosity, sensory pageantry (drawing on McCauley and Lawson 2002),[12] the innate desire to belong, and factors such as mass hypnosis and mob hysteria (147–9). Ritual provides, at any rate, a handy memory enhancer because it acts as a digitalized alphabet of behaviors enhanced by rhythm, rhyme, and the inclusion of incomprehensible elements. The latter encourages participants to fall back on 'direct quotation,' thus preserving accuracy under replication (149–50). This scenario has some possibility, but strikes me as being extremely simplified.

The big question at this point is: how do we get religion? Dennett argues that religion emerged with agriculture, where specialist guilds – again drawing on Boyer here – developed the idea of stewardship, i.e. the artful, sophisticated, and elaborated reflection on genealogies of ideas and behaviors. When folk religion, in other words, became thoroughly domesticated, and specialists became dedicated to actively preserving religious tradition (167–71). Drawing on Jared Diamond (1997: 276), Dennett claims that in order to carry out this domestication process, an alliance was struck between government leaders and priests by which ideologies and religions were constructed to justify their kleptocracies or government by theft. Every control system, Dennett argues, is designed to protect something, including itself.

But reflectiveness undermines control systems, so there is a need to anchor free-floating rationales as *represented* rationales, in other words, as a body of ideas that are publicly discussed, agreed upon, and nurtured (177). In this way, people become conscious stewards. A by-product of this selective process is the invention of team spirit. Represented rationales enhance survival in two ways. First, since believers are the chosen ones, they become imbued with resolution and confidence, thus securing individual effectiveness (following Dunbar 2004). Second, they create or strengthen bonds of trust, thus permitting groups to act more effectively (following Boyer 2001 and Burkert 1996).[13] Reflection brings with it the need for systematic invulnerability to disproof, a veil of mystery, and various sleights of hand. There is the need to stimulate fear of a higher power through the use of awesome displays which will discourage defectors (following Bulbulia 2004).

Dennett devotes a number of pages to organizational theories. He calls one type 'the ant colony model,' where the group is a kind of super-organism, and the other 'the corporation model,' where, according to David Sloan Wilson (2002),[14] selection occurs at many levels, including the group level. Dennett also discusses Stark and Finke's (2000) rational choice, market competition theories, but argues that the evolutionary process involves 'the differential replication of *memes*, not *groups*' (184). His hypothesis is:

> Memes that foster human group solidarity are particularly fit (as memes) in circumstances in which host survival (and hence host fitness) most directly depends on hosts' joining forces in groups. The success of such meme-infested groups is itself a potent broadcasting device, enhancing outgroup curiosity (and envy) and thus permitting linguistic, ethnic, and geographic boundaries to be more readily penetrated. (184–5)

Thus, there is no theoretical need of rational designers or competing groups, rather a cultural environment of competing ideas.

The final element necessary to religion is the most central one, namely 'believing in belief.' Once people commit themselves publically to particular ideas, a peculiar process of defense mechanisms fall into place, as psychiatrist George Ainslie (2001) argues, by which the myths we live by must not be disturbed at any cost (202–3). This is the source of the many baffling epistemic taboos found in religions around the world. Even when people lose faith, they either live on as if nothing has happened or else they cast around for alternatives. The actual belief that belief in God is necessary is hardly questioned (204–5). This belief was a paramount element in the development of the Abrahamic monotheistic religions, Dennett claims. The division of doxastic labor allows the experts to concern themselves with understanding dogma so that the lay people can do the believing (218). There is even room for agnostics to live comfortably with the belief in belief. I won't go into detail on Dennett's arguments on types of God beliefs and arguments about the existence of God. The important point is the *profession of belief* (226ff.). This argument leaves the back door open for Dennett's political agenda in the next section.

Critical remarks

According to Dennett, religion is bad and should be removed by legislation. I have addressed the political aspect of Dennett's book elsewhere (Geertz 2008). In many ways I agree with Dennett and Dawkins. I definitely do not, however, agree with their discursive strategy. Donald Wiebe is of the same opinion but for different reasons. He argues, as I do, that Dennett's rhetoric is detrimental to his professed aim to persuade religious people to embrace his point of view, but, Wiebe argues further, Dennett's assumption that scientific knowledge will *inevitably* provide solutions to the world's problems is untenable. Wiebe argues furthermore that by mixing his scientific and public intellectual agendas, Dennett may be causing unnecessary problems for the scientific student of religion (Wiebe 2008: 56–7), an abiding theme that Wiebe has argued for the greater part of his career (see for instance Wiebe 1999). Luther Martin, on the other hand, claims that critics in Scandinavia and elsewhere in Europe who dislike Dennett's hyperbole are guilty of 'neglecting his substantive arguments and maintaining that enchanting spell which Dennett argues continues to protect religious studies from scientific inquiry' (Martin 2008: 63). This is an absurd claim. Most Europeans have very little interest in the respectability problems of American religious studies. My own reasons are that I don't share Dennett's scientism or his triumphalism. In some ways you might call it a methodological smugness for which there is no basis. The value of evidence is entirely dependent on the value of the experiment, and the value of the experiment is dependent on the theories and questions that inform it. Because of this, the results, far from being 'explanations,' as is often claimed by cognitive scientists of religion, are in fact interpretations. Jeppe Sinding Jensen in his insightful discussion of explanation and interpretation, prefers the term 'explanatory interpretation' because the two procedures are complementary (2003: 236).

After some 150 years of experimental psychology – which is the basis of the cognitive science of religion, with a smattering of brain scans here and fieldwork there – what can we confidently (let alone triumphantly) claim to have explained? So far, hardly any of the theories and hypotheses of Boyer, Lawson and McCauley, or Whitehouse have been 'proven' in the natural sciences sense of the term. They are, however, good tools to think with.

Martin's castigation of Dennett's critics is, however, important because if friends and colleagues in the cognitive science of religion react in that way, we can expect no less of other, less friendly individuals. And perhaps our rejection of Dennett's style can be seen and used as a rejection of his arguments by colleagues and members of the public with religious agendas. Thus we have a public relations problem which needs to be addressed. My criticism of the above-mentioned triumphalism is among other things based on an abiding goal to persuade perceptive colleagues in the scholarly study of religion, who are not involved in the cognitive science of religion but who are curious, to look more carefully at this burgeoning field of inquiry. I have not been concerned with whether religious believers or religious scholars understand us. In that sense, I wholeheartedly share Dennett's and Martin's cry for a naturalistic study of religion, and as any alert reader will note, the substantive part of my 2008 article seriously addresses Dennett's evolutionary scenario described above.

Martin decries the fact that Dennett, who is a respected American philosopher, was not immediately welcomed by everybody as a natural ally. It is precisely the absence of respectable philosophy that is most disappointing about the book and which will turn off skeptical colleagues in other disciplines.[15] Thus the problem is not simply a matter of discursive style, it is equally and perhaps more fundamentally a matter of philosophical – perhaps even foundational – disagreement.

Richard Dawkins – the biologist meme-maker[16]

Richard Dawkins is a British ethologist and evolutionary biologist. He holds the Charles Simonyi Chair for the Public Understanding of Science at the University of Oxford and is a professorial fellow of New College, Oxford. He is famous (and infamous) for his book *The selfish gene* (1976) and his more important book *The extended phenotype* (1982). His book *The blind watchmaker* (1986) was a prolonged argument against the existence of a divine creator. He is also a world-renowned atheist. The book under consideration here, *The God delusion* (2006), extends his arguments against the existence of a divine creator. In justifying the title of his book, Dawkins quotes hippie author Robert M. Pirsig (*Zen and the art of motorcycle maintenance*): 'When one person suffers from a delusion, it is called insanity. When many people suffer from a delusion it is called Religion' (Dawkins 2006: 5).

The goal of the book is to show that the God Hypothesis is 'a scientific hypothesis about the universe, which should be analysed as sceptically as any other' (2). After a chapter describing the God Hypothesis in more detail (Chapter 2), Dawkins describes in chapters 3 and 4 arguments for and against the existence of God and claims to show that arguments for God's existence are spectacularly weak, whereas arguments against God's existence are singularly strong: 'Far from pointing to a designer, the illusion of design in the living world is explained with far greater economy and with devastating elegance by Darwinian natural selection' (2). Chapter 5 on the roots of religion will be discussed in detail below. Chapters 6–10 show that religious belief is not necessary for living a moral life and document how Christians, the Old Testament, and the New Testament are filled with morally reprehensible and shameful claims, ideas, and practices.

Dawkins spends Chapter 5, 'The roots of religion' exploring the evolutionary assumptions of an explanation of where religion comes from. Thus he asks the 'Darwinian question' as he calls it, 'What pressure or pressures exerted by natural selection originally favoured the impulse to religion?' (163). Because religion is wasteful, extravagant, and dangerous, there must be some benefit. 'Benefit' means, in Darwinian terms, 'enhancement of the survival of the individual's genes' (165). Dawkins argues that there are three other targets of evolutionary benefit: (1) group selection, (2) another individual, and (3) replicators. The chapter is a detailed discussion of these three possible targets. As for the first target, i.e. that religion may be beneficial at a group selection level, such a theory argues that religion is good at motivating individuals and instilling in-group solidarity and out-group hostility, thus enhancing the survival and sexual reproduction of the individuals of the strongest group. Dawkins admits that in principle this could happen but is skeptical of whether it is a significant force in evolution: 'When it is pitted against selection at lower levels – as when group selection is advanced as an explanation for individual self-sacrifice – lower-level selection is likely to be stronger' (170). But cheaters in the group would benefit more greatly by not sacrificing themselves. Dawkins quickly leaves the debate because he is a long-standing opponent of group selection theory, and he is more interested in expanding on the other two targets of evolutionary benefit.

The second target, another individual, is based on arguments put forward in his book *The extended phenotype* (1982): 'The individual you are watching may be working under the manipulative influence of genes in another individual, perhaps a parasite' (Dawkins 2006: 165). Dennett begins his book with exactly this type of argument. In the opening page Dennett describes the lowly ant climbing blades of grass, falling off, climbing again, etc., until it gets eaten by a herbivore. This seemingly wasteful and idiosyncratic behavior, it turns out, is commandeered by the lancet fluke, a parasite on the ant that must get into the stomach of a herbivore in order to complete its reproductive cycle (Dennett 2006: 3). Similarly, religious ideas are like the fluke in the brain of the ant. They invade humans, but the benefit is to the parasite and not the host. Dawkins argues that 'religious behaviour may be a misfiring, an unfortunate by-product of an underlying psychological propensity which in other circumstances is, or once was, useful' (Dawkins 2006: 174). What is that propensity? Or, as he states it, 'What is the primitively advantageous trait that sometimes misfires to generate religion?' (ibid.).

He mentions an example of the *kind* of thing he has in mind: children's brains are hardwired to believe and obey authorities. This is absolutely essential for their survival. The flip side is 'slavish gullibility': 'The inevitable by-product is vulnerability to infection by mind viruses' (176). As Dawkins argues, the child cannot distinguish between the truth values of 'Don't paddle in the crocodile-infested Limpopo' and 'You must sacrifice a goat at the time of the full moon, otherwise the rains will fail' (ibid.). Both come from respected authorities and are given as serious commands to which obedience is expected:

> The same goes for propositions about the world, about the cosmos, about morality and about human nature. And, very likely, when the child grows up and has children of her own, she will naturally pass the whole lot on to her own children – nonsense as well as sense – using the same infectious gravitas of manner. (ibid.)

In his review of Dawkins's book, Icelandic scholar Guðmundur Ingi Markússon argues that Dawkins's use of the notion 'by-product' does not coincide with the notion as broadly used in the cognitive science of religion:

> Due to evolved psychological dispositions, the human mind is *not* a general purpose learning device equally likely to pick up and pass on just any odd idea it may come across. Religious ideas are apt to excite our cognitive apparatus in specific ways and are thus particularly likely to be acquired, remembered and passed on (Boyer 2001). All of this is contrary to Dawkins' portrayal of children's minds and the roots of religion. (Markússon 2007: 370)

As a theory of the roots of religion, Dawkins' argument cannot explain the recurrent features of religious ideas and behavior. If children 'acquire, remember and pass on *anything* they are told ... there should be much more variation in the cultural complexes that we call religions' (ibid.: 371).

Dawkins refers to Boyer and Atran for other examples of the kinds of psychological by-products he has in mind. He gives a little more attention to psychologist Paul Bloom's view that children have a natural dualistic theory of mind, i.e. there is a fundamental difference between matter and mind. Religion, for Bloom, is a by-product of this view. Dualists conceive of disembodied spirits that inhabit bodies, thus allowing for ideas of spiritual personifications in the natural world (179–80). Similarly, Dawkins draws on psychologist Deborah Keleman, who argues that children are intuitive theists, assigning purpose to everything:

> Our innate dualism prepares us to believe in a 'soul' which inhabits the body rather than being integrally part of the body. Such a disembodied spirit can easily be imagined to move on somewhere else after the death of the body. We can also easily imagine the existence of a deity as a pure spirit, not an emergent property of complex matter but existing independently of matter. Even more obviously, childish teleology sets us up for religion. If everything has a purpose, whose purpose is it? God's, of course. (181)

Dawkins asks what usefulness dualism and teleology might have. To answer that question, he draws on Dennett's above-mentioned term *intentional stance*. Like Dennett, Dawkins argues that it enhances our ability to discern the intentions of others. The intentional stance speeds up decision-making in dangerous situations and in social situations (182–3). Dualism may underlie higher-order intentionality, although Dawkins is not prepared to push the point.

Dawkins then arrives at the question of whether there are ideas that are more spreadable than others because of some intrinsic appeal that triggers our psychological dispositions. This leads him to the third target of selective benefit, i.e. replicators. The benefactors in this case are the religious ideas themselves, acting somewhat like genes, or the more general term *replicators*. Dawkins notes that a gene can spread through a population 'not because it is a good gene but simply because it is a lucky one. We call this genetic drift' (189). Can the evolution of religion be understood as the cultural equivalent of genetic drift, he asks?

> I surmise that religions, like languages, evolve with sufficient randomness, from beginnings that are sufficiently arbitrary, to generate the bewildering – and sometimes dangerous – richness of diversity that we observe. At the same time, it is possible that a form of natural selection, coupled with the fundamental uniformity of human psychology, sees to it that the diverse religions share significant features in common. (189–90)

Dawkins comes to the conclusion that religions demonstrate a blend of design and natural selection. By this he does not, of course, mean supernatural design, rather he refers to the institutional aspects of religion, which are clearly well fitted to ensuring religion's own survival. Furthermore, natural selection may have favored a particular set of psychological predispositions that have produced religion as a by-product, but 'it is unlikely to have shaped the details' (190). This leads Dawkins to his central question: 'Are religions such stuff as memes are made on?' (ibid.).

Let us return to meme theory with the words of its originator. Dawkins's comments throw interesting light on how he understands the term and its processes. His main point is that survival or reproductive success does not have to benefit the individual. The benefit may very well go to the genes, or, in Dawkins's terms, the replicators, themselves. Dawkins chose the term 'memes' because he wanted to coin a term that resembled the term 'genes' and that underlined his point 'that the gene was [not] the only Darwinian game in town' (196). In fact, Dawkins explicitly states that the purpose of meme theory at this point 'is not to supply a comprehensive theory of culture, on a par with Watson–Crick genetics' (ibid.).

Memes are 'units of cultural inheritance.' They are replicators. A replicator is 'a piece of coded information that makes exact copies of itself, along with occasional inexact copies or "mutations"' (191).[17] Those replicators that are good are getting copied thrive and grow at the expense of less successful replicators. Some proponents of meme theory have pushed it much farther than Dawkins himself. Susan Blackmore, for instance, argues that brains, computers, radio frequencies, etc. are all receptacles being occupied by jostling memes (Blackmore 1999: 8, 204).[18] Some memes succeed and some don't. But this mechanical view of memes and their activities is not exactly what Dawkins has in mind.

Dawkins holds a more nuanced view that unfolds in his discussion of one of the criticisms raised against meme theory. The criticism is that memes suffer from insufficiently high fidelity as replicators. Dawkins responds, however, with the illustration of a carpenter–apprentice situation. It is quite clear from this and other examples (he reiterates for instance his origami example presented in the Foreword to Blackmore's book *Meme machine*, 1999) that even though details may vary, the basic rules are passed down essentially 'unmutated' through imitation-generations. For Dawkins, 'that is all that is needed for the analogy of memes with genes to work' (193). The valuable point I want to flesh out here, and which is also compatible with alternative views on the evolution of culture and religion, is that teachable skills that may spread epidemic-like through populations have in-built self-normalizing procedures, like recipes or written language (193–6). The second point Dawkins raises is that, like genes which collaborate with hundreds of other genes in a given developmental process, memes also collaborate in so-called 'memeplexes' (197). A gene is favored for 'the compatibility of its phenotype with the external environment of the species' and for its compatibility with other genes in the gene pool (198). The 'meme pool,' although much less structured than gene pools, is an important part of the 'environment of each meme in the memeplex' (ibid.).

Dawkins then introduces his memetic theory of religion:

> Some religious ideas, like some genes, might survive because of absolute merit. These memes would survive in any meme pool, regardless of the other memes that surround them. (I must repeat the vitally important point that 'merit' in this sense means only 'ability to survive in the pool.' It carries no value judgement apart from that.) Some religious ideas survive because they are compatible with other memes that are already numerous in the meme pool – as part of a memeplex. (199)

He summarizes his evolutionary theory of religion:

> In the early stages of a religion's evolution, before it becomes organized, simple memes survive by virtue of their universal appeal to human psychology. This is where the meme theory of religion and the psychological by-product theory of religion overlap. The later stages, where a religion becomes organized, elaborate and arbitrarily different from other religions, are quite well handled by the theory of memeplexes – cartels

of mutually compatible memes. This doesn't rule out the additional role of deliberate manipulation by priests and others. Religions probably are, at least in part, intelligently designed, as are schools and fashions in art. (201)

Critical remarks

Dawkins's exemplification of his arguments is problematical from a comparative study of religion point of view. For instance, immediately after the quotation above, he claims that Scientology and Mormonism are intelligently designed almost in their entirety. He also spends several pages describing cargo cults, based – alas! – on the reports of TV nature journalist David Attenborough's BBC documentary series *Quest in paradise*, rather than on academic studies which would have both supported and corrected Dawkins's arguments. The assumption is that recent religions, which give us the contemporary advantage of watching their development from scratch, are somehow different from established religions. I have argued elsewhere (1992) that such is not the case, but many others, such as Roger M. Keesing, for instance, do so as well. Keesing argues in his study of *kastom*, a contemporary pan-regional 'Melanesian way':

> [L]ong before Europeans arrived in Pacific waters, Melanesian ideologues were at work creating myths, inventing ancestral rules, making up magical spells, and devising rituals. They were cumulatively creating ideologies, which sustained male political ascendancy and resolved contradictions by depicting human rules as ancestrally ordained, secret knowledge as sacred, the *status quo* as eternal. We err, I think, in imagining that spurious *kastom* is radically different from genuine culture, that the ideologues and ideologies of the post-colonial present had no counterparts in the pre-colonial past. (Keesing 1982: 300–1)

There is ample evidence that all religions are designed and constructed, but also that they are designed and constructed from the bits and pieces of earlier religions, thus in a roundabout way supporting Dawkins's evolutionary summary.

The other point of criticism is Dawkins's list of religious ideas that fulfill his requirements for memes in meme pools. Briefly, his list consists of: survival of one's own death; martyrs enjoying virgins in heaven; heretics and blasphemers should be killed; belief in God is a supreme virtue; faith is a virtue; everyone should respect people's faiths; some ideas are not meant to be understood rationally; and music and scriptures are self-replicating tokens of religious ideas (Dawkins 2006: 199–200). This list is clearly idiosyncratic and based on limited knowledge of modern instances of Christian and Muslim fundamentalisms. Dawkins loses the most important point of his theory, namely, that we are dealing with recipes and rules that are passed on from generation to generation virtually unmutated, on the one hand, and details that might vary from environment to environment, on the other. Dawkins draws no distinction in the list between memes that have absolute survival value and memes that have survival value only against the right background. Perhaps survival of one's own death is a universal, but there are many other fundamental religious memes which have 'recipe-like' status such as purpose, meaning, authority, numbers, rituals, incantations, purity, sacredness, secrecy, foundational narratives, spirit possession, visions, miracles, penance, forgiveness, good, suffering, evil, and so on. He confuses things further by arguing that whole religions 'might be seen as two alternative memeplexes' (200). Here it seems that he has abandoned his careful distinction earlier in the chapter between proximate and ultimate causes. Proximate causes are the immediate mechanisms of a phenomenon, whereas ultimate causes are the reasons for a particular design. Thus the proximate cause of religious behavior may be neural activity in the brain, but the ultimate cause would be the natural selection pressure that favored it (168–9).

Wistful conclusion

My conclusion is more wistful (or grumpy moaning) than a summarizing statement. I raised this point in my 2008 article on Dennett, but it is worth repeating here since it also characterizes Dawkins. It would have been nice if both authors had been more cognizant of the groundbreaking insights in the cognitive science of religion. A supplementary wish is that it would have been nice if both authors had viewed the negative aspects of religion in a broader perspective, namely, as the negative sides of being human. Religions do not have a monopoly on tribalism, fundamentalism, terror, violence, bigotry, mass hysteria, deception, ignorance, pride, intolerance, murder, rape, child abuse, war, and so on, although they know how to use these forces. There is a lot of interesting literature on such things as the cognition of fundamentalism (Atran 2002, 2003, 2006; Malley 2004), memory, suggestion, and false beliefs (Rubin 1996; Rubin and Berntsen 2003; Berntsen and Rubin 2004; Spanos 1996), techniques used in the mind control and socialization of children, and so on. Then there are important topics left untouched by Dennett and Dawkins, such as the evolution of consciousness (which Dennett had written on earlier), theories of memory, the role of narrative, the development of persons and selves, embodied cognition, extended mind, the chemistry of ritual in general (not just placebo), and the development of language in general.[19]

Other, more cohesive, evolutionary accounts might also have been discussed such as those of Terrence Deacon (1997), Merlin Donald (2001), Michael Tomasello (1999), Robin Dunbar (2004), Stewart Guthrie (1993), Steven Mithen (1996), or any of the well-known evolutionary psychologists such as Jerome H. Barkow, Leda Cosmides and John Tooby (1992). Pascal Boyer and Scott Atran[20] could have been more comprehensively discussed.[21]

Omissions are the inevitable result of priorities. Dawkins's and Dennett's books are obviously not scientific literature on the evolution of religious ideas and behavior. Nevertheless for better or for worse, their ideas are worth consideration in this book.

Notes

1   Harris's book is *The end of faith* (2004). The paperback edition (published in October 2005) entered the *New York Times* bestseller list at number four, and remained on the list for a total of 33 weeks.

2   Cf. Shermer 1997; Eller 2004, 2007; Mills 2006.

3   Dennett claims that there is no science of religion and those who dabble in religion are theoretically innocent, small-minded backbiters in low prestige jobs (2006: 33–4), busily passing on 'a legacy of ever more toxic forms of religion to our descendants' (39).

4   Dawkins is aware of the problem, as this statement seems to indicate: 'Nevertheless, it is not obviously silly to speak of a meme pool' (2006: 192).

5   Their website, which, naturally, is in Danish, is at www.dsn.dk/. There is a good Wikipedia article on the Commission in English.

6   Icelandic was systematically 'cleaned up' via nineteenth-century nationalism, with Old Icelandic texts as paradigms. Thanks to Guðmundur Ingi Markússon for this information.

7   This section is a highly revised version of Geertz 2008. See Dennett's website at http://ase.tufts.edu/cogstud/incbios/dennettd/dennettd.htm.

8   This is a reprint of Dennett's article 'The new replicators' (2002).

9   On Guthrie's theory see Benson Saler's chapter in this volume.

10   Jaynes 1976: 223–54. Dennett describes the book as 'brilliant but quirky and unreliable' (133).

11   This part of his argument is doubtful. If any kind of intellectual reflection occurs during ritual, it usually is in the context of a sermon or exhortation addressed to the whole congregation. Memory management doesn't seem to occur among the ritual participants. Whitehouse (2000, 2004) has shown that imagistic modes of religiosity, dominant in oral cultures, encourage rather than discourage idiosyncratic reflection. There is very little check for errors in such rituals. Doctrinal rituals, on the other hand, like Protestant church services, excel in maintaining orthodoxy through repetition.

12   On Lawson and McCauley's (earlier) theory see the chapter by Steven Engler and Mark Q. Gardiner

13 On Burkert's theory see Gustavo Benavides's chapter in this volume.
14 On Wilson's theory see Joseph Bulbulia's chapter in this volume.
15 See Lars Albinus's excellent critique of Dennett's philosophical premises (2008). Albinus argues that Dennett's notions of science and religion are too narrow and that 'the classical problem of self-reference ... and the ungrounded attempt to argue for a moral standing on these premises' constitute serious weaknesses in Dennett's philosophical premises (23).
16 See Dawkins's official website http://richarddawkins.net/
17 Biologist Terrence W. Deacon has shown that making 'information' an intrinsic quality of the meme is wrong. Memes, like genes, Deacon argues, cannot be understood 'without considering their embeddedness in a dynamic system which imbues them with their function and informational content' (1999: 2). Genes are just patterns. What counts as information, Deacon claims, is context-dependent. For Deacon, memes are simply signs (physical patterns), and their information content is embedded in semiotic systems. In consequence, Deacon argues, 'genes and memes are not the locus of the replication process, nor are they somehow the functional unit of information. They are replicas not replicators. They are rather more like the concretion of information bottlenecks in a system' (1999: 2).
18 The ultimate memeplex, Blackmore claims, is 'our own familiar self' (219).
19 See my survey in Geertz 2004.
20 On Atran's theory of religion see Joseph Bulbulia's chapter in this volume.
21 See the recent collection of evolutionary theories of religion in Bulbulia *et al.* 2008.

References

Ainslie, G., 2001. *Breakdown of will*. Cambridge University Press, Cambridge.

Albinus, L., 2008. Dangerous ideas: the spell of *Breaking the spell*. *Method & Theory in the Study of Religion* 20 (1), 22–35.

Atran, S., 2002. *In gods we trust: the evolutionary landscape of religion*. Oxford University Press, Oxford.

Atran, S., 2003. *The strategic threat from suicide terror*. AEI-Brookings Joint Center for Regulatory Studies, Related Publication 03–33, December.

Atran, S., 2006. Genesis of suicide terrorism. *Science* 299 (5612), 1534–9.

Barkow, J.H., Cosmides, L., and Tooby, J., 1992. *The adapted mind: evolutionary psychology and the generation of culture*. Oxford University Press, Oxford.

Barrett, J., 2000. Exploring the natural foundations of religion. *Trends in Cognitive Science* 4, 29–34.

Barrett, J., 2004. *Why would anyone believe in God?* AltaMira, Walnut Creek.

Berkowitz, P., 2007. The new new atheism. *The Wall Street Journal*, July 16, online at www.opinionjournal.com/forms/printThis.html?id=110010341

Berntsen, D. and Rubin, D.C., 2004. Cultural life scripts structure recall from auto-biographical memory. *Memory and Cognition* 32 (3), 427–42.

Blackmore, S., 1999. *The meme machine*. Oxford University Press, Oxford; reprinted, 2000.

Boyer, P., 2001. *Religion explained: the evolutionary origins of religious thought.* Basic Books, New York.

Bulbulia, J., 2004. Religious costs as adaptations that signal altruistic intention. *Evolution and Cognition* 19, 19–42.

Bulbulia, J., Sosis, R., Harris, E., Genet, R., Genet, C., and Wyman, K. (Eds.), 2008. *The evolution of religion: studies, theories, and critiques.* Collins Foundation Press, Santa Margarita.

Burkert, W., 1996. *Creation of the sacred: tracks of biology in early religions.* Harvard University Press, Cambridge, MA.

Dawkins, R., 1976. *The selfish gene.* Oxford University Press, Oxford; reprinted, 1999.

Dawkins, R., 1982. *The extended phenotype: the long reach of the gene.* Oxford University Press, Oxford; revised edn., 1999.

Dawkins, R., 1986. *The blind watchmaker.* W.W. Norton and Co., New York.

Dawkins, R., 2004. *The ancestor's tale: a pilgrimage to the dawn of life.* Weidenfeld and Nicolson, London.

Dawkins, R., 2006. *The God delusion.* Bantam Press, London.

Deacon, T., 1997. *The symbolic species: the co-evolution of language and the human brain.* Allen Lane, the Penguin Press, London.

Deacon, T.W., 1999. Memes as signs: the trouble with memes (and what to do about it). *The Semiotic Review of Books* 10 (3), 1–3.

Dennett, D.C., 1991. *Consciousness explained.* Little, Brown and Company, Boston.

Dennett, D.C., 1995. *Darwin's dangerous idea: evolution and the meanings of life.* Simon & Schuster, New York.

Dennett, D.C., 1996. *Kinds of minds: toward an understanding of consciousness.* Basic Books, New York.

Dennett, D.C., 2002. The new replicators. In: Pagel, M. (Ed.), *Encyclopedia of evolution.* Oxford University Press, Oxford, E83–E92.

Dennett, D.C., 2003. *Freedom evolves.* Viking, New York.

Dennett, D.C., 2006. *Breaking the spell: religion as a natural phenomenon.* Penguin Books, New York.

Diamond, J., 1997. *Guns, germs, and steel: the fates of human societies.* Norton, New York.

Donald, M., 2001. *A mind so rare: the evolution of human consciousness.* W. W. Norton and Co., New York.

Dunbar, R., 2004. *The human story: a new history of mankind's evolution.* Faber and Faber, London.

Eller, D., 2004. *Natural atheism.* American Atheist Press, Cranford.

Eller, D., 2007. *Atheism advanced: further thoughts of a freethinker.* American Atheist Press, Cranford.

Geertz, A.W., 1992. *The invention of prophecy: continuity and meaning in Hopi Indian religion.* University of California Press, Berkeley, Los Angeles, London; revised edn., 1994.

Geertz, A.W., 2004. Cognitive approaches to the study of religion. In: Antes, P., Geertz, A.W., and Warne, R. (Eds.), *New approaches in the study of religion.*

Volume 2, *Textual, comparative, sociological, and cognitive approaches*. Mouton de Gruyter, Berlin, 347–99.

Geertz, A.W., 2008. How *not* to do the cognitive science of religion today. *Method & Theory in the Study of Religion* 20 (1), 7–21.

Guthrie, S.E., 1993. *Faces in the clouds: a new theory of religion*. Oxford University Press, New York and Oxford.

Harris, S., 2004. *The end of faith: religion, terror, and the future of reason*. W.W. Norton and Co., New York.

Harris, S., 2006. *Letter to a Christian nation*. Knopf, New York.

Hitchens, C., 2007. *God is not great: how religion poisons everything*. Twelve Books, New York.

Jaynes, J., 1976. *The origins of consciousness in the breakdown of the bicameral mind*. Houghton Mifflin, Boston.

Jensen, J.S., 2003. *The study of religion in a new key: theoretical and philosophical soundings in the comparative and general study of religion*. Aarhus University Press, Aarhus.

Keesing, R.M., 1982. Kastom in Melanesia: an overview. In Keesing, R.M., and Tonkinson, R. (Eds.), *Reinventing traditional culture: the politics of Kastom in Island Melanesia*. Special issue of *Mankind* 13 (4), 294–399.

Malley, B., 2004. *How the Bible works: an anthropological study of evangelical biblicists*. AltaMira, Walnut Creek.

Markússon, G.I., 2007. Book review: Richard Dawkins (2006) *The God delusion*. *Journal of Cognition and Culture* 7 (2), 369–73.

Martin, L.H., 2008. Daniel Dennett's *Breaking the spell*: an unapologetic apology. *Method & Theory in the Study of Religion* 20 (1), 61–6.

McCauley, R.N. and Lawson, E.T., 2002. *Bringing ritual to mind: psychological foundations of cultural forms*. Cambridge University Press, Cambridge.

Mills, D., 2006. *Atheist universe: the thinking person's answer to Christian fundamentalism*. Ulysses Press, Berkeley.

Mithen, S., 1996. *The prehistory of the mind: a search for the origins of art, religion and science*. Thames and Hudson, London.

Nair, R.B., 2002. *Narrative gravity: conversation, cognition, culture*. Oxford University Press, Oxford and New Delhi.

Ochs, E. and Capps, L., 1996. Narrating the self. *Annual Review of Anthropology* 25, 19–43.

Ochs, E. and Capps, L., 2001. *Living narrative: creating lives in everyday storytelling*. Harvard University Press, Cambridge and London.

Rubin, D.C. (Ed.), 1996. *Remembering our past: studies in autobiographical memory*. Cambridge University Press, Cambridge.

Rubin, D.C. and Berntsen, D., 2003. Life scripts help to maintain autobiographical memories of highly positive, but not highly negative, events. *Memory and Cognition* 31 (1), 1–14.

Shermer, M., 1997. *Why people believe weird things: pseudoscience, superstition, and other confusions of our time*. Henry Holt and Co., New York.

Siegel, D.J., 1999. *The developing mind: how relationships and the brain interact to shape who we are*. The Guilford Press, New York and London.

Siegel, D.J., 2001. Toward an interpersonal neurobiology of the developing mind: attachment relationships, 'mindsight,' and neural integration. *Infant Mental Health Journal* 22 (1–2), 67–94.

Skinner, B.F., 1948. 'Superstition' in the pigeon. *Journal of Experimental Psychology* 38, 168–72.

Spanos, N.P., 1996. *Multiple identities and false memories: a sociocognitive perspective*. American Psychological Association, Washington, DC.

Stark, R. and Finke, R., 2000. *Acts of faith: explaining the human side of religion*. University of California Press, Berkeley.

Stenger, V.J., 2007. *God: the failed hypothesis. How science shows that God does not exist*. Prometheus Books, Amherst.

Tomasello, M., 1999. *The cultural origins of human cognition*. Harvard University Press, Cambridge, MA.

Whitehouse, H., 2000. *Arguments and icons: divergent modes of religiosity*. Oxford University Press, Oxford.

Whitehouse, H., 2004. *Modes of religiosity: a cognitive theory of religious transmission*. AltaMira Press, Walnut Creek.

Wiebe, D., 1999. *The politics of religious studies: the continuing conflict with theology in the academy*. St. Martin's Press, New York.

Wiebe, D., 2008. Science, scholarship and the domestication of religion: On Dennett's *Breaking the spell. Method & Theory in the Study of Religion* 20 (1), 54–60.

Wilson, D.S., 2002. *Darwin's cathedral: evolution, religion, and the nature of society*. University of Chicago Press, Chicago.

16

Interventionist practices and the promises of religion

On Martin Riesebrodt,
Cultus und Heilsversprechen (2007)

Michael Stausberg

This chapter summarizes and discusses a theory of religion that – in terms of its metatheoretical and methodological framework – parts company with major current trends in the study of religion(s) and theorizing about religion. Let us approach the theory with a short note on the theorist and the development of his work.

From fundamentalism to a theory of religion

Martin Riesebrodt (b. 1948) is a German sociologist (PhD thesis 'The debate on theories in economic anthropology' [in German], Heidelberg, 1973). He served as the Associate Director of the Max Weber Archives at the Bavarian Academy of Sciences and Humanities and the Associate Director of the Ernst Troeltsch Archives (Augsburg University).

Large parts of his academic work are devoted to the work of Weber, be it as editor of Weber or of works on Weber and as interpreter (see e.g. Riesebrodt 1999, 2001a,b,c). Apart from Weber, he built his career on studies of political religion, in particular fundamentalism. In 1990, Riesebrodt published what to the eyes of the present writer is one of the most important studies of fundamentalism (Riesebrodt 1990). In the same year he became Professor of Sociology and Sociology of Religion at the University of Chicago (Department of Sociology and Divinity School). That was the time when, in Chicago, Martin E. Marty and R. Scott Appleby were running the Fundamentalism Project (1987–95).

Riesebrodt's first book (English translation 1993) is a comparative study of fundamentalism in the United States and Iran, in which he discusses and defends the value of a historically grounded intercultural comparison. He draws on Weber with regard to the method of forming concepts and

ideal-types (see also below).[1] His study also highlights important differences between Weberian and Marxist approaches to theorizing of religion.
Although the comparative analysis of fundamentalist movements had clearly
shown the importance of economic factors, social relations were seen as
more significant than the purely quantitative distribution of material goods.
Accordingly, Riesebrodt's analysis focused more on the 'subjective' expectations, experiences and interpretations of reality among historical actors than
on their alleged 'objective' class interests (1990: 251).

Riesebrodt has continued to publish and to co-edit publications on
fundamentalism, but at the same time his frame of analysis has widened
towards what he calls the 'return' (Riesebrodt 2000a) or the 'resurgence'
(Riesebrodt 2000b) of religion in contemporary societies. In his book on
'the return of religions' he starts to outline a new theory of religion – one
able to account for the complex situation of religion in modern societies
beyond a focus on essentialisms and secularization (Riesebrodt 2000a:
35–57). Moreover, he began to extend his analyses, in both space and time;
he did so in a period when globalization emerged as a key term and issue
in social theory. His global perspective on religion (see Riesebrodt 2003
[largely based on 2000a]) is aligned with an affirmation of the universality of the concept of religion, as embedded in a new theory of religion,
the full version of which was published in German in 2007. The German
title can be rendered as *Worship and the promise of religion*.[2] Some of
the main theoretical theses are conveniently summarized in an essay from
2008 (Riesebrodt 2008).

The book has four main parts. The first two chapters discuss the concept
of religion. The following two chapters discuss previous theories of religion (chapter 3) and his own theory (chapter 4). Chapters 5–7 empirically
substantiate ('verify') the theory. The last chapter draws conclusions with
regard to the future of religion. The theory owes much to Weber in terms of
method and metatheory, albeit less to his account of religions. Like Weber,
Riesebrodt embeds his theory in empirical and historical cases.

Relegitimizing the concept of religion

The first chapter is 'Religion as discourse'.[3] Here, he distinguishes
between four main epochs of discourses about religion: an Enlightenment discourse, a Romantic discourse, a secularization discourse, and
a postmodern discourse. Riesebrodt dismisses discourse theoretical and
postcolonial critiques, questioning their empirical data and the coherence of their arguments.[4]

Where the postmodern critique made much of the absence of comparable
cross-cultural equivalents for 'religion', Riesebrodt shifts the focus from

terms to social relations, where people make distinctions between different types of meaningful actions. Compare the case of music, where one would, following Riesebrodt, ask whether people distinguish between performances of music and other forms of performances – rather than whether any given culture has a separate *concept* of music.[5] In fact, Riesebrodt finds that distinctions between religious and non-religious phenomena tend to be universal. He points to two main forms of this distinction. To begin with, within given cultures people tend to, at least rudimentarily, distinguish ordinary from religious actions 'in the sense of actions that involve personal or impersonal superhuman powers' (42). These actions often 'require charismatically qualified specialists' (42). Second, the quasi-universality of the distinctiveness of religion is confirmed by the fact that adherents of various religious traditions keep on comparing their own religions to those of others (42). People actually make such comparisons, notwithstanding their alleged invalidity according to postmodern critique. The scholarly use of the term therefore merely refines common schemes of classification and differentiation (42).

The 'perception of difference' between religious and non-religious actions, actors, and institutions made by people in a variety of ordinary and extraordinary contexts is illustrated in the next chapter, the main thrust of which is a systematic empirically grounded analysis of different forms in which 'religious groups and institutions perceive each other as points of reference' (43). Riesebrodt introduces a helpful distinction between three forms of mutual (inter-religious) relations: demarcation, superposition (i.e. 'the appropriation of sacred places and times by subsequent religions' [55]), and assimilation (including incorporating elements from other religions and mutual borrowing). Religious actors from different traditions have looked on each other as potential partners or competitors (72). Riesebrodt claims that 'the appropriateness of the concept of religion' is also confirmed 'by the fact that all great empires, with their cultural and religious diversity, have conducted a politics of religion' (64), meaning that they have tried to regulate the religious field. Moreover, he notes that travellers since ancient times have described and compared religions. (Yet he admits that this often happens without any notion of religion, but since he is interested in the very acts of distinguishing and referencing this does not deter him.) Here – and throughout the book – Riesebrodt presents various examples from East and West, past and present, in order 'to justify the universal use of the concept of religion' (72), not as 'a category of the human mind' (72), 'but in people's social behaviour' (73). This is to be distinguished from 'a universal concept of religion: There can be no such concept, because this degree of conceptual systematization is obviously not universal' (44).

The limits of previous theories of religion

In the third chapter of his book, Riesebrodt provides an overview of a series of previous theories of religion, mainly from the classical period, but with some contemporary theories interspersed. The title of the chapter refers to these theories as 'scientific imaginations' of religion (perhaps a nod to a certain Chicago colleague). His presentation is organized around key metaphors of the theories under review. Such metaphors include 'religion as a gift of reason' (Herbert of Cherbury; Kant), 'religion as an experience of revelation' (Schleiermacher; Otto; van der Leeuw; Eliade), 'religion as projection' (Marx), 'religion as proto-science' (Tylor; Frazer; Boyer), 'religion as affect and as a way of controlling affects' (Marett), 'religion as brain function' (Newberg; Ramachandran),[6] 'religion as sacralised society' (Durkheim; Luckmann; Luhmann), 'religion as an interest in salvation' (Weber; Bourdieu),[7] and 'religion as commodity' (Stark).[8]

Finding value in all these theories (but singling out Weber as 'the most theoretically and empirically differentiated' [107]), Riesebrodt claims that his review illustrates the existence of 'more than one legitimate perspective on religion' (106). The multitude of perspectives could contribute to a more complex conceptualization of religion. (It remains unclear to what extent that is considered as an ideal, and if so, how that is followed up in his theory.) At the same time, he holds that many theories (or families of theories) share characteristic weaknesses. Some theories, for example, present religion as a purely individual affair. Theories that emphasize the societal aspect of religion are often functionalist, which he regards as unsatisfactory because functionalist theories are at the same time too broad and too narrow: they include phenomena that apparently serve the same function but are else generally perceived to be different (e.g. sports), whereas they exclude phenomena that do not serve the respective function, although these phenomena are generally acknowledged as religious (e.g. magic or divination) (110–12). By a priori assigning a given function and societal necessity to religion, functionalist theories resemble theology, and they deny individuals and societies the possibility of not being religious.[9] Last but not least, Riesebrodt dismisses the deductive approach of many theories, in so far as they are derived from general assumptions regarding human beings, society, or modernity (107).

Explanation as systematization of insider perspectives

Chapter 4 carries the same title as the book and contains the core of the theory. It starts with some meta-theoretical and methodological statements. To begin with, in contrast to functionalist theories, Riesebrodt holds that only substantial, i.e. content-based definitions will allow an adequate delimitation of religion as a theoretical object (108 [with a reference to Spiro 1966]). In other words, the definition should express the specificity of religion 'as a universal social phenomenon' (108). There follows a related qualification: 'any sufficient explanation of a given social phenomenon (such as religion) requires an understanding of its meaning' (108).[10] Religion can be conceptualized theoretically only in so far as 'its specific meaning clearly distinguishes it from other types of social action' (108).

If religion is a kind (or system) of meaningful social actions (or practices), to whom are these actions meaningful, and who establishes their meaning? Riesebrodt notes that there is a 'gap between religious internal and external scientific perspectives' (108). According to Riesebrodt, the latter explanations, by ignoring insider perspectives, are under pressure to justify their 'exalted' cognitive position. Unfortunately, he does not give any reasons for his scepticism towards outsider (external) perspectives and his privileging insider (internal) perspectives, nor is it clear what qualifies as an internal/insider perspective.[11] Moreover, an outsider/external perspective does not need to claim an 'exalted' position, but merely a different one; it addresses other audiences and issues, and it proceeds by other rules. Riesebrodt, however, does not advocate 'going native', but makes the case for interpretative explanations that arrive at their perspective by abstracting and systematizing insider perspectives, thus claiming no privileged or even 'objective' status for themselves' (109). Such interpretative explanations operate by transforming insiders' 'perspectives into an external [outsider] perspective that differs from the internal [insider] perspectives but does not contradict them' (109).

By adopting this strategy Riesebrodt hopes to overcome the insider/outsider divide that has haunted religious studies for quite some time (see McCutcheon 1999). However, it remains unclear what precisely he has in mind when he seeks not to 'contradict' insider perspectives; the ethical, methodological, theoretical, and philosophical implications of that goal would require further discussion. It seems that Riesebrodt's statements once again echo Weber's methodology, where Weber claims that one 'explains' action not by deducing it from psychic facts, but by deriving it from the expectations that subjects foster about objects and from the experiences that they are entitled to have (Weber 1988 [1913]: 432). We will soon find that Riesebrodt in fact focuses on expectations about religions and on different experiences with and within religions.

Even if he does not share them, Riesebrodt takes claims and promises made by religions at face value. In fact, for him, they are central to his theory of religion: his strategy is to 'systematise the self-portrayals of religions' as a 'sufficient foundation for the explanation of religion' (109). His promises to be a theory grounded in what religions themselves say about religion (not to be confused with how religious intellectuals, namely theologians, systematize their respective religions).

Definitions and distinctions

Unlike the case with his theory, Riesebrodt does not claim that his definition is built on insider views, or on self-presentations of religious claims, but merely that it is 'compatible' with the self-understanding of religions. A definition, he argues, should not be too remote from our everyday understanding. It should point clearly to the specific character of the phenomena to be defined, without implying their explanation.

Here is Riesebrodt's definition: 'religion is a complex of religious practices based on the premise of the existence of generally invisible personal or impersonal superhuman powers' (113).[12]

He refers to the assumed existence of these powers as 'the religious premise' (113). With 'premise' he seems to have in mind a starting point, an assumption, that allows for inferences. These inferences, however, are not logical conclusions but actions/practices. Practices are religious in so far as they, based on the 'religious premise', engage or refer to 'powers' that are qualified as 'superhuman' in so far as they are ascribed or attributed (by those sharing the religious premise) the capacity to influence or control such 'dimensions of individual or social human life and the natural environment … that are usually beyond direct human control' (113). The definition of religion thereby ultimately rests on the idea of (power to) control and (lack of) controllability, i.e. an anthropology of deficiency (i.e. based on the inability of humans to 'control' life and nature). Given the logical structure of the definition, these powers are the real defining trait of religion (see Spiro). Making references to or inferences from the existence of these powers provides a specific capacity for creating meaning. This, then, is the feature that distinguishes religion from other forms of social action (108; see Spiro 1966: 98). Given the supposed universal occurrence of religion, one would therefore need to postulate the universality of the notion of such powers.

The means of establishing contact with these powers are mediated by the respective 'religious imaginations' and the social and cultural parameters of their accessibility as learned through socialization. Riesebrodt distinguishes four main forms of establishing contact: interaction (e.g. prayers, chants), manipulation (e.g. spells, amulets[13]), fusion (e.g. ecstasy), and self-empowerment (e.g. contemplation); the latter two are usually the business of religious virtuosos. Riesebrodt subsumes these four forms of establishing contact under the category of 'interventionist' practices (114).

He distinguishes this category from two others types of religious practices, namely 'discursive' practices and 'behaviour-regulating' or 'regulatory' practices. While the former roughly correspond to what is generally known as 'ritual' or, to a lesser degree, 'worship', the latter two categories would, in language games familiar from Christianity, correspond to 'theology' and 'ethics' respectively.

According to Riesebrodt there are two main types of interventionist practices. On the one hand, there are 'general practices' that are performed by, or on behalf of, the laity (i.e. non-specialists). This category includes practices performed at times defined by the respective calendar ('calendrical practices'), at given moments in the life-cycle ('life-cycle practices'), as well as those performed irregularly whenever the need arises ('variable practices'). On the other hand, there are practices performed by virtuosos (specialists). These often present more 'radical' versions of the general practices, with regard both to the forms and the aims of performances. Riesebrodt devotes one chapter to each of these two categories of interventionist practices (135–210).

Riesebrodt distinguishes religion from 'religiosity' and 'religious traditions' (115; see 2008: 29–30). Religiosity (or religiousness) is not a synonym for 'religious practice' or attitudes but 'the subjective appropriation and interpretation of religion'. People are religious when they appropriate and develop their own understanding of given complexes, or systems, of religious practices. However, Riesebrodt maintains that one can be religious without practising any one given religion, and that people themselves can create subjective coherence beyond that provided by religions as institutionalized practices (115).[14] Contrary to a common understanding, Riesebrodt does not regard religions as extended forms of a basal religiosity, but holds that religiosity derives from religions. Where religiosity appears to be a smaller analytical unit than religion, religious tradition is more encompassing. It seems that Riesebrodt wants to solve several problems at the same time when introducing this term.[15] First, it is 'a theological category' (116), a normative and ideological construct that serves to create boundaries with regard to other religious traditions. Second, it is 'a classificatory concept that distinguishes among religious practices or complexes of practices on the basis of their key symbols and self-classifications' (116). The appearance of a cross in a ritual, for example, serves to identify it as Christian. Third, as an 'empirical category' it refers to practices and structures of meaning that are perceived to be long established (116). Finally, a 'religious tradition' is a more encompassing term than 'religion' since religious traditions also refer to ways of life and other 'traditional' elements that cannot be defined as religious in a stricter sense (2008: 29).

Interventionist practices as key to religions

Superhuman powers are the central feature of religions, and interventionist practices establish and maintain contact with these powers. Therefore, Riesebrodt argues for the centrality of interventionist practices for a theory of religion (while his rehabilitation of the validity of the concept of religion is mainly based on an analysis of discursive practices);[16] they unlock the inner logic of religion. Moreover, he claims that discursive and regulatory practices are grounded in interventionist practices, in logical, systematic, and pragmatic terms (127). Interventionist practices are 'the logical precondition of the other practices' (2008: 30), which would have no basis without the 'belief in the existence of superhuman powers and the possibility of communicating with them' (2008: 30–1; see 2007: 128). Emotionally and cognitively, they constitute, confirm, and dramatize the 'aura of factuality' (Geertz) of religious reality. Systematically, they constitute the points of reference for other practices, in particular discursive practices such as interpretation. Pragmatically, 'discursive practices become important' '[o]nly because interventionist practices provide protection against misfortune, means of overcoming crises and establishing means of salvation' (128). These accomplishments, achievements, benefits or effects of interventionist practices relate to the promises of religion more generally.

With his focus on interventionist practices Riesebrodt brings home the so-called 'performative turn' in the humanities to theorizing religion: 'In religion as in the theatre or opera we should focus on performances and the scripts that inform them' (2008: 33). According to Riesebrodt, there are three main sources and strategies to identify the meaning of religious practices: theologies and worldviews, generally the domain of intellectuals; subjective interpretations of individuals, typically 'instable, situational, and incomplete' (2008: 31); and 'liturgies', here not understood as (Christian) service or public worship, but more technically as 'rules and modes of interaction between humans and superhuman powers, transmitted orally or in writing' (2008: 31).[17]

The stable character of liturgies – one cannot help thinking here of Rappaport's 'liturgical orders'[18] – suggests their methodological value. Their fixed character as rules or norms (i.e. as regulatory rather than interventionist elements!) allows the scholar to use them as a basis for 'a comparative analysis of the meaning of practices across millennia and cultural boundaries' (128). Note, however, that what one is comparing is not the interventionist practices, which are the core of religion, but the scripts governing such performances.[19] These scripts are 'institutionalised structures of meaning' (129) rather than free-floating subjective interpretations or abstract worldviews.

Riesebrodt proposes to interpret liturgies in an ideal-typical sense à la Weber, which is to say as a construction, a 'utopian' thought-image; ideal-types are nowhere to be found in pure form in reality, but serve to 'measure' reality with regard to certain highlighted aspects (Weber 1988 [1904]: 190–5). Conceptualized as ideal-types, liturgies can be key to an analysis of the meaning contained in religious practices, 'though this does not imply that all acting subjects have appropriated and want to express this meaning in exactly this way. Liturgies express the meaning of religion, not of religiousness' (129). The extent to which ideal-typical and institutional meanings are appropriated or not by performers remains an empirical question. Yet in terms of theory Riesebrodt argues that 'the meaning inscribed in liturgies is fully sufficient to conceive religion theoretically' (130).

The promises of religion as pragmatic core

Methodologically, then, a comparative analysis of the liturgies/scripts as structures of meaning, or the 'logic', underlying the interventionist practices that constitute the core of religion will serve to unpack the 'supra-individual, objective levels of religion' (131) as the basis for 'a universal theory that transcends historical and cultural boundaries' (131).

In a comparative analysis of interventionist practices – or rather of the liturgies (scripts) governing them – one first encounters them on a culture-specific level, where superhuman powers and practices carry specific names. One first needs to account for these practices on this level. In a second step, this 'cultural interpretation of meaning' is transformed into a 'sociological interpretation of meaning' that operates on a more abstract level by selecting those aspects from the first level that seem theoretically relevant; the selection and transposition to the more abstract level is governed by 'a one-sided theoretical interest in certain aspects of the cultural meaning' (131). (However, note that Riesebrodt uses rules and norms of practices as his main data, i.e. acts of systematization; Riesebrodt's systematization of these systematizations therefore is a third- or fourth-level abstraction. Where Riesebrodt seeks to avoid a theological bias he risks falling into the trap of a ritualistic bias.)

He draws the following conclusion from this comparative one-sided ideal-typical abstraction and systematization of structures of meaning: 'All religions claim to have the ability to ward off misfortune, overcome crises, and provide salvation' (132; see also 2008: 33). Elsewhere he refers to this 'set of promises that all religions make' as 'a rather pragmatic core' (2008: 33). 'On this view, religion is primarily a promise of salvation' (2007: 132). He makes it clear that this is not merely 'a latent function of religious practices, but rather the meaning inscribed within the latter' (132).

Riesebrodt claims that 'the theme of averting misfortune, overcoming crises, and providing salvation appears throughout all types of religious practices in the most diverse religions, regardless of time, place, or specific cultural form' (134). The 'explanation' of religion announced by Riesebrodt turns out to be the identification of a shared, 'universal and central' (135) leitmotiv of liturgies. Misfortune or calamity (*Unheil*) and blessing or salvation (*Heil*) manifest themselves in three domains: nature, the body, and social relationships.[20] Crises are often attributed to superhuman powers. Blessing and salvation are sometimes promised for this world, sometimes for the next (132).

Religion and the social

For Riesebrodt it is the 'promise' of religions that lies at the heart of their ability to exert power and authority (132):

> For the purpose of theory-building I am interested not in the 'critical' external perspective that 'unmasks' religious ideologies and their involvement in power interests, but rather in an interpretive perspective that arrives at an explanation of religion by systematizing religious self-representations. In this way I seek to find out how religion comes to be capable of constituting authority and power at all. (184)

This, again, is part of the Weberian legacy: values, world images and ideas (or promises) can create – taking power structures into account – the track along which interests are articulated and behaviour is organized.

The credibility of his theory is strengthened, Riesebrodt believes, by being grounded in 'the respective meanings of religious practices and their liturgies themselves' rather than by drawing on outside impositions (134). He defends his straightforward, apparently uncritical and naïve reading of sources as a reasonable methodological strategy: 'I take the sources literally, because the logic of religions is revealed in these self-images' (184). In that sense, his theory is inductive. Accordingly, Riesebrodt does not want to draw conclusions for religion based on given theories of society or the social; rather, his theory 'is designed to read religious practice as a seismograph of the social' (2008: 38) since an analysis of interventionist theories and liturgies can 'inform us about the misfortunes to be averted, the crises in need of coping with, the temporal blessings hoped for, and the imagined eternal happiness' (2008: 38).

This analytical perspective can explain the 'recent global resurgence of religion' as a political and public force: 'From the point of view of my theory, one would look for misfortunes and crises created by historical transformations during this period' (2008: 38). This remark raises some important questions. Riesebrodt argues that an increase in misfortunes or crises would make 'promises' of overcoming them more attractive, resulting in a resurgence of religion. Note that his is not a functionalist theory, since he does not claim that religion has the inherent function of solving such crises, nor that religions actually do resolve crises. Rather, religions promise to achieve this, and this promise is not an abstract idea but is performed in interventionist practices and administered by institutions. The promise is the meaning of the practices. Yet what constitutes the plausibility of practices cum promises? Riesebrodt, as far as I can see, nowhere addresses that question. Following the logic of his argument, this must be the superhuman powers with which performers establish and sustain contact by engaging in interventionist practices. In social terms, however, other factors (such as crises) explain why more people revert to promises of religion in some given historical circumstances than in others. If the correlation between promise and needs is not one of function, maybe it is one of fit? If religion has been able to prosper universally and for millennia, is it unlikely that its promises and practices have been functional in the sense of catering to a set of needs? Would anybody have bothered with promises if such promises were implausible?

The genesis, reproduction and evaluation of religion

Some of Riesebrodt's remarks on the origin ('genesis') and reproduction of religion, outlined in the final chapter of the book, point in a similar direction. With regard to the 'phylogenetic' (i.e. evolutionary) question of the origins of religion Riesebrodt draws on Durkheim and, in particular, the German philosopher and sociologist Arnold Gehlen (1904–76). Gehlen argued that the human 'reduction of instincts' creates the need 'to regulate and institutionalize to a significant degree its internal and external relationships', in particular 'when people are confronted by their own powerlessness, as in the case of the mortality of their bodies, their lack of control over the natural environment, or the instability of social relationships' (240–1, see Gehlen, 1988 [1940; 15th edition 2009]). For Riesebrodt, religions, especially interventionist practices, are particularly apt to cope with these limitations:

> [T]he achievement of religious institutions is based on the fact that they maintain people's ability to act in situations where they are in fact powerless and incapable of action. In bringing threats into significant relation to superhuman powers, people can attempt, by communicating with these powers, to actively manage these situations, instead of panicking or sinking into depression. (241)

As especially powerful and effective ways of 'coping with contingency' (241), religions are potentially adaptive mechanisms, where adaptive (a term not used by Riesebrodt) refers to traits that promote survival and reproduction. Restoring agency instead of inaction and depression can be called adaptive in that sense. Riesebrodt holds that his theory of religion 'is thus completely compatible with a phylogenetic explanation of religion that underlies central sociological traditions' (241). It may well be so, but one also wonders how the phylogenetic (evolutionary) grounding of his theory relates to his metatheoretical and inductive methodological commitments, which eschew deriving religion from other social processes. While Riesebrodt does not explicitly take the step to social functionalism or evolutionary adaptationism, there seems nothing in the way of his theory's moving in that direction, given the asserted affinity and fit between the promises and effects of religion on the one hand and the specific biological need of humans on the other.[21]

When it comes to the ontogenetic level, that is the 'reproduction' of religion in the life of the individual, Riesebrodt refers to psychoanalytic theories as one way to better 'understand the universality and plausibility of the "religious premise" of the universal belief in the existence of superhuman powers' (241). In particular, he draws on Ana-Maria Rizzuto's classic *The birth of the living god: a psychoanalytic study* (1979).[22] Riesebrodt claims that these theories can be combined with his theory of religion and confirm its central thesis of the specific achievements of religion in 'warding off and overcoming crisis situations. Religion not only makes the unexplainable explainable, but also maintains people's ability to act in situations in which they run up against their limits' (243). The latter again seems to indicate an adaptive function for religion, but Riesebrodt paints an ambivalent picture:

> On the one hand, religion allows human beings to continue to act even when their capacities are actually insufficient. Religious practices offer humans a structure in situations in which they might oscillate between panic and depression. On the other hand, the institutionalization and internalization of religious ideas can also prevent people from rationally coping with their fate themselves when they are capable of doing so. (243)

The latter statement, of course, is a judgement based on the values of Western modernity, namely that it is better to cope with one's fate rationally (and individually) rather than within traditional structures of meaning.

Conclusion and criticism

These pages from the eighth and final chapter give a different twist to Riesebrodt's theory and make his project appear somewhat ambivalent. In fact, one could go so far as to say that Riesebrodt's book presents its readers with two different theories of religion. On the one hand, there is an outline of a theory that grounds religion phylogenetically and ontogenetically in human nature and assigns it a clear functionality with regard to crises and human agency. This theory explains the potential universality of religion. It deductively lays the ground for the necessary preconditions of religion, is based on preconceived theories of society and humans and is grounded in classic theories (Durkheim/Gehlen; Freud/Rizzuto). On the other hand, there is a theory that inductively proceeds by systematizing the almost universal occurrences of 'religion' (as conceptually established) and that challenges the legitimacy of theoretical outsider perspectives. This theory does not address the necessary preconditions of religion at all, but is based on sufficient preconditions. Riesebrodt introduces the deductive theory as a means to supplement the inductive theory, but does not explain how it is possible to unite two different theoretical strategies within one and the same theoretical framework. Where he anticipates a theoretical convergence, others may sense a contradiction, at least in a methodological and philosophical sense, with the deductive side impeding the plausibility of the inductive project, which proceeds on the basis of an analysis of what religions claim to be able to accomplish. Even if such a convergence were theoretically possible, Riesebrodt fails to explore this possibility. If one were to do so, one might also wish to consider other theoretical alliances instead of the somewhat dated options chosen in the book.

The inductive (side of the) theory makes up the main body of the book. It is the result of a systematic analysis of a wide range of cross-cultural data for religion. It offers a defence of the very concept of religion, a definition of religion, an interpretation and an explanation of religion. Note that, following Weber (and contrary to authors such as Geertz (see Segal 1999)), interpretation and understanding are not regarded as opposite but as complementary procedures: Weber conceived of sociology as a science that seeks to interpretatively understand social action and thereby causally explain it with regard to its course and effects (Weber 1988 [1921]: 542). Interpreting and understanding social action, however, directs attention to meanings, that is motives, intentions, and expectations. Meanings are causes; in order to explain what people do one must understand why they do it, that is the meanings people give to their actions subjectively and in shared, normative, symbolic and institutional frameworks. This is what Riesebrodt seeks to achieve with his systematization of liturgies and other data for religion (such as religious propaganda and conversion accounts): to establish the 'meaning', 'significance' and the 'logic' of religion.

With this sort of theory Riesebrodt is able to answer some of the main questions expected of a theory of religion. To begin with, his theory makes strong statements about the specific features and significance of religion, allowing for a clear distinction between religion and non-religion. He does that both at the level of definition and at the levels of interpretation and explanation. At the same time, Riesebrodt makes it clear that his theory

> should not be misunderstood as a determination of an 'essence' of religion. My theory does not seek to prove that all religions are 'ultimately' alike, but rather wants to make them comparable through reference to a general structure of meaning underlying them. (257)

It is understandable that Riesebrodt wishes to avoid being stigmatized as an essentialist, but it is difficult to come up with a non-essentialist reading of a 'general structure of meaning underlying' religions.

While his inductive meaning-systematizing theory is not in a position to state anything about the origins of religion, his 'second' phylogenetic/ ontogenetic theory is all about origins. Where his 'inductive' theory focuses on the promises and to some extent on the (self-proclaimed) achievements of religion, but emphatically objects to the very legitimacy of functionalist theorizing, his 'deductive' theory comes conspicuously close to a functionalist agenda. Finally, Riesebrodt makes a number of interesting statements and inferences about the structure of religion. Consider his distinction between different forms of practices and the pre-eminence of one of these types, namely the 'interventionist practices', or his elaboration on the practices of virtuosos as radicalizations of 'general practices'.

The interpretative-explanatory character of the theory granted, one still wonders whether the theory presents an end point or starting point for theorizing about religion. Riesebrodt takes for granted things that other theories seek to explain in the first place. Consider the key notion of 'superhuman powers'. Apart from the fact that Riesebrodt never argues for his choice of terms[23] one wonders why he does not discuss the findings of cognitive and evolutionary theories that point to cognitive constraints and evolutionary frameworks for human conceptualizations of these 'superhuman powers'. An explanation of the starting point for his 'religious premise' would be an important precondition and extension of the theory. Likewise his theory, based on self-portrayals of religions, simply takes it for granted that such powers easily achieve a certain fluency and plausibility and are able to generate commitments in social groups. These are important prerequisites for their ability to succeed in making such assertions, which should be addressed in a theory of religion. Similar concerns can be raised with regard to Riesebrodt's 'interventionist practices' or 'liturgies'. Even if he were right in declaring them the foundational mechanisms of religious universes, it will be difficult to appreciate this without a theory of ritual that could possibly account for ritual's capacities to operate in ways Riesebrodt, from the basis of assertions made by various religions, believes they do, how they achieve this, what makes them persuasive, etc. Given the importance of superhuman powers in the architecture of his theory, one wonders whether, as predicted by Lawson and McCauley (1990, 2002), rituals that involve such powers in more immediate ways than others would in turn constitute a superior class of interventionist practices. What qualifies practices to become effectively 'interventionist'? At times, Riesebrodt's theory of religion makes one think of a theory of insurance companies that would take the 'promises' of their products as their core feature and that would only allow for their self-portrayals as legitimate source of knowledge about them. While such promises make many people buy their policies, these promises alone are a long way from explaining how the industry works (and why it can fail, despite its promises).

Some doubts and further questions arise with regard to Riesebrodt's key terms, *Heil* and *Unheil*, only partially translatable as 'salvation' and 'misfortune'. Where these terms clearly make sense in a religious vocabulary, as theoretical terms they are probably as elusive as 'the holy', 'the sacred', *mana*, or other terms that previously cast their spell over the study of religion(s). The extensive criticisms of these terms would likely also apply to 'salvation' and 'misfortune.'

The term 'salvation' recalls Weber's concept of salvation goods (*Heilsgut*), a concept not systematically developed in his works (see Stolz 2006: 18–20). As analyzed by Stolz, for Weber a salvation good is either an end or a means to an end as defined by and embedded in religious worldviews and practices; they can be transcendent or immanent, set in the future or in the present, this-worldly or other-worldly, individual or collective, ascetic or contemplative, aspired to or provided by an external power. Salvation goods can satisfy different social and psychological needs. Stolz, in turn, proposes a new typology of religious goods based on general characteristics of goods, on distinctions between different kinds of situations and circumstances, and on a distinction between individual and social goods (2006: 21–8). Following up on this suggestion offers just one potential way to elaborate on Riesebrodt's rather vague core notions.

Riesebrodt's interpretation and explanation of religion is built on facts that can be reasonably described in terms of religion (in his model), and the theory is grounded in data, yet the proposed level of (second-, third- or fourth-level) abstraction makes the conclusions derived from the data look disappointingly shallow. His disclaimer that the practices of all religions are by no means 'exhausted by the structures of meaning I have identified' (145) fails to alleviate these concerns. Take the first example he presents: religious calendars (146–57). From a sketch of calendars in Western

('Abrahamic') and East Asian religions Riesebrodt draws the following conclusion:

> This brief outline has, I hope, sufficiently shown that the liturgies of calendrical practices in both the Abrahamic and East Asian religions promise to provide blessings and salvation, to ward off misfortune and disaster, or to help humans in overcoming crises. (157)

Statements of that sort seem to have distilled meaning to such a high degree that they appear insufficiently complex and almost banal. Even granted that the statement is not wrong, it simply leaves too many 'how' and 'why' questions unanswered. But if the meaning of theories is to stimulate further questions, then this may offer a good starting point for further theorizing.

Notes

1   Riesebrodt (1990: 9) critically remarks that Weber's studies led to a tendency to use the comparative method mostly in order to highlight the special development characteristics of 'the West'.

2   An English translation (by Steven Rendall) is in preparation with the University of Chicago Press; Martin Riesebrodt kindly made that translation available to me. This has saved me the trouble of translating the quotations into English (though I have not followed Rendall's translation in all cases). All page references are to the German edition. Note that the German word *Cultus* is somewhat antiquated and not used in contemporary academic German.

3   In one of his methodological papers, Weber had emphasized the discursive nature of all scientific cognition and knowledge (Weber 1988 [1904]: 195).

4   For the discourse theoretical critique, Riesebrodt refers mainly to Asad and to Dubuisson (but not to Fitzgerald); for the postcolonial critique he refers to Chidester, L. Jensen, King, and Sugirtharajah. He does not engage with the work of other defenders of the concept of religion such as Saler (2000, 2008).

5   It seems that very few societies have a concept (and a term) of music comparable to the Western one. See Nettl 2005 for interesting discussions of the question of ethnocentrism and universality in the study of music (ethnomusicology).

6   He holds that these theories face the problem that they admittedly cannot distinguish between religious and non-religious phenomena; that they have a Romantic notion of religion; that they reduce religion to the emotional states of virtuosos (mystics and shamans); and last but not least, that 'they are dreadfully naïve and simplistic as researchers in the field of religion' (96).

7   Here is his criticism: 'Bourdieu reduces religion to an instrument for pursuing this-worldly power interests and social advancement. Thus he concentrates on a dimension of religions that is certainly present but relatively unspecific to religion' (103).

8   This is his critique. First, the theory is inconsistent because it remains unclear whether its assumption of stable preferences is to be read in methodological or ontological terms. Second, the theory is tautological ('Whatever people do expresses their preference'), i.e. unspecific. Third, its model of human action is simplistic (106). Fourth, it only works 'for analyzing situations in which rational calculation is institutionalized. It is, however, unsuitable as a foundation for a universal theory of religion' (107). Finally, one of the main principles of the theory 'reveals an astonishing historical and cultural ignorance' (107).

9   He singles out Luckmann as a protagonist of that approach (112).

10   Here and throughout 'meaning' translates the German word *Sinn*.

11   Is being religious or pro-religious an internal/insider perspective? Is being anti-religious an external/scientific or an internal perspective? How about a German Catholic studying American Catholicism? Who defines the perspective of the observer? Maybe the perspective is less important than the type of knowledge one seeks to produce.

12   Riesebrodt 2008: 29 provides a shorter and somewhat different definition: '*a system of meaningful practices with reference to superhuman powers*' (italics in the original). This definition avoids the apparent tautology of defining 'religion' in terms of 'religious' practices. Riesebrodt refers to Spiro 1966 as a source of inspiration.

13   Riesebrodt argues that his definition of religion dissolves the problematic distinction between religion and magic (117). I agree with Riesebrodt that this distinction is often informed by value judgements and can be theological in nature. On the other hand, the distinction between 'religion' and 'magic' is, if not universal, at least widespread. Given Riesebrodt's metatheoretical and methodological programme one would expect him to systematize this distinction and to refine it analytically on a more abstract level rather than abandon it. Riesebrodt's desire to dissolve the category of magic recalls other scholars' desire to incorporate the concept of religion into wider categories such as culture.

14   This is logically inconsistent. For if religiosity means absorbing a religion and a religion is a meaningful complex or system of practices then religiosity must imply practising a religion.

15   I would have preferred to have a different term for each of these three communicative functions it is supposed to fulfil.

16   I owe this observation to my student Knut Melvær.

17   Riesebrodt claims that these 'represent the unity of theory and practice' (2008: 31). The unification of theory and practice is a leitmotiv for many theories of ritual; see Bell's metatheoretical analysis (1992).

18   See Rappaport 1999: 169 for definitions ('the more or less invariant sequences of rituals that make up cycles and other series as well'); see Stausberg 2003: 233–4.

19   For liturgies as scripts, see Riesebrodt 2008: 33.

20   Riesebrodt refers to Freud's *Future of an illusion* for this systematization.

21 Note that Gehlen's basic assumption of a 'reduction of instincts' is long since outdated, as is his theory of culture. It is rare for Riesebrodt to completely uncritically draw on this theory.

22 Other theories could have been considered; one might suggest attachment theory.

23 Given the relatively extensive debate about the concepts 'superhuman' and 'supernatural' (or the related concept 'transcendence') and the problematic legacy of the notion of power in the study of religion(s) this is somewhat disappointing.

References

Bell, C.M., 1992. *Ritual theory, ritual practice*. Oxford University Press, New York, Oxford.

Gehlen, A., 1988. *Man: his nature and place in the world*. Columbia University Press, New York.

Lawson, E.T. and McCauley, R.N., 1990. *Rethinking religion: connecting cognition and culture*. Cambridge University Press, Cambridge.

McCauley, R.N. and Lawson, E.T., 2002. *Bringing ritual to mind: psychological foundations of cultural forms*. Cambridge University Press, Cambridge.

McCutcheon, R.T. (Ed.), 1999. *The insider/outsider problem in the study of religion: a reader*. Cassell, London.

Nettl, B., 2005. *The study of ethnomusicology: thirty-one issues and concepts*. University of Illinois Press, Urbana, IL.

Rappaport, R.A., 1999. *Ritual and religion in the making of humanity*. Cambridge University Press, Cambridge.

Riesebrodt, M., 1990. *Fundamentalismus als patriarchalische Protestbewegung. Amerikanische Protestanten (1910–28) und iranische Schiiten (1961–79) im Vergleich*. Mohr-Siebeck, Tübingen.

Riesebrodt, M., 1993. *Pious passion: the emergence of modern fundamentalism in the United States and Iran*. University of California Press, Berkeley (English translation of 1990).

Riesebrodt, M., 1999. *Charisma* in Max Weber's sociology of religion. *Religion* 29 (1), 1–14.

Riesebrodt, M., 2000a. *Die Rückkehr der Religionen. Fundamentalismus und der 'Kampf der Kulturen'*. Beck, Munich.

Riesebrodt, M., 2000b. Fundamentalism and the resurgence of religion. *Numen* 47 (3), 267–87.

Riesebrodt, M., 2001a. Religiöse Vergemeinschaftungen. In: Kippenberg, H.G. and Riesebrodt, M. (Eds.), *Max Webers 'Religionssystematik'*. Mohr-Siebeck, Tübingen, 101–17.

Riesebrodt, M., 2001b. Charisma. In: Kippenberg, H.G. and Riesebrodt, M. (Eds), *Max Webers 'Religionssystematik'*. Mohr-Siebeck, Tübingen, 151–66.

Riesebrodt, M., 2001c. Ethische und exemplarische Prophetie. In: Kippenberg, H.G. and Riesebrodt, M. (Eds.), *Max Webers 'Religionssystematik'*. Mohr-Siebeck, Tübingen, 193–208.

Riesebrodt, M., 2003. Religion in global perspective. In: Juergensmeyer, M. (Ed.), *Global religions: an introduction*. Oxford University Press, Oxford, 95–109.

Riesebrodt, M., 2004. Überlegungen zur Legitimität eines universalen Religions-begriffs. In: Luchesi, B. and von Stuckrad, K. (Eds.), *Religion im kulturellen Diskurs / Religion in cultural discourse. Festschrift für Hans Kippenberg zu seinem 65. Geburtstag / Essays in Honor of Hans G. Kippenberg on the occasion of his 65th birthday*. Walter de Gruyter, Berlin, New York, 127–49.

Riesebrodt, M., 2007. *Cultus und Heilsversprechen. Eine Theorie der Religion*. C.H. Beck, Munich.

Riesebrodt, M., 2008. Theses on a theory of religion. *International Political Anthropology* 1 (1), 25–41.

Rizzuto, A.-M., 1979. *The birth of the living god: a psychoanalytic study*. University of Chicago Press, Chicago.

Saler, B., 2000 (1993). *Conceptualizing religion: immanent anthropologists, transcendent natives, and unbounded categories*. Berghahn Books, New York, Oxford.

Saler, B., 2008. Conceptualizing religion: Some recent reflections. *Religion* 38 (3), 219–25.

Segal, R.A., 1999. Weber and Geertz on the meaning of religion. *Religion* 29 (1), 61–71.

Spiro, M.E., 1966. Religion: problems of definition and explanation. In: Banton, M. (Ed.), *Anthropological approaches to the study of religion*. Tavistock, London, 85–126.

Stausberg, M., 2003. Ritual orders and ritologiques: a terminological quest for some neglected fields of study. In: Ahlbäck, T. and Dahla, B. (Eds.), *Ritualistics*. Donner Institute for Research in Religious and Cultural History, Åbo, 221–42.

Stolz, J., 2006. Salvation goods and religious markets: integrating rational choice and Weberian perspectives. *Social Compass* 53 (1), 13–32.

Weber, M., 1988. *Gesammelte Aufsätze zur Wissenschaftslehre*, 7th edition, ed. Johannes Winckelmann. Mohr-Siebeck, Tübingen.

17

Back and forth

Michael Stausberg

This set of discussions of individual theories highlights the diversity of current attempts to theorize religion. The evaluations range from solid endorsements through critical dissent to philosophical refutations. I will not lend my editorial voice to pronounce a verdict on the validity of any single theory among those considered in this book, but rather address some issues that may serve to put the various theories in a comparative perspective.

Conversations, trajectories, lineages

First of all, the reader may wonder whether the various theories can be read as part of a larger discussion. Clearly, many theories are grounded in wider theoretical discourses in different branches of scholarship. This is obvious and self-acknowledged in some cases, though less explicit in others.[1] But do the theories engage in conversations with each other? Apart from some exceptional cases (see below), this does not really seem to be the case – or at least not at any deep level. Some theorists seek to state their case or to explicate and refine their documented positions without engaging with the work of fellow theorists of religion. Lewis-Williams, Luhmann, Rappaport, and Rue discuss other theories of religion only tangentially.[2] Possibly these theorists, given their quite different academic disciplinary backgrounds, are not aware of the spectrum of earlier and competing theories – or they simply assign priority to their own theoretical projects.

Boyer's and Riesebrodt's surveys of earlier (lay and academic) theories, meant to give a clearer profile to their own theories, are remarkable exceptions. Guthrie devotes an entire chapter to demonstrating 'that present theories of religion are inadequate' (Guthrie 1993: 5), while at the same time acknowledging his intellectual debts (37). Stark and Finke contrast their own project, rhetorically presented as the 'new paradigm', with a summary sketch of some guiding assumptions of other and previous theorizing (= the 'old paradigm'). Dawkins rejects some large and unspecific groups of theories such as psychological explanations in general, but criticizes fellow biologist Wilson's group selection theory in particular (Dawkins 2006: 168–72).[3] Others are more receptive in their theorizing of religion. Pyysiäinen develops his theory in conversation with, among others, Boyer and Lawson and McCauley (and in explicit contrast to an earlier theoretical tradition epitomized in Durkheim and Geertz). Atran makes perhaps the most impressive attempt to map a theoretical landscape and to seek to integrate diverse bodies of theoretical work, often by pointing to what he perceives as their limitations. Dawkins's concept of the 'meme' is of crucial importance for Dennett's theory. Dennett seeks to incorporate what he has read of cognitive, evolutionary, and ethological theorists of religion including Burkert but mostly Boyer (who also draws on Dawkins),[4] and sees his project rather as an attempt to highlight 'a small fraction of the work that has already been done' by others (Dennett 2006: 312). As a biologist, Wilson criticizes the entire social science tradition of theorizing religion and singles out so-called rational choice theory, in particular Stark and Iannaccone. Wilson's project reads as if he wanted to put the social sciences on what he perceives as a more solid footing; evolutionary theory in general and group selection theory in particular are presented as having vastly superior explanatory power.

Even if there are some conversations and attempts at syntheses, there is so far no attempt to put the various theoretical agendas into a metatheoretical perspective – provided that this is at all possible, feasible, and desirable. In order to make that happen, however, one would probably need to redimension theoretical claims and premises, limits in empirical breadth, and ideological agendas. Let us first take up a thread from the introduction.

Varieties of 'theory'

Not all the theories discussed in the present volume spell out, or even discuss, the aims and scopes of a 'theory' of religion, as they understand it. Instead of analytically extrapolating their understanding of 'theory', let us look at some examples of those books that go beyond merely stating which questions a theory of religion should be able to answer (e.g. Guthrie 1993: 9). In fact, several notions of theory are hidden behind the seemingly homogeneous mask of a volume on contemporary theories of religion. The theorists have different backgrounds, and accordingly their theories point in quite different directions.

Lawson and McCauley – the latter a philosopher – require of a theory that it employs 'a common set of concepts and general principles' (Lawson and McCauley 1990: 174). These must then be organized in the architecture of a theory. 'In addition', they write, 'a *satisfactory* theory makes testable claims about universal constraints on the phenomena in some domain' (174 [my italics]). Lawson and McCauley then proceed to demonstrate why they think their theory adequately meets these requirements. In developing their concepts and principles, as well as in constructing the architecture of their theory, they draw on linguistic theory.

Riesebrodt, on the other hand, clearly situates himself in a different, viz. a Weberian, tradition of theorizing. In line with this, Riesebrodt advocates an interpretative (*verstehende*) approach and rejects explanations that as a matter of principle disregard insider perspectives (Riesebrodt 2007: 108–9). Instead, insider perspectives are generalized and systematized in such a manner as then to qualify as outsider concepts. Explanation is not contrasted with but informed by interpretation. Stark and Finke, albeit also sociologists, again set out from a radically different view of theory, namely a deductive model:

> To construct a *proper theory*, one postulates or assumes the axioms and then logically deduces propositions, some of which have empirical implications. One tests the theory, and thereby the axioms, by testing empirical predictions deduced from the propositions. (Stark and Finke 2000: 43 [my italics])

Their theory is thus, at least partially, presented as a series of 36 definitions and 99 propositions (see Stark and Finke 2000: 277–86). While some of these propositions are framed as if they were laws (e.g. Proposition 18: 'Magic cannot generate extended or exclusive patterns of exchange'),[5] others are formulated in terms of causal relations (e.g. Proposition 9: 'The greater the number of gods worshipped by a group, the lower the price of exchange with a god or gods'),[6] and others are presented as predictions logically derived from other propositions, indicated by the use of the future tense (e.g. Proposition 10: 'In exchanging with the gods, humans **will** pay higher prices to the extent that the gods are believed to be more dependable' [the last word bold in the original]). Predictions (or retrodictions) are also used as a method within evolutionary theory.

The evolutionary biologists (and other theorists building on evolutionary theory such as Rue), in their turn, bring their theoretical apparatus to theories of religion, including such terms as 'fitness', 'adaptation', and methods or sources of evidence such as arguments from 'design', comparison, and tracking the evolutionary process (Wilson 2002: 71–3). Evolutionary theory also builds on the distinction between proximate and ultimate causes.

In a metatheoretical reflection, Tweed emphasizes the importance of metaphors for theories. Consequently, he describes his own theoretical project in metaphorical terms, namely as 'embodied travel', 'purposeful wandering' (Tweed 2006: 11, 13), while at the same time pointing to the limitations of all metaphors (15). While Atran, a cognitive anthropologist, does not discuss the importance of metaphors for theorizing, he deliberately proceeds from a 'chosen metaphor for thinking about the evolutionary history and underpinnings of religion in particular, and culture in general', namely that of 'a mountain-valley landscape formed by different mountain ridges' (Atran 2002: 265).[7]

Critique and apology

Theories of religion are unavoidably selective (reductionist), and attempts to explain religion can be perceived (and are sometimes also intended) as attempts to explain *away* religion.[8] This is, however, not necessarily given by the theory-character of theories. Theories of language, for example, do not try to make us stop using language, nor do theories of syntax want us to stop using syntax. Having and speaking a language is perceived as taken for granted and as a completely unproblematic matter of fact, whereas having and professing a religion may not always appear as an equally normal option. All the theories discussed in the present volume, however, defend the idea that being religious is 'natural' in the sense of a possibility, or susceptibility, if not a necessity, open to all human beings as a matter of principle.[9] While relatively few speakers of a given language make it a point that theirs is a better language than that of other speakers (although learning a new language as an adult often entails the impression that one's second language is odd), religious people may be more prone to value judgements. Similarly, I have so far not come across the sentiment of offence expressed by humans as speakers of languages with regard to the terms used by linguistics when analyzing language. People investing in and committed to religion, on the other hand, may feel offended by certain ways of referring to religion. When Boyer repeatedly calls religion an 'airy nothing' (Boyer 2002: 3, 56, 379), this might well be perceived as offensive, even though it is an allusion to Shakespeare's *Midsummer night's dream* 'Turns them to shapes and gives to airy nothing / A local habitation and a name' (V.1).

The critique of religion put forward by eighteenth-century European philosophers was a breeding ground for early theories of religion. Several classical theories – most notably those of Marx and Freud – also stand in the tradition of critique. This tradition has been revived in some recent theorizing: Dawkins's book is more a weapon against religion than a detached theory. Dennett's aims appear to be somewhat modest: he promotes the idea of educating 'the people of the world, so that they can make truly informed choices about their lives' (Dennett 2006: 339). Even if not campaigning against religion as such, Dennett regards religion as a possible carrier of 'bad spells' (15) and as the source of 'toxic mutations' (332). The project thus amounts to an attempt to disarm religion. Burkert likewise concludes his book by claiming that '[t]he contents and prospects of religion remain thoroughly problematic – and fascinating' (Burkert 1998 [1996]: 179).

While Dawkins's theory has an explicit anti-religious agenda, Dennett's a sceptical thrust, and Burkert's a final note of warning, other theoretical projects point in the opposite direction. Beyond mere sympathy to religion in the sense of a humanistic respect and hermeneutical openness to the subject area, several books spell out religious visions. Consider Rappaport. Besides developing a theory of religion, his monumental volume *Ritual and religion in the making of humanity*, as was pointed out in the Foreword by Keith Hart, amounts to 'nothing less than to lay the groundwork for the development of a new religion adequate to the circumstances humanity will encounter in the twenty-first century' (Hart in Rappaport 1999: xiv; see also Wiebe 2004).

Stark and Finke's theory engages in ongoing polemics against 'liberal' or 'modernized' religion (and intellectuals, especially theologians), which they regard as 'clearly a failure on sociological grounds' (Stark and Finke 2000: 276). Their theory presents itself as a sociological apology for 'strict' churches and an American model of organizing the 'religious economy'.[10]

Newberg's theory claims to prove 'that the existence of an absolute higher reality or power is at least as rationally possible as the existence of a purely material world' (Newberg, D'Aquili, and Rause 2001: 155). Newberg claims to have outlined a 'framework within which all religions can be reconciled' and that can likewise 'reconcile the rift between science and religion' (ibid.: 168–9). He also points to the 'mythological' nature of science (ibid.: 171).

Wilson ends his book by stating that, as regards the future of humanity, he is

> encouraged by some of the examples of religious belief that we have encountered in the pages of this book, which combine hard-headed factual realism with the profound respect for symbols embodied in the word 'sacred'. Like the Nuer tribesman and the Balinese farmer, let us know exactly what our unifying systems are for, and then pay homage to them with overflowing belief. (Wilson 2002: 233)

Wilson also thinks 'that science might profit by becoming more religious along certain dimensions, as long as it remains nonreligious with respect to its stated goal of increasing factual knowledge' (Wilson 2002: 230).

Rue ends his book by pointing to the global ecological crisis and painting a doomsday scenario from which only 'significant changes in values and attitudes' (Rue 2005: 341) will be able to save humanity. According to Rue these changes will ultimately only be made possible by inspirations from mythical traditions or by people adopting the stance of 'religious naturalism' (363–8). This implies, and at the same time defends, the thesis that religion is something essentially 'good'[11] or, in a term Rue might prefer, 'fitness-maximising' (whereas it is something essentially 'harmful' for Dawkins and potentially so for Dennett).

Theorists of religion, especially American scholars,[12] are taking on the roles of critics or advocates of religion. They are actors in the notoriously disputed field of religion (especially so in the United States). Apparently they want their theories to become part of the public discourse on religion – though likely not because of a reflexive recognition that 'their' theories are public goods already entangled in public discourses. The 'engaged' character of recent theorizing and the public status of religion as a social fact in societies around the globe –not only in 'the West' – may also be one factor why attempts to 'deconstruct' the category are not discussed by contemporary theorists (Tweed and Riesebrodt being the exceptions that confirm the rule).[13]

Functions, transmission, constraints

Statements on the possible benefits or even necessity of some form of religiousness cannot be separated from general views on the functionality or adaptive value of religion. Apart from being a theoretical question, views on the functionality, adaptiveness, or naturalness of religion will have an impact on the evaluation of the future of religion in our respective societies. The widespread rise of atheism may be a challenge for theories based on the idea that religion is a natural phenomenon,[14] and the phenomena usually subsumed under the umbrella term secularization (mostly identified as a European phenomenon) have served as a point of departure for early sociological theories of religion; at the same time, sociological theory itself has since Comte been an agent of secularization. Readers cannot fail to notice that secularization is still a recurrent theme for those contemporary theorists writing from a sociological background (Luhmann; Stark and Finke; Riesebrodt), all of whom advance different interpretations and 'solutions'. In all other works, the concept is hardly mentioned at all, or if so, only marginally.

Given its alleged inherent logical difficulties, functionalism was declared dead as a viable explanatory strategy in theory of religion by Penner (1999 [based on Hempel 1959]). Lewis-Williams echoes that critique when he refers to 'the functionalist trap' (2005: 78) or 'the functionalist tautology' (79).[15] Riesebrodt also rejects functionalist explanations.[16] Rappaport and Luhmann, on the other hand, present functionalist theories. In his chapter, Robert Segal reconstructs how Rappaport's latest theory (1999) can be read as providing an unexpected answer to the problem his earlier (1968) theory faced with regard to Hempel's critique of functionalism. Luhmann had likewise published an earlier functionalist theory (1977) and maintains a functionalist programme in his later theory (2000). He conceives of religion not as beneficial to society as a whole, but as making possible the maintenance of the social system's fundamental modus operandi, namely communication, even in situations of apparent paradox, where communication faces its limits (Luhmann 2002 [2000]: 137–41). Where Luhmann rejects the strategy of grounding a theory of religion on the alleged needs of people, and while he limits his theory to one type of society only, Stark and Finke build their theory squarely on the assumption that 'religion is the only possible source of certain rewards for which there is a general and inexhaustible demand' (Stark and Finke 2000: 85). However, they do not conclude from this 'that religion is a universal aspect of human societies' (113), and they devise their theory in opposition to functionalism, which they hold to be circular (and part and parcel of the 'old paradigm'). Biological evolutionary theory, as outlined by Wilson, on the other hand, rereads rational choice theory as potentially functionalist (Wilson 2002: 81) and tries to save social science from social scientists by applying the conceptual apparatus of evolutionary theory to rehabilitate functionalism under the disguise of an adaptationist programme.

Wilson thus hopes to join forces with a social science tradition against the other strand in evolutionary theories of religion (Atran, Boyer) that regards religion as a by-product of evolutionary forces. This latter way of theorizing religion is consonant with a theory that considers religion as some sort of a parasite that infects its hosts and builds complex structures around itself (Dawkins). The challenge for these theories is then to explain how religions are able to perpetuate, to persist, and to be transmitted despite not being based on any specific primary needs or embedded in functional and adaptationist structures. They achieve this by drawing on a theory of culture, which regards cultures as clusters of successfully transmitted (= epidemic) mental representations (or 'memes') rather than as structures, patterns, or networks of actions, interactions, symbols, or meaning. Instead of looking for either the needs of people or the functions of religion within society and culture, these theories tend to focus on the biological (evolutionary) and mental (cognitive) constraints that predictably limit the perceived variety of religious forms and formations.

Comparing such features of selected theories brings the discussion to a metatheoretical level. A metatheoretical comparison of theories of religion would need to discuss not only their value judgements regarding religion (as positive or negative) but also their implicit or explicit assumptions regarding such fundamental issues as anthropology, cognition, culture, evolution, history, meaning, and society.[17] All such issues (some of which are discussed in various chapters of the present volume) would need to be addressed by an overarching 'grand' theory of religion, assuming such a theory could or should ever be attempted. This, however, would require another series of books.

Perspectives

Much groundwork therefore remains to be done. In reviewing contemporary theories one cannot fail to notice their mutual divergence and competition. Some key points have been commented upon. While it would at the present stage be a hopeless venture to even begin to integrate the present corpus of theories into some grand unified theory – probably a hopeless and questionable task – the range of theoretical insights and perspectives contained in these works cries out for at least a rough sketch of avenues of conversation. At the risk of a very subjective selection, let me highlight some points.

One crucial issue that needs to be discussed further is the various levels at which a theory of religion should be operative.[18] Although not exactly addressing this concern, Stark and Finke move in a similar direction by making an attempt to analyze religion on three levels of aggregation, which Alles calls the micro-, meso- and macroeconomics of religion. Analyzing the working of religion on the level of individual agents, from the point of view of religious groups, or even with regard to entire 'religious economies' (i.e. all religious activities going on in a society), requires different conceptual tools and theoretical strategies.

On a related note, when reviewing the various theories, one finds that several of them conceptualize religion in terms of different analytical units. The sample, varying with the theoretical objects engaged by the theories, includes memes, representations (including judgements), actions and decisions, emotions and experiences, narratives, groups, and social systems.

To a varying extent, all contemporary theories try to frame their theories in such a manner that they avoid the appearance of bias in favour of some specific form of religion.[19] Guthrie, Boyer, and Atran are especially prolific in referring to a wide cross-cultural sample.[20] Wilson reflects on sampling strategies to avoid bias (Wilson 2002: 157; further developed in Wilson 2005). Riesebrodt seeks to 'consider materials from traditions and periods that are as different as possible, without wandering through history and geography too arbitrarily' (2007: 143). He is especially concerned to represent cases from East Asia, as a counterweight to claims about Western specialness, and Burkert argues that basing one's dossier, as he does, 'on the earliest written evidence has the advantage of a distanced view, largely exempt from the tensions and anxieties encircling living religions' (Burkert 1998 [1996]: xi). Evolutionary theory and psychology, however, presume much longer temporal horizons, often referring to (reconstructed, hypothetical) situations from the remote ancestral past. In the case of Lewis-Williams, the attempt at finding a key to an interpretation of Neolithic 'art' amounts to developing a (neuropsychological) theory of religion.[21] Evolution is not only a keyword in evolutionary theory, i.e. in biology and psychology, but also in other theoretical contexts, including history and sociology. Luhmann, for instance, discusses several moments of religious evolution, including the impact of writing and the rise of religion as a self-generating and recursive ('autopoetic') system (2002 [2000]: 267); ultimately, the decisive process is that of differentiation of society into several functional systems, where religion is one of these functions (besides law, science, politics, etc.). This is what, in this particular theory, characterizes modern society. On this view, 'religion' as an autopoetic, functional system is a result rather than a premise of historical developments; in other words, there were religious discourse and institutions in earlier times, but religion as discourse and institution only emerged at some point in history, with 'modernity' as the standard candidate.

Some theories (Lawson and McCauley, Guthrie, Boyer, Pyysiäinen, Atran) analyze elementary cognitive mechanisms that trigger religious conceptualizations such as anthropomorphism, concept acquisition as well as transmission, and representation. The mainstream cognitive theories have inverted the relationship between what Bulbulia[22] calls eReligion (= religious cultural; external religion) and iReligion (= innate religion) towards an emphasis on the latter. Some theorists have engaged in polemics against the theoretical supremacy of the concept of culture. At the same time, however, it has become clear that culture matters to biology[23] – in fact biology seems to be all about culture – and that the relation between cognition and culture is probably less one of antagonism than of dialectics.[24] Even the brain, still regarded by many as the 'hardware' that autonomously engineers culture, can be described as a cultural artefact (Mithen and Parsons 2008). Moreover, while recent theories rightly point to the relevance of biological and cognitive processes largely beyond the control of consciousness, concepts and representations are difficult to conceive of in social terms without taking meaning into account. Moreover, religious conceptualizations operate as symbols, and symbolization in turn is one way of connecting cognition and culture. Last but not least, with Luhmann one would emphasize the importance of communication. Concepts and representations constitute 'religion' only as part of a string of communication,[25] the absence of which will not allow the religious representations to gain a social quality in the first place. The religious quality of communication will in turn probably depend on the kind of inferences it allows for, the kind of agency it involves, the concepts it engages, or the kind of memes it helps to reproduce (unless communication is merely the vehicle for memes to reproduce themselves).[26] Successful religious communication will be such that it kicks off further religious communication.

Religion is typically associated with cross-culturally recurrent features that promote the perceived ubiquity, or universality, of religion. Myth and ritual are the most obvious candidates, and there is a long theoretical legacy on the question of which of the two should be assigned priority and how they are interrelated. To some extent this legacy reverberates in contemporary theorizing. Rappaport is an example of an attempt to establish ritual as the generative principle of religion and 'liturgical orders' as establishing metaconventions; Riesebrodt places 'interventionist practices' or 'liturgies' at the core of religion.[27] Rue exemplifies a theory that places myth as the cornerstone of its edifice (which is itself, as analyzed by Seiwert, constructed as a myth).[28] Most, if not all, contemporary theories of religion carry theories of ritual and myth in their baggage. Another classic and recurrent topic is morality, including related issues such as exchange, gifts/giving, and commitment. Depending on their underlying theoretical approach, contemporary theories have analyzed several mechanisms and specific modes of operations for all these domains. The relation of these domains to the general category of religion, however, still seems to be somewhat undertheorized. In one way or another, most theories seem to presuppose that religion as a generic category is more than an assembly of single traits or features, but why and how this is so still remains to be elucidated, whether in systematic or historical terms. That is to say, the emergence of the modern category of 'religion' along with the differentia-tion of religion as a societal subsystem quite possibly created a historical (others might call it an evolutionary) framework or niche that assembles many of the features identified as 'religious' because of their direct or indi-rect reference to divine agents; in this light, religion is a modern systemic reconfiguration of religious premises (see also Beyer 2006 for a similar approach). This, of course, is but one of many open questions, and even if all the theories discussed in the present volume have their shortcomings, they and the critical evaluations presented here will hopefully have given food for further thought.

Notes

1 A case in point is Jeppe Sinding Jensen's discussion of the impact of Sperber's theory of culture on what he calls the 'standard' cognitive theory of religion. For some, Darwin figures as the most important theoretical ancestor. For Riesebrodt, Weber is the main theoretical resource.

2 Note that Luhmann in some contexts refers to Rappaport.

3 Wilson later launched a counterattack in the *eSkeptic* of July 4, 2007, see www. skeptic.com/eskeptic/07–07–04.html (I am unsure whether the date of publication, Independence Day, is merely a coincidence); Dawkins replied to Wilson in the *eSkeptic* of July 11, 2007: www.skeptic.com/eskeptic/07–07–11.html. Dawkins's reply does not add any new arguments. Both texts can also be downloaded from the authors' personal homepages.

4 See the chapter in this volume by Armin Geertz on this lineage.

5 One way to defend such a statement against empirical counterexamples is to tighten the definition of 'magic'.

6 As an empirical statement, this proposition seems flawed in the light of what we know about Hinduism.

7 This metaphor is reflected in the subtitle of the book.

8 Greeley 1996 [1995]: 5 suggests dividing social science theories of religion 'into two categories – those who sought to explain religion and those who sought to explain it away'.

9 The most reluctant way of acknowledging this is presented by Dawkins (2006: 169) when he argues that a Darwinian theory 'wants to know why people are *vulnerable* to the charms of religion and therefore open to exploitation by priests, politicians and kings'.

10 See also the chapter by Gregory Alles in this volume.

11 This is a point made by J. Ingersoll in her review, see *Religion* 38 (3), 285–6.

12 The notable exception is Dawkins. Dennett makes it clear at the outset that he is 'an American author, and this book is addressed in the first place to American readers' (Dennett 2006: xiii).

13 Riesebrodt 2007: 243 warns that potential benefits of religion should not be misunderstood as 'a cheap justification of religion, because the result is certainly ambivalent'.

14 See the chapter by Armin Geertz in this volume; Geertz has another article on this issue in preparation; see also Saler and Ziegler 2006.

15 He bases his critique on Friedman 1974.

16 For details see my chapter on Riesebrodt in the present volume.

17 Several of these issues are discussed in the present volume: for meaning see the chapters by Steven Engler and Mark Q. Gardiner (on Lawson and McCauley) and by Jeppe Sinding Jensen (on Boyer and Pyysiäinen); for culture see the chapters by Jeppe Sinding Jensen and Armin W. Geertz (on Dawkins and Dennett).

18 See also my Introduction.

19 This is not to say that all theorists have succeeded in that regard. For an instructive example, see Beyer's critical remarks on Luhmann's sample. See also the chapter on Stark and Finke by Alles, who points to the danger of dilettantism.

20 Boyer (2002: 12) makes this quite explicit: 'When we put forward general explanations of religion, we had better make sure that they apply outside our parish.'

21 See Donald Wiebe's chapter in the present volume. This theoretical project engages the notion of 'shamanism' as the prototypical early religion; critical (discourse) theory would probably seek to dismantle this construct – just as it would the Romantic notion of 'mysticism', which is often relied upon as the epitome of 'pure' religion.

22 See his chapter on Atran.

23 See, for example, the chapter by Bulbulia and Frean on Wilson in the present volume.

24 There is by now a relatively large body of literature on this point. See also Jensen in this volume.

25 Note that both Luhmann and Rappaport regard religion as ways to address the inherent 'risks' (i.e. the fragility) of communication.

26 Luhmann presents some other features of religious communication; see the article by Peter Beyer in this volume. Beyer's own work has, extrapolating from Luhmann, taken the shape of a theory of religion in global society (Beyer 2006).

27 Lawson and McCauley seek to outline 'a framework for a larger theory of religious systems' by analyzing the generative logic of 'ritual systems' (Lawson and McCauley 1990: 171). Atran makes much of ritual as mechanisms of emotional validation; he does not pay attention to myth.

28 Newberg and D'Aquili likewise assign theoretical priority to myth: 'All religions, in essence, are founded upon myths' (Newberg, D'Aquili, and Rause 2001: 56).

References

Atran, S., 2002. *In gods we trust: the evolutionary landscape of religion.* Oxford University Press, New York.

Beyer, P., 2006. *Religion in a global society.* Routledge, London, New York.

Boyer, P., 2002. *Religion explained: the human instincts that fashion gods, spirits and ancestors.* Vintage, London.

Burkert, W., 1998 (1996). *Creation of the sacred: tracks of biology in early religions.* Harvard University Press, Cambridge, MA, London.

Dawkins, R., 2006. *The God delusion.* Houghton Mifflin, Boston, New York.

Dennett, D.C., 2006. *Breaking the spell: religion as a natural phenomenon.* Viking, New York.

Friedman, J., 1974. Marxism, structuralism and vulgar materialism. *Man* (n. s.) 9 (3), 444–69.

Greeley, A.M., 1996 (1995). *Religion as poetry.* Transaction Publishers, New Brunswick, London.

Guthrie, S.E., 1993. *Faces in the clouds: a new theory of religion.* Oxford University Press, New York, Oxford.

Hempel, C.G., 1959. The logic of functional analysis. In: Gross, L. (Ed.), *Symposium on sociological theory.* Harper & Row, New York, 271–307.

Lawson, E.T. and McCauley, R.N., 1990. *Rethinking religion: connecting cognition and culture.* Cambridge University Press, Cambridge.

Lewis-Williams, J.D. and Pearce, D.G., 2005. *Inside the Neolithic mind: consciousness, cosmos and the realm of the gods.* Thames & Hudson, London.

Luhmann, N., 1977. *Funktion der Religion.* Suhrkamp, Frankfurt am Main.

Luhmann, N., 2002. *Die Religion der Gesellschaft,* ed. André Kieserling (originally published 2000). Suhrkamp, Frankfurt am Main.

Mithen, S. and Parsons, L., 2008. The brain as a cultural artefact. *Cambridge Archaeological Journal* 18 (3), 415–22.

Newberg, A.B., D'Aquili, E.G., and Rause, V., 2001. *Why God won't go away: brain science and the biology of belief.* Ballantine Books, New York.

Penner, H.H., 1999. What's wrong with functional explanations. In: Frankenberry, N. and Penner, H.H. (Eds.), *Language, truth, and religious belief: studies in twentieth-century theory and method in religion.* Scholars Press, Atlanta, 246–72.

Rappaport, R.A., 1999. *Ritual and religion in the making of humanity.* Cambridge University Press, Cambridge.

Riesebrodt, M., 2007. *Cultus und Heilsversprechen. Eine Theorie der Religion.* C.H. Beck, Munich.

Rue, L.D., 2005. *Religion is not about God: how spiritual traditions nurture our biological nature and what to expect when they fail.* Rutgers University Press, New Brunswick.

Saler, B. and Ziegler, C., 2006. Atheism and the apotheosis of agency. *Temenos* 42 (2), 7–41.

Stark, R. and Finke, R., 2000. *Acts of faith: explaining the human side of religion.* University of California Press, Berkeley, Los Angeles, London.

Tweed, T.A., 2006. *Crossing and dwelling: a theory of religion.* Harvard University Press, Cambridge, MA.

Wiebe, D., 2004. Can science fabricate meaning? On ritual, religion, and the academic study of religion. In: Light, T. and Wilson, B.C. (Eds,), *Religion as a human capacity: a festschrift in honor of E. Thomas Lawson.* Brill, Leiden, Boston, 89–103.

Wilson, D.S., 2002. *Darwin's cathedral: evolution, religion, and the nature of society.* University of Chicago Press, Chicago.

Wilson, D.S., 2005. Testing major evolutionary hypotheses about religion with a random sample. *Human Nature* 16 (4), 419–46.

Index

Page numbers in italics in entries for book titles and author names refer to references within a chapter devoted to that book and author. Page numbers in bold contain figures.

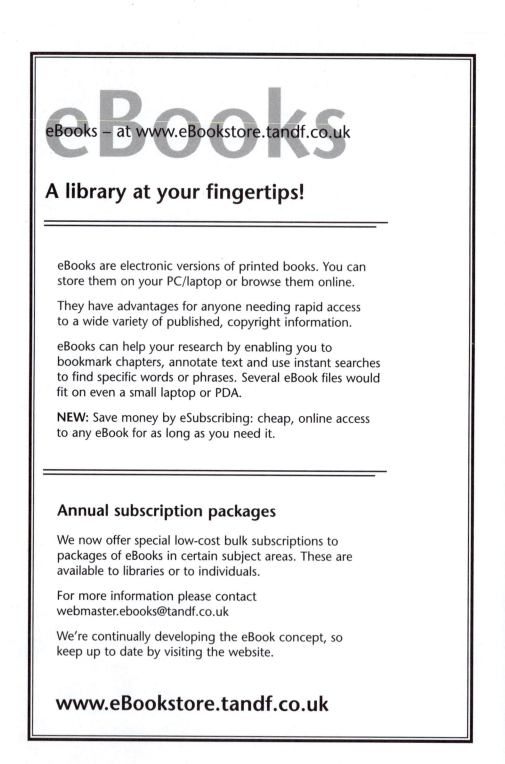